Hit Men

MULLER

TOP: *Walter Yetnikoff, president of CBS Records, the most powerful man in the record business. In his twenty-five years with the company, he transformed himself from a shy corporate lawyer into a brilliant, crafty rock warlord.*

BOTTOM: *Morris Levy, president of Roulette Records, was dubbed the "Godfather" of the American music business because of his ties to organized crime. "If a guy's a cocksucker in his life," Levy once philosophized, "when he dies he don't become a saint."*

Dick Asher, one of the few top record executives to take a moral stance against shady industry practices — only to be politically "executed" at CBS Records.

TOP: *Clive Davis brought CBS Records into the rock mainstream. After being fired from CBS, he pleaded guilty to tax evasion in 1976. He reemerged as the head of Arista Records, scoring immediate success with singer Barry Manilow—seen with Davis, above—and later on, Whitney Houston.*

BOTTOM: *Though outwardly self-effacing, Warner Bros. chairman Mo Ostin was as capable of waging war as his bitter enemy, CBS Records' Walter Yetnikoff. When Yetnikoff lured James Taylor from the Warner roster, Ostin retaliated by snatching Paul Simon from CBS.*

TOP: *After managing acts such as Laura Nyro and Crosby, Stills, Nash and Young, David Geffen created Asylum Records and, later on, the label that bore his name. In the process, he made himself very powerful—and immensely unpopular. A music attorney once received more than forty congratulatory telegrams for slugging him.*

BOTTOM: *Goddard Lieberson, the urbane and witty president of CBS Records in its pre-rock days, minted gold with the original cast album of My Fair Lady. Worshipped by his staff, he signed his letters "God."*

TOP: *Irving Azoff, MCA Records president, shown here with his wife, Shelli. Like David Geffen, Azoff was a former artist manager who enhanced his power by becoming a label boss. He was both feared and loathed. Nicknamed the "Poison Dwarf," Azoff once sent a former friend a live boa constrictor as a birthday gift.*

BOTTOM: *Allen Grubman, the industry's top lawyer, represented Bruce Springsteen, Madonna, Sting, George Michael, and other stars. Yet he was wary of offending CBS president Walter Yetnikoff. "Once I yelled at Allen," Yetnikoff said, and "he had to take three Valiums!"*

TOP: *Casablanca Records chief Neil Bogart, the king of disco, dead at thirty-nine. Motto: "Whatever it takes." He created a fad and nearly destroyed a large multinational in the process.*

BOTTOM: *Frank Dileo, the former bookie and CBS promotion executive who became Michael Jackson's manager. Jackson believed Dileo had a lot to do with the success of his megahit, Thriller.*

TOP: *Tough and unsentimental, Larry Tisch replaced Thomas Wyman as president of CBS Inc. in 1986, shunted Paley aside, and sold CBS to Sony for $2 billion.*

BOTTOM: *In 1980, Thomas Wyman, left, became the fifth man to serve as president of CBS Inc. under its chairman-founder, William Paley, right. He wound up as yet another of Paley's "disposable lighters."*

In February, 1986, NBC News exposed one of the music industry's darkest secrets in a special report on the Network, a group of independent record promoters with mysterious influence over radio. TOP: *Joe Isgro of the Network is captured behind the wheel of his Rolls-Royce by a hidden NBC News camera.* MIDDLE: *Fred DiSipio, another member of the Network, left, attending an industry dinner with his bodyguard, Big Mike, right.* BOTTOM: *DiSipio, left, hugs a close friend, future CBS Records executive Tommy Mottola, right.*

"Businessmen, they drink my wine."
—Bob Dylan, "All Along the Watchtower"

HIT MEN

*Power Brokers and Fast Money
Inside the Music Business*

Fredric Dannen

MULLER
LONDON SYDNEY AUCKLAND JOHANNESBURG

For my parents and for Ruth Fecych

This edition first published in 1990 by Muller
Random Century Group
20 Vauxhall Bridge Road, London, SW1V 2SA

Century Hutchinson Australia (Pty) Ltd,
20 Alfred Street, Milsons Point, Sydney 2061 Australia

Century Hutchinson New Zealand Ltd,
PO Box 40–086, Glenfield, Auckland 10, New Zealand

Century Hutchinson South Africa (Pty) Ltd,
PO Box 337, Bergvlei, 2012 South Africa

British Library Cataloguing in Publication Data
Dannen, Fredric, *1955–*
Hit men: power brokers and fast money inside the music business.
1. United States. Pop music recording industries. Pop music recording trades. Pop music recording industries & trades.
I. Title
338.4778163

ISBN 0–09–174633–7

Grateful acknowledgment is made to the following for permission to reprint previously published material:

William Morrow & Company, Inc.: Excerpts from *Clive: Inside the Record Business* by Clive Davis. Copyright © 1975 by Clive Davis. Reprinted by permission of William Morrow & Company, Inc.

National Broadcasting Company, Inc.: Excerpts from transcripts of NBC News broadcasts of February 24, 1986, and March 31, 1986, concerning payola. Copyright © 1986 by National Broadcasting Company, Inc. Excerpts reprinted courtesy of National Broadcasting Company. All rights reserved.

Straight Arrow Publishers, Inc.: Excerpts from "The Godfather of Rock-n-Roll" by Fredric Dannen (these excerpts constitute a portion of Chapter 3) from the November 17, 1988, issue of *Rolling Stone* magazine. Copyright © 1988 by Straight Arrow Publishers, Inc. All rights reserved. Reprinted by permission.

CONTENTS

THE DEPUTY AND THE PRESIDENT

CHARACTERS

WHATEVER IT TAKES

PART
FOUR

THE DEPUTY AND THE PRESIDENT...CONTINUED

PART
ONE

THE
DEPUTY
AND THE
PRESIDENT

THE
EDUCATION
OF
DICK ASHER

■

P INK Floyd booked five concert dates at the Los Angeles Sports Arena in February 1980 and sold them out. The Sports Arena was one of the largest indoor theaters in the nation, with a seating capacity of sixteen thousand. Pink Floyd, a psychedelic rock group from England, had just come out with a new album, *The Wall*. It was the band's first release in two years, and an instant smash. *The Wall* had climbed to the number one spot on *Billboard*'s album chart in January, and would not yield until May. This was a feat for any album, let alone a two-record set of unrelenting gloom. "This is very tough stuff, and hardly the hallmark of a hit album," wrote one rock critic. Yet *The Wall* was more than a hit; in record industry lingo, it was a "monster."

The band's contract with CBS Records called for a tour after each new release. The *Wall* tour, which required a stage crew of eighty and cost nearly $1 million in props, set a new standard for sheer spectacle. Each night a Spitfire aircraft dive-bombed the length of the concert hall and a forty-foot inflated pink pig danced in the air. The arena shook with quadraphonic sound. During the first half, the crew lugged four hundred man-sized bricks on stage and built a wall. By intermission it was four stories high and hid the band. The bricks, made of white polystyrene, formed a movie screen for surreal animated cartoons. At the show's end, the wall came crashing down.

Pink Floyd's concert was too elaborate to take on the road, so the tour was limited to four cities: Los Angeles, New York, London, and Cologne. As the first stop, Los Angeles became gripped by Floydmania. The *Wall* concert was instantly the hottest ticket in town.

Pink Floyd belonged to an elite category: the cult band. Its albums were not mere song anthologies but mini-operas. Most rock acts that make it big in the United States do so with a run of hit singles. For them, the object is to be heard on Top 40 radio. These stations have the most listeners nationwide, and play what they consider the forty most popular singles of the week, sometimes fewer. It's no exaggeration to define Top 40 radio as the fount of rock superstardom. Pink Floyd was a special case. Top 40 mostly ignored the band, which had built a vast following on album-oriented radio, stations that played album cuts instead of 45s.

Now and then, however, Pink Floyd recorded a song Top 40 could not ignore. Listeners would light up radio station switchboards with requests. It happened in 1973 with the song "Money" from the album *The Dark Side of the Moon*. It would happen again with "Another Brick in the Wall, Part Two," a cut from the *Wall* album.

CBS Records' Columbia label, the home of Pink Floyd, knew immediately that the song was a classic. Columbia released it as a single in late 1979, the first Pink Floyd 45 in years. It wasn't long before "Another Brick in the Wall" became a Top 40 favorite. By the week of February 8, 1980, *Radio & Records*, the leading industry tipsheet, calculated that 80 percent of the stations in its coast-to-coast survey were playing the song. At major Top 40 stations in every region of the country, "Another Brick" had risen to number one, getting the most airplay of any record that week. Out West, it was number one at big stations in Phoenix, Seattle, and Spokane.

The same week, Pink Floyd opened the *Wall* tour in Los Angeles. Given the mad scramble for concert tickets, the barrage of media attention, and the undiminished sales strength of the *Wall* album, one might have expected Los Angeles stations to flood the airwaves with "Another Brick in the Wall." But for some mysterious reason, L.A.'s four big Top 40 stations, which collectively had over 3 million listeners, refused to play the song at all. It was nothing less than a blackout.

∎

Dick Asher knew why. At least he thought he knew. If he was right, the implications were terrible. Only Asher, CBS Records' deputy president, and a few others at CBS were aware that "Another Brick in the Wall" had been earmarked for an experiment. Asher wanted to see whether it was possible to break a single on Top 40 without paying large sums of money to a handful of men known as independent promoters. More precisely, Asher wanted to *prove* it could be done.

The independent promoters were freelance record pluggers with an uncanny knack for getting Top 40 radio stations to play certain songs. They sold their services to any record company that could afford them. A few independent promoters were so effective that record companies kept them on retainer and paid them bonuses whenever they scored a station. At the time of Asher's experiment, the major labels were disbursing tens of millions a year to the top "indies." CBS Records, the world's largest record company, outspent all other labels on the service.

Asher was hoping that CBS could safely curtail its use of independent promoters. Business was bad despite Pink Floyd's monster album. In corporatese, the millions that CBS shelled out for independent promotion went "right to the bottom line"—that is, cut directly into profits. Yet if profits didn't improve, Asher might be forced to lay people off. It didn't seem right. How could a few indies be worth that kind of money?

CBS Records could not afford a replay of 1979, a disastrous year for the whole industry. CBS earned $51 million before taxes on sales of just over $1 billion. This was a drop of 46 percent in earnings from 1978. The industry's total sales slumped 11 percent to $3.7 billion, the first decline since World War II. Until 1979 the business was judged recession-proof. You couldn't make too many bad mistakes, because sales growth covered them up. So it seemed, anyway, to an industry drunk on the disco craze. After the phenomenal success of *Saturday Night Fever*, released in 1977, the public was thought to have an insatiable appetite for dance music. But it didn't. Record companies force-fed millions of albums to retailers and booked them as sales. But they weren't. Labels thought they could impose limits on the amount of unsold merchandise the racks could return. They couldn't. Unwanted records thundered back by the ton. The record industry had become the victim of its own hype.

This was the battleground onto which Dick Asher had been dropped, and he was not happy about it. As deputy president of CBS Records, Asher's mission was to cut costs and restore profits.

It had been John Backe's idea to make him deputy. A former air force squadron commander, Backe was chief executive officer of CBS Inc., the broadcasting company that owned CBS Records. He liked Asher.

Dick was an ex-marine, balding, rawboned, somewhat introverted, though no doubt qualified for the job Backe had given him. Asher had a law degree from Cornell and had demonstrated that he could rescue a troubled operation. In 1972 he took over CBS Records' money-losing English label and steered it into the black. Three years later, Dick was bumped up to president of the entire international division. By 1979 he had been away from American record operations for seven years. He hadn't missed them.

Dick accepted the deputy president post, as he later put it, "kicking and screaming." He didn't need the aggravation. But Backe appealed to Dick's loyalty, and Dick was nothing if not a company man. Asher worried that the deputy post, which had never existed before, would be an affront to his boss, CBS Records president Walter Yetnikoff, another lawyer. It would look like a demotion for Walter. Backe didn't see it that way. He considered Walter smart and capable, and believed no one could better manage CBS Records' artist roster. Artists loved Walter; he carried on like a rock star himself sometimes. Walter was a superb negotiator, a skill crucial for the head of an entertainment company.

The problem with Walter Yetnikoff was that he was hard to control. He refused to show up for work before eleven, though he would stay late into the night, banging away at the phone, screaming in Yiddish. Walter never wrote memos; his secretary couldn't even *type*. Backe thought CBS Records needed a counterweight to Walter's wildness. He knew the record business ran hot and cold, and that you had better keep your costs down. Backe felt Asher understood this, too. He was certain that Dick and Walter would make a good team, and promised to resolve any conflict.

Dick had other misgivings. He found the American record division insufferably arrogant. "They thought they knew everything there was to know about the business," he later remarked. The domestic labels treated the foreign division like a poor relative, and Dick resented it. CBS Records' American artist roster was indeed unmatched. The Columbia label boasted Barbra Streisand, Bob Dylan, Bruce Springsteen, Billy Joel, Neil Diamond. CBS Records' Epic label had Michael Jackson and Boston.

Asher felt he had to fight to get the American company interested in his overseas acts. One artist Dick championed was a Spanish singer named Julio Iglesias. He was vindicated when Iglesias's albums sold millions of copies in the United States. "Not chopped liver," he pointed out.

Asher knew he was a poor politician, though he was probably worse than he realized. The rank and file hated the new deputy on sight. To them, he was a spy sent down from Corporate, that mysterious enclave on the thirty-fifth floor of Black Rock, CBS headquarters in Manhattan. Dick did not help his cause with diplomacy. He detained people in endless meetings and wore them down with interrogation. He thought CBS Records was out of control and that no one was accountable. He would make them accountable.

Asher set out right away to cut perks. He issued stern directives: buses instead of limos, less dining at fine restaurants, fewer trips. People grumbled, but Dick was adamant. When his eye fell on a huge ledger item, the millions being spent on independent promotion, he was less certain what to do. It baffled him. Who were these guys? Why were they paid so much? Of course, Dick knew what independent promotion was. He had been one of the first to use outside consultants to help plug records to radio. But that was a long time ago. Before Dick went to London in 1972, indie promotion was a small expense. You might hire a freelance promoter to work a record for, say, $100 a week, because your internal staff was overloaded. In seven years the decimal point had moved three spaces. It now ran you as much as *a hundred grand* to hire a top promoter for one pop song. The service had gone from a tiny line item to the company's biggest expense after salaries.

Dick knew that good Top 40 promotion was crucial and difficult. Each big record company had Top 40 promoters on staff in every region of the country. The staff promoters called on stations in their territories and attempted to urge new singles on the program directors, the radio people with power to add a song to the playlist. Top 40 radio was a paradox, though. It alone could make a hit record in most cases, yet it strived to play only records that were *already* hits. No Top 40 station wanted to be first on a new song, and this made the program director a tough sell. Each month the PD was assaulted with more than two hundred new singles, but the station did not have that many slots to fill on the playlist—not even forty slots, because most of the list carried over from week to week.

It became a Darwinian struggle to get a record added. You could beg and plead that you were going to lose your job (some did), but program directors could not be moved by sympathy. Top 40 stations lived and died on ratings. You plied programmers with reasons (It's a real funky tune, just right for an urban audience). You plied them with statistics (The song tested well at stations in Topeka and Omaha). The PD wanted to be assured, though, that the single was a *priority*. The record company was going to be behind the artist. It was going to lay out huge sums for a concert tour, hang displays in record store windows, and take out full-page ads in *Rolling Stone*.

Asher's employees told him that if the local rep made these assurances every week about all the records in his satchel, it started to wear thin. But if you hired an indie promoter who specialized in that region, he was believable. He was, in effect, a lobbyist. He had no loyalty to any one record company. He came armed with one or two 45s from each label, not a whole stack. These records obviously *were* priorities, if only because the company paid the promo man so much money to work them. In the seven years Asher had left the American scene, his people told him, the weekly barrage of new product had become too much for Top 40 stations. They wanted to deal with the independents. No wonder indies cost a lot: You were in a bidding war for their services. There was nothing sinister about it, and there wasn't much you could do to keep the price from going up and up. If you wouldn't pay, it wasn't a priority.

This explanation gave Dick Asher pause. He did not have an ounce of promotion experience himself. He was blunt and a bit awkward and would have made a deplorable salesman. But he understood that in the record business, promotion was the game. The pop-music business had a golden principle: There was an enormous amount of money to be made with a hit record, and no money to be made without one. You might have a hundred artists on your pop roster, but most of them were going to lose money. A handful of stars, the Billy Joels, the Michael Jacksons, the Barbra Streisands, compensated for all the losers. Your job was to develop your unknown artists, the "baby acts," until their albums went gold (half-million sellers) and platinum (million sellers).

You were dependent on Top 40 radio for that. People did not buy pop music they had never heard. But it was axiomatic that for each single in the Top Ten, you could sell a million albums. So promotion, the art and science of getting songs on the air, drove the record business. Not marketing, because no amount of advertising or even good reviews and publicity were enough to sell millions of albums. Not sales, because record stores only reacted to demand and did not create it. Even the best A&R—artist and repertoire—staff in the world couldn't save you if radio gave you the cold shoulder.

Dick immediately formed some dark suspicions about independent promotion, but he put them aside. He had other worries that had nothing to do with possible illegality or even the high price. It was simply dangerous to have a power base like that outside your company. The more powerful it became, the harder it was to control. It was a slap in the face of your own people. Dick kept insisting to the heads of promotion at Columbia and Epic, If your staff can't do the job as well as the independents, get rid of them and hire better people. They told him he was missing the point.

It became imperative for Asher to prove them all wrong. But how to do that? By taking a single and breaking it without independent promotion. Easier said than done. If he chose a new group for his experiment and failed to make the pop charts, what did that prove? It was hard to break a new act under the best of circumstances. If he picked a star act, he was asking for trouble. The torturing would start right away. He could see it: The artist's manager or lawyer would blow up, and it was always a variation on the same theme—One Career. My act has only One Career. How dare you make my act an experiment. *My act could sign with another label.*

So when Pink Floyd's *The Wall* hit the album charts and rose to number one, Dick believed his prayers were answered. Normally, you could not have a hit album without a hit single, but Pink Floyd was not normal. Pink Floyd's manager, Steve O'Rourke, was barely conscious of Top 40 radio. He'd probably never *heard* of independent promotion. He would not torture. From a commercial standpoint, it hardly mattered if *The Wall* generated a hit 45 or not. Your objective was to sell albums; you never made much money from singles, even hit ones. If Asher used Pink Floyd, his experiment carried little financial risk. Dick

9

already knew which song he would target: "Another Brick in the Wall." Columbia had barely released it as a 45 when some Top 40 stations started playing it without any promotion at all.

Equally obvious was the city in which to try this experiment: Los Angeles. Pink Floyd had chosen L.A. as the place to kick off the new concert tour. Dick sat down with Columbia head Bruce Lundvall and formulated the plan, then reviewed it with his own boss, Walter Yetnikoff. They were all in agreement. CBS Records would not put independent promoters on "Another Brick in the Wall" in Los Angeles. If any L.A. Top 40 station added the song, no indie could demand payment. Los Angeles was a key market, a trendsetter market. When programmers went on a song in Los Angeles, it wore down the reluctance of stations in other cities to take a chance.

Los Angeles had four large Top 40 stations at the time of the *Wall* tour: KEARTH, KFI, KRLA, and KHJ. Asher was fairly confident that at least some of these stations would add the song to their playlists during the tour. He was wrong.

Bob Hamilton picked the records at KEARTH. He could not be persuaded to play "Another Brick in the Wall" for the duration of the Los Angeles tour. Nor could John Rook of KFI. Hamilton and Rook were not the only holdouts. KRLA would not play the song. KHJ would not play it, either.

Individually, you could draw no conclusions. There were many good reasons for a Top 40 station not to play a record, even one that was already a hit. A station might decide the song simply didn't fit its format. But the overall effect of all the big Top 40 stations holding off on the song—well, it was just plain weird.

So striking was lack of Top 40 exposure in a town where everyone under thirty seemed to be wearing a Pink Floyd T-shirt that Steve O'Rourke, the group's manager, took notice. Why, he asked, don't we hear our song on the radio? Asher did not tell O'Rourke the reason, but someone did; Dick never found out who. O'Rourke got a quick lesson in independent promotion and decided he wanted it. CBS could not long resist pressure from one of its biggest acts. The experiment acquired a second phase. Dick rescinded his ban on independent promotion in Los Angeles and waited to see what would happen.

Columbia Records hired the indies one morning soon after the Los Angeles concert dates ended, and by that very afternoon "Another Brick in the Wall" was on the Top 40 airwaves in L.A. It was unbelievable. By mid-March KFI reported the song at number 1, KEARTH at number 3, and KHJ at number 9. A month later "Another Brick" remained the top song at KFI and KEARTH. KRLA never played the record, so for the purposes of the experiment, the station was meaningless.

But the result was clear. It conjured images of the stone wall on stage, standing impenetrable until unseen hands brought it crashing down. How many bands, Asher wondered, could book five back-to-back dates in one of the largest indoor halls in America and pack them in every night? How could you blackball any rock act so popular? It was not a possibility that Dick had even allowed for, because until now he had imagined that independent promotion was at worst a powerful positive force, not an invincible negative one. Only when he considered the implications of what had happened in Los Angeles did Asher realize what he was up against.

■

They were called the Network, an informal alliance of the dozen or so top independent promotion men. The Network was rumored to have been formed at a summit meeting in New York in 1978. The term surfaced, apparently for the first time, in a November 1980 *Billboard* article. It was probably coined by its own members; a few independent promoters even had "The Network" embroidered on their golf shirts. *Billboard* identified some of the key men of the Network in 1980. Among others, the magazine named Joseph Isgro of Los Angeles; Fred DiSipio of Cherry Hill, New Jersey; Gary Bird of Cleveland; Dennis Lavinthal of L.A.; Jerry Brenner of Boston; and Jerry Meyers of Buffalo.

Though the term "Network" conjured images of a powerful, secret society, it referred to the tendency of the promoters to work as a loosely knit team. Each member had a "territory," a group of stations over which he claimed influence. If a record company wanted national airplay for a new single, it could choose to hire one of the Network men, who would in turn subcontract the job to the other members of the alliance.

The Network was mostly a phenomenon of Top 40.* To a lesser degree, it promoted records to "urban" radio, an industry euphemism for stations with a predominantly black audience.

---

* For several years, the preferred term for Top 40 has been CHR, or contemporary hit radio, to reflect that such stations often play even fewer than forty records at a time. "Top 40" is used throughout this book to mean CHR.

There were non-Network indies who promoted to Top 40 and urban stations, but they were not nearly as well rewarded. There were also indies who worked country and album-oriented stations. The money in these formats was apparently not great enough to interest the Network.

The two leading figures of the Network were Fred DiSipio and Joe Isgro. According to one estimate, DiSipio, who worked out of a squat office building in a shopping center near Philadelphia, had influence over ninety key stations. One station DiSipio routinely took credit for was KEARTH of Los Angeles, one of the Pink Floyd holdouts. It might seem odd that a man who worked in Cherry Hill, New Jersey, could deliver an L.A. station, but the Network promoter's territory often had nothing to do with where he lived. Joe Isgro of Los Angeles took credit for records added at L.A.'s KFI—another station in Asher's experiment—but also KAMZ in El Paso and WCIN in Cincinnati.

Not long after the Pink Floyd incident, Asher began to encounter Isgro and DiSipio, mostly in social situations. He found them distasteful and dealt with them as little as possible. Joe Isgro, a native of Philadelphia and only thirty-three at the time of the *Wall* tour, could have passed for a hood. He wore black shirts and custom-made suits and gold jewelry, and flashed big wads of C-notes. He employed two beefy British bodyguards. Isgro was broad-shouldered, with furtive eyes, a pencil mustache, a perennial three-day beard. He referred to himself as a "street guy." It was hard to imagine him making it as a promoter, let alone one who could afford a marble-floored mansion in the San Fernando Valley and a Rolls-Royce Corniche. He was humorless and menacing. Isgro said he was haunted by his tour of duty in Vietnam. He kept a box full of photographs of the Vietcong he had slain.

Fred DiSipio was twenty-one years older and more polished than Isgro. He was short, spectacled, and appeared to wear a rug. He had a rapid-fire repartee and a surprising command of Yiddish. "Freddy could open the shul and close it," said one man who heard DiSipio speak. DiSipio also had a reputation for discouraging competition. Like Isgro, he went around with a huge bodyguard, Big Mike.

It seemed incredible to Asher that the record industry was paying millions to these "grade-B movie characters," as he called some of the promoters and their retinue. After emerging from his seven-year cocoon running CBS Records UK and then the company's entire foreign operation, Dick had not expected to find men like Isgro and DiSipio as power brokers in the American record business.

Asher had been involved with the music business for a long time—since 1958, in fact, as a young associate at a mid-sized New York law firm—and had seen a lot. This Network business was something new, yet disturbingly familiar at the same time. Shortly before the fifties had ended, payola—a contraction of "pay" and "Victrola"—became a household word when disc jockey Alan Freed went down for taking bribes to play records on WINS. Asher long remembered the public outcry, the congressional hearings, the ruined careers. Freed, who became a symbol of the payola scandal, drank himself to death in 1965.

But payola did not go away. It was rampant again in the early seventies, which brought a fresh round of scandals. Even then it persisted. Payola was an unpleasant fact of life, but never all that noticeable at the corporate level. It was pretty much a nickel-and-dime affair. After all, how much did it take to bribe a low-paid record-picker at a radio station?

Indie promotion in the eighties, however, was not a matter of nickels and dimes. Asher did a quick calculation. CBS Records was spending $8 million to $10 million a year on the indies. This meant the entire industry was probably laying out at least $40 million. Dick had no idea what percentage was being used to bribe radio stations, but if the indies could keep a monster group like Pink Floyd off the air, it had to be a significant amount.

In time, indie promotion would be dubbed the "new payola," which indeed it was. Perhaps a better term would have been "institutionalized payola."

During the seventies, the record business had coagulated into six large multinational companies, of which CBS and Warner Communications were the biggest, and a handful of key independent labels. But unlike other businesses—such as car manufacturing or fast-food restaurants—bigness provided few competitive advantages in records, at least in terms of having hits. In fact, it could be a disadvantage. The small labels were often quicker to spot a new trend, and they could make a record as cheaply as a big company. And radio airplay was free to the label with the best record.

The large record companies understood on some level that if radio airplay were not free, it would mean a major competitive edge. The big companies had budgets sufficient to outbid the small labels for airplay. Payola had always been the means to put a price on free airplay, but it had never been institutionalized. To get a lock on pop radio across the nation would take a big outlay of cash. The large companies had the money, but they could not allow their staff people to make payments to radio stations. It had become too risky. The antipayola statute of 1960 was feeble and rarely enforced. But the seventies gave rise to the Racketeer Influenced and Corrupt Organizations statute, known as RICO, which can inflict heavy penalties on a company that engages in bribery. In the words of a law journal study on the "new payola": "The threat of RICO liability created an incentive for record companies to retain independent contractors for record promotion in order to insulate themselves from imputed criminal liability or complicity."

The Network proved the ideal insulation. Membership in the Network did not necessarily mean you were a payola conduit. Some top indies had clean reputations. Other Network men, however, plied station program directors with cash, cocaine, expensive gifts, and hookers. The former program director of a medium-sized California radio station, for example, admitted in 1987 that he had taken about $100,000 in cash from an independent promoter over a three-year period. Every week he got a "birthday card" in the mail, delivered to a post office box he had set up under an assumed name, as instructed by the indie. Each week he added three or four songs for the promoter and found between $500 and $1,000 in his birthday card.

There were other methods of delivering the payoff money. One promoter stuffed the money in empty cassette boxes. Others used record jackets. "There are programmers," one label executive laughed, "who take the record up in the sleeve and go like this." He held an imaginary 45 to his ear and shook it. "Sounds good, sounds good. I like it, I like it."

The Network served its purpose. After 1978, records put out by small labels began to vanish from the Top 40 airwaves. But indie promotion was a two-edged sword. At first the big labels were bidding against the small ones, but before long they were bidding against each other. The price of indie promotion rose steadily. By 1985 it was costing the industry at least $60 million and perhaps as much as $80 million a year. A label might spend as much as $300,000 to promote one record.

This was vastly more money than was needed to rig the airwaves. The leftover millions made a few top indie promoters exceptionally rich. Meanwhile, a few label bosses expressed fears that indie promo dollars were being kicked back to some vice-presidents of promotion at the record companies, the men who disbursed funds to the Network. Mo Ostin, head of Warner Bros., said in a deposition, "There was . . . a suspicion that [the indies] could be corrupting promotion men who might work for us," although, he added, "we had no indication that that had happened." One former promotion VP, requesting anonymity, confirmed that 10 percent was a typical kickback, and admitted taking money. "I didn't steal enough," he said. "I'm real fucking sorry; I saw many an opportunity." Vice-president of promotion, he added, "is a *very* valuable job. And nobody ever gets nailed. You know why? They're all working for public companies. Nobody breathes a word of what happened."

Though institutionalized payola remained a good deal for the Network, the bribe-takers at radio stations, and promotion VPs on the take, it eventually turned into a very bad deal for the labels that had created it. The $60 million to $80 million in annual outlays might not sound oppressively large, but it was for the record business. Despite its powerful influence on culture and fashion, recorded music is a relatively small industry. Americans today spend about the same amount on breakfast cereal—$6.3 billion a year— as they do on compact discs, tapes, and records. In 1985, the U.S. record industry grossed no more than $4.5 billion and made pretax profits of perhaps $200 million—and this is a generous estimate.*

Therefore, in 1985 the U.S. record industry was spending at least 30 *percent* of its pretax profits on indie promotion. By then it had become a financial crisis, one of the worst an industry has ever brought upon its own head.

Even before it became unbearably expensive, the Network was not a good investment. For all its power, the Network could not make a hit record. No one could do that except the marketplace. You could saturate the airwaves with an uncommercial song and have some moderate success, but in the end you could not force people to buy a record they did not like. It is easy to find examples of "turntable" hits: records that got loads of airplay but

---

* Maybe too generous. That year, four of the nation's six largest record companies lost money or were only marginally profitable.

did not sell. Consider Carly Simon's hit single "Jesse," on Warner Bros. Records. Said an executive at a competing label, " 'Jesse' is legendary as one of the most expensive singles of all time in the amount of indie promotion money spent on it. I don't know the actual number, but if you told me $300,000, I wouldn't blink. The amusing thing is, it was top ten, it got a lot of airplay, but they didn't sell any albums. It was perceived as a hit record. But the album was a stiff. So was it a successful project? Not for anybody. Except for the independent promoters. You can't blame them for taking the money."

In fact, the Network's power came not from its ability to make a hit record but to *prevent* one. This was deliberate, since the Network was the means to deprive small labels of access to the Top 40 airwaves and increase the market share of the large labels. Unfortunately, market share isn't worth anything if you can't acquire it profitably. In business, a company that buys market share at a heavy price is tagged with the unflattering name of "loss leader." The Network was the ultimate loss-leader deal.

Some of the record companies felt they had no choice but to hire the indies. Dick Asher, for example, complained that "it wasn't payola, it was extortion—the price you had to pay to be in business." Said Elliot Goldman in mid-1986, when he was president of RCA Records: "You got the feeling you had to hire them so bad things wouldn't happen."

To make matters worse, the Network became adept at getting money for nothing. "I call them claim-jumpers," said Paulie Gallis, a non-Network indie promoter who had got his start in radio in 1948. One time, in the late seventies, Gallis, who worked on retainer for Motown Records, persuaded a friend at a radio station in Tallahassee to add a Motown single to his playlist. A promotion executive at Motown called Gallis to thank him but said he was unable to pay him a bonus for landing the station. "He says, That station belongs to somebody else, and I have to pay *that* guy," Gallis recalled. "I said, What do you mean it 'belongs' to somebody else? Wait a minute! Are you that fucking stupid? You're going to pay a guy for a station that *I* got?"

The Network men, some of them, were obstinate about being paid, and you did not want to cross them. This seemed especially true of Fred DiSipio. "The line about Freddy," said one promotion vice-president, "was that if he flew in a plane over an antenna, he claimed the station. Any time he could do one, he would turn it in. I admit, I allowed him to intimidate me." It always came down to the Network's ability to stop a hit.

What's more, when a Network indie demanded a bonus for delivering a station, it was hard for record companies to verify that the station was playing the song in question. The standard contract given to a Network promoter by a record company entitled him to a bonus, or "spiff," of up to $7,500 each time a station in his "territory" told *Radio & Records* magazine, the industry's top tipsheet, it had added a specific song. If a radio programmer was reluctant to add a song because he feared it would hurt his station's ratings and endanger his job, he could still help a Network promoter get his spiff by lying to *Radio & Records*. This common ruse was called the "paper add." (An alternate ploy was to add the record, but only during off hours—say, after 2:00 A.M. This was known as putting a record into "lunar rotation.")

Paper adds infuriated *Radio & Records* publisher Bob Wilson, a scrupulously honest man who valued the integrity of his charts. After he discovered the practice in the late seventies, about the same time the Network came into being, he issued a warning that stations caught reporting songs they never played would be bumped from *R&R*'s Top 40 survey. Wilson so warned a number of offending stations, including KEARTH, after program director Bob Hamilton reported a Doobie Brothers song he never put on the air. Hamilton's KEARTH was one of the stations that had held out on "Another Brick in the Wall."

As Dick Asher learned more and more about the Network and its methods, it heightened the sense of eerie dislocation he had felt on returning to U.S. operations after his long absence. Why, he kept asking himself, did the industry allow it to continue? Why was everyone around him so complacent? Surely, Asher figured, his boss and longtime colleague Walter Yetnikoff, another attorney, would share his concerns about independent promotion. He was in for a surprise.

DICK AND WALTER

∎

MARTIN Richard Asher had known Walter Yetnikoff since 1966, when Dick joined CBS Records as head of business affairs, and Walter was general attorney. They had much in common, or so Dick believed. Both were New York–bred Jews who had attended Ivy League law schools and married their college sweethearts. Dick was one year older than Walter. In the early days, Walter was shy and introverted, a fair description of Asher as well.

For a decade, their career paths tracked one another closely. In 1975 Yetnikoff bequeathed to Asher his post as head of CBS Records International to become president of the entire record company, the world's most powerful. Suddenly "king of the grooves," as Walter put it, he began to reinvent himself in the mold of a street fighter. He was forty-two at the time. For most people, this is late in life for a transformation, but most people do not suddenly find themselves baby-sitting some of the world's biggest rock stars. Walter adapted. He became wild, menacing, crude, and, most of all, very loud. "Nobody," he once boasted, "out-*geschreis* me."

Perhaps Walter had come to understand the record industry's unusual set of values. The business reveres only two types of people. One is the "record man," the person with an innate sense of a hit record. The other is the colorful "character," the streetwise hustler and inveterate gonif. These were the attributes of the pioneers who built the modern record industry from its post-Depression ruins. Walter was no record man and had no hopes of becoming one, because the most powerful executive in the music business was tone-deaf. So he admitted in an interview, before hedging a little: "I mean I can't *sing*. My ear is okay, but somewhere between the ear and the throat there is something missing." As a self-made character, however, Walter won the industry's deepest respect.

Unfortunately for Dick Asher, he fit neither category, and the industry tended to undervalue him. He was merely a good administrator. Wherever he went, profits went up, while many record men and street characters lost money. For the record business, this was not reason enough to be admired. Asher simply was not flamboyant like Ahmet Ertegun of Atlantic Records, or David Geffen of the label that bore his name, or the "new" Walter Yetnikoff. He recognized this, calling himself "a moth among butterflies." To a certain extent, his lack of pizzazz made him stand out in the record business.

There was something else. Attitudes toward artists among the industry's power elite vary from contempt—quite prevalent—to fandom. But Asher was simply *in awe* of artists. He once explained why he worked his employees so hard: "Think about what it takes to be an artist, to get up onstage and open your viscera and expose it to the world. If you're going to put bread on your table from the efforts of these people, at least give them the best you've got." He meant it. One of the ironies about Dick, though not surprising if you consider the psychology of rock stardom, was that artists didn't like him very much. Walter Yetnikoff browbeat rock stars and they loved him for it.

"I'm not sure artists want to hang out with old guys like me," Dick said. "If I wasn't the head of a record company, maybe they wouldn't want to talk to me on the street. No reason why they should." Some artists were fond of him—Julio Iglesias, for one. But Asher had worked hard to break Iglesias in the United States, and like Dick, he was a lawyer and businessman. Frank Zappa considered Asher the most ethical label boss he had met. But his admirers were few. Artists like Michael Jackson and Neil Diamond and Billy Joel wanted to deal with Yetnikoff instead.

Employees seemed to care for him even less. It troubled Asher and was hard for his friends to understand. They knew Dick to be fundamentally decent, loyal, and honest. He wanted to be liked, but he made people uncomfortable. He was clumsy. "Dick can't eat lunch without having Chinese food on his tie," said Vincent Romeo, a man who worked for him. Some people found him dull. "Walter used to call Dick Asher the most boring man in the world," Romeo said. "Dick can't go from A to B by the shortest route. In business, people think that's devious. He's not devious at all, he's just a *bad fucking storyteller*."

Dick was an officer in the marine corps and even looked like a famous military man, Alexander Haig. He was built like a linebacker, a position he had played at Tufts University before earning his law degree. Asher had a tough, almost grizzled exterior, a sharp nose, and brushed his hair to one side to cover the bald spot. He spoke in a slow, gravelly voice.

Football remained his passion. Once a talent scout from the Green Bay Packers made some inquiries about Asher and a teammate to the Tufts coach. Dick was electrified. He said his parents would kill him, he had already been accepted to law school, but he was ready for the Packers. His coach laughed him out of the office. Many years later, Asher confessed he would probably leave the music industry, where he had spent his adult life, if someone would make him coach of the New York Giants.

The surest way to set off his temper was to be insubordinate. Al Shulman, a salesman who ran CBS Records' special products division, found this out. Shulman was a smooth operator—"he could sell ice to the Eskimos," said one admirer—but he had an unfortunate habit of doing things without company approval. One time he ran counter to an Asher directive, and Dick found out about it. The moment Dick raged into his office, Shulman pulled his chair back, sensing trouble. Asher went straight for his desk— a large, heavy desk weighed down with papers—and turned it over.

"Dick could be a formidable enemy," said attorney David Braun. "He's built like a bull. There are certain things you do not do to Dick. You don't threaten him and you don't lie to him." Asher once had Braun and lawyer John Mason in his office to discuss contracts for the Jacksons. Braun represented Michael Jackson individually, and Mason did legal work for the rest of the group. "John wanted more than Dick was willing to give, and he kept pushing," Braun recalled. "I was behind Dick, leaning against the cabinet. It was late in the afternoon and we were having a drink. And John said the wrong thing to Dick. He said, If you don't give me what I want, I can't guarantee that my clients won't develop a *throat problem*. Dick got nuts. I could see the short hairs on the back of his neck stand up. He started turning beet red. GET OUT OF HERE! GET THE FUCK OUT OF HERE!

DON'T YOU EVER SAY THAT TO ME! And he threw John out of the office."

Braun admired Dick's integrity; he just wished he were more fun. One time Epic threw a party on a Friday afternoon to celebrate a couple of hit singles. Braun and attorney Joel Katz, who between them represented some of CBS Records' biggest acts, were in a good mood and decided to crash the party. Braun noticed Asher fixing him with an ice-cold stare. When the celebration was over, Braun dropped by his office. Dick, he said, are you pissed at me? Nah, Asher assured him, it's those Epic guys. I gave them strict orders: *no outsiders* at the party. Braun couldn't believe it. Here he thought he was doing CBS a favor. Walter Yetnikoff, out of town that day, would probably have been thrilled to see two important lawyers make a special trip to Black Rock just to share in the *naches*, as they say in Yiddish. That was Dick for you.

Asher had a zest for minutiae, and it could drive attorneys crazy. While Yetnikoff made rapid decisions, Dick took his time. "Four hours was nothing to him," one attorney recalled. "It was excruciating." When a recalcitrant lawyer gave Walter *tsuris*—heartburn—he would hiss into the phone, You know what your punishment is? From now on, you get to deal with Asher!

Dick's meetings were long and frequent. He would pack a conference room and sit in the middle of a long table, flanked by his personal support staff. Since he was deputy president, they were known as the "Posse." Everyone feared them. At meetings, the Posse came armed with volumes of notes. Asher would look around the room and ask technical questions. For many, it was an ordeal. Susan Blond, a highly strung publicist at Epic, said she crammed for these meetings, trying to memorize chart positions, dates, figures. "You never knew what he was going to ask," she said. "Sometimes you felt like you were justifying your entire existence."

■

Walter Yetnikoff inspired fear as well, but in a different way. His tantrums were legendary. He shattered glassware, spewed a mixture of Yiddish and barnyard epithets, and had people physically ejected from the CBS building. One time a rival label president signed an act he had wanted. "Walter worked himself into a fury," said an eyewitness. "He was weeping with rage, he was screaming and banging on the walls: I'LL DESTROY HIM! I'LL

DRIVE HIM OUT OF THE INDUSTRY! It was embarrassing and frightening."

It became the record industry's version of the Hamlet enigma: Was Walter mad, or did he feign madness? The consensus was that he was crazy like a fox. His outbursts were calculated to keep people off guard and give himself an edge. "When he has a fit," said an employee, "he knows damn well why he has it." He used crudeness the same way. Yetnikoff signed the Beach Boys to CBS for several million dollars in 1976; four years later, they had not recorded one new album. He summoned them to his office for what they probably hoped would be a pep talk. It wasn't. "Gentlemen," he began, "I think I've been fucked!"

The heart of Yetnikoff's persona was his Brooklyn Jewishness. An outsized number of label bosses were Jews from Brooklyn, but Walter wore his ethnicity like a gabardine. He looked like a cross between a rabbi and a man who sold piece goods on Seventh Avenue. He had a full beard, a thick head of black hair, a stocky build. His eyes were narrow, Slavic.

Walter grew up in the shadow of the Brooklyn El. His father, a man he never spoke of with much affection, was a housepainter. He had fonder memories of his Russian immigrant grandfather, a tailor who kept a needle in his lapel to his last days and cautioned Walter against law school. Jews are always in flight, he warned, and your fancy diploma won't help you in Lithuania. As a tailor, you can make a nice living. Walter ignored the advice and worked his way through Columbia University Law School, where he edited the law review.

Walter fit in well with the record business, which was culturally Jewish, but he stuck out at CBS Inc., which was not. The broadcasting company's aging founder and chairman, William Paley, appeared ashamed of his own Jewish origins, and he had made CBS a WASP sanctuary. Walter was fond of Paley nonetheless. "I tried to get Paley to adopt me," he said. "My son the lawyer." For a time, Walter served on the CBS board. Once, in the middle of a stuffy speech by a CBS director, Walter leaned toward Paley, the only other Jew in the boardroom. I know what you're thinking, he stage-whispered. Aren't the goyim boring!

The goyim. With Walter, it was always Us versus Them. When CBS Records had its annual convention in London, Walter forbade his people to stay at the Dorchester Hotel because it was Arab-owned. During the 1978 convention, Walter roomed at the

Grosvenor House and was irked to find out that the sheik of Qatar had the suite next to that of Epic general manager Ron Alexenburg. Walter and Alexenburg leaned against the wall and heard bleating; the sheik required fresh goat's milk. "Walter said, What *is* this shit!" Alexenburg recalled. "So we took Johnny Winter's record, 'Rock and Roll,' and we blasted it. When they told us the sheik was checking out the next day, we laughed ourselves silly."

Yet at least one of Walter's friends had strong doubts about his religious sincerity. "It's nothing more than him playing Jewish delicatessen clerk," he said. "It means nothing. Somebody ought to call him up on that." One of Walter's inconsistencies was that he dated only gentile women, preferring well-endowed blondes. Before his twenty-five-year marriage broke up in the early eighties, he had already begun to amass a stable of such girlfriends—his "shiksa farm."

No one ever doubted Walter's brilliance, however. He could glance through a thick contract and absorb complex details. "I was in a meeting with Walter once," said Susan Blond, "and he had to decide the fate of five projects. Walter went like this: yes, no, no, yes, no. He could tell with the minimum amount of information what was going to work and what wasn't." He rarely kept notes. "He writes things in matchbook covers," attorney David Braun once mused aloud. "Millions of dollars in deals, scribbled inside of matchbook covers."

Though tone-deaf, when communicating with rock stars, Walter had perfect pitch. "You have to be sensitive to what is too easily called artistic temperament, which I think I understand completely," he said. Walter saw himself as the artists' "rabbi, priest, guru, banker for sure, adviser, friend, psychotherapist, marriage counselor, *sex* counselor . . ." He soothed Michael Jackson with Talmudic wisdom and schmoozed until three with Billy Joel. "Sometimes," he said, "I can't believe the places I find myself."

If Asher was deferential toward artists, Walter was the opposite. Yetnikoff recalled his first meeting with Epic star Cyndi Lauper. "We had a big fight over her women's lib routine. I'm a bit of a male chauvinist pig. She told me I was, and I said, Are you crazy? You're out of your mind. I said, You see over in the corner, a pile of hay and straw? Go sit on it, have your period and come back when you're finished!" Lauper appeared to adore Yetnikoff.

"My wife had an uncle like Walter," said David Braun. "He

could literally tear up tickets the cops gave him and they would laugh. I had an uncle like Dick Asher. He would do it once and get arrested. There are just people on earth that can get away with a lot more. Walter's one of them."

Because of Walter's outrageous public persona, his friends claimed the real Walter was hidden to the outside world. The private Walter, they said, was a different man—in fact, a mensch, the supreme Yiddish compliment, one who is noble and generous and upright. His attorney and best friend, Stanley Schlesinger, said he knew no softer touch than Walter. It was not hard to find examples of his kindnesses. When an employee wrenched his back at a convention, Walter upgraded him to first class on the flight home at his own expense and looked after him with avuncular care. "You know what my problem is?" he once confided. "I'm too *nice.*"

There was indeed evidence that Walter's bravado, like his Jewish militancy, was a put-on: He was constitutionally unable to fire. CBS Inc. president John Backe recalled, with much amusement, that Walter could not even dismiss his chauffeur, though the driver was not reporting for work. "Walter had to have the personnel man fire him," Backe said.

In 1979, when the industry recession made layoffs a necessity, Walter got his then number two man, CBS Records U.S. president Bruce Lundvall, to issue the pink slips. On June 29 of that year, fifty-three CBS Records employees in New York, Los Angeles, and Nashville were let go. The belt-tightening wasn't over. On August 10, 1979—they called it "Black Friday"—CBS Records dismissed another 120 people. The company was in shock.

Two months after Black Friday, Dick Asher stepped in as deputy president at John Backe's insistence. Backe knew that further cutbacks might be necessary, and that Walter would have trouble making them—yet another reason for the appointment. Dick abhorred having to fire people, but if he had to do it, he could. One of the main reasons Dick did not want the deputy job was that he dreaded another Black Friday.

To help Walter save face, Backe maintained the fiction that Dick's appointment was Yetnikoff's idea. Asher believed it—or wanted to. "I was very naive," Dick said in retrospect. "I mean, Walter and I had always gotten along. He was my friend. I thought it *was* his idea; it wasn't until much later that I learned the truth from Backe."

By now, the differences between Dick and Walter had become painfully acute. Before long, if you were on the eleventh floor of Black Rock to conduct business with CBS Records, you got the distinct feeling that it had become two companies: Dick's and Walter's. "They divided the floor off," said David Braun. "The area between Dick's camp and Walter's camp was called the Demilitarized Zone. Between them were accountants. CBS has partitions, and you can change the configuration of the floor. And they partitioned it off so you literally felt you were walking from one camp to the other. It was very funny. Walter walled off his end and sealed it with a locked door."

The door was Debbie Federoff's idea. She was Walter's secretary at the time. "I had it put in when Dick moved downstairs," she said. "It had a two-way mirror. Walter couldn't stand Dick around, so the door was always closed and we could see who's coming. We never liked Dick. He was a nice man, but he went on and on. He was a *nudzh*. Walter, nyah nyah nyah, he would be in Walter's office every two seconds. I don't think Dick was Walter's personality type. Too straight. Dick always had a tie on. We used to call him Deputy Dick."

Bob Jamieson, a member of Asher's Posse, long remembered the friction between his boss and Walter Yetnikoff. "It never got personal, it was business. But they didn't agree: strategies, moves, artists to go after. Dick and Walter are both strong-willed. At night, they'd have a meeting in Walter's office, and it would get boisterous: I THINK YOU'RE WRONG, GODDAMN IT! When you're disagreeing with Dick, it can be head-for-the-hills time. He can get *very* loud."

To Dick's surprise, one of his early disagreements with Walter concerned independent promotion. It was an important financial issue if the company was to avoid further layoffs. And after the Pink Floyd incident, the matter took on a new urgency for Dick. For starters, Dick felt that bribery was morally wrong, not a common stance in the record business. When record executives even admit that payola exists, they tend to defend it on the following grounds: a) it is no different from political lobbying; b) corruption in government is worse; c) corruption on Wall Street is worse.

But morality was less an issue than legality. CBS Inc. could lose its vital broadcasting licenses if caught breaking the law. As head of International, Dick had been forced to fire a valued employee of long standing because the man had paid off a customs agent in Brazil to get machinery delivered in time for Christmas production. The man hadn't stolen any money; bribery was a way of life in Brazil. But Congress had just passed the Foreign Corrupt Practices Act, and the CBS board insisted that the man be let go.

Dick began to ask Walter, as one attorney to another, whether he believed CBS was adequately protected if independent promotion turned out to be a front for bribery. All contracts given to indie promoters contained a warranty clause that forbade payola. This was well and good. But the billing system at CBS for the independents was, to say the least, unorthodox.

"The promoters," Asher recalled, "would send a bill for services rendered, and the bill would have a bunch of little papers stapled to the side. There was a piece of paper for each station claimed by the promoter. Let's say the bill was for $20,000. If the price was $2,000 per station, there'd be ten little slips of paper stapled to the bill."

Someone in CBS Records' promotion department would make sure each of these stations was in fact playing the company's newest release. Then he would tear off the slips and discard them, so the actual bill that got filed didn't look as if it were on a per-station basis. Apparently, the billing system had arisen out of concern that an indie promoter might one day be found to have improper influence over a specific station. A bill showing CBS had paid the promoter to deliver that station could put the company in a bad light. "So here we are," Asher said, "paying $10 million a year in tear-off receipts that get thrown away."

Asher had even darker fears. Though he admitted his knowledge of organized crime was "somewhat less than my knowledge of Buddhism," he did not want to rule out the possibility of mob involvement. "Walter kept saying, What do you mean? How do you know? And I said, Walter, I don't really know anything. But if the industry is spending $40 million or $50 million a year, that's sizable enough, I think, to attract organized crime. Of course, I had nothing to support that."

Walter later ridiculed the idea of a Mafia connection to the Network, and he seemed far more comfortable with the top indies than Dick Asher was. Indeed, as Dick became a chief adversary of indie promotion, Walter evolved into one of its staunchest advocates. "They get results," Walter explained in a 1986 interview. "The indies are *mensches*, you understand?"

■

The rise of the Network was hardly an event without parallel in the record business. In fact, if the story has a moral, it is that the "new" record business of today, with its sophisticated multi-nationals, is no different from the "old" record business of the buccaneering fifties. And it is in the fifties that this account must begin. With the advent of rock and roll, a new ruling elite took charge of the record industry. They were the so-called pioneers of rock, the independent businessmen who created the first labels to record the new music. These men established the shaky moral foundation on which the modern record industry is built.

Their legacy, three decades later, would be an industry held hostage by the Network. This was progress, indeed. If the early rock and roll labels were unspeakably crooked, at least they did not spend tens of millions in protection money. It would take the big, lawyerly corporations of the eighties to bring that about.

PART
TWO

■

CHARACTERS

■

LULLABY
OF
GANGLAND

■

ROCK historians tend to romanticize the pioneers of the rock and roll industry. It is true that the three large labels of the fifties —RCA Victor, Decca, and Columbia, which CBS had bought in 1938—were slow to recognize the new music. So were the publishers of Tin Pan Alley. It took independent businessmen like Leonard Chess of Chess Records in Chicago to put Chuck Berry on vinyl, and Syd Nathan of King Records in Cincinnati to record James Brown.

The pioneers deserve praise for their foresight but little for their integrity. Many of them were crooks. Their victims were usually poor blacks, the inventors of rock and roll, though whites did not fare much better. It was a common trick to pay off a black artist with a Cadillac worth a fraction of what he was owed. Special mention is due Herman Lubinsky, owner of Savoy Records in Newark, who recorded a star lineup of jazz, gospel, and rhythm and blues artists and paid scarcely a dime in royalties.

The modern record industry, which derives half its revenues from rock, worships its early founders. It has already begun to induct men such as disc jockey and concert promoter Alan Freed into the Rock and Roll Hall of Fame. When veteran record men wax nostalgic about the fifties, they often speak of the great "characters" who populated the business. Morris Levy, the founder of Roulette Records, said proudly, "We were all characters in those days." The term is probably shorthand for "Damon Runyon character." It signifies a Broadway street hustler: tough, shrewd, flashy, disreputable. Levy denied this last attribute, but Levy is a man who has spent his life denying things.

In the dominion of characters, Levy was king. He loomed larger than most of the other pioneers, and as each of them fell by the wayside, he remained a potent institution and a vibrant reminder of where the industry had come from. In 1957 *Variety* dubbed Levy the "Octopus" of the music industry, so far-reaching were his tentacles. Three decades later, another newsman called him the "Godfather" of the American music business. His power had not diminished.

Morris Levy started Roulette in 1956, after a decade in nightclubs (he owned the world-famous Birdland). Roulette was one of several independent record companies that put out rock and roll. It featured Frankie Lymon, Buddy Knox, Jackie and the Starlights. As rock became the rage, the big labels discovered that the independents were bumping them off the singles charts. So they opened their checkbooks and bought the rock musicians' contracts or acquired the independents outright. In 1955 RCA Victor paid Sun Records $35,000* for Elvis Presley. By the end of the decade most of the independents were gone; the founders had cashed in their chips. Atlantic Records in New York remained a going concern but in 1967 became part of Warner-Seven Arts (later Warner Communications). Levy kept Roulette. It continued to grow and absorb other independent labels and music publishers and even a large chain of record stores.

Morris's power came from copyrights. He understood early in the game that a hit song is an annuity, earning money year after year for its lucky owner. His very first publishing copyright was the jazz standard "Lullaby of Birdland," which he commissioned for his nightclub. Every time a high school marching band played "The Yellow Rose of Texas" at the Rose Bowl, Morris got paid, because he owned that copyright, too. "It's always pennies—nickels, pennies," Morris once said of his song catalog. "But it accumulates into nice money. It works for itself. It never talks back to you."

Nice money, indeed. By the eighties, Morris Levy was worth no less than $75 million. A major share of his wealth came from his music publishing empire, Big Seven, which had thirty thousand copyrights. Sunnyview, his two-thousand-acre horse farm along the Hudson River in Columbia County, New York, was

---

* Plus a $5,000 signing bonus.

valued at $15 million. In the seventies, he took over a small chain of bankrupt record stores, which he renamed Strawberries. A decade later he turned down a $30 million bid for the chain. Not bad for a man who was tossed out of elementary school for assaulting a teacher.

Much harder to quantify was another source of Morris Levy's wealth and power: a lifelong association with the Mafia. A Sephardic Jew (or "Turk," in his words) from the poorest section of the Bronx, Morris was never a member, but he did business with several crime families. The Genovese family of New York cast the longest shadow over his career. Morris always disavowed mob involvement; when the subject of his well-known gangster friends came up, he was fond of pointing to a framed portrait of himself with Cardinal Spellman, remarking: "That don't make me a Catholic."

Morris endured over a quarter-century of government "harassment," as he called it, but seemed immune from prosecution, even after a policeman lost an eye to him in a 1975 brawl, and after two business associates were murdered, apparently by the mob. (His brother Zachariah, better known as Irving, was murdered as well, in January 1959. He was stabbed to death at Birdland by a collector for mob loan sharks after ordering the man's prostitute wife from the club. Despite legend, it was not a gangland hit.) Morris's string ran out at long last in 1988, when he was convicted along with a Genovese underboss on extortion charges and drew a ten-year sentence. He was sixty-one years old.

Morris's gangster ties were never a secret to the record business. To say that few held it against him is an understatement. The industry, which knew him as Moishe, revered him. He was chairman emeritus of the music division of the United Jewish Appeal and a key fund-raiser for other music charities. His philanthropy was not the only reason, or even the main reason, the business embraced him. It went much deeper. Morris reverberated with the industry's street mythos. He looked like Big Jule in *Guys and Dolls*—large, stocky, with an enormous neck and huge, hamlike hands. His voice sounded like sandpaper in the glottis.

In another trade besides vinyl, a man like Morris Levy might have been a pariah. The record business has never shrunk from the mob. At the end of World War II, the industry's best customers were jukebox operators, and many of them were mafiosi. Since the Depression, the Mafia has played a key role in artist management and booking (especially of black performers), pressing, and independent distribution.

In the record business, to be close to dangerous men like Levy is to take on some of their attributes and accrue some of their avoirdupois. It confers far more status than, for example, an MBA, which is perhaps even a liability.

Walter Yetnikoff found this out early in his career. According to Morris, "One of Walter's first assignments at CBS as a young kid was to collect $400,000 off me. He collected it. See, that was the beginning of his rise at CBS." Walter grew fond of Morris and spent time at Levy's farm. Yetnikoff invested money in Malinowski, an improbably named Irish racehorse that Morris owned and stabled there. (Morris also sold shares in horses to rock stars Billy Joel, Daryl Hall, and their managers.) At the end of a long, abusive day, haggling on the phone with lawyers and managers, Walter would call Moishe and unload his troubles. One time Morris demanded three dollars for "psychiatric consultation"; Walter sent a check, which Levy framed and hung. Morris believed that Walter was the last of the great characters, a member of his dying breed. "Walter could be a throwback," he said.

"Throwback" was the wrong word. Walter, after all, is only six years Morris's junior. It is well to remember how young the American record industry is and how rapidly it has grown up. In 1955 the industry's total sales were about $277 million. Revenues have increased over 2000 percent, and today's key record executives and lawyers and managers are not even a generation removed from the founders. Nor are they much different.

■

On a day in early 1987, Roulette Records' offices on the eighteenth floor of 1790 Broadway could have been mistaken for those of a rundown CPA firm, had it not been for the gold albums and rock posters on the walls. Facing Morris Levy's cluttered desk was an old upright piano. A sign on the wall proclaimed, O LORD, GIVE ME A BASTARD WITH TALENT! Just above it was a hole drilled by federal agents, who had snuck into Levy's office in the middle of the night and planted an omnidirectional microphone. The ceiling had two holes, each for a hidden video camera. Morris was in good spirits, considering that the previous September he had been nabbed by two FBI agents in a Boston hotel room and indicted for extortion. Never a sharp dresser, Morris was arrayed in blue jeans and an old polo shirt and had several days' worth of stubble. He leaned across the desk and began to tell his story.

"One of my first jobs in a nightclub was at the Ubangi Club. That was in '43 or '44. I was just sixteen years old. I was a check-room boy. Then I became a darkroom boy. The camera girls would go around clubs taking flash photos. You were in a room in the back of the club, and you got the negatives, and you developed 'em and had 'em ready in fifteen minutes for the customers. Before that there, I was a dishwasher and a short-order cook. I worked in a restaurant called Toby's on the corner of Fifty-second and Broadway. The kids from the checkroom at the Ubangi used to come up for coffee, and they're the ones who told me about it. So I tried the checkroom and the darkroom, one led to the other, which is sort of the way your whole life goes.

"I became good at the darkroom. I advanced with the people I worked for and became a head guy, setting up darkrooms around the country. We had the rights to a lot of clubs. In Atlantic City, there was Babette's, the Dude Ranch, the Chateau Renault. In Philadelphia, there was the Walton Roof, the Rathskeller, Frank Colombo's. In Newark, it was the Hourglass; in Miami, there was places like the 600 Club, the Frolics Club, the 5 O'Clock Club. New York itself had two hundred nightclubs, probably. You could go out any night of the week and see any one of a hundred stage shows or dance bands. It was a different world.

"When I was seventeen, I joined the navy. I was away for a year. I got out in '45 and went back into darkroom work. I tried my own concession, in Atlantic City, and went broke.

"Then an opportunity came up. There was a guy out of Boston who opened up a big place called Topsy's Chicken Roost on Broadway, under the Latin Quarter. And he wanted out. So I got my old bosses to buy the club off him with no money down, and for that I got a small piece of the club and a big piece of the checkroom. We were a chicken restaurant. We served as much as a thousand chicken dinners a night, for $1.29. And we opened up a little lounge there called the Cock Lounge. Billy Taylor played there, Sylvia Sims, and other acts like that. It was a groovy little spot.

"In the beginning of '48, Symphony Sid and Monte Kay came down about running a bebop concert. We put the bebop in on a Monday night, there was a line up the block. We had Dexter Gordon or Charlie Parker or Miles Davis. They did two nights a

35

week, and then it grew to three nights a week, then six and seven nights a week. That's where Billy Eckstine got started. It was really fabulous. We became the Royal Roost, the first bebop club in the city.

"Then the three partners decided to move to a much bigger place. They moved to the old Zanzibar, which seated like twelve hundred people, and opened up Bop City. And when they moved over, they forgot about me. I felt I got screwed. I stayed with the Royal Roost, I tried to run it, but it ran into the ground.

"About three months later, Monte Kay came to me about opening up competition for Bop City. We opened Birdland at Fifty-second and Broadway on December 15, 1949. But we found out that Bop City was so powerful, we couldn't get an act unless they didn't want it. Harry Belafonte worked Birdland for like a hundred a week. But we had great difficulties booking the club.

"We finally came up with a Machiavellian move against Bop City. Every time we reached for an act, they would get it. So we went to the big booking agents and said, You've got a band we want: Amos Milburn and his Chicken Shackers. Which really don't belong in a jazz joint. We picked another band that played tobacco barn dances. And they said, We'll get back to you. And being that we tried to book those two bands, they grabbed 'em and put 'em into Bop City. We got ahold of Charlie Parker. So we sort of stunk out their place and got tremendous goodwill at our place. From that point on, we drove Bop City into the ground. Everybody wanted to work Birdland."

Morris next discovered publishing. "I was in my club one night, and a guy comes in from ASCAP [the American Society of Composers, Authors, and Publishers, a performing-rights agency] and said he wanted money every month. I thought it was a racket guy trying to shake me down. I wanted to throw him out. And then he came back again and said he's going to sue. I said, Get the fuck outta here. I went to my lawyer and I says, What *is* this guy? He keeps coming down, he wants money. My lawyer says, He's entitled to it. By act of Congress, you have to pay to play music. I said, Everybody in the world's gotta *pay*? That's a hell of a business. I'm gonna open up a publishing company!"

Morris called it Patricia Music, after his first wife. (He would marry and divorce four more times and father three sons.) Patricia Music's first copyright was "Lullaby of Birdland." "I went to

George Shearing, I says, Write me a theme and record it. It's probably one of the most recorded pieces in the world.

"And during that period, I opened up other nightclubs and restaurants, like the Embers, the Round Table, the Down Beat, the Blue Note, Birdland in Florida. . . ."

Colorful as it is, Morris's account of his early days in nightclubs omits some details. He failed to mention the wiseguys who were his silent partners. He did not explain where the money came from to open Birdland, though he said Morris Gurlak, a hatcheck concessionaire who had employed him and his brother, Irving, donated a few thousand dollars. Some years after Birdland opened, New York police investigators put together a dossier on Levy. They believed that Morris and Irving took over Birdland from mobster Joseph "Joe the Wop" Cataldo. When Levy and Morris Gurlak opened the Round Table Restaurant, a steak house on Fiftieth Street, in 1958, police sources identified some of the other partners. One was Frank Carbo, the so-called "underworld commissioner of boxing," a convicted killer with ties to Murder Incorporated. Another was John "Johnny Bathbeach" Oddo, a *caporegime*, or captain, in the Colombo family.

Morris's ties to Mafia figures can be traced back at least to when he was fourteen and a hatcheck boy at the Greenwich Village Inn. There he won the favor of Tommy Eboli, future head of the Genovese family and a future partner in records. As a club and restaurant owner, Morris is thought to have fronted for Genovese soldier Dominick Ciaffone, also known as Swats Mulligan. Swats had a nephew, Gaetano Vastola, who went by several nicknames: "Corky," "the Big Guy," "the Galoot." Morris did business with Vastola for thirty years; the Big Guy was convicted in 1989 as an accomplice to the same crime that brought Levy a jail sentence. Swats was proud of his nephew; a federal wiretap once caught him bragging, "This kid could tear a human being apart with his hands."

The Genovese family, which became central to Morris's life, is one of the five large Mafia families of New York, the others being the Gambino, the Lucchese, the Bonanno, and the Colombo. The Genovese faction makes money the old-fashioned way: illegal gambling, loan-sharking, drugs, prostitution. It also has a grip on legitimate enterprises like garbage collection, the New Jersey waterfront, Teamsters locals and other unions, and the Fulton

Fish Market in lower Manhattan. The concrete industry in New York is under Genovese domination.

The family has a bloody history. Law enforcers trace its roots to the Castellammarese War of 1930, which raged between forces headed by Salvatore Maranzano and Joe "the Boss" Masseria. The war ended in 1931 when Joe the Boss was lured to a Coney Island restaurant by one of his own lieutenants, Charles "Lucky" Luciano, and shot dead. This left Maranzano the *capo di tutti capi*, or boss of bosses—but not for long. A few months later, four men posing as police officers walked into Maranzano's Park Avenue office, shot him, and slit his throat. The assassins had been sent by Lucky Luciano, who thereby seized command of what was then called the Luciano family. When Lucky went to jail in 1936, his underboss, Vito Genovese, took over. The family has since borne his name. Genovese soon fled to Italy to escape prosecution, and Frank Costello assumed control. When Genovese returned to New York in 1945, he began plotting to depose Costello.

A decade later, Costello was allowed to step down, a rare privilege in the Mafia, which has perhaps the world's worst retirement program. It was a reward for his observance of the mob's sacred *omerta*, or code of silence. Costello had refused to identify the man who tried to kill him. On May 2, 1957, Costello entered the lobby of his Central Park West apartment building when a gunman called his name. As he turned around, a bullet grazed his skull. He was discharged from Roosevelt Hospital a short time later, very much alive. The gunman's identity was no secret. He was Vincent "the Chin" Gigante, a former club boxer and Genovese soldier on the make. Chin was indicted for the murder attempt, but Costello cleared him.

Genovese regained control of the family, only to die of heart failure in federal prison in 1969. The reins passed to Tommy Eboli, who, among other dubious achievements, was Gigante's boxing manager. Around that time, according to police files, Morris Levy sold Eboli a half share in Promo Records, a New Jersey company, for $100,000, and placed him on the payroll at a salary of $1,000 a week. Promo Records specialized in cutouts: old, unsold albums dumped wholesale by record companies into the hands of discount merchandisers. The mob has long liked cutouts because they can be counterfeited easily: You buy a thousand and press several thousand more yourself. Promo was never charged with any crime, but Eboli and Morris kept complaining of government harassment. Customs agents stopped them both in 1971 as they returned from a vacation in Naples. Eboli insisted he was a legitimate businessman. A year later, he was mowed down by gunfire in Brooklyn.

Morris saw nothing untoward in his having run a business with Tommy Eboli. "Yeah, so?" he said. "Here's a guy that wanted to do something legit. He treated it legit. We were investigated every three weeks, we never had a bad record in the place, because if we did, we would have gone to jail together. So? So what?"

Vincent Gigante, the man who allegedly bungled the hit on Frank Costello, is a year younger than Morris Levy. He and Morris were boyhood friends in the Bronx. The FBI saw Gigante as the key mob figure in Morris's background, the man to whom he owed the most allegiance. Just before Morris was indicted in 1986, the FBI supposedly warned him that Gigante might have him killed out of fear that he would become a government witness—precisely what the feds wanted Morris to do, to no avail.

Gigante stood about six feet tall and, at the time of the Costello hit, weighed close to three hundred pounds. He listed his occupation as tailor. In 1959 he was convicted of heroin trafficking and did five years. This was his last term in jail. After serving his sentence, he rose up the family ranks to *caporegime*, operating out of a social club on Sullivan Street in New York's Greenwich Village. By the eighties, he was underboss to family head Anthony "Fat Tony" Salerno, a man Morris once described as a "close friend." Unfortunately for Salerno, the FBI had grown sophisticated in the use of room bugs and long-range microphones. Salerno was convicted of being a member of the mob's ruling commission and began serving a hundred-year sentence in 1986. This left Vincent Gigante in charge of the Genovese family.

By 1986 Gigante was one of the few Mafia dons not in prison or under indictment. Lawmen expressed admiration for his craftiness. It seemed Gigante had found the ideal defense: insanity. The boss of one of the nation's most powerful crime families walked around Sullivan Street in bathrobe and slippers. He regularly checked into a mental hospital. When FBI agents served him with a subpoena in his mother's apartment, he retreated into the shower with an umbrella.

But at 2:00 or 3:00 A.M. most days, the Genovese boss became a different man. He would shed his baggy trousers and rumpled windbreaker for finer clothes. His trusted aide, Dominick "Baldy

Dom" Canterino, would drive him to a four-story brownstone on East Seventy-seventh Street, the home of Chin's mistress, Olympia Esposito, and their three illegitimate children. When the neo-Federal brownstone was declared a landmark in 1982, it belonged to Morris Levy, who had bought it for $525,000. He sold the building to Olympia Esposito the following year for a reported $16,000.

■

"George Goldner," Morris said, tasting the name. Goldner! One of the greatest A&R men in the history of rock and roll. It is impossible to imagine New York rhythm and blues without him. He discovered and produced Frankie Lymon and the Teenagers, Little Anthony and the Imperials, the Flamingos, the Cleftones, the Chantels. . . .

Goldner formed his first label, Tico, in 1948, to record Latin and mambo music, and hit it big with Tito Puente. In 1954, on his Rama label, he recorded "Gee!," a song by the Crows that was one of the first R&B hits to cross over to the white pop charts. He gratefully named his third label Gee, and promptly put out Frankie Lymon's "Why Do Fools Fall in Love?" On subsequent labels, Goldner introduced the Four Seasons and made some of the earliest recordings of the Isley Brothers. In 1964 Goldner formed Red Bird Records with producers Jerry Leiber and Mike Stoller, and had hits with the Shangri-Las and the Dixie Cups. He kept starting new labels for a reason. A compulsive gambler, he was forever selling his old labels to Morris Levy for desperately needed cash.

"He liked horses," Morris said. "He always needed money. Any degenerate gambler needs money all the time. It's like being a junkie, isn't it? It's a shame, because George knew music and knew what could be a hit. But if he was worried about the fifth race at Delaware and working the record at the same time, he had a problem. George was a character, and a victim of himself."

Morris met Goldner after inducing Tito Puente, who played at Birdland, to switch from Tico Records to RCA Victor. Levy produced some records for RCA in the fifties. "George came to see me. I never met him before. He says, You took away my number one act, you really hurt my label. I said, Jesus, George, I didn't realize it, I'm sorry. Because I really didn't do it to hurt the man. He says, Well, maybe you can help me. . . ."

Goldner had a plan, and it concerned the Crows' new song, "Gee!" Morris had been putting the jazz acts that played Birdland into package tours and sending them on the road. In so doing, he had set up what he called "the best payola system in the United States." He explained, "Whenever our jazz concerts played a city, I would hire a couple of disc jockeys in the town to emcee the show. They got money for that, which was legitimate. George had this new record by the Crows, and he says, You know a lot of the black jockeys in America. So I helped him get his record played. He says, Let's become partners. With me making the records, and you getting 'em played, we'll do a hell of a business. So we did. And that was the beginning of Gee Records."

One year later, in 1956, Morris created Roulette. It was launched as a rock and roll label but also recorded Birdland stars such as Count Basie and Joe Williams. "I formed Roulette," Morris said, "because George kept telling me I didn't know nothing about the record business, and it aggravated me. And I says, Okay, now I'm gonna form a record company that *I'm* gonna run. The first records on Roulette were by Buddy Knox and Jimmy Bowen. They hit number one and number eleven within five weeks. [The songs were "Party Doll" and "I'm Sticking with You," respectively.] George got disillusioned and we bought him out." So Roulette picked up Frankie Lymon, the Valentines, the Harptones, the Crows. Goldner came back in the mid-sixties and sold Morris his subsequent labels, Gone and End. Roulette now had the Chantels, the Flamingos, the Imperials.

Around this time, another man central to the history of rock and roll entered Morris Levy's life. His name was Alan Freed. He was a trombone player from Salem, Ohio, who worked as a disc jockey, first in New Castle, Pennsylvania, then Youngstown and Akron. He had a drinking problem and a penchant for trouble. In Akron, Freed left one station for another before his contract expired and was legally barred from broadcasting in the city for a year. He moved to Cleveland and settled at WJW in 1951.

In the early fifties, pop radio was dominated by crooners like Perry Como and Andy Williams. It dawned on Alan Freed that America's youth was disenfranchised by this music because it was hard to dance to. As legend has it, he dropped by a Cleveland record store and became a convert to rhythm and blues. Freed bombarded his growing white audience with the first R&B it had ever heard—LaVern Baker, Red Prysock, Big Al Sears. Freed howled while the records played, beat time on a telephone book, and provided a rapid, raspy commentary: "Anybody who says rock and roll is a passing fad . . . has *rocks in his head, Dad!*" He was so popular that in 1954, WINS in New York acquired Freed and his program, "The Moondog Show."

Freed was promptly sued by a blind New York street musician, Louis "Moondog" Hardin, for infringing his name. Hardin won an injunction, and Freed sulkily agreed to retitle his show. Freed went to P. J. Moriarty's, a Broadway restaurant, and sat down with some of the people who had welcomed him to New York: song-plugger Juggy Gayles, manager Jack Hooke, Morris Levy. "Alan was having a few drinks and bemoaning the fact that he had to come up with a new name," Morris recalled. "To be honest with you, I couldn't say if Alan said it or somebody else said it. But somebody said 'rock and roll.' Everybody just went, Yeah. *Rock and roll*." The WINS program became "Alan Freed's Rock and Roll Show," and a musical form acquired a name.

Freed set up shop in the Brill Building on Broadway. He had begun to host rock and roll concerts, a lucrative endeavor, and who was better at booking concert halls than Morris? "At that time, I used to take the Birdland stars on the road," Morris said. "So he came to me, Alan, and says, I want you to be my manager.* I said, My deal is fifty-fifty. He says fine. About five days later, the manager of WINS says, Moishe, we have a problem. Alan Freed's been in town a week now, and he's already given away a hundred and twenty percent of himself! He had a lot of talent, but he was also a little *nuts*."

Morris remained Freed's manager nevertheless. "The first show I did with Alan Freed was two nights at the St. Nicholas Arena. Which I think at that time held seven, eight thousand people. He made four announcements, six weeks before the dance, and $38,000 came in the mail. I says, Oh my God. This is crazy. Well, it was two of the biggest dances ever held. The ceiling was actually dripping from the moisture. It was *raining* inside the St. Nicholas Arena. I'm not exaggerating."

Encouraged, Morris booked the Brooklyn Paramount, a large movie house with a stage. Under the standard arrangement, the Paramount kept half the proceeds over $30,000 but guaranteed $15,000 for the promoters. Morris had other ideas. He waived the guarantee in return for an escalating percentage of the box office that would reach 90 percent at the $60,000 mark. No Paramount

---

* More likely, according to people who knew Freed, Morris encouraged the DJ's original manager, Lew Platt, to make himself scarce.

show had ever grossed near that amount, so the terms were granted.

"Alan stopped talking to me, because people had steamed him up that I sold him down the river by not taking a guarantee. As a matter of fact, one big agent bet me a case of Chivas that we're gonna get killed. Well, we opened up the first day, and there's lines in the streets, and the pressure's so great at the door that we start to cut out the movie. Alan and I pass each other in the hallway. I says, How's it goin', Alan? He makes a face. I says, Hey, Alan, let me ask you a question. You wanna sell your end now for twenty thousand? He says, What do you mean? We're making *money*? I says, Alan. And I told him what we're gonna make for the week. And he started talking to me again."

When Morris formed Roulette Records, he gave Freed 25 percent of the stock. Freed promptly sold his shares to "some wiseguys from around town," Morris said, bending his nose with his index finger to signify that the men were hoods. Who were they? "That's none of your business. And I got hold of Alan, and I said, Gimme back my fucking stock. Here's your contract with the shows, but we're not partners no more."

The payola scandal of 1960 destroyed Freed's life. He was indicted on May 19, along with seven others, and charged with taking bribes to play records. Freed admitted he accepted a total of $2,500, but said the money was a token of gratitude and did not affect airplay. He forgot to mention that the Chess brothers of Chicago let him stick his name on Chuck Berry's first hit, "Maybellene," and that he stood to gain by playing it often. Freed paid a small fine, but his career was over. By 1965 he had drunk himself to death.

"Bullshit charges," said Morris, reflecting on the scandal. "Freed got indicted because Freed stuck himself out in front. I had stopped talking to Freed because we'd had an argument for a few months. But when he got in trouble, he did call me. And I told him, I'll help you. But do me a favor. Go home and don't talk to nobody. And before the day was over, I was walking down the street, and the *New York Post* was sitting on the stand, and there's this big interview with Alan Freed. He had already talked to Earl Wilson, the columnist. And I called and said, What the fuck did you do? Did you see the size of the type? The type was the same size when World War II ended."

Payola was not illegal, in fact, until after the scandal. Commercial bribery was a crime in New York, though, and that statute proved Freed's undoing. The government tried to nail Roulette on the same charges but had no luck.

"Oh, yeah, they tried to break my balls with everything," Morris said. "They put their special agents in New York, they harassed the shit out of me. The government came in and seized our books. I went before the grand jury, and they were hot, because on my books there was a loan to Alan Freed of $20,000. And the D.A. wanted to show it was for payola.

"Now, Alan had once come to me, he wanted $20,000 that he needed for taxes. And I gave it to him from Roulette, it was no big deal. And at the end of the year, I said to my comptroller, Take that off the books, we're never going to get it back anyway. And then Alan and I had an argument in February. So I said to my comptroller, Put it back on the books, fuck him, I'm going to make him pay it. Then, about four months later, I said, Ah, take it off, fuck him. And it's really on the general ledger just like that, about five times, on and off and on and off.

"So the D.A. makes a statement, see, this shows you how payola works, this $20,000. So he's questioning me. And I says no, it's not payola. I got mad, I got glad, I got mad, I got glad. He says no, it's because he played your record. I said, Not so. He played my records anyway. So when he got all through, he starts to make a speech. This will show the people of the grand jury what kind of money and how rampant it is. So he said, You're excused. And I says to him, I got something to say. He said, *You're excused*. So one of the jurors said, Let him talk. So what is it? I said, You know, we just had a laugh here about $20,000—which was a lot of money then—and we just had some fun. But you didn't take into account that Alan and I are partners in the rock and roll shows, and we make $250,000 a year each on that. So me giving him twenty or him giving me twenty is really no big deal. Well, he got so mad he said, *You . . . can . . . leave . . . now!*"

The government tried to get Morris to sign a consent decree, admitting he had done wrong in giving payola. He refused. "People said I was an idiot, and I had plenty of grief because of that," Levy said. "But I liked myself better for not signing it."

■

"Payola" is a word the record industry has bestowed on the English language. The term's familiarity has led to a common perception—unfortunately true—that the business is full of sharpies and opportunists and crooks. But as crimes go, payola is no big deal if the government's enforcement effort is an indication. After Freed's commercial bribery bust in 1960 and congressional hearings on payola the same year, Congress passed a statute making payola a misdemeanor offense punishable by a maximum fine of $10,000 and one year in prison. To date, no one has ever served a day in jail on payola charges. The law is hardly a strong deterrent.*

Worse, the 1960 statute unwittingly laid the groundwork for the "new" payola of the Network. Because disc jockeys had proven so easy to bribe in the fifties, the selection of records at a station was passed to the higher level of program director. This meant, of course, that a bribe-giver needed to seduce only one person rather than several to have a station locked up.

Even the commercial bribery laws were fairly toothless; Morris was probably right when he said that Freed would have beaten the charges had he been less belligerent. The legions of radio people and record executives called before the congressional payola hearings of 1960 made a mockery of the law's ambiguity. Unless it could be shown that they took money to play specific records, there was no illegality. So no one disputed receiving cash and gifts, just what the boodle was for. It magically turned into thank-you money. Thanks for giving my little ol' record a spin, pal—even though I never asked you to.

The men who presided over the hearings were not bowled over by the logic of this explanation. It drove some of them to sarcasm. One congressman demanded of a record executive, "Is it not a fact that these payments were payola up until the time that this investigation started? Then suddenly they became appreciation payments or listening fees or something else?"

Rock historians like to gripe that the hearings were an attack on rock and roll. Maybe they were. But the congressmen heard expert testimony that payola could be traced back at least to 1947, when the record business began to take off. It even existed in the Big Band era. "It was customary for the song plugger to walk up to a [band leader] and slip him an envelope with some money in it," one witness testified. No doubt some politicians believed that were

---

* The FCC weakened the statute even further in 1979 by ruling that "social exchanges between friends are not payola." This loophole makes the statute virtually unenforceable.

it not for payola, radio would be playing Frank Sinatra and Dinah Shore instead of Screamin' Jay Hawkins. "Do you think without payola that a lot of this so-called junk music, rock and roll stuff, which appeals to teenagers would not be played?" one congressman demanded of a disc jockey. "Never get on the air," came the solemn reply.

The committee called to the stand a Boston disc jockey named Joe Smith. He wasn't much at the time, but Smith would go on to become the president of three big labels: Warner Bros., Elektra/Asylum, and, in 1986, Capitol-EMI. Smith never showed much talent for business—in his last two years at Elektra, the once-booming label lost $27 million—but he sure was funny. He turned up on daises year after year as the industry's favorite roastmaster, its Don Rickles. (He once introduced Seymour Stein, president of Sire Records, as "the man who is to the record industry what surfing is to the state of Kansas.") In 1960 it was Joe Smith who got roasted, by Representative Walter Rogers of Texas.

Rogers: Well now, you got a note that says "thank you" and it had a check with it for $175. . . .
Smith: I accepted it as a gift, and why they sent it to me, I cannot tell you, sir. . . .
Rogers: Did you report it as earned income?
Smith: Yes, sir.
Rogers: If it was a gift, you did not have to report it as income. The government owes you some money. . . .
Smith: Sir, I want no more truck with the government after today, I assure you, sir.

Smith was small potatoes, however. The committee was more interested in Richard Wagstaff Clark, better known as Dick Clark, the host of ABC-TV's *American Bandstand*. It was impossible not to compare him with Alan Freed, if only because both men played a seminal role in bringing rock music to white teenagers. Since Freed's last radio job in New York was at WABC, he and Dick Clark had worked for the same parent company. However, as one congressman pointed out to Clark, "ABC fired *him* and retained *you*."

Dick Clark and Alan Freed were different sorts. Freed was rumpled, loud, and a drunkard. Clark was the All-American Boy.

46

In fact, ABC picked Clark for *Bandstand* in 1956 because of his clean image; a drunk driving charge had forced the resignation of the original host. But if you placed their outside interests side by side, Clark and Freed began to look more alike. Clark had a piece of so many companies that could profit from his television program—thirty-three in all—that the committee had to draw a diagram to keep track of them. He had interests in music publishers, record-pressing plants, and an artist-management firm. He had equity in three Philadelphia record companies. He had a third of a toy company that made a stuffed cat with a 45 rpm (the "Platter-Puss"). George Goldner gave him copyrights. Coronation Music assigned him the rights to "Sixteen Candles," a rock classic. He managed Duane Eddy and played his songs endlessly on *Bandstand*. He accepted a fur coat, necklace, and ring for his wife. He invested $175 in one record label and made back more than $30,000.

In the end, the committee chairman pronounced Clark "a fine young man." He was allowed to divest his companies and walk away. By the eighties, Dick Clark was still host of *American Bandstand*, as well as *The $25,000 Pyramid*, and *TV's Bloopers and Practical Jokes*. He owned one of the biggest independent production companies in Hollywood. He had a Rolls-Royce, a Mercedes, a Jaguar, and a house in Malibu. *Forbes* put his net worth at $180 million.

Morris Levy, for his part, was not asked to testify before Congress. One hot topic of the 1960 hearings concerned Roulette Records, however. The previous May a disc jockey convention was held at the Americana Hotel in Miami Beach, drawing over two thousand industry people. The biggest event was an all-night barbecue hosted by Roulette, featuring Count Basie. Roulette spent more than $15,000 on the bash, half of it for bourbon (two thousand bottles' worth, according to hotel ledger books). Basie started swinging at midnight and didn't stop until dawn, at which point Roulette served breakfast. The event became known as the three B's, for bar, barbecue, and breakfast. A *Miami News* headline on May 31, 1959, read FOR DEEJAYS: BABES, BOOZE AND BRIBES.

■

Morris was not a man deterred by stern laws, let alone feeble ones like the payola statute. His contempt for authority had begun as a child. When he recorded Frankie Lymon's "I'm Not a Juvenile Delinquent"—and substituted his name for Lymon's as author—

there was irony at play, because he *was* a juvenile delinquent. All his frustration exploded in one incident at school—an event, he later said, that "changed my whole life."

"I was very bright. I could get an 'A' in any subject I wanted to, without working at it. I really could. Read a history book at the beginning of the term, take the test, and get an 'A.'

"But I had this one teacher, she had no business teaching school. Miss Clare. We had her for homeroom. Must have been seventy-five years old, never got fucked in her life, probably. And she hated me. One day she gave us a math test, and everybody failed it very bad, except for me and another person. She says to the class, you're not gonna do homeroom this period, you're gonna do math because of the poor showing. So my hand shot right up, and I says, What about those who *passed* the test? She looks at me and says, Levy, you're a troublemaker. I'm gonna get you out of this classroom if I have to take your family off home relief.

"And I got up—I was a big kid—took her wig off her head, poured an inkwell on her bald head, and put her wig back on her fucking head. Walked out of school and said, *Fuck* school. Never really went back to school after that there. I was sentenced for eight years to [reform school] by the children's court. And when we got the [welfare] check on the first of the month, I used to mail it back to the state, or the city, or whoever the fuck it was. That's what a teacher can do to you. This bitch had no fucking *humanity.*"

Miss Clare had said the wrong thing. Morris was painfully embarrassed to be on Board of Child Welfare, though he was more than eligible. His father and oldest brother had died of pneumonia when he was a baby. After his middle brother, Irving, joined the navy, he lived alone with his mother in a Bronx tenement. She worked as a house cleaner and suffered from high blood pressure, diabetes, and lockjaw so severe that her front teeth had to be knocked out so she could take food. "Every sickness in the world just came at once on this lady," Morris sighed.

Morris made up for his childhood poverty but never shook the law of the street and the arrogance it entailed. He saw nothing wrong, for example, in putting his name on other people's songs so that he could get writer's as well as publisher's royalties. When Ritchie Cordell wrote "It's Only Love" for Tommy James and the Shondells, Roulette's biggest act of the sixties, "Morris," he said, "gave me back the demo bent in half and told me if his name wasn't on it, the song didn't come out."

Morris was not alone in believing this was his right. "He's entitled to everything," said Hy Weiss, who grew up with Morris in the East Bronx and became a fellow rock and roll pioneer as founder of the Old Town label. "What were these bums off the street?" Nor did Weiss see anything wrong with the practice of giving an artist a Cadillac instead of his royalties. "So what, that's what they wanted. You had to have *credit* to buy the Cadillac."

No performer, however big, was sacrosanct to Morris Levy. John Lennon found this out. Lennon's last album with the Beatles, *Abbey Road*, included his song "Come Together," which sounded similar to Chuck Berry's "You Can't Catch Me," a Levy copyright. Morris sued, but backed off when Lennon proposed a settlement. His next solo album would be a compendium of oldies, including three songs Levy owned. Recording began in late 1973, but the project stalled. Morris interpreted the delay as a breach of settlement. He had dinner with Lennon, who promised to complete the oldies album. Morris let Lennon rehearse at Sunnyview, his farm in upstate New York, and took him and his eleven-year-old son, Julian, to Disney World. He asked Lennon if he could borrow the unedited tape of the songs he intended for the album —just for listening. Morris then released the songs as a TV mail-order album, *Roots*. More litigation followed, but Lennon prevailed, and *Roots* was withdrawn.

Morris is also listed with Frankie Lymon as author of the hit "Why Do Fools Fall in Love?" and other songs he did not write. Sued for back royalties in 1984 by Lymon's widow, Emira Eagle, Morris was pressed to explain under oath how he helped write the tune. "You get together, you get a beat going, and you put the music and words together," he testified. "I think I would be misleading you if I said I wrote songs, per se, like Chopin."

Whether or not Morris took advantage of artists, he never allowed others to take advantage of him. "If you screw him," said one former friend, "he'll always get revenge." Morris was known to administer his own brand of frontier justice. "Given where we came from," said Hy Weiss, "we were capable of a lot of things." For his part, Weiss claimed he once hung a man out a window to settle a business dispute. Another time, Weiss said, he and Morris drove to Rockaway, New York, with a baseball bat, "to bust up a plant that was bootlegging us."

Morris could become violent if provoked, as he demonstrated on the night of February 26, 1975. He, Father Louis Gigante (the Chin's brother, a Bronx priest), Roulette employee Nathan McCalla, and a woman friend of Levy's, identified as Chrissie, were leaving Jimmy Weston's, a Manhattan jazz club. Three strangers approached Chrissie, and one made a flirtatious remark. Morris took offense, and a fight ensued. Two of the men turned out to be plainclothes police detectives. McCalla held the hands of Lieutenant Charles Heinz while Morris punched him in the face, costing him his left eye. Morris and McCalla were indicted for assault, but the case was inexplicably dropped before coming to trial. Heinz brought a civil suit, which was settled out of court. "Morris told me, Louie, I didn't know the cop was hurt," Father Gigante said, years later. "I just fought him."

Nate McCalla was commonly thought to have been Morris's "enforcer" until he disappeared in the late seventies. He was found murdered in 1980. A former army paratrooper, McCalla stood over 6' and weighed 250 pounds. Morris was so fond of Nate that he gave him his own record label, Calla, which recorded soul singers Bettye Lavette and J. J. Jackson. Morris also gave him a music publishing company that McCalla, a black man from Harlem, called JAMF—for Jive-Ass Mother Fucker.

"If I was going to describe Nate, I'd recall the song 'Bad, Bad Leroy Brown,' " said an attorney who did legal work for McCalla. "He had hands like baseball gloves. But he was as gentle as a Great Dane." Most of the time, that is. Once, in the mid-seventies, McCalla went to Skippy White's, a record store in Boston, to collect a delinquent debt. Said an eyewitness, "Nate had a medieval mace and chain, and was slinging it against his hand. He said, 'Where's the boss?' The boss immediately wrote a check."

Though it is not known why McCalla was killed, Washington, D.C., homicide detectives think they have some clues. In 1977 a rock concert was held at the Take It Easy Ranch on Maryland's eastern shore. The concert was sponsored by Washington disc jockey Bob "Nighthawk" Terry, but law officers believe the Genovese family had a financial interest. According to a police report, tickets were counterfeited by two men, Theodore Brown and Howard McNair, and the concert lost money. Brown and McNair were shot dead. Terry vanished, and his body has never been found. McCalla, who was traced to the scene of the concert by the FBI, disappeared soon afterward.

In 1980 McCalla turned up in a rented house in Fort Lauderdale, dead of a gunshot wound in the back of his head, which had literally exploded. Police found him slumped in a lounge chair in front of a switched-on television. The rear door was ajar and keys were in the lock. McCalla had been dead for at least a week and was badly decomposed, a process that had accelerated because someone had sealed the windows and turned on the heater. No suspects were apprehended. Just before the murder, a neighbor saw a bearded, heavyset white stranger pull up to McCalla's house in a Blazer truck. Beyond which, deponent knoweth not.

■

On October 29, 1973, the music division of the United Jewish Appeal feted Morris Levy as man of the year. The testimonial banquet was held at the New York Hilton, and thirteen hundred people turned out to shower love on the man they knew as Moishe. The crowd was a *Who's Who* of the record business. The guests dined on sliced steak and listened to the bands of Harry James and Tito Puente. They sang "Hatikvah" and "The Star-Spangled Banner." There was dancing. A row of saxophonists did synchronized swan dips; a soprano warbled "I Don't Want to Walk Without You, Baby." Speeches were made. "This man is beautiful," gushed UJA official Herb Goldfarb, introducing Morris. Father Gigante hugged Morris and described him as "a diamond in the rough." There was more music. A calf wearing a garland of flowers was wheeled onto the dance floor in a wooden crib. It began to moo plaintively.

"Jesus Christ!" It was Joe Smith, the former disc jockey from Boston who had become the industry's favorite emcee. He was then head of Elektra Records. "I'm the president of a big record company. I'm supposed to follow a *cow*, for Christ's sake. The priest [Gigante] comes on with that *mi corazon* crap, and now I gotta follow a cow, too."

Morris had personally requested that Smith do the roasting. Smith looked out over the dais he was to introduce and saw most of the surviving characters of Morris's generation and a few of their widows.

"The thought of coming up to honor Morris Levy," Smith began, "and to introduce and say something complimentary about this crowd up here tonight, is the most difficult assignment I've ever faced. . . . They have different styles, they have different personalities, they have different approaches to the business. But two things all of these ladies and gentlemen on the dais have in common: They cheated everybody every time they could. And they are the biggest *pain in the ass* people to be around. . . . I would tell you that with this group of cutthroats on this dais, every one of you would be safer in Central Park tonight than you are in the ballroom of the Hilton Hotel."

This got a tremendous laugh, but Smith seemed dismayed.

"Morris is not laughing too hard," he said, "so I think I'll move onward and not stay into that too long."

"Bye, Joey!" cried a voice from the dais.

"That's it, huh?" Smith replied. "I said either tonight I'm a hit, or tomorrow morning, I *get* hit, one or the other."

"You asked for it!"

Smith turned his attention to Hy Weiss, Morris's old neighborhood pal, who was in the back row. "Sorry about the seating arrangements," he said. "Hymie was assigned not to the table, but to room 328, where he's gonna line up the hookers for the party afterwards." There was laughter and applause. "I must tell you that Hymie Weiss, in addition to being a leader in the record business, invented the famous fifty-dollar handshake with disc jockeys. And, as always, tonight he said hello and gave me fifty. And I told him, I haven't been on the air for fifteen years, for Christ's sake."

(Weiss never denied the "handshake"; he was proud of it. He later bragged, "I was the payola king of New York. Payola was the greatest thing in the world. You didn't have to go out to dinner with someone and kiss their ass. Just pay them, here's the money, play the record, *fuck you*.")

Smith continued introducing the dais. "Art Talmadge is the president of Musicor. Began his career with Mercury Records in 1947, where he learned to skim cash, moved on to [United Artists], where he did it good to them. They found out where the leak was. . . .

"Now, one of the biggies enters in here. Cy Leslie, chairman of the board of Pickwick. *Great* rip-off organization. It'll repackage this *dinner* tonight and sell it.

"Another representative of a great tradition and a name in the industry is Elliot Blaine. . . . He and his brother Jerry . . . formed Cosnat Distributing and Jubilee Records back in 1947 and introduced the four bookkeeping system—with four separate sets of books. . . . And it took those guys ten years to find out they were screwing *each other*, with the distributing and Jubilee. . . .

"Mike Stewart, president of United Artists Records, a former actor—*bad* actor. Found four dummies from Canada, the Four Lads, milked them for everything they were worth. And he now sits with a big house in Beverly Hills, and they're working an Italian wedding in the Village tonight. . . ."

Smith saved Morris for last. "I take this opportunity to extend my own personal best wishes to Moishe, a man I've known for many years, admired, and enjoyed. And I just got word from two of his friends on the West Coast that my wife and two children have been released!"

The laughter was uproarious.

■

In 1988, fifteen years after the UJA dinner, Moishe Levy was convicted on two counts of conspiracy to commit extortion. The music industry did not turn its back on him. Before his sentencing, Morris requested and received testimonial letters from the heads of the six largest record companies to present to his parole board and the presiding judge, Stanley Brotman. Bruce Repetto, the assistant U.S. Attorney from Newark who had nailed Morris, countered the letters with allegations, not brought out at the trial itself, that Roulette had been a way station for heroin trafficking. Brotman overlooked the drug allegations but still gave Morris ten years.

The case had begun innocently enough. In 1984 MCA decided to unload 4.7 million cutouts—discontinued albums—including past hits by Elton John, the Who, Neil Diamond, and Olivia Newton-John. Morris had been, in his day, the biggest-ever wholesaler of cutouts. MCA asked $1.25 million for the shipment, which came to sixty trailer-truckloads. Morris signed the purchase order and helped arrange for the records to go to John LaMonte, who was in the cutout business with a company called Out of the Past, based in Philadelphia. LaMonte, incidentally, was a convicted record counterfeiter.

On the surface, it looked like a simple deal, but it wasn't. A number of alleged mafiosi, including Morris's old pal Gaetano "the Big Guy" Vastola, all converged on the deal, expecting to make a "whack-up," or killing, of in some cases a hundred grand apiece. So they said, anyway, in conversations secretly monitored by the

FBI. It was never clear how they would have made this whack-up, since the deal went sour. And when it did, violence and an extortion plot followed.

Though a roughneck with no evident musical ability, Vastola had a number of years' experience in the music business. This was due in part to his association with Morris. Back in the fifties, Vastola often hung around Alan Freed's office at the Brill Building, possibly keeping an eye on him for Morris. Vastola managed a few early rock groups, including the Cleftones, and apparently had an interest in Frankie Lymon and the Teenagers. And he was an owner of Queens Booking, a big agency mostly for black acts in the sixties. One Queens Booking client whom Vastola also set up with a horse farm was Sammy Davis, Jr.

Under normal circumstances, Morris's dealings with Vastola might never have come to the attention of the FBI. But he was unlucky. Other members of Vastola's crew got involved with drugs and gambling, and the FBI won court approval to eavesdrop on the suspects' conversations. As the reels started turning on FBI tape recorders, the U.S. Attorney's Office in Newark grew curious about this MCA cutout deal.

Morris was also unlucky in the choice of John LaMonte to receive the cutouts. LaMonte turned out to be a deadbeat. His refusal to pay Morris back for the records—he said they were all *schlock* and not the ones he ordered—ruined everybody's plans. There would be no whack-up at all unless LaMonte could be persuaded to pay.

Vastola, who had joined Morris in picking LaMonte to get the records, was furious.

"Moishe, Moishe," the FBI heard him say, "you knew this guy was a cocksucker before you made the deal, didn't you?"

"That's right," Morris agreed.

"Why did you make the deal with him?"

Because, Morris explained, he had believed LaMonte was "a *controllable* cocksucker."

Vastola, the man who "could tear a human being apart with his hands," was beginning to sweat. Evidently, he had to answer to higher powers in the mob hierarchy. On the phone with his cousin Sonny Brocco, a fellow conspirator, he fretted about "what they're doing to me . . . including the Chin."

He saw only one way out. "Sonny," Vastola said, "I don't like the way this thing is going with this kid [LaMonte], I'm telling you now. . . . I'm gonna put him in a fuckin' *hospital*. I'm not even going to talk to him. I don't like this motherfucker, what he's doing. . . . I mean, what are they making, a *asshole* out of me, or what?"

Morris was angry, too. "Go out to that place, take over the kid's business," he proposed.

"I'm ready to go over there and break his ass," Vastola said.

On May 18, 1985, Vastola confronted LaMonte in the parking lot of a New Jersey motel and punched him in the face. LaMonte's left eye socket was fractured in three places, and his face had to be reconstructed with wire. True to his word, the Big Guy had put him in the hospital.

But LaMonte still would not pay.

Relations between Morris and Vastola became strained. The two men and another conspirator, Lew Saka, met at Roulette Records on September 23, 1985, to try to sort out the mess they were in. FBI video cameras and bugs preserved the meeting for posterity.

Saka, for one, could not believe LaMonte's nerve. "He still has the balls not to come up with the money like he was supposed to," Saka clucked. "He busted his jaw, he broke it. . . ."

Morris was convinced that LaMonte would not pay because he had a side deal with Vastola's cousin, Sonny Brocco.

"As far as I'm concerned," Morris said, "the one that fucked us with him is Sonny Brocco. I say that flat out, too. What do you think of that? Because he was the one who sat in that fucking chair at the first fucking meeting last year, looking to him what to say. And that's the first time this kid [LaMonte] ever got up on his ass and got enough nerve to even talk back."

"Sonny Brocco's dying," Vastola said.

"Fuck him!" Morris said.

"I went to see him at the hospital in isolation."

"What's he done, *nice* things for people, Sonny Brocco?" Morris demanded. "A lot of people are dying. Let me tell you something about me. If a guy's a cocksucker in his life, when he dies he don't become a saint."

Matters went downhill from there, and Morris finally felt it necessary to call a mediator. The man he phoned was Dominick "Baldy Dom" Canterino, the Chin's chauffeur and right-hand man.

"I'm sorry to do this to you, pal," Morris said.

Vastola began to muse aloud about the prospect of jail. He had done time twice already—for extortion. It seemed to be one of his sidelines.

"We're gonna wind up in the joint," Vastola said. "Me, I know definitely."

"I'm hotter than all of youse," Morris replied. "They'd love to get me. You know that." The government had been after him, he said, for twenty-five years.

When he arrived and took his place at the meeting, Baldy Dom was treated with deference. He listened to Vastola and Levy relate their problems with John LaMonte and then asked the obvious question: "Who gave him the records?"

There was a pause.

"The original deal?" said Morris.

"Yeah," said Canterino.

Somehow it seemed prudent to blame alleged West Coast mob figure Sal Pisello, yet another party to the transaction.

"The original deal was finally closed with Sal and him," Morris said. "Sal closed the deal with him. The deal was blown up and I said fuck it all. . . ."

"He says get rid of it," Vastola nodded.

"Sal closed the deal," Morris repeated.

"Right," agreed Lew Saka.

"Sal closed the deal with him and now we all have to live with it," Morris said. "The truth's the truth. Sal did close the deal with him."

Despite such blatantly incriminating conversations, Morris had been predicting for over a year that he would win his case. He seemed genuinely shocked to have lost it. It had been his plan, after he was acquitted, to sell Roulette and his farm and move to Australia. Now, he would have to wait at least three and a half years before he became eligible for parole. In the meantime, he did sell all his music holdings, at long last, for more than $55 million.

"The music business was a beautiful business," he said, adding that he, Morris Levy, was the last of a breed. "The government will finish burying me off. The government don't like the mavericks and impresarios. It used to be Horatio Alger stories, now they want no-talent bums. Stick your head up above the crowd, you get it chopped off."

■

Morris was wrong about being the last of a breed. If the label bosses of today are not quite as intimidating as he was, it isn't for lack of trying. Morris's more genteel contemporaries of the fifties, whose careers preceded rock and roll, are the real vanished race. When Morris formed Roulette, for example, a man of dignity and charm named Goddard Lieberson was in command of CBS Records. He was *not* a Damon Runyon character, not even remotely. Though his legacy would be felt at CBS Records well into the Yetnikoff era, his approach to the business would not.

4

Goddard and Clive

GROUCHO Marx was in New York with talk show host Dick
Cavett. Tell me, Dick, he said, would you like to have dinner with
a man named Goddard Lieberson? Cavett said he would be delighted. Okay, Groucho shot back, I'll try to find one. As it happened, he did know a Goddard Lieberson, a *bon vivant* who also
mingled with Jacqueline Onassis, John Gielgud, Richard Rodgers,
and Somerset Maugham. It was Lieberson who introduced Noel
Coward to the Las Vegas vice squad. One might encounter him at
a bathhouse in Tokyo, on a safari in Kenya, or in the royal men's
room at the palace in London. When he was not roaming the
globe or delighting café society, Goddard Lieberson also found
time to be president of CBS Records.

He became CBS Records' head man in 1956, the year Morris
Levy launched Roulette. It is hard to imagine two business contemporaries with less in common. Goddard came from the rural
town of Hanley, England, the son of a manufacturer of rubber
heels. He was graduated from the Eastman School of Music as a
classical pianist and composer and wrote music criticism as "Jo-
hann Sebastian." As Morris Levy recorded bebop and rock and
roll, Goddard Lieberson signed Vladimir Horowitz and Leonard
Bernstein to the CBS Masterworks division and produced the orig-
inal-cast album of *My Fair Lady*.

Goddard Lieberson must not have guessed in the fifties that
he was becoming a relic, that the future of his business belonged
to men like Morris. Perhaps it was apparent to him by the time he
retired in 1975. In the fifties and early sixties, Lieberson conquered
popular taste by recording Andy Williams and Tony Bennett and

Mitch Miller's "sing-along" albums, but the rock revolution left him behind. Corporations that wanted to make it in the post-fifties record business had to recruit from Morris's circle, or at least find executives who spoke the language.

Goddard was far removed from Levy's world. CBS did not record rock and roll in the fifties, and there were few bribes for disc jockeys who played Bach or Cole Porter. In Lieberson's day, however, the mob had a grip on independent distribution of records. Goddard was not naive about this. In a convention speech, his personal art form, Goddard told the story of fictional pop singer Joe Gamm. Gamm had no talent, he said, but this had not stunted his recording career, "since his father, Charlie Gambino, owns two recording companies, five one-stops, seven record stores, two armored cars, and four submachine guns. Joe Gamm's records have never been pirated. . . ."

Such *méchant* humor was a Lieberson trademark. One time CBS Records held a double-entendre contest; Goddard won with this entry: "I love you, Truman Capote said, tongue in cheek." When a doctor instructed him to send a stool sample through the mail, he observed that the Columbia Record Club had been doing this for years. He introduced a vice-president, Ken Glancy, to a dinner audience as "that rare combination, a practically unknown combination, I would say—a charming, cultured, witty man, an astute businessman . . . *and a gentile*." He signed his letters "God."

This last jest was appropriate; his employees worshiped him. Goddard Lieberson was tall and distinguished, with a high forehead, a strong nose, gray temples. He spoke in a resonant baritone and puffed a pipe. Goddard married ballet dancer Vera Zorina and served on the board of the Metropolitan Opera. He had his shirts custom-made in London and his handkerchiefs monogrammed. He demonstrated, said his friend Walter Cronkite, "impeccable taste in all things: in black tie at the opera, in mufti at a board of directors meeting, in slacks at a recording session." Music attorney John Eastman once sat down with Lieberson wearing a blue suit and clashing gray socks. "He spent the whole meeting staring at my *ankles*," Eastman recalled years later.

In sum, Goddard Lieberson was perfectly tailored for a corporation like CBS, the "Tiffany" network. The men he served, chairman William Paley and president Frank Stanton, seemed obsessed with style. Paley covered the walls of the executive floor with de Koonings and Rouaults; Stanton hired world-famous architect Eero Saarinen to design Black Rock and hand-picked the Canadian granite and smoked glass. Depending on whether Paley or Stanton took the corporate jet, the interior decor was redone to that man's personal taste. Something of a snob, Paley had little time for people who did not meet his standards of elegance. Goddard Lieberson was one of the few CBS employees Paley entertained in his own home.

This was no small honor, because William Paley was somewhat larger than life. His story has been told innumerable times: son of a German-Jewish cigar-maker . . . bought the money-losing CBS radio network in 1927 for a million or so . . . built it into one of America's largest media corporations . . . made CBS a "national trust" with an all-star news division headed by Edward R. Murrow, but also a merchant of the "vast wasteland" with low-brow entertainment like *The Beverly Hillbillies* . . . married Babe Cushing, the sister-in-law of Jock Whitney and Vincent Astor . . . imposed mandatory retirement at sixty-five but stayed on as chairman well into his eighties. . . . Paley was a man accustomed to getting what he wanted. He tossed out chief executives, as some wag put it, like "disposable lighters" and fired his personal attorney of forty years the morning after the man disagreed with him in public. Paley's exquisite taste permeated CBS; so did his cold-bloodedness.

Lieberson was himself a political animal. Classical A&R man Thomas Shepard worked for Goddard for fourteen years; after he left to head RCA's Red Seal division, they met at concerts without shaking hands. "There's a story going around that at the beginning Goddard took me under his wing," Shepard said. "He never took *anybody* under his wing." Shepard remembered something else about Goddard: his commitment to quality. Goddard believed, said Shepard, "that we were deriving a lot of profits out of the music business, and it was our responsibility to plow something back." Lieberson recorded "important" music that sold poorly, such as the jazz of Duke Ellington. His CBS Legacy Series issued one blue-ribbon album a year, including a Civil War commemorative and a set of records on the Irish uprising. Lieberson even put out records guaranteed to lose money, like the complete works of serial composers Arnold Schönberg and Anton von Webern.

He got away with it because under him CBS Records had some enormous commercial successes. None was bigger than the original cast album of *My Fair Lady*, which sold 5 million copies worldwide in 1957, more than any previous LP. This was all the more impressive considering the nation had at the time only one fifth the stereo sets it has today. Moreover, Goddard had persuaded Paley to have CBS Inc. finance the show; for $500,000, CBS became the sole backer of a musical that earned the company $32 million. CBS Records' pop roster made good money and included prestige acts such as Barbra Streisand, Tony Bennett, and Rosemary Clooney. In jazz, CBS Records had Miles Davis; in country, Johnny Cash; in gospel, Mahalia Jackson; in folk, Pete Seeger.

It was a showcase of talent, and nearly all of it was on Columbia, known as "Big Red" for the label's color. In Lieberson's time, CBS Records and Columbia were synonymous. The Epic label, future home of Michael Jackson and Cyndi Lauper, had few acts of note; some people called it "Mediocre Orange." Columbia had the cream of the roster and a proud history. The Columbia Phonograph Company was cofounded in 1887 by Alexander Graham Bell; its first stars, recorded on wax cylinders, were John Philip Sousa and the United States Marine Band. When William Paley bought Columbia Records in 1938 for $700,000, it did a roaring trade in "race" records, with black artists like Bessie Smith and Ethel Waters. But it was not the biggest record company in the thirties and forties; that honor fell to RCA Victor.

Lieberson would help change that. His successes in Broadway musicals and mainstream pop enabled Columbia to overtake RCA Victor as the leading label by the late fifties. He added to RCA's indignity by abetting the successful launch of the long-playing record, invented in 1948 by CBS scientist Peter Goldmark. RCA had earlier fumbled with its own version of the LP.

Goddard had joined Columbia as an A&R man the year after CBS bought it, and he never lost sight of his calling. The A&R man was a redoubtable figure in Lieberson's day. A&R stood for artists and repertoire, and it meant artists and repertoire. The A&R man (he was always a man) did not merely discover talent. He picked the songs and arrangements and supervised the recording sessions. Rock and roll changed A&R, because rock musicians wrote or at least chose most of their material. A rock group went into the studio with an independent producer, and the record company might be barred from the whole record-making process. This was frustrating, because a rock album could take months or even years to complete. In Lieberson's time, the company A&R man brought a Frankie Laine or a Guy Mitchell into the studio and cut a record in a day or two. With the advent of rock, to be an A&R executive meant going to clubs, listening to demo tapes sent by top lawyers and managers, and saying no most of the time. In the rock era, the joke went, A&R stood for Arguments and Recriminations.

Probably no A&R man has ever been as powerful as Mitch Miller was under Goddard Lieberson. He was a classical oboist who met Goddard at the Eastman School in the thirties. Miller's first A&R post was at Mercury, where he produced the Fine Arts Quartet and other classical acts. In 1948 he turned his talents to pop. Miller found the song "Mule Train" for Frankie Laine; it sold a million and a half copies. He produced Patti Page and Vic Damone. He switched to Columbia in 1950, and within two years it was the biggest pop label. Goddard told Miller to discover new talent, and he did: Rosemary Clooney, Tony Bennett, Mahalia Jackson, the Four Lads, Johnny Mathis, Guy Mitchell, Johnnie Ray, Jerry Vale.

With his King Faisal beard, Mitch Miller became a household figure, thanks to the NBC television program *Sing Along with Mitch*, which, when canceled in 1966, still had a remarkable 34 share. Miller asked Boy Scouts, Girl Scouts, Kiwanis, and Rotary members what they sang at parties. He took his list and assembled four-part choruses, backed by ukeleles and accordions, to perform the songs. His sing-along albums for Columbia sold 20 million copies, well into the rock era. This fact was not lost on Mitch Miller because he was the living repudiation of rock and roll. He loathed it.

Though Miller left Columbia in 1965, the company took some time to overcome his deep-seated feelings about rock. That year CBS Records' "contemporary" roster consisted of Bob Dylan, Chad and Jeremy, Paul Revere and the Raiders, Simon and Garfunkel, and the Byrds—period. Columbia's two biggest rivals at the time, RCA Victor and Capitol, had Elvis Presley and the Beatles, respectively, but overall they were no more committed to rock than CBS. It seemed too scruffy a musical form to last very long.

Not everyone in Goddard's A&R department felt this way, least of all John Hammond. Some people believe Hammond was the greatest talent scout of all time. What is certain is that Hammond was the ultimate WASP in a preponderantly Jewish profession. His mother was a Vanderbilt, and he grew up in an eight-story mansion off Fifth Avenue. Early on, he developed a passion for jazz, blues, and civil rights. Hammond dropped out of Yale and wrote jazz criticism. He went to Alabama to cover the infamous Scottsboro Boys trial for *The Nation*. He worked for Mercury and Vanguard before settling at Columbia in 1937, just before CBS bought the label. Hammond wandered into a Harlem speakeasy one night in 1933 and discovered an unknown singer of seventeen named Billie Holiday. Forty years later, Bruce Springsteen came to his office at CBS for an audition, and Hammond gave him the nod. In between, Hammond discovered Charlie Christian, Count Basie, Teddy Wilson, Bob Dylan, Aretha Franklin, and George Benson.

Around Columbia, Bob Dylan was known as "Hammond's folly." Hammond's antennae must have been finely tuned, because he discovered Dylan playing backup harmonica and guitar —badly—at a rehearsal for Texas folksinger Carolyn Hester. Hammond invited Dylan to audition as a soloist and immediately signed him to Columbia. At that time, Columbia had weekly product meetings; Hammond came to one with a tape of Dylan's "Talking New York Blues." The A&R staff was underwhelmed. Some of the older men on the staff did not think Dylan could sing or play. Hammond later said he never had any trouble with Mitch Miller on Bob Dylan, but Miller left Columbia before the folksinger grafted an electric guitar to his sound and became a rock artist.

Bruce Lundvall, the future president of the Columbia label, was a young marketing man in the early sixties. He long remembered the bitter feuds in the A&R department over rock and roll. "I would go to A&R and planning meetings, and these *fights* would break out," he said. "People were yelling and screaming at one another about whether CBS Records should be in rock."

Lieberson's CBS Records was not a large company. As the sixties began, the entire staff worked out of five floors at 799 Seventh Avenue, except for small outposts in four foreign countries. This was still a far cry from the CBS Records of the late eighties, when the company maintained branch offices in Los Angeles and Nashville, and had subsidiaries in about fifty foreign countries.

Sales and distribution were a primitive affair. Inventories were kept and processed on hand cards—no computer networks just yet. CBS used distributors of televisions and other household goods to deliver its LPs and singles to retailers. A Philco distributorship handled CBS Records in Atlanta, and that was one of the better arrangements. The record company's dealer in Memphis was big in shotguns. This system did not work well. Salesmen whose main concern was TVs or steam irons or firearms did not have much feel for record albums. Meanwhile, many of Columbia's smaller competitors were at the mercy of independent distributors. This had its problems, too, since an indie distributor might disagree with a label on the sales potential of a new record and refuse to ship it in quantity.

Enter Bill Gallagher. He was executive vice-president under Goddard Lieberson, and he invented what was known as the branch system. In simple terms, Gallagher created a distribution network owned and operated by CBS. Before long the other major labels followed CBS's lead. Gallagher didn't know it, but he had dealt independent distribution a mortal blow. For this he deserves a special mention in the history of recorded music. One by one, the little labels would turn to the big labels to distribute their records, finding them on the whole more reliable than the independents. It took a while, but by the early eighties independent distribution was dead. Gallagher's revolution would make the major labels more powerful than ever.

Gallagher was a stocky man much feared and respected at Lieberson's CBS Records. Since Lieberson was "God," Gallagher was known as "the Pope." Meetings with Gallagher were called "confessions"; if you left his office, someone might ask whether you had kissed his ring. Everyone saw Gallagher as Lieberson's heir apparent. He probably was, until another, even more ambitious man arrived on the scene. Gallagher's rival would lead CBS —or *drag* it, as he later claimed—into the forefront of rock once and for all. His name was Clive Davis.

■

One of the supreme compliments in the record business is to call someone a "great record man." It's a simple expression, but it conveys multitudes. You can be a top record *executive* with a firm grasp of contract law and accounting and management principles and not qualify as a record *man* at all, let alone a great one. (Boy's club that it is, the industry has no such term as "record woman.") To earn this tribute, you must have "ears," which is not quite the same thing as having good taste. In short, you must be able to tell a hit record. A person who claims to know which songs will become hits and is right often enough develops an aura equal to that of a stock-picker on Wall Street who consistently beats the Dow Jones index.

More important than hit records are the hit artists that make the charts with regularity. A great record man should be able to point to artists he discovered and signed and nurtured who had staying power. No one ever disputed, for instance, that Berry Gordy fit the bill. He was the Detroit automotive worker and songwriter who founded Motown Records in 1959 and launched Diana Ross and the Supremes, the Jackson Five, Stevie Wonder, the Temptations, Smokey Robinson, and many others.

Then there was Ahmet Ertegun, the Turkish-born jazz and blues buff who cofounded Atlantic Records in 1948, and sold it to Warner Communications two decades later. He had Great Record Man written all over him. He was jaunty, and bald, and had a goatee, and shone as a raconteur. He could order a bottle of wine from a headwaiter in perfect French, then turn to his jazzman dinner guest and slip into black jive. Ertegun was one of the original characters of the record business, but the one with the most class. In time he and his interior designer wife, Mica, moved into social circles where Goddard Lieberson himself would have felt comfortable—in short, as Morris Levy groused, "he went *legit.*" Ertegun recorded some of the early R&B greats, including Ray Charles and Wilson Pickett, and in the sixties and seventies he had not lost the magic, as he proved by signing Crosby, Stills, Nash and Young and Led Zeppelin and Bette Midler.

Ahmet's sidekick at Atlantic, Jerry Wexler, was another G.R.M., for sure. Wexler humiliated Columbia Records with Aretha Franklin. Columbia did not know what to do with her once John Hammond signed her. The A&R staff stuck her in front of an orchestra and gave her middle-of-the-road pop standards. When Wexler got her on Atlantic, he knew exactly what to do with the gospel singer, and said so: "I put her in the church."

Clive Davis was not a likely candidate for this hallowed band. He was a Harvard-educated lawyer who eventually made it to the top of CBS Records through talent, timing, and feral political infighting. This might have been enough for most people, but Clive Davis also wanted to be a great record man. Yet, as he later admitted, "I had no A&R training, no claim to having 'ears.'" Clive worked hard at it, as he did at everything, and in time he managed to convince the record industry that he *did* belong in the company of Gordy and Ertegun—and Goddard Lieberson.

Comparisons were inevitable. Lieberson managed to look stylish without appearing vain; Clive looked vain. At first he emulated Goddard with expensive suits and flowing pocket handkerchiefs. As he began to move CBS Records into rock, he put on Nehru jackets and other "mod" clothes. These would have appeared even sillier, but Clive was only in his thirties and seemed younger. He had a boyish face; some described it as cherubic. Goddard, naturally enough, spoke with a Continental accent; his first four years had been spent in England. Clive sounded faintly of Oxford, too, and no one knew why, since he came from a middle-class Jewish neighborhood in Brooklyn. His tongue occasionally betrayed him, though: To Clive, Aretha Franklin was Are*ther*.

There is no question that Clive Davis developed ears, just as there is no disputing that CBS Records grew into a rock powerhouse under his presidency. More than one person has remarked that had Clive been content to rest on his laurels, he might have won the industry's love as well as its respect, for much could be said in his favor. Clive was passionate about his work. As he grew confident of his creative instincts, he was not afraid to tell a big-name artist that a song had to be done over or that a new album was not very good. He knew every detail of CBS Records' operations, down to the daily sales figures. Clive inspired his people to work hard, and he was a fine teacher. One of his young assistants, Alvin Teller, who went on to become a label president, still recalls how Clive defined his job: "Just *learn*."

Yet Clive did not inspire loyalty. The company simply gagged on his inflated self-importance. The record business has never seen anyone so stingy in sharing credit as Clive Davis. His 1975 autobiography, *Clive: Inside the Record Business*, gives the impression that he, singly and alone, signed, molded, and marketed every major pop act CBS Records had during his eight-year reign. The people who worked for him at CBS did not love him for it.

"That ego was *unbearable*. Everything Clive said was genius," remarked Jack Craigo, Clive's head of sales. CBS Records was much too large to be a one-man show the way, say, Motown was in the sixties, and all the world seemed to understand this except Clive. Joe Smith got a good laugh introducing him at a convention. "Let me read the official biography," Smith recalled saying. "Clive was born in a manger in Bethlehem. . . ." He did not grow humbler with time. A close aide quipped not long ago that Clive Davis thought they had named the CD after him.

Whatever became of his accent, Clive maintained that Brooklyn had made him "competitive" and "flinty" and instilled in him "the idea that dignity and fairness must be joined with a clear definition of one's own standards." He came out of Crown Heights, a tight community off Eastern Parkway, with memories of Ebbetts Field, the corner candy store, and double features on Saturday. Clive's father, Herman, was an electrical contractor who later went on the road selling shirts and ties. He described his mother, Florence, as "a dark-haired, gregarious, vivacious beauty."

Clive was a classic overachiever. He went to New York University in 1953 on a full scholarship and made president of his freshman class and the student council. He graduated magna cum laude and advanced to Harvard Law School on *another* full scholarship. Clive had no time for music, though he loved Broadway show tunes. He didn't care for rock and roll. Upon graduating from Harvard in 1956, he joined a small New York law firm at a salary of $4,500 a year. Two years later, he moved up to a large, white-shoe firm, Rosenman, Colin, Kaye, Petschek, and Freund. Sam Rosenman was counsel to Franklin Roosevelt and Harry Truman; Ralph Colin's clients included William Paley and CBS.

The job was not what Clive had hoped. He didn't mind the fifty-hour workweek, but he resented that Rosenman and Colin brought in most of the business and left the young associates to service their accounts. Clive hadn't endured Harvard Law to carry someone else's briefcase into court. En route to the office one day in 1960, he found himself choking back tears. He began to weigh a job offer from a former colleague at the Rosenman firm, Harvey Schein. He was general counsel for Columbia Records, and would soon be setting up CBS Records International. Schein wanted Clive to be his assistant counsel. Ralph Colin advised Clive not to go. He frankly thought Davis was too Ivy League for a shuck-and-jive business like pop music. After a bit of soul-searching, however, Clive Davis, twenty-eight, joined Columbia.

One of his first assignments was to keep Bob Dylan on the label. When John Hammond signed him, Dylan was twenty and a minor under New York State contract law. The folksinger said he had no parents to countersign for him, which was untrue. After his first album bombed, Dylan sent Columbia a letter declaring his contract void. Hammond, who had never before been double-crossed by an artist, handed the letter to Davis. Clive asked whether Dylan had used the CBS studio since turning twenty-one. Six or seven times, Hammond told him. In that case, Clive said, Dylan had affirmed his contract. Dylan was forced to rescind his letter. A year later, Clive had a run-in with Dylan over his song "Talkin' John Birch Society Blues." Columbia would not record it because it equated Birchers and Nazis, and that was deemed libelous. Clive had to break the news to Dylan, who took it badly. Not wishing to seem illiberal, Clive regaled Dylan with stories of how he'd worked for Adlai Stevenson in the fifties and been a campus radical at Harvard. "Bullshit!" Dylan said, and stalked out of the room.

Almost immediately, Clive caught the eye of Goddard Lieberson. Goddard liked lawyers. His number two man, Norman Adler, was a former general counsel. Goddard watched Davis go into overdrive when the Federal Trade Commission sued the Columbia Record Club for antitrust (CBS won the case). Clive drew up Broadway show contracts and went to opening nights with Goddard. He worked weekends and made sure Goddard knew it. He took night classes in antitrust and copyright law. When Harvey Schein moved into International, and CBS's chief counsel tried to give Schein's job to someone else, Goddard said no, he wanted Clive Davis.

Clive was in awe of Goddard—in awe of his elegance and the cult of personality that surrounded him. To this day, Clive can describe Goddard's wardrobe in detail. Clive marveled at the way Goddard bent the corporation to his lifestyle, which no one else could do at Bill Paley's CBS. Goddard was a privileged soul because he moved in the same glamorous circles as Paley. Clive could not get too close to Goddard—no one could. Lieberson was an aloof executive, not interested in building a team. He liked to pit people against one another, Clive observed, "so that he could lie back and take a rest while his underlings struggled for position and power." This would prove fortunate for competitive and flinty Clive Davis.

Bill Gallagher, the marketing executive they called "the Pope," *had* built a team, one that was large and loyal. He had masterminded the label's wholly owned distribution network, and a huge field force, which had not existed before, owed its allegiance to him. This gave Gallagher leverage over his own boss, Norman Adler. All the same, marketing wasn't everything. Columbia's lifeblood was A&R, and A&R reported directly to Goddard Lieberson.

For the moment, anyway. This was a period in American corporate history known as the "go-go years," when it was faddish to take over smaller companies whose products had little or nothing to do with your own. History would prove that this was basically a dumb idea. Empire builder that he was, Paley urged CBS divisions to look for takeover targets. Columbia Records picked up Fender Guitars and Creative Playthings, an educational toy company. The label would soon move into drums and loudspeakers as well. What these products had to do with records was more theoretical than real. Columbia was becoming unwieldy, and the Harvard Business School was called in to sort it out. By the time the consultants put down their pencils, they had advice that Lieberson hadn't counted on: Combine marketing and A&R.

Columbia was abuzz. Goddard did not care to relinquish artists and repertoire to Norman Adler—a lawyer, after all. Instead, he gave Columbia A&R to Bill Gallagher and Epic A&R to that label's general manager, Len Levy. They were Adler's men, but on A&R decisions they would now report to the president. It was pure Lieberson. He had complied with the Harvard study *and* left Adler in the cold. A week later, in June 1965, Goddard summoned Clive Davis to his executive suite. He came right to the point. Would Clive accept the new post of administrative vice-president? His salary would be doubled, and he would be Adler's equal in rank. He would oversee Gallagher and Levy on everything, including A&R. Clive did not need to be asked twice. "I was stunned," he wrote. "I suddenly had the job everyone coveted." He was thirty-three.

Bill Gallagher was stunned, too. It was the beginning of a two-year power struggle between him and Clive. Had Gallagher realized how ambitious a foe he had in Clive Davis, he might have spared himself the agony and resigned immediately. Lieberson, for his part, had no idea that Clive Davis had A&R aspirations. Goddard only gave him the job, Clive later admitted, because he "needed a buffer between him and all these people under him. He didn't like to have to deal with too many things that were distasteful, or unpleasant, or too detailed. He was traveling abroad a lot of the time." Clive Davis may have been cut out for many roles, but being a buffer was not among them. Within a few years, he would elbow his mentor aside, leaving Goddard the head of CBS Records in name alone. Clive confessed with a sly smile, "The original job that he gave me, he never envisaged building, I don't think, in the way that it took place."

Clive's title was indeed ambiguous, and this was deliberate. Whenever Clive bullied Gallagher, the marketing man would step into Lieberson's office and sound off. Goddard would tell him to calm down, that Clive was just an *administrator*. If Clive was right about Goddard, he wanted to provoke a donnybrook without getting himself involved. Clive's strategy, however, was to force Goddard to take sides. "Goddard," he explained, "would *never* have given Columbia as a company to Bill Gallagher."

Clive noticed that the Columbia A&R staff had qualms about Gallagher. Mitch Miller had just retired on his sing-along millions, and the department was leaderless. With Goddard's blessing, Clive ordered Gallagher to replace Miller with a new head of pop A&R. Gallagher was stung. He had wanted to try his own hand at the job. He stalled the appointment for months, and the A&R staff began to grumble. Clive went to Goddard, using the controversy to have his title upgraded to vice-president and general manager. No more administrative handle. Gallagher proposed one of his former salesmen for the A&R post; Clive rejected the appointment —testily. Another nominee, another veto. Meanwhile, Clive clamped down hard on Len Levy of Epic. He appointed a loyalist to run Epic A&R and told Levy to stick to marketing.

Clive was so strong a general manager that in 1967 Goddard bowed to the inevitable and made him Columbia president. Goddard was still head of the records group, but Clive was in control. Bill Gallagher and Len Levy resigned. Clive noted that both men moved in and out of several jobs after that. "This is really very sad," he wrote with thinly disguised glee. "A&R can be an addiction. It derailed both Gallagher and Levy, at least temporarily, and their stories serve well as a warning to others in the industry."

Though Clive was now the undisputed head of Columbia, the label was still rife with Gallagher loyalists who resented the young attorney. But at least two top men owed their jobs to Clive. Their names were Walter Yetnikoff and Dick Asher.

Clive had tapped Walter to be his assistant in 1961 while general attorney. Like Clive, Walter got his start as a young attorney at the Rosenman law firm. Walter was twenty-eight, shy, and very

"Brownsville," which was not a compliment. Clive had shed his Brooklyn accent and become an immaculate if flashy dresser. Walter talked like Walter and had a couple of ill-fitting suits. (In law school, he had worn sweaters with holes in them.) Clive's original assessment of Yetnikoff was that he was "rough around the edges."

Walter never forgot his first impression of CBS Records. The Rosenman firm, he said, "sent me to CBS around Christmastime to do a file search. Very boring. But [Columbia] was having a party. Lots of girls around, music, lights being turned off. I thought, this looks like a fun place.

"About a week later Clive Davis offered me a job to be his assistant at $1,500 more than I was getting."

Walter had wanted to practice "law with a capital L," as he put it, and he had to mull the offer. "I went back to the firm and said, Are you going to make me a partner? I'd been there three and a half years. And they said, Well, you know, bring in some *business*. Who do you know? I said nobody."

In the end, the glamour of show business won out. Best of all, Walter said, Clive "gave me my own secretary—and the most exciting thing, a telephone with four buttons on it!"

When Clive leapfrogged over Bill Gallagher in 1965, he recommended Walter for general attorney. Goddard was not so sure. In dress, speech, and manners, Walter Yetnikoff was the antithesis of Goddard Lieberson. "I wouldn't say Lieberson disliked him," Clive said. "But if one had to judge by superficial appearances, it was a question of whether he was just a good second man as compared to a first man. I remember vouching that he was a first man." So Walter moved up into Clive's old job.

A year later, in 1966, Clive was still feuding with Bill Gallagher. Though Gallagher was losing, the wear and tear of political infighting was beginning to show on Davis. Now and then he poured out his frustration to a lawyer his age, thirty-four, in private practice with his own firm: Asher, Beldock & Kushnik.

Dick Asher was fond of Clive, and he had a high opinion of Columbia. He was sorry to hear of Clive's political troubles. Each time they had a business lunch, which was a frequent occurrence, Dick would say to Clive, Look, if it gets to be too much, join my firm. And Clive would tell him, I'll take you up on that someday.

A day came in 1966 when Clive invited Dick Asher to lunch but would not discuss the agenda. Dick was sure that Clive was going to tell him he had had it with Columbia, so he went to his partners and said, Look, he's a very good man and I think we should welcome him aboard. Much to Asher's shock, Clive instead proposed that Dick join him at CBS as vice-president of business affairs. Dick gave him a flat no. He was making a lot of money and had his own firm. Clive said that was too bad, and perhaps Dick could recommend someone else. He gave qualifications, Asher said, that were "somewhere between Superman and Jesus Christ," and Dick was flattered to think Clive held him in such high regard. The hook was baited. "I guess he upped his offer and was persistent," Dick said, "because I ended up going over there."

Business affairs was a key position, for that was where the contracts were drawn. Clive would give Asher a list of artists to sign or renew, and it would be up to him to get it done. Clive needed someone he could trust, because in 1966 he had a crisis on his hands. Three important artists were up for renewal at once: Andy Williams, Barbra Streisand, and Bob Dylan. The first two did renew, but it looked as though Columbia would lose Dylan. Manager Albert Grossman and lawyer David Braun had worked out a deal for MGM to get Dylan for a 12 percent royalty. Columbia paid 5 percent and could not match MGM without setting an ugly precedent, so it had to come up with a complex contract full of compensating goodies. Just as keeping Dylan had been one of Clive's first tasks, it was now Dick Asher's.

Dick finally worked out the details with Grossman and Braun and delivered the contract to Dylan in upstate New York. It was an odd time in the singer's career, because he had had a motorcycle accident and been out of public view for months. There were rumors in the press that he was a quadriplegic or brain-damaged.

"I drove up to Albert Grossman's barn in Woodstock with the contract," Asher said. "Dylan pulled up in a blue Ford station wagon, looking like a suburban husband. It shocked the hell out of me.

"I was a Dylan fan and we were talking about his new record. I said, What's it going to be like? He thought a while and said, Oh, further down the road. I said, What does that mean? He thought some more and said, I guess just further down the road. The next album was *John Wesley Harding*, and the only way you could describe it was further down the road.

"I came back with the contract and was immediately besieged. What does he look like? Can he talk without slurring his words? I didn't realize that no one had seen Dylan since his motorcycle accident. All of a sudden, I found myself a center of attention. I was not used to that."

■

When Clive took over as president of Columbia in 1967, it was a far cry from a rock and roll label, Dylan or no Dylan. Whether rock was a pot of gold was still an open question. One thing was clear, however: The music that had sustained Columbia for so long was showing signs of tired middle age.

In fact, Columbia was in deep trouble. Pretax earnings had flattened to about $5 million a year, and even this sum was in jeopardy. After eleven gold albums, Mitch Miller's sing-along series was played out. Johnny Mathis left Columbia for Mercury. The Top 40 format was taking hold around the country, and it was turning away from Broadway show tunes. Columbia felt it. In 1958 the Rodgers and Hammerstein musical *Flower Drum Song* was only a moderate success on the stage, but the album sold 600,000 copies, thanks to a Top 40 single from the score, "I Enjoy Being a Girl." *Mame* ran for three years, but the Columbia album sold poorly—no hits on Top 40.

Rock had dominated the singles charts for a decade. Elvis Presley had already recorded sixteen number one hits; the Beatles held the entire top five one week in 1964. Motown artists like the Supremes and Mary Wells were making the singles charts, and Columbia acts like Doris Day were not. Clive would nevertheless write that rock "wasn't the music of the masses. Not yet." This was bad history but good accounting. If you looked at the album charts, middle-of-the-road, or MOR, pop still held sway in the sixties. One of the biggest album acts of 1965, for instance, was the Tijuana Brass. And albums, then as now, were the real money-makers. Rock was regarded as a singles format, the Beatles notwithstanding, and therefore possible for the major labels to ignore.

This was about to change as Clive ascended to Columbia's presidency. The Beatles led the way with their landmark 1967 album *Sgt. Pepper's Lonely Hearts Club Band*, which sparked the psychedelic movement, making rock an album medium. The year bore witness to the Summer of Love and the rise of new San Francisco acts such as the Grateful Dead, the Electric Flag, and Quicksilver Messenger Service. Meanwhile, Jimi Hendrix and the Jefferson Airplane had begun recording. The new sounds caught a generation of college-educated baby boomers, and when they began to buy albums, the amount of money they spent was unprecedented.

Clive was in the right place at the right time. He was young and had not yet asserted his musical tastes. No one identified him with the music of Lieberson's generation. Many of the new rock acts already had large followings, yet were still available—and cheap. Clive made the decision to go after them wholeheartedly. As a result, CBS Records would make a quantum leap in power and profitability.

It is too easy to dismiss Clive's pro-rock business strategy as an obvious move. For one thing, he was bucking an unfriendly constituency at CBS, which was still largely bound to Mitch Miller's way of thinking. "It's hard to overestimate how much of a change in the mentality of the company Clive really achieved," Dick Asher said. "He made a statement to the salesmen once that if they weren't reading *Rolling Stone*, maybe they were in the wrong business. Today that sounds funny, but in those days it was heresy. The A&R staff had clandestine meetings. They were planning revolts because Clive was ruining the company."

Furthermore, if Clive's strategy was so obvious, it should have been applied at RCA and Capitol, which had been CBS's two closest competitors. Even though RCA and Capitol had Presley and the Beatles, neither company embraced rock with conviction until far too late in the game. In 1967 CBS, RCA, and Capitol each had about 12 or 13 percent of the market. By 1970 CBS's market share had risen to 22 percent. RCA and Capitol have had difficulty making a profit since the sixties. CBS's after-tax profits doubled to $6.7 million in 1968, rose to $10 million in 1969, and exceeded $15 million in 1970. Meanwhile, the labels of Warner Communications—Warner Bros., Atlantic, Elektra, and, later on, Asylum—pursued rock with a fervor equal to Clive's. Warner would soon become CBS's toughest rival.

Though Clive was smart enough to spot the rock trend, he could not leave it at that. He turned it into an epiphany akin to Joseph Smith's discovery of the Book of Mormon. (His autobiography opens, "I sensed change. I don't know, even now, precisely how I knew. . . .") Clive claimed he got religion at the Monterey Pop Festival of 1967. He would never have gone but for Lou Adler, a rock industry pioneer from Los Angeles and one of the producers of the three-day festival. Clive had made a deal for Columbia to distribute Adler's label, Ode Records, and the first record was a hit: Scott McKenzie's "San Francisco (Be Sure to Wear Flowers in Your Hair)."

At Adler's request, Clive went to Monterey, anticipating a mostly social weekend. Instead, Clive proclaimed, Monterey marked "the creative turning point in my life." He added that the festival "changed me as a person," which is undoubtedly true; Clive needed an image to set him apart from Goddard Lieberson. He was still very much in his mentor's shadow. Monterey, which *Newsweek* dubbed "hippie heaven," gave him what he required. After Monterey, he was *hip*. "It was clear that a social revolution was occurring, clear that a musical revolution was occurring," he said. Established talent played the festival, including two Columbia acts, Simon and Garfunkel and the Byrds. But there were relative unknowns as well, including Hendrix, the Steve Miller Band, Laura Nyro, and Big Brother and the Holding Company.

Clive sat up and took notice of Big Brother's lead singer, a young Texan named Janis Joplin. She was barely known outside of San Francisco. Joplin and her band were under contract to Mainstream Records—and a rapacious contract it was, too—but had no albums out. She was a mesmerizing performer who sang blues in a voice soaked with Southern Comfort. The audience loved her. If Clive was entranced, so was another businessman in the audience, manager Albert Grossman, whose clients included the Electric Flag and Bob Dylan. As Clive negotiated to get Big Brother out of its Mainstream contract and onto Columbia, Grossman became the band's manager. It took a year, but Grossman delivered Big Brother to Clive for a quarter-million dollars, then a large sum for an unproven act.

Joplin was not the only rock act that Clive pursued after Monterey. His head of business affairs, Dick Asher, was kept busy. "Clive came back to New York all pumped up," Dick said. "He thought it was incredible that these bands were known to all these kids and not to us. He had a virtual hit list, and most of them had no recording contract. I took over the role of the bounty hunter, continually on a plane to San Francisco." Dick helped Columbia acquire the Electric Flag and Santana, among others. But of all the San Francisco acts, his favorite was Janis Joplin. He still recalls her exact words when Albert Grossman introduced Asher as the man who had drafted her contract: "I hope you didn't fuck us too much."

When Clive at last presented Big Brother with the contract in the tenth-floor conference room of Black Rock, he wanted to apologize for the setting. Artists like Robert Goulet and Andy Williams felt at ease in the antiseptic building, but here were five flower punks from San Francisco. Joplin, who had a weakness not only for booze and controlled substances but promiscuous sex, suggested that she and Clive consummate the deal by sleeping together. Clive demurred. He did promise that CBS Records was far less formal than it looked. At this point, one of the band members stood up from behind the conference table and revealed himself to be completely nude. Well, Joplin said with her trademark cackle, this is how informal *we* are.

Big Brother may have cost a lot, but it paid off. The first album, *Cheap Thrills*, sold a million copies. This was at least partially due to a hit single, "Piece of My Heart," an old blues song first popularized by Erma Franklin. Clive said he not only picked the song for Top 40 release but edited it. He felt the album track was too long, and the hook phrase—"take another little piece of my heart now, baby"—not repeated enough. The edited version went to number 12, and Clive took this as proof that he now had ears. Joplin's last single, "Me and Bobby McGee," was a hit, too. It did not need Clive's editing. It was 1970, and she had just died of a drug overdose when her producer sent Clive a test-pressing of the song. Clive said the first time he heard it, he wept.

In the three years between Monterey and Joplin's death, it seemed Columbia could do no wrong. After Big Brother, the next monster act signed to Columbia, in 1967, was Blood, Sweat and Tears. The group's first album had excellent reviews and poor sales. Then lead singer Al Kooper quit the group and Canadian David Clayton-Thomas, who had more of a Top 40 feel, replaced him. The second album yielded four gold singles and sold almost 4 million copies. Clive congratulated himself. "I had trusted my musical instinct and it was working!" he wrote.

Next came Santana, Chicago, Laura Nyro, Johnny Winter, and Edgar Winter. These were all baby acts when they were signed; they had little or no prior success. They came cheap. Aside from Big Brother, Columbia rarely had to pay more than $25,000 for any new act, so profits were bigger and the excitement of breaking them was greater. After 1970 Clive began to raid established acts, and there were fewer unknowns of note, though two stand out: Billy Joel and Bruce Springsteen.

Unfortunately, by the time Clive published his memoirs in 1975, the notion that others had helped discover and break all these acts seemed to elude him. Almost everyone who had worked under Clive was offended, some more than others. Dick Asher, who in many ways idolized Clive, merely shrugged. Walter Yetnikoff fumed.

When the book came out, Walter said recently, "everybody ran to the index to see whether their name was there. Mine was there *once*. I was a 'bright young lawyer.' Of course, I was a little *pisher* at the time, so I was not important! . . . And the book is so ponderous! *Oy vay*, please, enough! [Breathlessly:] 'I went to the Monterey Pop Festival, and I was instilled with Love, and Joy, and the Flowers were in the Air. Then I came to Los Angeles, and a Cop stopped me. Can you believe what they did to the Love . . . ? Then I signed this, and I signed that. . . .' What *is* this bullshit?"

Recently, Clive was asked about his oft-criticized failure to share credit. He seemed taken aback.

"If there's fallout, I feel bad about it," he said. "I know I go to every extra length [to give credit]. . . . But what A&R man signed an artist that I claimed to have signed? What A&R man would have said that he should get half credit for signing Blood, Sweat and Tears? Or Santana? Or Chicago? Or Billy Joel? . . .

"When I recite my signings, it could [sound like] immodesty. I don't do it for that. That happens to be the list. I mean, this is a very clear-cut list of important, major trendsetting artists that I would bend over backwards to share the credit with any person who had a meaningful role. . . ."

Well, what about Bruce Springsteen? Everyone knew legendary A&R man John Hammond had signed him to Columbia, but in an *Audio* magazine interview Clive seemed to suggest otherwise.

"I've clearly indicated that John Hammond brought him to my office," Clive allowed. "But I said no to a number of John Hammond signings. People tried to make it sound as if he had the right to sign an artist. Well, that was just not the case. John Hammond obviously has an illustrious career of major names. But in between the major names, there was a long history of artists that sold nothing. . . .

"The reason I would claim credit for Bruce Springsteen is that he could not have been signed were it not for my hearing him, seeing him, and signing him. . . . Springsteen came to my office for a final audition. I heard his material, I believed in him, *I* signed him. So I'm more than happy to share—more than share—with John Hammond."

■

Dick Asher's skill at business affairs may have failed to win public praise from Clive, but it did not go unnoticed in the industry. In 1970 Capitol Records, based in Hollywood, offered Asher the job of vice-president of its East Coast division. Dick accepted. The move was a disaster. Asher was extremely grateful when Clive took him back in mid-1971.

Walter Yetnikoff also had reason to be grateful to Clive. In 1971 Harvey Schein, the man who had brought Clive to CBS Records, quit as head of the international division. Clive was probably happy to see him go. When Clive bid for an artist, he often needed monies from International, and Schein was a notorious tightwad. With Schein gone, Clive could fill the international post with someone who owed him fealty. He chose Yetnikoff.

Walter had not yet overcome his awkwardness. After Monterey, he briefly gave in to Clive's urgings to "look the part." "I bought some suede boots with zippers and let my sideburns grow," Yetnikoff recalled. "I felt like an ass." At a CBS convention at the Grosvenor House in London in the early seventies, Walter was asked to emcee an evening of music. "He was tongue-tied," Bruce Lundvall remembered. "It was a very different Walter Yetnikoff from the man you see today. Clive was backstage posturing, as Clive will do, and he was very annoyed that Walter was not getting on with the introduction of artists. Then Walter froze for a minute and Clive had to bail him out."

After Clive's post-Monterey successes, bad news struck, the worst of which was Joplin's death in 1970. The same year, Simon and Garfunkel split up. Sly Stone's drug problems kept him out of the studio. Andy Williams and Johnny Cash had popular TV shows, and their records made fortunes into the late sixties. Now, their programs were being canceled. In three years, the record group's earnings had quintupled. Clive had too much at stake to see his hot streak end. He had just been elected to the CBS board of directors, and he loved showing the board his sales charts, which looked, he said, like "inverted lightning bolts."

Clive knew perfectly well that CBS president Frank Stanton would take mandatory retirement in three years, and Clive was an ambitious man. He later denied ever having designs on Stanton's job, but this is directly contradicted by those who knew him well then. Clive, in fact, used to pass notes to other CBS directors just before board meetings, inviting them for cocktails. Clive knew CBS Records could coast for a year or so, but after that sales would slip unless he did something drastic. "I became very intense," Clive wrote, and "embarked on the heaviest talent-raiding campaign ever conducted in the history of the music business."

It was an important moment in the history of CBS Records. By the time "tone-deaf" Walter Yetnikoff took over some years later, the company had completed its transition from the A&R company to the *deal* company. But it began with Clive Davis, lawyer turned record man but lawyer nevertheless.

Talent raiding was a game best played by the big labels, because it cost a lot up front. If you broke a baby act, the money was terrific, but most times you failed to break the act and lost money. Though profits were smaller if you bought proven talent, unless you paid too much, at least some profits were guaranteed. RCA Victor's $40,000 purchase of Elvis Presley's contract from Sun had turned out to be a pretty good deal. The big oil companies had the same idea. Buy small oil companies, because in the long run it's cheaper to purchase known reserves in the ground than to drill for crude.

Clive had already proven he could break new talent. Now, he would show that as a businessman he was smart and lucky, which in business are synonymous. Columbia got the R&B group Earth, Wind and Fire at a low price just before it took off. It picked up Ten Years After and Herbie Hancock. Clive's best deal made Capitol Records look foolish. In 1973 Columbia paid about a million for Pink Floyd, just before the group's *Dark Side of the Moon* album lifted it from a small cult band to a multiplatinum act. So Columbia got itself four back-to-back smash albums, culminating with *The Wall*.

In 1970 Clive heard Neil Diamond perform at a record convention and resolved to get him. Diamond was then on MCA and had two years left on his contract. His lawyer, David Braun, said Neil was willing to make a five-year, ten-album deal with Columbia, but wanted $425,000 an album. Up until then, the top rate was about $150,000 an album. Clive was aghast.

Elliot Goldman had taken over business affairs from Asher when Dick moved over to Capitol. Goldman did a quick calculation. The royalty rate that Braun wanted was not out of line.

Unless Diamond sold less than 225,000 copies per album, Columbia would at least break even. He could not imagine an artist of Diamond's stature doing less than that, so he advised Clive to accept the terms. "Braun told me later he was in absolute shock," Goldman said. "He couldn't believe he got an answer so quickly."

When Clive and Elliot Goldman brought the contract to a Los Angeles recording studio, they wondered whether they were signing Neil Diamond or the Treaty of Ghent. Diamond had decorated the studio with old tapestries and suits of armor, and he signed the contract with a quill pen. It was a wonderful joke, but the record industry felt the deal itself was a bigger one. Word of the huge advance got around quickly. As it happened, the joke was on the industry. Diamond's next album was the soundtrack of a flop movie, *Jonathan Livingston Seagull*, and though it did not yield one hit single, it sold 2 million copies and paid for the entire deal.

So Clive was both smart and lucky and, as usual, selfish with praise. When he told the story of how Columbia got Neil Diamond, he tended to leave Elliot Goldman out of it.

■

It was Clive Davis's custom to hold a singles meeting every Wednesday at eleven o'clock. He would play for all department heads the songs chosen for release that week. He wanted the staffs of sales and merchandising and publicity and business affairs—everyone in the company—to know what his priorities were. It was impermissible to talk or leave the room or read a newspaper while music was being played. If the song did not get the reaction Clive wanted, he played it again. Afterward, he fired questions around the room. "It was like being back in school," said one survivor. "Not even high school—grade school." "There's a story," Walter Yetnikoff laughed, "that once at a singles meeting, Clive said, Who here thinks he can pick a single? No one's going to respond to that. He says, See, that's the problem, I have to do everything myself."

Success was going to Clive Davis's head. Dick Asher, newly returned from Capitol, did not like what he saw. "I thought Clive was terrific; I really did," Dick said. "But I didn't think he walked on water and, at times, I would tell him to his face, Come on, Clive, you're a fat kid from Brooklyn. Which, of course, he'd laugh about; we'd all laugh.

"But after a certain point in time, he got carried away with himself. To people who had been with him a long time, he was becoming close to insufferable. It was no longer fun to be with him. And maybe sensing that, he surrounded himself with sycophants. People who just agreed with him. Whatever he said was wonderful."

One of Clive's biggest sycophants was Columbia's head of public relations, Bob Altshuler. Davis thrived on interviews, and Altshuler was only too happy to prime the press with stories of Clive's genius. Another member of Clive's inner circle was artist relations head David Wynshaw, who was essentially a high-level gofer. If an artist needed entertaining, Wynshaw was the man Clive dispatched.

In 1972, the last full year of Clive's tenure at CBS, he sent Dick Asher to London to turn around the money-losing British label. It was a relief to be out of the home office. Even in London, Asher got a taste of Clive's insensitivity. Dick called the fifteen heads of all CBS's European labels to a meeting at the cramped London offices on Theobalds Road. It was scheduled for 10:00 A.M., and Clive was to be there. They sat in a small room for three hours and waited. Dick kept running to the window. Finally, at one o'clock a stretch limo pulled up, and Clive emerged with some members of his entourage.

Clive did not seem to realize that others felt ill-treated at his hands. He was sure of one thing, though: *He* was being ill-treated by CBS Inc. Most of all, he believed he was underpaid. In 1970 he made $100,000 a year in straight salary and got a bonus of $40,000 more. But everything is relative. "Clearly, I wasn't starving," Clive wrote. "Yet it seemed ridiculous to be making Columbia tens of millions of dollars of new profits and getting much less compensation than the president of Capitol Records—which was losing money."

He saw artist managers and lawyers, who earned commissions off their clients, becoming millionaires. This was due in part to Clive's own high-priced bidding for top acts. He had made others rich—but *he* was not rich. And CBS was cheap with amenities, he felt. In Los Angeles, Clive had to audition artists in the Rodeo Room of the Beverly Hills Hotel, which might be set up for a bar mitzvah reception. Couldn't CBS lease a house out there or something?

Clive felt impoverished when he looked at Warner Communications. Warner paid big salaries, and it knew how to spend on perks. And why not? It was making a fortune in rock music. How, Clive wondered, could he compete with Ahmet Ertegun of Atlantic, when Ahmet had access to the Wickey Bird, Warner's jet ("Wickey" was a derivation of WCI, or Warner Communications Inc.). When the Rolling Stones were shopping for a new label, Ahmet was wining and dining and flying lead singer Mick Jagger all over the place. And he got the deal.*

While the people under Clive grumbled that he seemed to care only about his own treatment, a man ostensibly over him was grumbling, too: Goddard Lieberson. In 1970 Goddard had been made a CBS corporate vice-president. He no longer dealt with records day to day, but had a vague job that paid well but signified little, a reward for service that the navy calls a "sunset cruise." Since that time, Clive had occasionally offended his former mentor. For example, Clive staged a concert of classical music at Radio City Music Hall in New York without Goddard's participation. But Clive did permit Lieberson to maintain a ceremonial role. When CBS Records held a convention, Lieberson made the closing remarks, and no one minded that a bit. "Goddard was so much fun to listen to," Yetnikoff said. "Much more fun than Clive. Clive, you had to be careful, you might get a short-answer test later."

At the CBS Records convention in London in 1972, however, Clive decided it was time to break with custom. He tried—unsuccessfully—to preempt Goddard and give the closing address himself. Goddard was livid. He could not forgive Clive for this final insult, and it would have lasting repercussions.

■

In 1971 CBS president Frank Stanton was bumped up to vice chairman. If Clive had hopes of replacing Stanton, they were quickly dashed when Paley picked Charles "Chick" Ireland, an executive from International Telephone and Telegraph, for the job. But a few months later, Ireland died of a heart attack. Evidently, Bill Paley, who seemed immortal, needed to find a younger man for the high-pressure job of running his broadcasting empire.

He found such a man in Arthur Taylor, a choice that astonished CBS. Taylor was only thirty-seven years old. Rumor had it

* Actually, Jagger chose Atlantic because he loved its R&B catalog. "I think Jagger would have liked to be on *Excello*," Ahmet said, naming a tiny funk label. "We were the closest he could get to Excello and still get five million dollars."

that Paley had been impressed by an interview Taylor gave to *Corporate Financing* magazine. He was a man with remarkable credentials on paper, at least for one his age. He taught Renaissance history at Brown University; then, in his early thirties, became the youngest-ever managing director of First Boston, a bulge-bracket Wall Street firm. After that, Taylor was named executive vice-president of the International Paper Company.

The day Paley offered Taylor the job, the young man phoned his attorney, Stanley Schlesinger, for advice. Schlesinger, who later became Walter Yetnikoff's lawyer and best friend, told Taylor not to take it. Bill Paley, he said, reminded him of one of his father's clients in the garment business, a man who was past retirement age but could not let go. Paley would not give Taylor a contract, and Schlesinger felt the job offered no security. Taylor knew it was sage advice, but he couldn't turn down the job. CBS was practically a national trust, and Arthur Taylor's ambition was to be secretary of state one day.

Clive Davis didn't take to Arthur Taylor. Here was a man even younger than Clive—by three years. Taylor had no background in media or entertainment. The company from which he'd been plucked, International Paper, was smaller than CBS Records, and Taylor had not even been its president. Oddly enough, Davis and Taylor had much in common. Taylor was another overachiever who had shed his accent. He had come from Rahway, New Jersey, but now he talked like a pedant. (He pronounced the "t" in *often*.) Taylor was not Jewish—Bill Paley did not hire Jewish presidents— and yet he spoke Hebrew and Yiddish. At the bar mitzvah of Stanley Schlesinger's son Kenneth, Taylor was the only one who could read the service. It was a colossal joke on Paley, in fact, because Arthur Taylor fervently *wished* he were Jewish, while Paley behaved like a man who wished he were not.

Clive let Taylor know exactly how he felt. He was outspoken, often to the point of rudeness. When Taylor spoke to Clive about the record division, Clive was often heard to remark: "That's a dangerous assumption." And sometimes: "You don't know what you're talking about." Taylor liked to run a management forum for the heads of all the CBS divisions. Clive rarely came. When he did, he would stare out the window.

To make matters worse for Clive, 1973 was shaping up to be a bad year for CBS Records. He had made rosy projections, and now it looked as though he would not meet them. The corporation was putting pressure on him, and he was putting pressure on his people.

One of them, Jack Craigo, the vice-president of sales, felt abused. "Initially, Clive and I had a good relationship," he said. "But then his projections didn't work, and his phone calls became very nasty. Don't your people listen to you? Why can't you put out more records? And so on. Then he started to fire questions at me at the singles meeting, and I started hitting the ball back. People were coming to the meetings because they could see sparks beginning to fly. I had the answers, and when I didn't, I brought people with me who did. So finally, I told my wife, I'm not continuing. I will not stay under these conditions.

"And then one day, all of a sudden, I came back from a radio convention, and I didn't have the problem anymore. But there was a whole new set of problems."

5

NEWARK

■

THE intercom sounded in Ron Alexenburg's office. Alexenburg, the chubby vice-president of promotion for Columbia, was one of Clive's fair-haired boys; the previous year Davis had made him one of the record group's two youngest VPs, at twenty-nine. *Mr. Alexenburg, a voice said, please come up to the CBS boardroom immediately. The boardroom,* Alexenburg mused. What was that all about? He rode the elevator to the thirty-fifth floor, where the mystified senior staff of CBS Records had assembled. Alexenburg took a seat next to Walter Yetnikoff. At the head of the table stood a somber Arthur Taylor, and with him was Goddard Lieberson and a teddy-bearish, middle-aged man Alexenburg did not recognize. The one person missing in the sea of faces was Clive Davis.

"That's when I knew," Alexenburg said later. "You ever get that? A *buzz?* I turned to Walter, and I said, *They've fired Clive.* Walter laughed."

Alexenburg had guessed right. Taylor read a press release that CBS was about to put on the newswire. Clive Davis had been terminated. The new president of Columbia was teddy-bearish, middle-aged Irwin Segelstein, a CBS television executive. Goddard Lieberson, sixty-one, was coming back from his "sunset cruise" job in corporate CBS to head the records group once more. Goddard said a few words, but they were lost in the general melee. He opened CBS Records' annual sales convention about a month later, however, with a line few could forget: "A funny thing happened to me on the way to my retirement."

■

At forty-one, Clive Davis was the foremost executive the record industry had ever seen. He'd become like the man in the cartoon who hails a taxi and, asked his destination, explains that it really doesn't matter—he's wanted *everywhere*. Despite the constant demand, Clive turned down million-dollar offers to leave CBS, purely out of "loyalty" and "devotion." He slaved eighteen-hour days to bring in new talent. "And no one at the corporate CBS level," he wrote, "seemed to have the foggiest notion that this might be a difficult, possibly even superhuman task." For loyally completing this task, he wanted to be sufficiently rewarded. His total CBS compensation for 1972 came to $359,000, and at the time this was *very* big money. But Clive believed he was entitled to more, and according to a CBS lawsuit served on him the day he was fired, he got it.

Altogether, CBS accused Clive Davis of wrongfully obtaining over a six-year period at least $94,000, leaving a trail of phony invoices. CBS found itself paying $53,700 for renovations to his Central Park West apartment. In addition, $20,000 in corporate funds were spent on a bar mitzvah reception at the Plaza Hotel for his eldest son.* CBS money was also allegedly used to help rent a summer home in Beverly Hills. Clive was not only a division president, but a member of the CBS board of directors. When the false invoices were uncovered, Arthur Taylor confronted Clive, who denied any wrongdoing. Taylor did not believe that Davis was giving him the straight story. So, with the full support of Bill Paley and the rest of the board, Taylor sacked him.

The record industry was shocked, but then, expense account indiscretions were apparently not a serious matter to the music business. Exclaimed a Warner executive at the time, "CBS is idiotic to bust a president of one of the major profit-making divisions for a mere hundred G's!" Clive was appalled by the publicity, though he conceded that some of it was favorable, particularly the opinion that "the expense account charges were absurd in light of the tens of millions I'd made for [the company] and the millions I would have received had I gone elsewhere."

Unfortunately, a bigger scandal was brewing in the record industry. CBS had uncovered the phony invoices as the result of a widening investigation by the U.S. Attorney's Office in Newark, a probe that became known as Project Sound. Allegations began

---

* Federal prosecutors would later put the bar mitzvah tab at closer to $18,000.

to surface in the press that CBS Records had bribed black radio stations and done business with an organized crime figure. The smell of payola was in the air.

Clive would eventually be convicted only of tax evasion. He would never be indicted for payola. To this day, Clive maintains that Project Sound was a witchhunt, a view shared by many other industry people. The Newark investigation was an ordeal from which CBS Records would not soon recover, and which Davis would long remember.

The broader scandal had its roots in a 1971 "custom label" deal that Clive made with two black record producers from Philadelphia, Kenny Gamble and Leon Huff. Both men had ties to Motown Records, having played backup for Diana Ross and the Supremes. When Clive heard from them, their rhythm and blues Philadelphia International label was a mini-Motown in search of financing.

As Clive knew too well, Columbia had conquered the pop charts but done little to crack the rhythm and blues charts. CBS Records was weak in R&B. Sly Stone recorded for Epic, but Columbia had lost Aretha Franklin to Atlantic. Clive observed around 1970 that more and more R&B albums were crossing over to the pop charts: Curtis Mayfield's *Superfly* album, for example, and Motown acts like the Supremes and the Temptations.

The separate designation of pop and R&B bears explaining. Pop in the record industry is a euphemism for white; R&B means black. Until 1949 *Billboard* listed music by black artists as "race" records, but then a staffer named Jerry Wexler coined the term rhythm and blues. This is about all that has changed (though the industry has found other euphemisms, including "soul" and "urban"). A rock record by a black act is automatically R&B—regardless of its *sound*—unless white radio plays it and white people buy it, at which point it is said to "cross over" to the pop charts. Since white record buyers outnumber blacks by a large margin, a crossover hit means a bigger payoff.

When Gamble and Huff called Clive in 1971 to propose a production and distribution deal, he was receptive. Clive closed the deal with a budget of $5,000 per single and $25,000 per album. The risk was small but the reward great. Within nine months of inking the CBS agreement, Philadelphia International exploded with Billy Paul, the O'Jays, and Harold Melvin and the Blue Notes. The Blue Notes featured singer Teddy Pendergrass, who subsequently had a hit solo career on Epic. Gamble and Huff provided four of Columbia's nine gold singles in 1972. The O'Jays' first two albums sold a combined three quarters of a million copies. Gamble, Huff, and staff producer Thom Bell became instantly famous for having created the "Philly Sound," with its lush string arrangements and strong percussion.

Encouraged, Clive signed another distribution deal, this time with Stax Records of Memphis, the R&B label of Isaac Hayes and the Staple Singers. Columbia invested $7 million in Stax, but the hits didn't come and the deal lost money. Stax may have been distracted by cash-flow problems, the result of living too high off the hog. When Columbia's Jack Craigo and Ron Alexenburg flew to Memphis and saw the Stax parking lot, they did a double take. "I said, Jesus, this must be a Lincoln Continental dealership," Craigo recalled. "There had to be fifteen of them there. Sure enough, everyone in that company of any import had a two-door Lincoln."

Columbia's venture into R&B was a success overall, thanks to Philadelphia International. Yet before the hits started to roll in, the Gamble-Huff deal almost disintegrated. Columbia had retained the right to promote the custom label's records, but Kenny Gamble was convinced that CBS had no idea how to promote a black single. He made suggestions, but Clive would not adopt them. Exasperated, Gamble and Huff called for a meeting with Clive and brought in Philadelphia International's attorney, Eric Kronfeld.* The sitdown took place in the CBS dining room in late 1971. Kronfeld announced that his clients were fed up with Columbia's promotion efforts and wanted out of the deal. "Clive was ashen," Kronfeld said. "It was the first time anyone had asked to leave Columbia."

Clive agreed to let Philadelphia International do its own promotion. He also approved quarterly payments from CBS to help support the R&B label's promotion effort. Gamble and Huff had their own promotion man, Harry Coombs; now, Coombs could work the records as he and Philadelphia International saw fit. Not long after that, black radio began playing the O'Jays and the Blue Notes and Billy Paul, and white radio caught on. Unfortunately for all concerned, Harry Coombs dealt in payola. So, for that matter, did Kenny Gamble.

---

* Clive later retained Kronfeld for personal legal services.

Meanwhile, a former business partner of Kenny Gamble's struck a promotion deal with Clive. Kal Rudman worked out of his home and later had an office suite just off Route 70 in Cherry Hill, a Philadelphia suburb. He published a powerful Top 40 tipsheet, *The Friday Morning Quarterback*. *FMQB* was a mimeographed, stapled sheaf of about fifty pages sent to Top 40 program directors. It told them which songs, in Rudman's opinion, were going to be hits.

Rudman was not demure about the reason for *FMQB*'s success. "What makes me so powerful?" he said. "I am almost always right." Since he lacked formal musical training, Rudman could only explain his hit-finding ability in terms of galvanic skin response. "I get goosebumps," he told a reporter, rolling up his sleeve. He was serious.

Rudman, who kept a cream-colored Cadillac and a driver, had come a long way from his past life as a $10,000-a-year teacher of retarded children at F.D.R. Junior High in Bucks County. His transition to pop music began in the fifties, when he moonlighted as a graveyard-shift DJ on WCAM. On the air, he was Kal "Big Beat" Rudman, "the wildest child on the radio dial" and "the round mound of sound." (He stood five and a half feet and weighed two hundred pounds.)

Rudman's life changed for good in 1967 when he and Kenny Gamble started Excel Records, a precursor to Philadelphia International, and put out a million-seller by the Intruders, "Cowboys to Girls." (It is not known whether Rudman had a financial interest in Philly International.) Rudman made a $100,000 profit, and the following year he quit teaching and broadcasting to start *FMQB*.

He never quite lost his disc jockey palaver. It carried over into headlines like M-O-N-S-T-E-R and KAL-Q-LATIONS. The red front page of his tipsheet forecasted which "GO-Rilla" hits would get "top phones"—the most listener requests—and which songs would "die like a dog."

By the seventies, Rudman was a wealthy man. He sold subscriptions to his programming guide for $150 a throw and advertising for $2,000 a page. Rudman nevertheless chose to pick up extra money by taking retainers from record companies to plug their records as an independent promoter. In 1972 CBS Records paid Rudman $44,000 for promotion services. Warner, MCA, and Capitol were among his other customers. Often his tipsheet touted the very records he had been hired to promote, but Rudman did not see a conflict. "You cannot read the sheet and know who's paying me and who's not," he said. "I only take money when I know the record is good. If I can't deliver, then my ass is grass. It's consultation at the highest level. My field is music; I'm a music junkie; we all serve the artist."

When Rudman dropped by Black Rock one Wednesday morning in the early seventies to attend a Columbia singles meeting, the event was captured by *The New Yorker* in a "Talk of the Town" column. Clive, who made a habit of being the last to enter a room, arrived wearing a brown suede suit and a purple shirt and tie, and his assembled staff was waiting for him. He played a number of cuts, and everyone listened intently. Kal Rudman closed his eyes and nodded and puffed an enormous cigar. At the end of each song, people held their comments until Clive had rendered his judgment ("Just a pretty album cut, not a single"; or "It's got the hook, but it doesn't have the lyric communication, I think"). Then Clive talked about the R&B group Free Movement and its current release, "I Found Someone of My Own."

This was Rudman's cue to speak up. "I was eminently involved in the entire history of the record," he bragged. "This record was an R&B hit with no pop exposure, except in a couple of places in the Midwest. I talked the record up strenuously. I got the program directors at KQV and WIXZ in Pittsburgh to listen. I got it on *both* stations. I put it in my sheet. I called the promotion men sissies for not promoting the record. In two weeks, there was a complete breakout! . . . You've got a million-seller! This is a memorable day! We are seeing the birth of a super group!" History will note, however, that despite Rudman's indie promotion efforts, the song was no million-seller.

Rudman eventually got his weight down, but the size of his ego remained vast. "How do you define a legend?" he said of himself. "I'm a dichotomy. To an extent. I don't want to overdramatize that or get carried away with it. . . . To a lot of people I am an enigma. The enigma is enveloped in a paradox, and the whole thing is totally surrounded by a paradigm. . . ."

There was nothing enigmatic, however, in Kal Rudman's importance in the development of the Network. Though Rudman himself eventually left the indie promo business, it was he who first grasped the basic principle of the Network's power. He articulated it in 1970 to Jerald Wagner, the young promotion director for Ampex, a tape company attempting to cut a swath through records.

"I was all of twenty-six," Wagner recalled. "And as soon as everybody figured out that I could quote unquote be trusted, then I could get into open conversations with Kal—to a point. I was talking to Kal one day. And I said, Kal, I'm really pissed at you. He said, Why? Because I read your asinine sheet every week, like everyone else, and you call this one light and that one heavy, and you just sit there behind your fucking typewriter. And I'm out there on the front lines. And I just wonder if you can really get a record played.

"He answered me perfectly—shut me right up. He said, Jerry, you may or may not be right. But let's assume I cannot get a record played. Do you think I can *keep one* from being played? Kal, have a good day. *Touché*, Kal. Guys like that never go away, except when they want to."

Clive's promotion agreements with Philadelphia International and Kal Rudman would come back to haunt CBS. A man who worked for Clive—his closest aide, in fact—would implicate CBS to federal investigators in connection with those agreements. Clive must surely have looked back on the selection of this aide as the worst hiring decision he had ever made.

His name was David Wynshaw. He was a bouncer-sized Brooklynite in his early fifties with a sales background in ready-to-wear clothing and real estate. In 1960, the same year Clive Davis joined Columbia, the record company hired Wynshaw as a sales representative in Los Angeles. He next became branch sales manager in New York. "Wynshaw wasn't a very good branch manager," recalled sales vice-president Jack Craigo. "He had no accountability for finance and money."

Wynshaw moved from sales to artist relations sometime in the sixties, and in that role he caught Clive's eye. Clive made Wynshaw his personal aide and gofer par excellence, while allowing him to keep a hand in artist relations. Wynshaw had a knack for getting tables at fully booked restaurants and nightclubs. Before long, Wynshaw had a number of unofficial and unflattering titles around CBS Records, among them, "Clive's pimp," the "royal procurer," and "Dr. Feelgood." "I loved it," he said of his job as Clive's right hand. "I took all the artists around town when they came in. I'm known at the Copa and the Waldorf. . . . I liked the action."

Wynshaw carried a gun. One day he showed it to Jack Craigo, explaining that he and Clive were out late at night and needed protection. Look, Craigo admonished Wynshaw, something's going to happen and you're going to pull that gun out and shoot Clive in the foot. And that will be the end of your job.

But Wynshaw apparently liked danger. He had grown close to Pasquale Falconio, better known as Patsy Falcone, an associate of the Genovese family, the crime syndicate that played a leading role in the life of Morris Levy. Falcone had ties to the music world as partner of Frank Campana, a manager of black and country acts. Like Dave Wynshaw, Campana had worked in artist relations at Columbia, but left to set up a management firm in the early seventies. Campana and Falcone managed Broadway star Ben Vereen and two of Columbia's Nashville acts, Lynn Anderson and Tommy Cash. Another client was O. C. Smith, whose single "Little Green Apples" was a runaway hit for Columbia in 1968.

O. C. Smith hired Patsy Falcone under troubling circumstances. The singer had run up a gambling debt and received death threats from West Coast mobsters. He turned to Dave Wynshaw for help, and Wynshaw alerted Falcone. Falcone in turn called Genovese underboss Anthony "Fat Tony" Salerno, the future head of the family. Salerno put a stop to the death threats, and Falcone took over as Smith's manager. Falcone played a more personal role in protecting another CBS artist, Jeff Beck, who had got phone calls from fanatics vowing to shoot him onstage. Falcone and two other men served as round-the-clock armed bodyguards for Beck.

With the help of Dave Wynshaw, Falcone bilked CBS Records. The two men set up sham companies in North Bergen and Fort Lee, New Jersey, with names like Del-Tone Trucking, Sutton Travel Bureau, and Limousine Service. CBS unwittingly paid more than $75,000 to these nonexistent operations.

Wynshaw was adept at other matters as well. He was very good at concocting false invoices. The most notorious instance concerned an October 1972 bar mitzvah reception at the Plaza Hotel for Fred Davis, the eldest child of Clive's first marriage. (Clive wed a second time, in 1966, to Janet Adelberg.) There were scores of guests, and most of them were business people: CBS Records employees, artists, managers, lawyers, agents. Clive could not separate his private and business life, and the reception was a case in point. Therefore, Clive's supporters insist, it was proper for CBS to pick up the $18,000-plus tab, which included the cost of engraved invitations from Cartier and the services of Skitch Henderson's orchestra. Arthur Taylor later said that had Clive explained beforehand that the bar mitzvah party would be an industry good-will gesture, CBS might have agreed to help with the bill. Instead, the receipts were dummied to fool the company auditors. The lion's share of the bill was charged to a nonexistent party for Broadway star Liza Minnelli, whom Clive had just signed.

In perhaps the most unconsciously funny passage of his book, Clive wrote, "It had never occurred to me that Wynshaw was anything but a selfless person totally dedicated to making my life free to handle the business of the company. . . . I was shocked by the thought that he might have been secretly duping me for years."

According to prosecutors, Wynshaw also charged $1,200 in jewelry for Janet Davis to a CBS petty cash account at the Century Plaza Hotel and turned the cost of a *bris* for another of Clive's sons into fictitious bills related to Johnny Mathis. CBS was also maneuvered into paying for airfare and lodging for Clive's family, housekeeper, and even his beagles, Charlie and Bimbo.

None of these matters might ever have come to light had the Newark authorities not been paying close attention to Patsy Falcone. It seemed Falcone had interests outside of music. He was also a heroin smuggler. Having become aware of this, the Newark authorities, working with the Royal Canadian Mounted Police, zeroed in on Falcone's heroin operation in Montreal. The Newark strike force won court approval to tap Falcone's phone in Fort Lee. Acting on overheard information, the Mounties grabbed ten kilos of heroin at a Montreal pizza parlor. On February 6, 1973, eight suspects, including Patsy Falcone, were indicted in federal court in Newark on smuggling and conspiracy charges. When Falcone was arrested, authorities found on him an address book containing David Wynshaw's phone number. Confronted with this information, Wynshaw soon became a cooperating witness. He was never charged in the drug case.

The Newark strike force warned the CBS brass of Wynshaw's ties to Falcone. Alarmed, CBS began investigating Wynshaw and turned up evidence that he was misusing company funds. On April 9, Clive telephoned Wynshaw at a restaurant and ordered him up to Black Rock. Wynshaw dashed back to Clive's office and found him waiting with CBS attorneys. "They mentioned the invoices," Wynshaw recounted. "Then Clive said they had to talk further and he asked me to leave." The next morning Wynshaw was called up before CBS attorney Mallory Rintoul. As Wynshaw told it, "Before I could say anything he held his hand up and said: It's too late. You're out." Wynshaw went to see Clive, "and all Clive would say was, you're not to go to your office." He did anyway and found the door padlocked.

Though his closest aide had just been fired, Clive betrayed no outward sign that his own job was in jeopardy. From Sunday, April 29, to the following Saturday, Clive hosted Columbia's *A Week to Remember* at the Ahmanson Theater in Los Angeles. By then he knew he was a subject of Newark and CBS investigations. The concert series showed the strength and diversity of CBS Records' roster under Clive; it may have been the apotheosis of his presidency. There were twenty-one acts altogether. Clad in a white suit and white patent leather shoes, Clive mixed and matched, Bruce Springsteen with the Mahavishnu Orchestra, Loudon Wainwright with Miles Davis, and so forth. In R&B, he presented Earth, Wind and Fire, Billy Paul, and the Staple Singers; in country, Lynn Anderson and Charlie Rich; in classical music, Anthony Newman. Bill Cosby and Richard Pryor were the emcees. Clive had the concerts filmed so that highlights could be shown at CBS Records' sales convention in July.

During his stay in California, Clive also worked to free Billy Joel from his onerous contract with Family Records. Joel's first album, *Cold Spring Harbor,* had been a failure. He and his band members went six months without getting paid; Joel claimed the record label suggested they live on peanut butter and jelly. In despair, Joel dropped out of sight and got a job playing piano and singing in a Los Angeles bar, the subject of his song "Piano Man." In the meantime, he hired a music lawyer who initiated talks with Columbia. When Clive sat down with Joel in L.A., he later wrote, "I had to push the company investigation out of my mind."

On Wednesday, May 23, Clive Davis conducted his last singles meeting at CBS Records. In the middle of it, Paul Simon, who had by then split with Art Garfunkel to become a solo artist, stalked in unannounced. Clive considered Simon among his closest friends on the CBS roster, and was delighted by the surprise visit. It would prove an omen. As Ben Fong-Torres of *Rolling Stone* recounted the meeting:

> Simon slammed a book onto the table in front of the president, telling him: "You need to read this book more than

anyone I know." Davis glanced at the volume—*The Life of Krishna*—as Simon spun around. "Wait, stay," urged Davis. Simon continued out through the door.

The next day, Clive held his final staff meeting. When it was over, he asked marketing head Bruce Lundvall to stay behind. "We were pretty close," Lundvall said. "He told me, They're out to get me, and I'm not going to have much longer here. And I haven't done anything wrong. He was absolutely shattered. It was horrible."

Arthur Taylor had been president of CBS for only ten months, and now he had a crisis on his hands. CBS Records under Clive had grown to represent one third of the corporation's profits. Taylor could not allow the record division to self-destruct. The Newark prosecutors had convened a grand jury. A member of the federal strike force came to see Taylor in April with a list of CBS people who were subjects of the grand jury probe. It comprised the entire senior staff of CBS Records U.S.—seventy-three people, including Goddard Lieberson. Taylor was aghast. "I was consulting experts—lawyers, Mr. Paley, Frank Stanton, and other people—to see how we could hold the record company together," Taylor recalled. "Mr. Paley went off two days after that to China. That left me, the grand jury in Newark, and some very upset people.

"When Wynshaw was arrested," Taylor continued, "his office was opened and we found meticulous records of wrongdoing. With that information, I started to have a number of discussions with Clive Davis, and in my judgment, he told me no truth at all. And I had the data in my desk. Had he told me the truth, there might have been a way to save him. I don't want to defame the man, but he did not come clean with me. That alone was the reason the board decided to dismiss him. I've always been credited with the decision, but it was the board's.

"If you're a junior clerk and you steal three hundred bucks, maybe the first time they let you put it back. But if you steal and you're a senior officer and director of the company, and the documents showing the defalcation are before the lawyers and prosecutors, and you still try to dissemble your way out of it—that doesn't cut in American corporate life." (Clive's version differed. He insisted that Wynshaw's invoice scams had been perpetrated without his knowledge or consent.)

Taylor still worried about losing Clive Davis. Clive had convinced Taylor that he was the glue holding CBS Records together. Could Clive really take artists with him? Was he critical not only to the label's creative vision but also its day-to-day operations? Taylor posed these questions to Goddard Lieberson. Goddard assured him that Clive Davis was *not* indispensable. The company was deep in executive talent, he said, and there were big days ahead for Columbia Records. If Goddard had any good words for Clive, "I'm the one he would have said them to," Taylor remarked, "because I'm the one that could have done something. But his position was that the company was not going to fall apart if Clive left."

The Memorial Day weekend came and went. On Tuesday, May 29, Clive arrived at the office and went through his usual morning routine: cornflakes at his desk, forty-five minutes with the mail, a meeting with the advertising department. Walter Yetnikoff claimed to have been the last person to meet with Clive before he was fired. "He doesn't remember it that way in his book," Walter said. "But I was."

In his book, Clive recalled the events: After the morning ritual, he conferred with business manager Michael Levy.

Levy and I had finished up and moved into small talk when my intercom buzzed. CBS president Arthur Taylor's secretary came on.

"Mr. Davis," she said, "could you come up to see Mr. Taylor?" . . .

I felt a little apprehensive. A sudden call to the president's office makes you wonder.

Taylor's office is on the thirty-fifth floor. He had two lawyers with him—and the meeting lasted about two minutes. It was calculated to last no more. I don't remember the exact words he said—perhaps I've blocked them—but the intent was clear. I was being told to leave the company.

"I'm in shock," I said, perhaps more than once. It was all I could think of.

"We'd like you to return to your office," Taylor continued, "and take whatever you'd like to take with you, and leave immediately."

That was it. That was the end of my love affair with Columbia Records. It was numbing; it seemed incredibly cold-blooded. I couldn't *believe* it. But that was it. There was nothing left to say. I turned on my heel and walked out of the office.

At the door, I was met by two CBS security men and served with the company's civil complaint against me, alleging ninety-four thousand dollars' worth of expense-account violations during my six years as president. The security men fell into step with me, and we took the elevator down to my eleventh-floor office. . . .

In the office, I took my checkbook, a few papers and other personal effects and loaded them into my attache case. I told my secretary, Octavia, the news, and left quietly without seeing anyone else. . . .

[At home] the telephone rang all afternoon. I was surprised at how fast the news had traveled. But I answered none of the calls, leaving my housekeeper to take messages. Beyond that, the afternoon seems mostly a blur. Friends, family members, and a number of people from Columbia and the industry came over and, in effect, sat *shiva* with me.

■

On the Thursday evening before Clive got fired, Irwin Segelstein was at the "21" Club with Oscar Katz, a CBS Television vice-president. Gruff, paunchy, bearded, and forty-eight years old, Segelstein was the CBS Television Network's number two programming executive, just below Fred Silverman. Arthur Taylor learned Segelstein's whereabouts and called him at "21." I'm just having a drink with Oscar, Segelstein told Taylor. Why don't you join us? No, Taylor said, come to my office. Irwin finished his drink and hurried to the thirty-fifth floor of Black Rock. "Arthur said there was some problem," Segelstein recalled, "and he couldn't tell me any of the details, but how would I like to run the CBS record company? I said, Why the hell would I want to do *that*?"

Segelstein protested that he knew nothing about the record business. Taylor gave him a short briefing paper on the industry that he had requisitioned from the records group on becoming CBS president. When do you need an answer? Irwin asked. Tomorrow, Taylor said. So Irwin went home and sprawled in a chair and read the primer. His wife and children were not home. The more he thought about the offer, the more attractive it seemed. Why not? he told himself. If you won't try something new in middle age . . . His wife arrived, and Irwin suggested she sit down, he had some news. "She probably thought I was about to ask for a divorce," he said. Instead, he told her he had been asked to take over CBS Records. "Her reaction was, Shit, just as I've gotten to know all the TV affiliates and their wives. And my kids laughed that the old man was being asked to get involved in rock and roll, since my personal record collection was Broadway cast albums and cantorial music."

Taylor had to go outside the record company for a new chief executive because everyone *in* the record company was a suspect in the Newark investigation. He picked Segelstein, he said, because "he was an outsider, he was honest as the day is long, and he was a mensch." All the same, Taylor knew Irwin would need help. He asked the strike force to hurry its investigation of Goddard Lieberson; Taylor wanted to bring him back as head of the records group, with Irwin running the crucial domestic operation. In short order, the feds cleared Goddard.

Irwin has long remembered the hastily assembled staff meeting on May 29 to proclaim his arrival, Lieberson's return, and Clive's departure. "Goddard and I were wheeled in," he said, "and Arthur made the announcement. There were stunned faces around the room. It was the first time I met Walter Yetnikoff. He looked glazed."

■

Dick Asher was in London running CBS Records UK when the news of Clive's termination reached him. He was crushed. Despite Clive's arrogance, he was still Dick's idol, the man who had transformed the label of Robert Goulet into the label of Janis Joplin. Clive had invited Dick and his wife, Sheila, to the infamous bar mitzvah reception at the Plaza, but Asher said he couldn't afford to fly in just for the weekend. Clive told him not to worry, the company would pay his airfare. Still he declined; it seemed a waste of corporate funds. Now, Dick realized that Clive's offer had been made without company approval. He nonetheless sympathized with Clive and thought the firing tragic.

It also created a potentially difficult problem for Asher. He lacked an employment contract, and if the new regime let him go for being a Clive loyalist, he literally could not afford to move his family back to the United States. Dick did not know Goddard Lieberson well. Fortunately, Goddard had heard good things about him, and soon he called and assured Dick not to worry, there would be no bloodletting. "It was a classy thing to do," Dick said, "and very much appreciated at the time."

∎

David Wynshaw was proving a cooperative witness. Shortly before being dismissed from CBS, he gave grand jury testimony in the Falcone heroin case. Wynshaw then appeared before the payola grand jury and made accusations about CBS Records. His detractors said he was lying to save himself from prosecution.

Wynshaw alleged that CBS Records had a hidden budget of $250,000 a year for payola to black radio stations. He claimed CBS payola had begun in 1971, when Columbia made production and distribution deals with Gamble and Huff's Philadelphia International and Stax Records in Memphis. He implicated tipsheet publisher Kal Rudman, suggesting he was a conduit for payoffs to black radio. (Rudman was incensed when this charge surfaced in *The New York Times*. His reply: "I'm as clean as the Board of Health!")

Around this time, Fred Ferretti of the *Times* caught up with Dave Wynshaw at the Park Avenue office of his attorney, Robert Arum.* Wynshaw paced the room and gestured forcefully.

He pictured himself [Ferretti wrote] as a man without professional friends since he was discharged. He has been seeking work since, in between his grand jury and strike force meetings. Twice during the interview he phoned prospective employers. "All those guys who kept telling me when I was with Columbia how much they wanted me. . . ." He shrugged. "My phone hasn't rung." Nor has he heard from his former superior, Mr. Davis. "But maybe his attorney has told him not to call me."

It was the start of a paranoid six months at CBS Records. The corporation provided counsel for all employees on the suspect list. But Taylor had no idea who would survive the investigation and who would not. "There was a tremendous amount of backbiting and people denouncing each other," Taylor said. "It was like being in a communist state when it falls down. Everybody had every-

---

* Interestingly, Arum, who was also a boxing promoter, later made a lucrative deal with CBS Sports.

thing terrible to say about everybody else, and nobody had anything good." The records group viewed Segelstein with suspicion, fearing he was some corporate pit bull. No one in records could be promoted or get a job elsewhere until he was cleared. Employees believed their phones were bugged. Meanwhile, the grand jury subpoenas kept rolling in.

Jack Craigo was furious—at Clive Davis. First Clive had made his life miserable for not meeting unrealistic sales projections. Now, he and others were being harassed because Clive was suspected of having broken the law. One Saturday morning Craigo visited one of his salesmen in Cincinnati and witnessed his interrogation by a Justice Department official and an IRS agent. "I saw how ruthless the IRS could get," Craigo said. "A lot of people at CBS were not pining away because Clive had left. But they were really pissed off that they and their families were being subjected to this bullshit because of Clive's indiscretions." Craigo had a point.

The tension at CBS Records told in July 1973, when the label held its annual sales convention at the Cow Palace in San Francisco. The theater lobby was awash in television camera crews and print reporters. Journalists tried to interview salesmen and promotion people; the news networks attempted to force cameras into the auditorium. The most emotional moment came when Jim Scully, the branch manager in Cleveland, accepted an award. "He broke down crying onstage," Bruce Lundvall recalled, "saying, We're honest people, we're good people, and I'm tired of this fucking investigation. We've worked real hard all our lives, and now my kids think I'm part of some *Mafia* organization, and this is bullshit!" Scully got a standing ovation.

For Arthur Taylor, there was a more emotional moment at the convention. He was about to ascend the tiny stage of the big, dark theater when a California state trooper stopped him, saying he had just got word that Taylor would be shot during his speech. Taylor froze. If he chickened out, he was afraid it would reflect badly on him—but who wanted to take the chance? Then Goddard Lieberson took his arm and suggested they walk down to the stage together. He introduced Taylor and stood by his side as the CBS president made his remarks. Taylor never learned whether the death threat was genuine.

Adding insult to injury for many records employees, one of the camera crews that attempted to force its way into the auditorium was from CBS News. The news division at Black Rock had jumped on the Clive Davis story, in fact, perhaps wishing to prove its independence. In at least one case, the news division went absurdly overboard. In London in October 1973, a network reporter called Dick Asher, claiming he had "irrefutable proof" that CBS Records was involved in drug trafficking, and that London was the hub. Asher was speechless. Such was his respect for CBS News that he was prepared to shut the London company down until he could find the culprit. It developed, however, that an employee in London had used the news pouch to ship a hard-to-obtain asthma remedy to another employee in Brazil.

For the record company, the ultimate blow came on August 11, 1974, when CBS News aired a one-hour special, "The Trouble with Rock." It ran only two days after Richard Nixon's resignation, and centered largely on the Clive-Wynshaw-Falcone scandal, by now over a year old. The first half presented an uninspired history of rock and roll and the growth of the music business. In the second half, the investigative news team, Emmy-winning Stanhope Gould and Linda Mason, a producer for Walter Cronkite, presented new details about the Clive Davis affair. There was also a brief look at Morris Levy and Roulette Records. Other highlights included an interview with an anonymous ex-employee of CBS Records, who spoke of getting drugs for artists; and Mick Jagger's assertion that "I'm sure there's other industries in America that are far dirtier than the record industry."

The broadcast marked the beginning of Walter Yetnikoff's hatred of CBS News. On a recent afternoon in his office at Black Rock, he was still seething. "That piece of *shit!*" he said. "They found some kid with long blond hair [the ex-employee], who was here for three months, and he made some idiot statement, you know, the record people, blah blah blah blah blah. The biggest scandal to hit the record business, *Clive Davis*? Is that the worst that's ever been done? My God. The industry ought to get the Order of the Meritorious Star of David, plus the Cross!"

Walter was not alone in his contempt for the news coverage of the scandal. Irwin Segelstein felt the same. He had come out of programming, and programmers tend not to be enamored of news people. At CBS there was always tension between the people who dreamed up the cop shows and sitcoms and the news division. Irwin began to see the record employees as victims. People who had feared he would prove a fiery reformer soon discovered the contrary. In a year's time, Irwin Segelstein had become immensely popular at CBS Records.

"Everyone thought Irwin had been sent down to spy on us," said Bruce Lundvall. "Instead, he ended up loving the people in the record division and defending them to Arthur Taylor. One day I was in Taylor's office with Goddard and Irwin, and the investigation was getting very hot. And Taylor was just wild. He says, Look, I want you to get rid of all these vice-presidents; this investigation is getting out of hand, and I'm tired of it." Segelstein, Lundvall recalled, made some speech about how his mother hadn't come to this country in steerage to have her son waive people's constitutional rights. "Then Irwin said, If you think I'm going to fire anyone, you can go *fuck* yourself. And Irwin was not a profane man. Goddard and I stood up next to him, and we said, We second the motion. It was unbelievable. Taylor backed down."

Clive, however, did not share in the record division's support of its employees. Goddard Lieberson was writing him out of the company's history with a vengeance. PR man Bob Altshuler, too, had turned on him. Clive could not believe it. It probably never dawned on Clive that Goddard was merely paying him back for trying to smother his reputation after taking over Columbia. Now, if for no other reason, Clive had to write his memoirs to set the record straight—as he saw it. Clive overcompensated for his hurt feelings by taking credit for *everything*, including CBS Records' phaseout of monaural albums. "Are you kidding?" Lieberson said when he heard about that boast. "The decision was made *years* before he was in that job."

Clive devoted his last chapter to the indignity of seeing his reputation dismantled.

Suddenly [he wrote], there was nothing special or unusual about the unprecedented growth that had occurred. . . . After all, Goddard Lieberson said, Columbia was important in rock before Davis was there. . . . Lieberson, truly a master politician, wrote me a personal letter saying, in effect, Clive, please don't believe what you read in the papers; I'm not saying these things at all. And then the stories kept coming. . . . Were all the interviewers stupid or hard of hearing? . . .

Artists could no longer mention me in their liner notes. . . . The films taken at the Ahmanson Theater . . . were edited to eliminate every single shot of me. This was quite a feat, since I had hosted the shows. . . . Watching this from the sidelines was sometimes amusing, but mostly very sad. Was *this* the company I'd given so much of my life to?

Clive's explanation for the snub was that Goddard had to prove to Wall Street that the loss of Davis would not sink CBS Records. This was naive on Clive's part. Almost every top manager who left the company before Clive and after him was "Stalinized" —purged from the record books. The company that became CBS Records had spent all but its first decade under William Paley, and it had grown up arrogant. Clive was correct, though, in accusing Lieberson of playing a double game. "After Clive got fired," recalled Elliot Goldman, then one of Davis's closest friends, "Goddard used to say to me, Why didn't Clive come and ask for my help? I could have helped him. He should have come to his *rabbi*."

■

Project Sound was in full force by late 1973. It had been intended as an inquisition into payola and "drugola," a word someone coined to describe the use of cocaine as a payoff. Jonathan Goldstein, the U.S. Attorney in Newark, was a student of history. He knew the last big payola shake-up, in 1960, had focused on the bribe-takers (disc jockeys) rather than the bribe-givers (record companies). He felt this was wrong. Goldstein, who had a reputation for being tough and incorruptible, wanted to corral the executives this time. Radio people would not be prosecuted, he said, unless they perjured themselves.

Goldstein's office found itself coordinating a grand jury probe of the record business in four cities. The Newark grand jury was hearing testimony about R&B label Brunswick Records and its president, Nat Tarnopol. He was a well-known industry figure who had produced shows at the Brooklyn Paramount with Alan Freed and managed and recorded soul singer Jackie Wilson. In Philadelphia, there was an investigation of Philadelphia International; and in Memphis, the authorities were building a case against Stax Records, the other black label distributed by CBS. Los Angeles was conducting a probe of a local promotion man.

Newark subpoenaed Philadelphia International's financial records. After months of delays, an IRS agent went out to collect them. When the authorities unpacked the carton of documents, they were astonished. It was the most graphic paper trail of payola that one could imagine. The payoff money came from the quarterly checks for promotion support given Philadelphia International by CBS. "Every time they got a check," one government lawyer recalled, "they cashed it, went out on the road, and gave the money to radio programmers in hotel rooms. We had lists of the amount of money paid and who it was paid to."

Did this discovery warrant a payola indictment against CBS? If Clive Davis gave Philadelphia International the promotion money with the understanding that it was to be used for payola, there was a case. If he merely *suspected* the funds would be so used, then he was guilty of cynicism, which was not an indictable offense. Given Clive's intimate knowledge of the record business, it was hard to believe the third possibility: that he neither knew nor suspected a thing. A payola case against CBS was no trivial matter; the outcome could affect the network's TV licenses. Wynshaw had testified to a payola fund for black radio at CBS, but Wynshaw was not an ideal witness. He would probably be crucified on the stand.

As matters developed, Newark lost jurisdiction over Clive Davis anyway. Because of the tax aspects of the case, it was transferred to Manhattan, where Clive had filed his returns.

On June 24, 1975, nineteen people were indicted in four cities, Davis among them. Clive was charged only with filing false income tax returns for three years. The six-count indictment alleged that Clive had failed to pay tax on a number of expenses paid by CBS, including the infamous bar mitzvah reception. David Wynshaw was indicted for mail and wire fraud. Gamble and Huff were accused of spending "in excess of $25,000" to bribe program directors. The seven senior executives of Brunswick Records, including Nat Tarnopol, were indicted for taking $343,000 in kickbacks from retailers, to whom they allegedly sold records below wholesale price; and for using part of the funds to pay off radio stations. Tarnopol was also indicted for conspiring to cheat the IRS and for wire fraud. Despite Wynshaw's accusations, no charges were brought against tipsheet publisher Kal Rudman.

The Newark grand jury was not quite through. In July 1976, it handed down a perjury indictment against Frankie Crocker, program director of WBLS, a black station in New York. U.S. Attorney Goldstein had promised that no radio man would face payola charges if he told the truth to the grand jury. But if any witness lied, he would have to suffer the consequences. As Goldstein saw it, Crocker lied.

On September 15, 1975, Crocker appeared before the grand jury and was asked about independent promoter Ellsworth Groce, aka Rocky G, who worked on retainer for Capitol and other record labels.

Q. Have you ever received cash from Rocky G?
A. No.
Q. Never?
A. Well, yeah, I received cash from Rocky G, but not—you asked me if I ever received *cash*. I guess you better clarify that. . . .
Q. Let me clarify it, then. When you were program director and he was a promotion man and—
A. Oh, no . . . he's never given me cash for records. That I would have remembered. . . . I don't take money for records.

Crocker also had denied accepting payola from Harry Coombs, the promotion man for Gamble and Huff's Philadelphia International. Evidently, the grand jury reached a different conclusion, because Crocker was indicted for perjury.

Crocker's trial began the following year in Camden, New Jersey, in the same squat courthouse and post office building that would house the Morris Levy trial a decade later. To the consternation of Assistant U.S. Attorney Robert Romano, when he put Coombs and Rocky G on the stand, they denied that any money they might have paid Crocker was payola. "They wiggled around and around and tried to make it look innocent," Romano recalled. The case looked better for Romano when he produced another witness who insisted he had paid Crocker to get his records played: Charles Bobbit, a combination bodyguard and promotion man for soul singer James Brown.

Crocker's appearance on the stand did not help his case. He showed up each day in a different expensive suit. Romano had already introduced Crocker's tax returns to show that his income from radio was small, yet the programmer lived on Sutton Place and drove a Rolls-Royce. Romano also found that Crocker had understated his age on his passport application. When Romano asked Crocker to give his correct age on the stand—a routine question—he refused to answer, despite a direct order from district judge Frederick Lacey. "Crocker's arrogance came across very emphatically," Romano recalled.

James Brown proved an equally recalcitrant witness. However, during one deadlock in the questioning, Judge Lacey leaned over the bench and asked him if he could think of any reason a record promoter would pay money to a radio man. Caught off guard, Brown said the only reason he could think of was to get one's records played. Romano was delighted by the poor showing of the defense witnesses. He was sure he had nailed Crocker. He was wrong.

Indeed, after all the final verdicts had been delivered in Project Sound, it was clear that the operation had been a failure. Frankie Crocker was found not guilty on Count 2 of the indictment, which involved statements he had made about Harry Coombs, but was convicted on Count 1, which related to Rocky G. However, the third circuit court of appeals overturned the conviction on the grounds that Charles Bobbit's testimony should not have been used to prove Count 1, since he was not mentioned in the indictment. Crocker would have faced a second trial, but the Newark office dropped the case as part of a deal in which Crocker pleaded guilty to a misdemeanor tax charge in New York. He paid a $2,500 fine, but received no jail term.

Nat Tarnopol was acquitted of thirty-eight counts of mail and wire fraud, but found guilty of one count of conspiracy, in a 1976 jury trial. He was sentenced to three years in jail. Then his conviction, too, was overturned on a legal technicality. Though he was tried again in 1978, the proceeding ended in a mistrial, and the government ultimately dropped the case. The loss was a sad blow because Tarnopol was a notorious abuser of artists, on a par with Morris Levy. He had taken ruthless advantage of Jackie Wilson by designing contracts that left the singer perpetually in debt to Brunswick, even as his records made hundreds of thousands for the label. The writing credit for Wilson's "Doggin' Around" is listed to Paul Tarnopol, Nat's son, who wasn't born when the song was recorded. Even the appellate judge who overturned Tarnopol's conviction took pains to note in his decision that "there was evidence from which a jury could find that artists were defrauded of royalties."

Kenny Gamble pleaded *nolo contendere* and was fined $2,500. The charges against Leon Huff were dropped. David Wynshaw pleaded guilty to conspiring with Patsy Falcone to defraud CBS and was sentenced to a year in jail. Falcone was given a two-year term to run concurrently with his ten-year sentence for heroin smuggling.

Clive Davis made out far better than Wynshaw. He pleaded guilty on May 24, 1976, to one count of his indictment: not paying taxes on $8,800 worth of vacation expenses in Jamaica, California, Florida, and Europe that had been charged to CBS. The government dropped the other five counts. At Clive's sentencing four months later, federal judge Thomas Griesa wrestled with the question of whether Clive had participated in a "blatant scheme of fraud" against CBS, but ruled that "in the absence of a trial" it was his duty to give Davis the benefit of the doubt. Griesa imposed the maximum fine, $10,000, but no prison term. The judge denied he was being lenient, though Clive could have received up to five years in jail. Griesa also reprimanded the news media for subjecting Clive to "appalling" publicity that connected him, for example, with payola. The charge that Davis pleaded guilty to had nothing to do with payola, the Mafia, or Wynshaw's fraudulent schemes, said the judge.

In November 1977 Clive quietly settled the civil case brought against him by CBS. Terms were not disclosed. After taking the better part of a year to write his autobiography, Clive was named president of the record division of Columbia Pictures, which he renamed Arista. He had immediate success with singer Barry Manilow. Within a year, the CBS Record Club gave Arista $1 million for the mail-order rights to its albums. In 1980 the T. J. Martell Foundation, a music-business charity run by a CBS Records executive, named Clive Davis its "Humanitarian of the Year." Clive did not allow these facts to go unnoticed.

Yet despite his success in avoiding jail and even greater success in rebuilding his career, Clive never recovered from his firing. "Clive was permanently damaged," said Elliot Goldman, who became his number two man at Arista. "He'd always had this fantastic ability to rationalize events even on the small things to make himself look right and good. Now, Clive is constantly writing his obituary because he cannot reconcile himself to the fact that whatever he does, 'Clive Davis, comma, convicted of wrongdoing' will be a paragraph in his life story."

Dick Asher, too, believed Clive was a changed man. The old Clive Davis he knew had been unflappable. One time in the early seventies, Clive was groaning to Dick that business was terrible.

Then a reporter from one of the trade papers arrived for an interview, and Clive asked Dick to stay and listen. To Asher's amazement, Clive began to paint a glowing and convincing picture of financial well-being at CBS Records. Dick knew he could not have pulled off such an act if his life depended on it.

About six months after Clive was terminated, Dick came back from London and saw his former boss for the first time since the scandal had broken. "I was riding in a car with him," he said, "and Clive was trying to put on a brave face. But his hands were shaking. And his voice was quavering. He was blinking. He used to be the picture of self-assurance. And I just know that Clive Davis today is a different person than he was before he was fired."

■

On a recent afternoon at Arista Records, Clive Davis reflected on the scandal that got him thrown out of CBS.

"Someone who worked in the record division I had never hired [David Wynshaw] claimed there was wrongdoing—payola—in the record industry and CBS itself. Wynshaw had been caught in large-scale defalcations of his own, which I never found out. And he lured the officials in New Jersey into believing there was a major, highly publicizable problem in the record industry, more specifically CBS. His lawyers believed if they shot enough bullets in different directions, they'd come up with something to lighten his sentence.

"It was a terribly irresponsible thing to do, and it led to the expenditure of several million dollars on the part of the government, claiming they'd come up with incredible disclosures. To protect their government-licensed business, CBS was forced to divest me. Not because they knew of anything; they had to have some person take the rap.

"And since [the government] could find nothing wrong within CBS, relating to me or anybody else, they had to create the impression they'd come up with something to justify the millions spent. So the same day they brought indictments against these few little minor record company officials, they brought one against me on the subject of taxes, involving the same matter of the CBS complaint. To do so on the day of the payola situation was a horrendous misuse of justice. There never would have been an indictment brought against me on any of those other issues, because I would never be a part of any wrongdoing.

"When I won 'Humanitarian of the Year' from the Martell

Foundation, it was said that during those horrendous, lonely years, when the industry went through this mammoth investigation, that the industry was fortunate that someone like myself was the symbol. It was like the McCarthy years, where everybody had an ax to grind, and could find nothing. And I had to bear that, in effect, for the industry. I'm not saying it to martyr myself. But it's unfortunate. I would not want to have to do it again."

Though Clive could be faulted for his lack of contrition, perhaps he had reason to be scornful of the government. If everybody was so guilty, why had Project Sound stumbled so badly?

There is no simple answer. Clearly, the government made errors. But part of the problem was the weakness of the federal payola statute, which calls for a maximum fine of $10,000 and no more than a year in jail. In this context, Kenny Gamble's punishment was harsh.

By failing to send a single person to jail for payola, the government may have done more to set the stage for the Network than had it never mounted Project Sound. "Everyone was so scared," recalled one prominent industry figure. "But then it turned out the government was so *inept*. Things got much worse after that."

6

WALTER'S WAR

∎

ONLY by a twist of fate had paunchy, bearded, middle-aged Irwin Segelstein, a man with no background in music, become overnight one of the most powerful men in the record business. The checkbook had passed from Clive's hand to Irwin's, and now he was the man who made the deals. He was the one the artists' lawyers and managers were clamoring to see or reach on the phone. But Irwin was not someone to throw himself into what Clive called the "creative wars." He would not let the power of his position go to his head. "One thing I did know," he said. "If I allowed myself to get involved in the creative side of the music business, I should be fired."

The CBS Records Clive had left behind was a juggernaut. Under him, CBS had assembled a pop roster that would sustain the company well into the eighties. Its market share was nearly double that of the nearest competitor, RCA, although the labels of Warner Communications were beginning to come on strong and would soon prove a serious rival.

In another respect, however, Clive had left CBS Records in poor shape for a successor. Because of his autocratic ways, there was a management vacuum at the top. He had refused to appoint a head of Columbia in 1970 after succeeding Goddard as group president. Clive admitted wanting to reserve for himself the power to sign artists to Columbia, so he held posts of both Columbia president and group president. Now that he was gone, Irwin was de facto president of Columbia and could not appoint a creative head of the label. Until the Newark investigation was over, no one was promotable. In creative matters, Irwin had to depend heavily on Kip Cohen, the head of pop A&R.

But only two months into Irwin's presidency, Cohen quit. Irwin replaced him with Charlie Koppelman, formerly head of CBS Records' music publishing division. Koppelman's effectiveness was somewhat limited, Segelstein recalled, because he was busy "wheeling and dealing, rather than being an A&R man." Such were the consequences of having no president of Columbia with creative ability. (The job would eventually go to Bruce Lundvall, but not until late 1975.)

The Warner labels would never have had the same problem if, for example, Warner Bros. chairman Mo Ostin had suddenly left the company and been replaced by a TV executive. Though Ostin was in principle the head man of all the Warner labels, he was not a monarch like Clive Davis. In 1973 there were at least five people besides Ostin with checkbook power: Joe Smith at Warner Bros.; Ahmet Ertegun and Jerry Wexler at Atlantic; Jac Holzman at Elektra; and a relative newcomer named David Geffen at Asylum. Warner was fully prepared to exploit the demise of Clive Davis.

CBS still had a big advantage over Warner in distribution, but this would not last long. Under the guidance of Clive's corporate enemy, Bill Gallagher, CBS had been the first record company to build distribution branches. In the early seventies, Warner set up its own distribution arm, WEA Corporation (for Warner, Elektra, and Atlantic). WEA was still primitive when Clive left CBS. But over the next two years, WEA would be able to hire a number of key people from shell-shocked CBS and become a virtual equal.

Distribution is no small matter. It is one of two essentials to launching a national pop star, the other being radio play. First you must "advertise" your artist's records by getting them heard on the radio. Having created a demand, you must see that the records are delivered to stores in time to meet the demand. It is a bit like trying to launch a new brand of toothpaste. The most effective national advertising is worthless if you cannot get shelf space for your product in stores across the country.

When Clive joined CBS, distribution was open to any record company, big and small. There were dozens of independent distributors you could hire to get rack space for your records in stores. By the end of the seventies, six "major" labels had begun to emerge as the oligarchs of the record business: CBS, Warner, RCA, Capitol-EMI, PolyGram, and MCA. (In 1986 RCA became part of BMG—Bertelsmann Music Group—when the West German media conglomerate Bertelsmann took it over.) They were called major labels because they did their own nationwide distribution.

By the late seventies, the majors found they needed more market share. This was only natural. Once you have set up sales branches, warehouses, and shipping depots across the map, you need tremendous volume to keep them running at capacity. A huge "pipeline" must be filled all the time or else it does not pay for itself.

The majors found that 5 or even 10 percent of the U.S. pop market was not enough. They had to have 10 to 15 percent. So they began to buy small labels and even a few large ones. Capitol-EMI bought Liberty Records and United Artists Records; MCA bought ABC-Dunhill. Beginning in the late seventies, the majors also began to make deals to distribute every independent label of size or importance. Today, Motown is distributed by MCA, Virgin by WEA, Def Jam by CBS, and so forth. Independent distribution is virtually dead. The term "oligopoly" is an apt one to describe today's record business: Most American record stores get nearly all their wares from six suppliers.

Think of them—CBS, Warner, BMG, Capitol-EMI, Poly-Gram, MCA—as the six sovereign states of pop music. Today, there is virtually no American pop singer or rock band of national stature that a major does not, in one way or another, have a piece of. The days are gone in which a pint-sized company like Vee Jay can launch the Four Seasons with independent distribution. (With the advent of the Network, the majors would lock up both the "advertising" and the "shelf space," and their control of the industry would be complete.)

Artists looking for a record deal have nowhere as many labels to choose from as they had in the sixties, because the overall number of independent labels has shrunk drastically. "When I shopped demo tapes at the beginning of my career fifteen years ago," a former artist manager said in 1986, "I had twenty-five places to go. Now, there are only six majors left." It translates into less choice for consumers. The record industry puts out about two thousand albums a year, half the number of a decade ago.

Even to speak of the Big Six is to make the record business sound less concentrated than it really has become. Far out in front there are the Big Two. As of this writing, the U.S. record business is a $6.3 billion pie, and a whopping one-third of it belongs to CBS and Warner. Their combined domestic sales are probably about $2 billion a year. The imbalance of power is the direct result of Clive's CBS and Ostin's Warner having been the first record companies to recognize the potential of album rock.

Today, CBS and Warner can be viewed as the record industry's equivalent of the world's two superpowers. Which is which depends on your point of view. ("After I left CBS," said Jack Craigo, "I found out that Warner referred to us as the communists.") The two companies exert hegemony over the business. There are no lasting price increases unless they approve of them. It is impossible to introduce a new format—the cassette single, to use a recent example—unless they go along. CBS and Warner even win an outsize share of Grammy Awards, thanks to the power of their block voting.

The supremacy of CBS Records dates from Clive's presidency. During his tenure, Clive felt Warner creeping up on him. In the disarray at CBS that followed Clive's firing and the Newark investigation, Warner rose rapidly to become CBS's equal. There are CBS loyalists, Craigo among them, who feel that Warner might never have caught up with CBS had it not been for Project Sound. This is probably unfair to Warner, though there is no question that CBS lost momentum during its two years under Irwin Segelstein. After all, he first had to learn the business.

■

Goddard Lieberson, the man who might have been able to help Segelstein the most, was proving an absentee landlord. Already past retirement age, Goddard had come back to CBS Records to find it heavily weighted in music for which he had no great affinity. He promised to press on with CBS Records' successful move into rock, but vowed to scale back the high-priced bidding for talent, which he felt had got out of hand. He also cut down on perks. "There was a little too much Louis Quatorze going on," he said. That was about the only guidance he provided for Irwin Segelstein. "I could walk in to his office and say, Here's what is happening, what do I do now?" Segelstein recalled. "But he did not get into the nitty-gritty. Goddard was usually on the phone talking to the great and near-great."

So Irwin turned more and more to Walter Yetnikoff, his corporate equal. Walter was the head of the less glitzy division, CBS

Records International. As such, he was one of the few ranking record executives at Black Rock who was not a suspect in the Newark investigation. As Irwin became frustrated by the inquiry, which he felt was hurting innocent people, it was often to Walter that he would vent his anger. "I would rant and rave," Irwin recalled, "and Walter would rub me down." Walter, for his part, seemed genuinely fond of Segelstein. Irwin was "Jewish the way I am," Walter said.

If Walter had thoughts of moving up the ladder, it must have been obvious to him that Irwin was not a serious long-term rival. Segelstein had made it clear that eventually he wanted to go back into television. It must have been equally apparent to Walter that Goddard Lieberson did not plan to remain group president for much longer. The thought of becoming the top man at CBS Records tempted Walter. "I guess I wanted it," he admitted recently. "But I don't think I ever thought I was qualified. I do now, but I didn't then. Now, I think I'm overqualified."

During this time, Walter made himself more visible to Arthur Taylor. At seven or eight in the evening, it was common for Walter to drop by Taylor's office for a chat. The subject often turned to issues of foreign currency—the strong dollar versus the weak yen —and international financing. Taylor, who had been a managing director of a Wall Street investment banking firm, was an expert on these subjects. He was pleased and flattered that Walter sought his advice. Asked by a reporter whether he ever felt Walter was deliberately schmoozing him, Taylor laughed. "I used to see twenty people a day," he said. "If I tried to sort out who was politicking, I'd never have gotten anywhere."

Walter insisted, however, that he was *not* campaigning for the job. In fact, he said, when Goddard stated his intention to step down, Walter tried to dissuade him.

"Goddard didn't like the corporate thing, he didn't want to do it anymore," Walter recalled. "He wanted to write, he wanted to live in Santa Fe, blah blah blah. And I tried to talk him out of it. So if I had designs on the job, I would have been crazy, right? Somewhere in the back of my head, there was probably a little thing saying, You could probably do it, you could probably do it, wouldn't it be great? But I didn't plan it. I may have wanted it and been afraid of it, but I didn't plan it.

"And I remember saying, Goddard, you can't go, what am I going to do without you? And he said, Can you get me out of all of these meetings? I told him I would try. So I went up to Arthur Taylor and said, I think Goddard ought to stay, it's good for the company.

"Now, if I was plotting, this was completely contrary to my self-interest. I may have been thinking, Wouldn't that be something! But I certainly wasn't manipulating in any way. I'm not manipulative—I don't think. I'm blunt, and I talk too much, but I'm not manipulative. And Taylor says, Well, you can get him out of a lot of these meetings, but he still has to go to the board meeting.

"So I went back to Goddard and said, I did it for you, here you are. You're out of all the meetings—but you do have to go to the board meeting. He said, I'm not going to do it. I said, Come on, you can't leave. . . ."

But he did retire, in early 1975. Goddard did not know it at the time, but he had only two years to live. He contracted cancer, and it galloped.

"I was very angry about him dying on me," Walter said. "I'm serious. Because I thought Goddard had beaten the system. He had left CBS when he wanted to leave, not when *they* wanted him to leave. He'd had some awkward years in the Clive era, when Clive kept pushing him to the side. But now he was back on top. He left with a sterling reputation, and he left to do what he wanted to do. He was, I think, quite a happy man, certainly one of the most gracious, funny guys on the face of the earth. And he was doing what he wanted to do. He had financial security. He . . . beat . . . the . . . system. And then the motherfucker *died* on me! It sounds facetious, but I was really pissed."

The decision to give Lieberson's job to Walter Yetnikoff may have been made aboard Arthur Taylor's forty-foot yawl. Taylor was an avid yachtsman and often went sailing with his attorney, Stanley Schlesinger, who also represented CBS in the Newark investigation. Fortunately, Taylor was able to handle the boat alone, because Schlesinger resisted working as a crew member. It was aboard the yacht that Stanley met Walter Yetnikoff. They took an instant liking to one another. Stanley found Walter somewhat shy—a word frequently used to describe Yetnikoff at that time— but exceptionally bright. Walter also shared Schlesinger's aversion to the physical demands of sailing, preferring to take it easy.

Taylor had to replace Lieberson with a new head of CBS Records, and he knew the decision was a crucial one. He was considering Irwin and Walter, but also a number of people from outside the company. Schlesinger began to urge Taylor to choose Walter. Stanley's argument, as the lawyer remembered it, was that in addition to being smart, Walter was "irreproachable and honest —qualities that were terribly important at the time, because of the Newark situation."

Taylor was already inclined toward Walter, and he soon offered him the position. Schlesinger thereby gained in Walter not only a lifelong friend but an important client. In May 1975 Walter ascended to group president of CBS Records—the "Fuhrer's job," as he called it. Exactly how the decision was made depends on who's telling the story. Walter preferred a version that depicted him as a lady-killer. "I got it because Arthur Taylor's assistant, a lady, liked me," he said.

Possibly to his own surprise, Irwin was a bit disappointed. Only a month later, a programming job opened at CBS, and he accepted it. He had mixed feelings about leaving the record division. Irwin was afraid that if he stayed out of programming too long, people in television would forget about him. On the other hand, he had wanted to remain in records long enough to learn the business and make an impact, and he thought four years would be the right length of time. Nonetheless, after two years as head of CBS Records U.S., Irwin Segelstein moved back into broadcasting. Walter invited him to attend the CBS Records annual sales convention in California that July. "Somebody saw me come in, and all of sudden they were all rising, giving me a standing ovation," Irwin recalled. "Walter was pushing me up. That was one of my most gratifying moments."

In retrospect, Arthur Taylor called his appointment of Walter Yetnikoff "a brilliant choice—maybe the best management decision I ever made." He was speaking in 1987, when CBS Records was having a banner year. Taylor quite naturally used a financial yardstick to measure the quality of top management. In business, chief executives often refer to quarterly earnings as their "report card."

By these standards, Taylor himself had proved an "A" student as president of CBS. By 1976 earnings were at an all-time high. Yet, for some reason, William Paley began to wonder whether his appointment of Taylor had been a good move after all. Perhaps, as has been suggested by Paley biographers, Taylor was a bit *too* successful as CBS president, and the old man began to feel stirrings of mortality. Paley was by then seventy-five. In any case, Schlesinger had been exactly right about Bill Paley when he warned Taylor that CBS's founder and chairman would have trouble letting go. For in October 1976, much to Arthur Taylor's surprise, Paley fired him.

"I think when Paley began to hear people saying how well I was doing, he couldn't tolerate it," Taylor said. "My reaction was to redouble my efforts, but at that point, nothing I did was enough. It was like sleeping next to an elephant. You treat the elephant gingerly, because he may roll over on you. That's what happened to me."

Paley saw things differently. "I'm just a bad picker, I guess. I thought I had someone good in Arthur Taylor. He was young, articulate, ambitious, aggressive—but he just didn't work out."

To replace Taylor, Paley reached within the corporation and offered the job to John Backe, then head of CBS's publishing division. Backe (rhymes with "rocky"), the former commander of an air force bomber squadron, had performed well with the publishing unit. Among other achievements, he had added Fawcett Publications and *Woman's Day* magazine to the CBS fold. So at age forty-three, Backe took Taylor's place as the number two official of the broadcasting giant. Unlike Taylor, however, Backe insisted on the more vaunted title of president *and* chief executive. Evidently, Backe felt this gave him more job security than Taylor had had. After all, you couldn't be too careful with Paley. The old man could be capricious.

■

Walter Yetnikoff was not kidding when he said he had doubted his qualifications to run CBS Records. He was coming into the title after a two-year interregnum, during which CBS Records had stagnated and the Warner labels had gained considerable ground. It was to Clive Davis, not Irwin Segelstein, that he would be compared. It was not going to be easy.

The industry was watching him. And for the first year or two, it liked what it saw. "Walter was beloved in our community because he was so humble," said attorney Eric Kronfeld. "He would say his power was completely tenuous and depended on the whims of Bill Paley. It was not personal power. That very statement and attitude were so different from everyone else in the record business that people warmed to Walter. He was the little guy coming to the top. You just loved him. You wanted to *do* for him."

This was still the Walter Yetnikoff who only a few years earlier had become tongue-tied before an audience at a London convention. He was ethnic—Walter had *always* been ethnic—but he had yet to turn his heritage into a badge of militancy. He was not the Walter Yetnikoff who, in the middle of an interview with a reporter, would pause to demand, "How do you feel about Jews?" The boisterous, wild, combative side of Walter was yet to emerge.

Walter's promotion had left his old post vacant. To no one's surprise, one of Walter's first official acts as group president was to name Dick Asher the new head of CBS Records International. Dick had spent the last three years in London running the CBS label there, and he had done a good job. Now, Dick was coming back to New York.

Dick and Walter, while never intimates, always got on well. They were a year apart in age, and both had married their college sweethearts. They attended the bar mitzvahs of each other's sons and went to concerts with their wives at the Fillmore East. Since Dick had joined CBS in 1966, they had worked closely together. When Asher was head of business affairs, Walter was general attorney; Dick negotiated contracts and Yetnikoff drafted them. When Dick moved over to CBS Records UK, Walter was his immediate supervisor. And now, Walter, at the first opportunity, had given Dick a major promotion.

But not long after Dick returned to New York, he and Walter had their first serious argument. It was over Clive Davis. Clive had just pleaded guilty to tax evasion, and was about to be sentenced. The only CBS people who had made their feelings about Clive known to the judge were from the company's legal department, and what they had to say was wholly negative. Clive was hoping to persuade some of his old colleagues to write testimonial letters to the judge. Asher had not been his first choice, since Dick had been in London during the final years of Clive's presidency. But most of the other people Clive had appealed to for a letter—Dick assumed this included Walter Yetnikoff—had rebuffed him. Asher unhesitatingly agreed.

"I told Walter I was writing the letter," Dick recalled. "And he said to me, Arthur Taylor won't like it. You're gonna get your ass fired for this. And Walter threatened and tried everything to get me not to write the letter. He said Clive was arrogant, that I shouldn't do this for him. I said, Wait a minute, Walter, I'm really doing it for *me*. In many ways, Clive was good to me, so how could

I turn my back on him when he was in trouble? And I said to Walter, You know, you really ought to write a letter yourself, because Clive did a lot more for you than he did for me. Walter wasn't even going to become the head of the law department after Clive was made president. They were trying to push someone else in. And Clive really fought to get Walter in there.

"Anyway, I wrote the letter. And I copied Walter and copied Arthur Taylor on it, and never heard anything about it. Eventually, I asked Walter what happened. He said Arthur Taylor didn't agree with it, but he could understand why I did it."

Without a doubt, Walter harbored ill will toward his former boss. Among friends, Walter did a devastating imitation of Clive— his pseudo-Continental accent, his preening mannerisms. The enmity appeared to be mutual. Walter said that shortly after replacing Goddard, "I turned to Clive for advice. I knew what he was going through, but still I needed his advice, and I think he gave me bad advice because unconsciously he still couldn't let go of what he had been at CBS. Once you work for someone, it is very hard for that someone to accept you as an equal. To them, you are always their employee. I think Clive gave me very bad advice. He said, Don't sign *this* artist, sign *that* one. Exactly the reverse of what ultimately proved right. He was pretty pissed off at CBS, and with good reason, but he didn't help me very much."

In 1978 Clive was invited to give the keynote address at the NARM convention, the record industry's most important yearly gathering. NARM is the National Association of Recording Merchandisers; its annual convention brings the record companies and retailers together. It was an important moment for Clive, who had become president of Arista, signaling his reemergence as a leading industry figure after his disgrace. Unable to resist, Clive took a couple of shots at CBS. "Walter went fucking crazy," said the president of a record chain. "He summoned the NARM board to his hotel suite the next day. So we all went up there. And Walter put on a performance that was extraordinary. Screaming, yelling, I'M GOING TO PUNCH CLIVE DAVIS IN THE NOSE! I'm sitting there saying, This is the president of the biggest record company in the *world*? He threatened, if they didn't throw Arista out of the organization, he would pull CBS out."

Walter knew from the outset that he could not compete with Clive on Clive's terms. It did not matter that both men had gone to Ivy League law schools and risen through the same legal firm.

They were men of very different sensibilities. Walter was not going to make himself an A&R executive. What would he be? A distinctive personality is essential if one is to be a powerful label boss. Irwin Segelstein had failed to establish one—that was, arguably, his great virtue: He was content to be Irwin Segelstein. Mo Ostin at Warner preferred to be faceless, but Warner was different, really a collection of nation-states. All the Warner labels had powerful, high-profile leaders.

Yetnikoff recalled pondering what he should do. "So I have to follow Clive and Goddard. Terrific. I have to develop my own image. The first thing I did was take a piece of yellow paper and write down everything everybody thought I should do. I would then go home at night, look at the yellow paper, and choose what I wanted to do. How do you forge your own image? Difficult.

"Unconsciously, I picked a fight with Warner Bros. So now I have a big flag out that says 'Fuck Warner Bros.' I have all the troops rallying around the flag, using the excuse to go in and steal artists under the banner of 'Fuck Warner Bros.'

"It was like I'd created a nation. Follow Walter? No one knew who I was. So unconsciously I made a war out of it. I believed in the cause, and now I had an army behind me."

Take out the word "unconsciously" and the account rings true. It was the start of Walter's War, as Jack Craigo dubbed it, and the origin of Walter's new image. At first, people who thought they knew Walter were amazed. There he was at a CBS convention, literally handing out GI boots. He did, indeed, have signs made up that said FUCK WARNER. At a meeting one day, Walter went on a tirade about the Wickey Bird, the Warner corporate jet. Craigo and Bruce Lundvall had been chasing talent in Texas, only to find that Ahmet Ertegun of Atlantic had been there the day before—*on the Wickey Bird!* It was a fighter plane, Walter declared, with machine guns! . . .

From playing General Patton, it took only a few modifications for Walter to round out his new image. "When Walter took that job, who was he?" said Elliot Goldman, the CBS business affairs head who followed Clive to Arista. "He was a lawyer who didn't have Clive's creative talent or Clive's polish. All of a sudden, he has great notoriety because of his war on Warner. And goddamn it, it *worked*. So now Walter's got to sustain the bluster. It worked because we're in the entertainment business, and people love power and the aura of power. As a result of acting that way—

throwing plates across the room—Walter stirred this enormous fear. Lawyers became afraid: I can't ask Walter for that! He'll get angry at me!"

The war applied to all the labels, including Atlantic, though it happened that Walter was fond of Ahmet Ertegun. For some reason, however, he felt nothing but animosity toward quiet, self-effacing Mo Ostin. "It became quite vicious," Craigo said. Yetnikoff kept in his office a statue of a circus strong man with a sign, THE MENSCH WITH SPILKAS—the man with jitters—and addressed it as Mo. He rarely passed up an opportunity to disparage Ostin or his management style.

The man Walter loved to hate was short and slight, bald and spectacled. His features were somewhat rodentlike. Mo Ostin kept his picture out of the trade magazines for the most part, never gave interviews, and rarely attended industry functions. He had entered the music business as Frank Sinatra's accountant. In 1963 Sinatra sold a small label he owned, Reprise Records, to the Warner film company, which had created the Warner Bros. label five years earlier. The labels were merged, and Ostin was chosen to run the latter half of what was then called Warner-Reprise.

Warner Bros. Records had begun inauspiciously. From 1958 to 1962, it lost an estimated $3 million a year. The film company toyed with closing down the record operations but feared it would never collect the money owed by its slow-paying independent distributors. Then, in 1963, Warner signed comedian Allen Sherman and folk trio Peter, Paul and Mary. Hit albums by Bill Cosby completed the turnaround. Meanwhile, Reprise began to score middle-of-the-road hits with Dean Martin, Nancy Sinatra, and Trini Lopez.

Mike Maitland, then the head of Warner Bros. Records, brought in industry funnyman and former disc jockey Joe Smith as a promotion executive a few years later. Smith signed the Grateful Dead, and Warner was on its way to becoming a rock company. Meanwhile, Seven Arts, a small film producer and distributor, acquired all of Warner Bros.—films and records—in 1966. The purchase encumbered Seven Arts with debt, and it resolved to sell the Warner holdings, but not before adding Atlantic Records to the fold in 1967. That year, the Warner movie and music operations found a stable owner in the Kinney Corporation.

Kinney must have seemed an unlikely parent. It was run by Steve Ross, an ambitious young man from Flatbush. He had taken over his then-wife's family business, funeral parlors, and expanded into car-rental agencies and parking lots. In 1967 he exchanged $10 million in preferred stock for the Ashley Famous talent agency. Entranced by the entertainment business, Ross soon took over Warner-Seven Arts, as it was then called.

Ross imparted his management style to the inchoate group of Warner labels. Business magazines often prate about "corporate culture," but it does exist—a deep-seated belief in the way things should be done. The Paley culture was autocratic, and it filtered down to CBS Records, but Steve Ross believed in delegation. Despite his background in hearses and car lots, Ross proved a good manager of creative people and well suited for the entertainment business. The film and record companies outgrew Kinney's core business so quickly that in 1971 Ross renamed it Warner Communications.

Mo Ostin shared the Ross philosophy of decentralization. Outside of distribution, the Warner labels competed with one another head-to-head. Though an accountant by training, Ostin signed acclaimed singer-songwriters such as Randy Newman, James Taylor, and Van Morrison. Warner under Ostin also picked up Jimi Hendrix and Black Sabbath.

By 1976 Mo Ostin had long since proven himself a record man. Walter had proven nothing. Soon this would change.

The first shot in Walter's War was fired that year. The battle began during the NARM convention in Florida, in a room at the Diplomat Hotel. Yetnikoff had just been told that Mo Ostin had disparaged him in some offhand remark, and he was in a tearing rage. He turned to attorney Nat Weiss, whose Nemperor label was distributed by CBS, and swore vengeance. There had to be some way, Walter kept insisting, to get back at Mo. After a few minutes of listening to his friend's fulminations, Weiss suddenly got an idea. Excuse me, Walter, he said, I have to make a phone call. Weiss found a public phone and rang his most famous client, James Taylor, whose contract with Warner would soon be up for renewal. James, Weiss said, I think I know a way to get a million dollars an album.

Yetnikoff was thrilled with the idea of plucking James Taylor from Warner Bros. He had been CBS Records president for less than a year, and had not yet distinguished himself with a major signing. To take an artist from Warner—one of its superstars, no less—would be the icing on the cake. In early 1976, Taylor was at the height of his popularity, having gone platinum with Warner albums such as *Sweet Baby James* and *Gorilla*. The deal Yetnikoff worked out with Nat Weiss—a guaranteed $1 million per album and a $2.5 million advance—was steep by 1976 standards, even for a hit act. But this was war.

The signing finally took place at Nat Weiss's apartment on Manhattan's Upper East Side, just before year-end 1976. It almost fell through. Taylor was scheduled to arrive at 11:00 P.M. but showed up an hour late with his manager, Peter Asher (no relation to Dick). The singer was distraught. Mo Ostin and other Warner executives had begged him to reconsider. Presently, Taylor broke down crying, saying he didn't think he could go through with the deal. Walter, holding a blank contract and a check for $2.5 million, was apoplectic. "He was staring daggers at me," Weiss recalled. Well, Peter Asher said, breaking the stunned silence, you have to respect James's feelings. WHAT ABOUT MY FEELINGS? Walter demanded. After hours of cajoling, Taylor finally acknowledged he had made a commitment. He signed the papers at about 4:00 A.M., and everyone collapsed from exhaustion.

Walter did not have long to gloat, however. Mo Ostin got his revenge only a year later by taking from Columbia an artist who was an inextricable part of the label's history: Paul Simon. The singer's 1970 album with Art Garfunkel, *Bridge over Troubled Water*, had sold 8 million copies worldwide, making it the first CBS recording to outdo *My Fair Lady*. Though Simon's solo albums, after his 1970 split with Garfunkel, had not matched those of the duo in sales, they nonetheless did well commercially and critically. In 1975 Simon won the best-album Grammy for *Still Crazy After All These Years*.

Simon had a reputation around CBS for being difficult. In fact, said Debbie Federoff, Yetnikoff's secretary at the time, "Walter hated his guts." Though losing so prominent an artist was unthinkable, the friction between Walter and Paul Simon was evident when his contract came up for renewal. Simon liked to sit in on the negotiations, which were handled by his close friend and attorney Michael Tannen. In late 1975, Walter had Simon in his office, and the bargaining session soon deteriorated into acrimony. Walter phoned Arthur Taylor and said he wanted Simon barred from the building. Catching on that Walter was playacting as a negotiating technique, Taylor said all right, he would instruct the security guards to lead Simon out the door and not allow him back. For how long? Walter said. Until eternity, Taylor replied. Hah! Walter said to Simon, I have Arthur Taylor on the line, and he says you're out of this building until eternity—until you're *dead*!

Before the session ended, Paul Simon had renewed his contract with CBS. But it was evident that Simon did not like Walter as much as he had liked Clive Davis. Clive, who knew a well-crafted song when he heard one, was an unabashed Simon fan. So, too, it turned out, was Mo Ostin. Ostin had made it clear to Mike Tannen that if ever Paul were free, Warner would be very interested.

Simon's contract with CBS came up for renewal again in late 1977. The negotiations were long and protracted and frequently nasty, but in the end Simon and Tannen believed they had worked out all the crucial terms of a deal. They were wrong. "Walter thought we reneged on basic terms, and Paul and I believed he had reneged on basic terms," Tannen said. "In any case, the deal fell apart. Walter called me at one point in the middle of all this and said, There's no deal for Paul Simon. I remember that very well. He said, Paul does *not* have a deal."

In February 1978, Tannen got on the phone with Mo Ostin, and within twenty-four hours, he had an agreement in principle to move Simon to Warner Bros. Warner soon found it had acquired not merely a singer-songwriter but also a matinee idol manqué. Paul Simon wrote and starred in a 1980 Warner Bros. movie, *One Trick Pony*, which bombed. Sales of the soundtrack album were equally disappointing.

Despite his personal distaste for Paul Simon, losing an artist of his caliber to Warner Bros. Records was more than Walter Yetnikoff could bear. He was furious and, according to a suit filed by Simon in November 1978, vowed that CBS Records would "destroy Simon's professional career," out of "anger and retaliation" for his plans to desert the label for Warner Bros.

Simon still owed CBS one more studio album under his previous contract. His lawsuit alleged that Walter had vowed to reject it, regardless of merit, in order to entangle him in litigation and prevent him from recording. Simon also charged that CBS was withholding royalties, and that Walter had discouraged other CBS artists from recording with him. Simon claimed, too, that CBS had failed to promote and distribute his new single, "Stranded in a Limousine," which sounded like a surefire hit, if ever such a thing existed. The song barely cracked the charts. CBS denied all the allegations. *

Before long, the Simon suit was settled out of court. Years later, Walter's friend and attorney Stanley Schlesinger, who represented CBS in the Simon matter, claimed victory. He noted that Simon had paid CBS Records $1.5 million. He failed to point out that Simon never did deliver his final CBS album, so that the "settlement" was in fact a buyout of his old contract.

Simon got a kind of fantasy revenge against Yetnikoff in *One Trick Pony* by casting Rip Torn as Walter Fox, a bearded, demonic record company executive. Toward the end of the movie, Jonah Levin, the rock musician portrayed by Simon, seduces and sleeps with Fox's blond shiksa wife. In an interview in *Playboy*, Simon referred to the "trauma" of the "terrible personal battle between me and Walter Yetnikoff," and suggested that it had contributed to a severe case of writer's block. Simon's career did stall for several years after the label switch, but in 1986 he released *Graceland*. It took the best-album honors at the 1987 Grammys, more than a decade after Simon had won for *Still Crazy* and two decades since his first runaway hit, "The Sounds of Silence." There could be no question about Simon's artistic fertility, and despite the financial loss of the film *One Trick Pony*, which several hit albums would not recoup, it is doubtful that Warner regretted the deal.

Yetnikoff was, if anything, angrier at Mike Tannen than at Paul Simon. He found Tannen distasteful, and was not alone in this assessment. Tannen was short, puckish, smart, and ruthless. His father, Nat Tannen, had been a prominent music publisher who virtually cornered the market on country songs by founding Acuff-Rose, named for two clients. Nat died of a heart attack when Mike was five, and one of Nat's best friends, attorney Harold Orenstein, virtually adopted the boy. Orenstein helped get Tannen through law school, then took him on at his firm, which handled such prestige clients as the estate of songwriter Frank Loesser and Simon and Garfunkel. Tannen did not get along well with Orenstein's partners, however, and decided to move out on his own. He took Paul Simon with him. "I watched Michael steal Paul

---

* Though in a recent interview, Walter admitted, "At the beginning, if [Simon] wanted an artist of mine to cooperate in a project, I would forbid it."

Simon, and I let him get away with it," Orenstein said, still stung by Tannen's ingratitude. "He's a louse." ("It's outrageous for him to say that," Tannen replied. "Paul wanted to leave the firm.")

No one could deny that Tannen was shrewd. Beginning with Simon, Tannen built probably the most powerful music law practice of the seventies, representing, at various times, the Rolling Stones, John Lennon, Billy Joel, Merle Haggard, Stephen Stills, and Bruce Springsteen. After bringing Paul Simon to Warner Bros., Tannen won the right to produce the movie *One Trick Pony*.

No wonder Yetnikoff hated him. In retaliation, Walter decided to punish Tannen with eternal banishment from the CBS building. He had barely instituted the ban, however, when Marvin Cohn, the head of business affairs, called with unpleasant news. Tannen had just become the attorney for Billy Joel. "Walter turned orange and purple at the same time," said industry veteran Jerald Wagner, who was with Yetnikoff when the call came in. "But Walter's no dummy. Memo rescinded; Tannen is allowed back in the building." Yetnikoff had been outfoxed—for the time being.

Meanwhile, the war was far from over, and it proved costly for both CBS and Warner Communications. In the late seventies, Ostin renewed Warner's deal with Rod Stewart on handsome terms—ten albums at $2 million apiece—in the mistaken belief that Stewart's manager, Billy Gaff, was holding talks with Yetnikoff. Said Gaff, "I've never seen a deal made so quickly." Around the same time, CBS and Atlantic engaged in furious bidding for Off Broadway, a rock group from Chicago. Atlantic won the auction at a high price—and the band faded after one album.

CBS did not fare much better. Though the James Taylor deal probably earned a profit, Yetnikoff made two other superstar acquisitions in the late seventies that bombed: Paul McCartney and the Beach Boys. Chances are good that he did the deals at least partly to prevent Warner Communications from getting them.

CBS offered McCartney an unheard-of enticement, a publishing company that held the copyrights of one of America's greatest songwriters, Frank Loesser. Walter had originally bought Frank Music, as it was called, to enhance CBS Songs, the music publishing arm of CBS Records. "When the Frank Loesser catalog was sold by the estate to CBS, Mr. Yetnikoff promised it would be the jewel in the crown [of CBS Songs]," said Harold Orenstein, the estate lawyer and Mike Tannen's early mentor. "He lied. Okay, he might have meant well at the time. But when it came to the competition as to who would get Paul McCartney when he left Capitol, the only thing CBS could give him that the others couldn't was copyrights. Lee Eastman [McCartney's father-in-law and a music attorney] was always copyright hungry."

It is hard to overstate the value of Frank Music. Loesser wrote the words and music to *Guys and Dolls* and other Broadway classics; his catalog included gems such as "Spring Will Be a Little Late this Year," "Standing on the Corner," and "Once in Love with Amy." McCartney did make five albums for CBS, and one of them, *Tug of War*, was a big hit. But after that, he re-signed with Capitol, and Frank Music was his to keep. One source close to McCartney believed CBS lost $9 million on the ex-Beatle.

Looking on from the sidelines, Mitch Miller, the former pop A&R boss under Goddard Lieberson, was appalled. CBS, he said, "just by sitting on its fanny would take in a million dollars a year just in performance rights on Frank Loesser's catalog. . . . If I were a Columbia stockholder, I would sue for dilution of assets. . . . But that goes to show, when the lawyers are making the decision, and a lawyer is president of the company instead of a musician. . . ."

Miller's point was well taken. CBS under Goddard Lieberson had been the A&R company. Clive had continued the tradition better than anyone had had a right to expect. Now, Walter— "tone-deaf" Walter—was forging a much different CBS Records. The *deal* company. From the sidelines, Clive derided what he called Walter's "banking deals." No creative vision was needed, just a checkbook. Clive, of course, had made such deals himself: Neil Diamond, Earth, Wind and Fire, Pink Floyd. In retrospect, he had not spent so much, however big the guarantees may have seemed at the time. Clive had set the precedent all the same.

Well into the eighties, the Yetnikoff regime would not distinguish itself for breaking new American acts, Cyndi Lauper notwithstanding. There would be several notable successes from CBS Records UK: the Clash, Elvis Costello, George Michael, and others. But for the most part, the emphasis would be on buying rather than discovering talent, including the Rolling Stones, snatched from Atlantic in 1983. In the meantime, Warner Communications would inherit the A&R company mantle from CBS and introduce new American stars such as Prince, Madonna, Talking Heads,

Anita Baker, and Tracy Chapman. "Warner is probably the best record company in terms of career development," a CBS man recently confessed. "They're sympathetic to groups that take a long time to break. Talking Heads would never have made a nickel on CBS Records."

Walter's War cooled but never ended, though recently Yetnikoff admitted feeling "sort of stupid" for having waged it in the first place. Whether he meant it, the war not only forged his identity but left a permanent mark on the industry.

Setting aside the personal ill will, Walter's War was a bidding contest between the two industry superpowers that raised the ante for the whole industry. The cost of talent—especially established talent—reached dizzying new heights. The "outrageous" $425,000-an-album deal that Clive had made for Neil Diamond in 1970 seemed like a pittance by the end of the decade.

The result was a business driven by bigger and bigger deals. Even Warner's success at developing talent was only impressive when measured against CBS's lack of success. Walter had used the might of CBS to impose his style of business on the industry, though in fairness, he could not have done so had Mo and Ahmet and the other Warner bosses refused to bid against him.

By the end of the seventies, the record business was no longer one in which music men like Goddard Lieberson were likely to rise to power. Now, it was the day of the dealmaker. The top label bosses would be the men who could grasp the concept of "front-end points" and "cross-collateralization" and "recoupable items." They did not have to be lawyers, however. In fact, the two men who would come closest to matching Walter Yetnikoff's power in the eighties were former artist managers. Their names were David Geffen and Irving Azoff.

THE TROIKA

■

THERE was no denying it, he had a golden touch. Whether David Geffen was investing in real estate or Magritte paintings or the careers of rock musicians, his instincts rarely failed him. By the eighties, he was one of the few music-industry people to make the Forbes Four Hundred list of wealthiest Americans, with an estimated net worth of close to $500 million.

David Geffen was not a universally loved figure in the record industry. He was vain, arrogant, and an incorrigible gossip. Music attorney Brian Rohan once slugged him in the Polo Lounge of the Beverly Hills Hotel, and received more than forty congratulatory telegrams the next day.

Though he never completed college, Geffen claimed to have learned the rudiments of business from his mother, a manufacturer of bras and corsets. He got his start in show business in 1964 at age twenty-one by landing a job sorting mail for the William Morris Agency. Since the agency required that all employees, however menial, have a college degree, Geffen forged a letter from UCLA. Years later, Geffen would teach business at the university and be elected to its board of regents. The irony was not lost on him.

Soon Geffen moved to the Ashley Famous agency, concentrating on the pop musicians nearer his age than the movie directors and screenwriters he had handled at William Morris. In 1968 he was introduced to Laura Nyro, an eccentric dark-haired young singer and songwriter. Convinced of her talent, Geffen quit Ashley Famous to become her manager. With a shrewdness that would characterize his entire career, Geffen created a publishing company for her songs, Tuna Fish Music—named for her favorite food—and assigned himself 50 percent of the equity, the standard publisher's share.

Clive Davis had seen Laura Nyro at Monterey, but she had performed so badly he barely noticed her. When Geffen brought her to CBS for an audition, she insisted on switching off all the lights and playing by the glow of a television set. She performed for Clive many of the songs that would constitute her Columbia album, *Eli and the Thirteenth Confession*. "I was knocked out!" Clive wrote, explaining why he signed her immediately. Nyro's lushly orchestrated albums were too self-indulgent to sell well, but her songs became hits for Barbra Streisand ("Stoney End"), Blood, Sweat and Tears ("And When I Die"), the Fifth Dimension ("Stoned Soul Picnic"), and Three Dog Night ("Eli's Comin' ").

Geffen sold Nyro's publishing company to CBS for $4.5 million worth of CBS stock in 1969, keeping half the proceeds. Despite his windfall, he was so furious with Clive that he wouldn't speak to him for a year. Had Clive been able to close the deal sooner, when CBS stock was higher, Geffen would have made a million or so more. In any case, Laura Nyro soon faded into history, but Geffen was on his way up.

Geffen had become the manager for David Crosby, Stephen Stills, and Graham Nash. Each belonged to a separate band and was under contract to a different label, but they wished to record together. Stills, a member of Buffalo Springfield, was on Atlantic Records. Geffen went to see Jerry Wexler at Atlantic to ask for a release for Stills so that he could deliver Crosby, Stills, and Nash to Clive's Columbia. Wexler physically ejected Geffen from the office. The next day, Ahmet Ertegun called to apologize and asked Geffen to come see him. "He was the most charming person I'd ever met in my life," Geffen said. "He just sucked me right in. Because of Ahmet, as soon as I got Crosby, Stills, and Nash free of all their other contracts, I signed them to Atlantic." A year later, in 1970, Neil Young joined the group, and Crosby, Stills, Nash and Young were on their way to superstardom.

As a manager, Geffen was hell on wheels. He prided himself on getting the highest rates for his acts. In his 1978 *New Yorker* profile of Ahmet Ertegun, writer George W. S. Trow described Geffen holding court at a table in the Majestic Hotel, discussing the Rolling Stones, who had just been signed to Atlantic:

"Their last tour was a joke," [Geffen] said. "What did they get out of it? *Tell* me. Stephen Stills got one hundred thousand dollars for one night at the L.A. Forum. The Stones only got seventy-five thousand. Think about that," he said. One person who thought about that, presumably, was Stephen Stills, who was sitting one place away from David Geffen.

"I love Ahmet," Geffen explained to Trow. A short time later, Trow watched Ahmet and David Geffen squabble over a $50,000 advance Geffen wanted to cover studio costs for Nash and Crosby —five times what Ahmet intended to pay. "Why don't you concede for once," Geffen said testily. After they bickered and called each other "chintzy," Ahmet said, "Whatever happens, I'm your friend and I love you, but don't squeeze the juice out of every situation."

Geffen was discovering, however, that it was not fun to be a manager. "I didn't like being called in the middle of the night, I didn't like being so closely involved with [the artists'] personal lives," he said. Before long, he worked out a deal with Eliot Roberts, who managed folksinger Joni Mitchell. They pooled their clients and formed the Geffen-Roberts management company. Roberts handled the day-to-day management, while Geffen stuck to negotiating deals.

The next client they picked up was singer-songwriter Jackson Browne. Geffen could not get him a record deal, even at Atlantic. As Geffen recalled, he went to Ahmet and said, "I'm the guy who brought you Crosby, Stills, and Nash. I'm doing you a favor. And he said, You know what? Don't do me any favors. I said, You'll make millions with him. And he said, You know what? I got millions. Do *you* have millions? I said no. [Geffen must have forgotten about his share of the Nyro publishing sale.] He said, Start a record company and you'll have millions. Then we can *all* have millions."

Soon after that, in late 1970, Geffen created a label using some of the proceeds of the Nyro publishing sale as start-up capital. He called it Asylum, and the label's first artist was Jackson Browne. He soon added Linda Ronstadt, Joni Mitchell, and the Eagles. A year later, he sold Asylum to Warner Communications for $7 million but remained its president. In 1973 Elektra founder Jac Holzman retired, and Warner chairman Steve Ross suggested merging Elektra and Asylum and making Geffen head of the combined company. Geffen accepted. But by 1975, Geffen was already bored with the job. Ross agreed to appoint him vice-chairman of Warner Bros. Pictures that year, bequeathing Elektra/Asylum Records to Joe Smith. Geffen, who liked to make quick decisions, found the movie job too bureaucratic. "It was a nightmare," he said.

The year 1976 brought a bigger trauma for David Geffen. After a tumor was removed from his bladder, Geffen was diagnosed as having cancer. He went into self-imposed retirement, collecting Tiffany lamps and teaching business part time at UCLA and Yale. In 1980 he took new medical tests and found he did not have cancer after all. He was thirty-seven and unemployed. Mo Ostin called and suggested he might wish to start another label—to be distributed by Warner, of course.

"I didn't know what to do," Geffen said. "I hadn't worked for four years. I had gone from being a top-level executive in show business to being retired. I thought about it a great deal and decided to go back to the business I knew the very best, the record business, and start from scratch once again. The people I was competing against in 1970 when I started Asylum Records were the same people I'd be competing against in 1980. They were considerably older, and I was still pretty young. I thought, If I could do it then, I can do it now."

(He had a point. The record industry is notorious for recycling its senior executives. By the eighties the majority of top label bosses were middle-aged men, many of whom had been unexceptional industry leaders in the seventies.)

Geffen named his new label after himself. The first months of Geffen Records in 1980 were even splashier than the early days of Asylum, but less auspicious. He signed and paid dearly for two established stars, Elton John and Donna Summer. Both eventually left the label, having failed to earn out. Geffen's career had not been notable for bad deals; even the Tiffany lamps he had collected when he thought himself at death's door went for $1.2 million at an auction. A third superstar deal, for John Lennon and Yoko Ono, did pay back. In December 1980 Lennon was assassinated, and the Lennon/Ono *Double Fantasy* album sold 3 million copies.

Geffen had learned too much about the movie business as an agent and executive to leave it behind, so he went into film production. His movies were distributed by Warner Bros. Pictures. Geffen Films was responsible for *Risky Business*, *Lost in America*, and *Beetlejuice*, among others. He rounded things out by investing in theater, coproducing the hit *Dreamgirls* with Michael Bennett, and financing Andrew Lloyd Webber's *Cats*, one of the top-grossing Broadway shows of all time. Toward the end of the eighties, Geffen hit the jackpot with heavy metal acts like Guns N' Roses and Whitesnake, and revenues more than doubled in two years, to an estimated $175 million in 1989.

Geffen Records' U.S. market share was not large, but David Geffen had reemerged as one of the most powerful people in the record business, if one accepts the definition of a power broker as a person who can make things happen. As owner of one of the Warner labels with a foothold in movies and theater, his reach was great.

On a recent summer morning, Geffen reflected on his career. Short, trim, and athletic, Geffen had the face of a Nice Jewish Boy, disturbed only by a belligerent lower lip. He wore a polo shirt and chinos and white sneakers and reclined in an Eames chair, a telephone at his feet. His office was large and airy, with a plush sofa, but no desk or writing table. It was so informal that the effect was oddly intimidating.

"When I started Asylum Records in 1970," Geffen recalled, "everybody said, Oh, it can't be done, you can't start a record company from scratch in 1970. And then in 1980, when I started Geffen Records, people said, Oh, well, *this* time he sure won't be able to do it. And here it is, Geffen Records is probably as profitable as any record company in the world. At the risk of appearing self-congratulatory, I've done it twice in the last two attempts. I'm certainly as successful or as wealthy as anyone in the business. So it's not like I'm doing this so I can make it. I made it long ago. I use my intuition. I invest in myself. I'm basically in the David Geffen business. . . ."

Geffen lamented the dearth of management talent in the record industry. "I think the fact that the record business hasn't brought along a host of new executives is unfortunate. It does not speak well for the record business."

High on the list of people he did not admire was Clive Davis. "I'm not a fan of Clive Davis's. I don't speak to him. I haven't spoken to him for many years. He's an egomaniac, is what he is. He tends to *lecture* you. I think I'm as good a record executive as there is in the world, and I think highly of other people in the record business and have good relationships with most. But he's such an arrogant fuck that he's of no interest to me. His ego has caused him nothing but trouble over the years. It's why he got fired from CBS. He thought he could bend the rules because he was so omnipotent. He elected himself to be a spokesman for the industry, and he enjoys that role and functions in it happily. I don't find myself a spokesman for anybody but myself."

Geffen was interrupted several times with phone calls. One call was from Geffen's former mentor and idol Ahmet Ertegun, who wanted some advice on Florida real estate. Geffen warmed perceptibly. But after a few minutes, the subject obviously had changed, because Geffen was out of his Eames chair, enraged. The matter at hand was Crosby, Stills, Nash and Young, the group that had brought Geffen and Ahmet together and helped establish the young manager as a major figure in the business. CSNY had long since split up, and Neil Young was then recording for Geffen Records as a solo act. (Young moved over to Reprise a year later, cursing Geffen Records for treating him, he said, not as an artist, but rather as "a product [that] didn't fit in with their marketing scheme.") Ahmet was planning a one-shot Crosby, Stills, Nash and Young reunion album for 1988 release on Atlantic. Evidently, Geffen wanted 50 percent of the proceeds, and Ertegun did not see the logic of this, as he had three of the four band members under contract.

"Listen, Ahmet!" Geffen seethed, coiling himself in the phone cord, his voice rising in pitch and volume. "Crosby, Stills, and Nash are OLD FAT FARTS! The only one with any TALENT is Neil Young!" Ahmet did not think so. "I can't *believe* we're arguing about this!" Geffen said. "It's too silly to argue about. . . ."

■

Geffen had advanced from one of the industry's top managers to one of its foremost label bosses. Another man did the same. He was more ruthless than Geffen, probably more powerful, and even shorter. His name was Irving Azoff.

Azoff got his start at Geffen-Roberts after dropping out of college and gaining experience as a booking agent for REO Speedwagon and Dan Fogelberg. After Geffen created Asylum and left the management business, he helped Azoff set up his own company, Front Line, by bequeathing him the Eagles. Front Line became the top management firm in the history of rock, representing, at one time or another, Dan Fogelberg, Steely Dan, Don Henley, Boz Scaggs, New Edition, Warren Zevon, Jimmy Buffett, Jackson Browne, Stevie Nicks, and Heart.

Azoff stood 5'3" on a good day. Friends called him the "Poison Dwarf." He was easily one of the most loathed men in the music business. His tantrums were extraordinary; even Walter Yetnikoff's were no match. Azoff once tore a television from the wall of a hotel and threatened to hurl it through a window because the staff could not silence construction men on the curb below. When Azoff found the service too slow at a chic Beverly Hills restaurant in 1974, he set his menu on fire. "Irving's got a fast burn and you don't want to be in front of it," said Dennis Fine, former publicist for the Eagles. "I don't know how much is real and how much is an act, but Irving is *very* good at intimidation."

The quintessential Irving Azoff story involved manager Michael Lippman, whose clients at one time included David Bowie and Melissa Manchester. It was Lippman's fortieth birthday, and he was being feted on the tennis court of his Beverly Hills home. Once among Lippman's closest friends but lately an adversary, Azoff was not one of the guests. So Azoff hired a delivery man to present a giftwrapped box to Lippman, and inside was a live boa constrictor. Azoff had gone to extra trouble to insult the manager's wife. The enclosed card read, "Happy birthday, Michael. Now you have two of them!"

Needless to say, Azoff's artists loved him. Most every rock star wants an SOB for a manager. Azoff made sure he was always beating up the record company, deservedly or not. "He was a master at creating a problem and then riding in on a white horse," said a former employee. "He would agree on something, let it go forward, and after it was done, call the artists and scream and yell that the record label had fucked it up. Then he'd ride in and solve the problem. Irving could do that all day long. He had total retention on every level and could tap dance and maneuver his way out of the tightest corners."

If anyone in the business was an intellectual match for David Geffen and Walter Yetnikoff, it was Azoff. "Irving is as fast mentally as it gets," said Bob Buziak, who worked for Front Line Management and went on to become president of RCA Records U.S. He described Azoff as a telephone virtuoso. "He can speak to more people in the course of twenty-four hours and retain more than anyone I've ever seen." And when Azoff wished to turn on the charm, Buziak said, there was no better schmoozer in the business. "Irving can take someone and have them locked up in fifteen minutes. That's a gift."

In 1983 Azoff followed Geffen's example and became a label boss, taking command of MCA Records in Hollywood. Though one of the six major labels, MCA Records had been scratching for profit for several years. Wags called it the Music Cemetery of America. It had Olivia Newton-John and some country artists of note, but not much else to support a national distribution system. Lew Wasserman and Sidney Sheinberg, the powerful heads of MCA Corporation, which owned Universal Studios, may have even considered dumping the record company. Instead, they turned it over to Azoff—after Walter Yetnikoff declined the job.

MCA Records was already familiar with Azoff and his tactics. One of his clients, country-rock singer Jimmy Buffett, recorded for the label. A dispute between Azoff and MCA over Buffett had erupted into a lawsuit. As Azoff remembered it: "I alleged they were so inept they didn't legally constitute a record company at all."

Azoff wasted little time overhauling MCA Records. He let go all but five of the forty-six acts on the roster. Within a year, he had worked out a deal to distribute Motown Records, past its glory days but still the home of Stevie Wonder and Lionel Richie, and possessing the most valuable R&B catalog in the world. Eventually, MCA bought Motown with some outside investment partners. Meanwhile, MCA broke a multiplatinum baby act, Tiffany —a teenage girl who built a following by singing in shopping malls.

Azoff bragged in a number of press accounts that he had turned MCA Records around. Profits under him soon rose to the tens of millions, as opposed to losses when he moved in. However, MCA did not break out the financial results of its record group separately, so it is possible that the real source of profits was another business placed under Azoff: videocassette distribution.

Azoff had ratcheted up his power by taking over a major label, but he was not interested in taking a pay cut. Though label heads are more powerful, top managers usually make more money. So Azoff took the MCA job but kept Front Line Management and his custom label at Warner, Full Moon, which featured Chicago and Joe Walsh. He also owned Facilities Merchandising, a company that sold rock "merchandise"—T-shirts and the like. Though

MCA agreed to pay Azoff $500,000 a year, it was no secret that he derived greater annual income from Full Moon alone.

Then, in 1986, Azoff sold his three companies to MCA for $15.7 million, despite an apparent conflict of interest. Here was a major label owning an artist management firm. Jimmy Buffett and New Edition, two MCA acts, happened also to be Front Line clients. There was some minor commotion in the trade press. (Geffen, who despised Azoff anyway, complained to *Rolling Stone*, "For MCA to be in the management business—it's shocking. They'll be dealing out of self-interest!") Azoff called his detractors "small-minded" and "crybabies," and the controversy died down in a few weeks.

As MCA Records chief, Azoff had acquired power to rival David Geffen's. He now had ties to Universal Studios, a movie company even larger than Warner Bros. Pictures. Azoff found he could get parts for singers Glenn Frey and Waylon Jennings on the TV show *Miami Vice*, which was shot at Universal. Yetnikoff, based in New York, was still the foremost man in the record business, due to his company's enormous market share. But CBS had no influence in movies, and it rankled Walter that Azoff and Geffen, both based in Los Angeles, did. An unnamed source, identified as a top recording artist representative, told *The Wall Street Journal*: "Yetnikoff, Geffen, and Irving are the only three individuals in this business with real clout. Geffen won't like it, but I think Azoff controls more [top artists]."

∎

Yetnikoff, Azoff, and Geffen were more alike than any of them cared to admit. All three were brilliant, ruthless, and loud. They all had the dealmaker's philosophy, which is that favors were meant to be traded. They seemed more preoccupied with the accumulation of power than any other label executives in the business. And they recognized in themselves a troika of sorts; at times vicious competitors, at other times shrewd allies.

Walter maintained an odd love-hate relationship with Geffen and Azoff, but the latter two merely hated one another. Geffen said of Azoff, "I don't wish to have him in my life, even for a second. I set him up in business; I gave him the Eagles to manage. He's just done so many bad things to so many people, including me, that at one point I said, Enough! Who *needs* this? What he is, is devilish. And that's interesting on some level, but not nearly as interesting as intelligence, or charm, or wit, or real, true ability. Irving is involved in some drama of self-importance. And he thinks that in order to be powerful or important, you have to fuck with people. Or frighten them, or be awful to them, which I find unacceptable behavior."

Walter appeared fonder of Azoff, though the contract renegotiations for Front Line artists on CBS were often high-decibel affairs. "Once," Azoff said, "we screamed for two hours, then ended up throwing darts for the points on Dan Fogelberg."

Yetnikoff, who took pleasure in needling Azoff, once characterized him facetiously to a reporter. "I'm waiting to get Irving on the stand," he said. "I would just like to ask him, what's your name? And he'll say Irving Azoff. And I'll say, you're lying, you *always* lie. Irving's problem—and he's not a bad guy—is that it's not a character flaw, it's a genetic defect. Irving lies when it's to his advantage to tell the *truth*. He just can't help it."

"Walter?" said Irv Azoff. "Dennis the Menace as Attila the Hun."

The three-way rivalry of Walter, Irving, and David reached comedic heights in the Boston affair. Boston was a rock group created in the studio by Tom Scholz, a musician who had studied engineering at MIT and done technical work for Polaroid. A staunch perfectionist and a bit of a nerd, Scholz assembled some session musicians and began to lay down the tracks of songs he had written. Whether the other four members of Boston were merely taking orders from Scholz was a matter of dispute, but no one denied that he was the key creative force. In 1976 the group signed with Epic, by which time they had completed their first album, eponymously titled. *Boston* was released that year and sold over 8 million copies, at the time the most successful debut album in history.

CBS pressed Scholz for a follow-up, and two years later, in 1978, he and his musicians completed *Don't Look Back*. Scholz complained that he had been rushed, and that only the first side of the album met his standards of perfection. *Don't Look Back* sold 4 million units, which qualified it as a monster hit. It still had done only half as well as *Boston*, which to Scholz was proof that it was only half a record, and that the B side was a botch. He vowed never to let this happen again.

It is hard to overstate Tom Scholz's obsessiveness in the studio. On one occasion, he redid a drum track seven hundred times before he was satisfied. It wasn't only his fellow recording artists who found Scholz difficult. Yetnikoff despised him, probably more than any CBS artist since Paul Simon. To advertise Boston's first album, Epic had devised a slogan that Scholz hated: "Better music through science." Scholz called Walter at home and informed him that the slogan had better be changed—or else. Yetnikoff was enraged. Success did not make Scholz more diplomatic toward his company president. "He told me from time to time that I could go fuck myself," Walter said. "He'd complain about the color of the sky, all sorts of things."

After touring for a year, Scholz began work on his third album. By 1981 it was nowhere near completion. Yetnikoff and Scholz had a face-off, and the words allegedly spoken by Walter would later be contested in a lawsuit. Scholz claimed he admitted his album was taking a long time, but promised to finance it himself provided CBS did *not* cut off his royalties. Scholz said Yetnikoff agreed but refused to put it in writing. "You don't need it in a letter, you have got my word," Scholz recalled Yetnikoff saying.

Only a year later, Boston was notified that its royalty payments were about to be suspended. Scholz wrote Walter a six-page letter in October 1983. It said, in part, "Apparently some people at Epic feel I should be punished for my refusal to sacrifice quality and deliver a record that's compromised by haste. In fact, I will *never* foist a second-rate record on the public to fill CBS's pockets or my own." This was the last straw for Walter. A week later, CBS filed a breach-of-contract suit against Scholz, his fellow musicians, and his former managers.

By late 1984, the album still wasn't finished, and more than $3 million dollars in royalties generated by the *Boston* album had been withheld by CBS. Scholz no longer had enough money to continue recording, so his failure to deliver the album and end the litigation seemed a certainty.

But Scholz had another career to fall back on. He had already rented some office space near his home to incorporate Scholz Research & Development, a company to market his musical inventions. He hit pay dirt with two electric-guitar attachments: the Power Soak and the Rockman. Scholz could afford to hire a top attorney and fight back.

The man he hired was Don Engel. Yetnikoff knew him well, because Engel had extricated Teena Marie from a rapacious contract with Motown and delivered her to CBS. Walter was delighted. "I was Walter's fair-haired boy," Engel said. "He told people to hire me."

Now, Walter didn't like Engel so much. Engel took Walter's deposition and tried to get him to admit he had promised not to cut Scholz's royalties. It was rough going. Noting that the stenographer was a woman, Walter began the session by trying to unnerve her. Some people say Don Engel's a cocksucker, he told her. I don't agree; I'm only here because he's a friend of mine. After four hours, Yetnikoff had not budged on any of the key points, but admitted he was "getting a little upset" with Engel's relentless interrogation.

The lawsuit took an ugly twist when Scholz began shopping for another label to put out his third album, which by 1985 was about finished. Yetnikoff issued a written warning to the other five major labels that none of them should dare sign Boston until the lawsuit was settled. He proposed, however, that CBS would be willing to let another record company put out the album for $900,000 and a royalty of twenty-five cents per unit.

Two label bosses were particularly eager to sign Boston: David Geffen and Irving Azoff. But for several months, neither of them made a move. "We claimed," said Engel, "that Yetnikoff made various threats to them and entered into a three-way conspiracy. Neither would sign my client until we settled with him. And my client was not going to be blackmailed into the settlement CBS wanted."

CBS denied any conspiracy. But Azoff testified to a "personal understanding" between him and Walter that MCA would not negotiate for Boston, provided Geffen didn't, either. Walter, he testified, assured him that Geffen would not defy him, because CBS, not Warner, did Geffen Records' international distribution. CBS could withhold the money owed Geffen as retaliation for breaking the Boston embargo.

As it happened, Don Engel knew both Geffen and Azoff personally. Aside from being Scholz's lawyer, he also represented disco queen Donna Summer and had delivered her from Casablanca Records to Geffen in 1980. Another of his clients, Olivia Newton-John, recorded for MCA. Engel got to know the two men even better in 1985 as he took their depositions in the case of CBS v. Boston. It did not take Engel long to conclude that there *was* a deal between Walter and the two West Coast labels chiefs not to sign Scholz.

Aware of the intense hatred between Geffen and Azoff, Engel decided to play one against the other. Initially, Azoff had expressed willingness to work out a deal for Scholz but then backed off, saying he would have to wait for a settlement. Unknown to Azoff or Walter, Geffen did negotiate a contract for Boston, but each time he was to sign it, he demurred until a future date. Engel realized that Geffen was very reluctant to buck Walter. (Geffen later explained, "I'm not in the business of incurring lawsuits—certainly not with my *friends*.") So Engel let word leak to MCA that he was about to make a deal with Geffen. "It was the dirtiest thing I did," Engel admitted, "but every word I said was true. We *were* about to sign with Geffen. He just kept postponing it."

Believing he had been double-crossed, Azoff said he was prepared to make an offer. Engel explained he did not wish to go through another grueling negotiation, but that Azoff could have the exact deal he had worked out with Geffen. Azoff took it.

Walter went berserk. "This means war," was how CBS Records' head of business affairs, Marvin Cohn, characterized Yetnikoff's reaction. Immediately, CBS withdrew a license for one of its masters that MCA wished to use on a compilation album. Within a few days, CBS had filed suit against MCA and Scholz to prevent the new Boston album, which was now complete, from being released. That was not all. In a fit of colossal arrogance, Walter saw to it that the suit named Don Engel as a defendant.

This did not sit well with the judge, none other than Vincent Broderick, the former New York City police commissioner who had defended Clive Davis. Broderick ruled that the inclusion of Engel in the lawsuit raised the "absolutely outrageous and frightening suggestion that an attorney who represents a client in litigation or in negotiation is at risk for actions he takes in the course of the representation of that client." Taking his cue from Judge Broderick's remarks, Engel countersued CBS for malicious prosecution.

In 1986 Judge Broderick denied CBS's move for an injunction against the new Boston album, and it came out that year on MCA as *The Third Stage*. It sold 4 million copies.

■

Though artist management had made them rich, it was only a matter of time before Geffen and Azoff leaped the bargaining table to become label presidents. Almost all top managers and lawyers in the record business secretly hanker to run a label. However powerful the artist representatives may be, the label bosses are the ones who hold the checkbook.

Lawyers and managers never forget, meanwhile, that their power is tenuous. Artists may fire them or, even more likely, fall from the charts. The average career of a rock artist is cruelly brief; five years is an achievement, and twenty years is a miracle. For every Paul Simon and Stevie Wonder, there are dozens of flash-in-the-pan acts like Frankie Goes to Hollywood and Meat Loaf. This makes artist representatives an insecure lot.

Record labels are happy to exploit this insecurity. The result is a much too cozy relationship between labels and artist representatives. The reps know that the labels will help them win future clients and hold on to their existing ones if they don't make too many waves.

This is especially true of attorneys. Once, a lawyer could afford to antagonize a record label, because there were legions of them. If your client had talent, you could always get him a deal somewhere. Nowadays, to get into a punch-up with a major label —worse yet, to sue—can be hazardous to a lawyer's career. This tends to divert the attorney's loyalty from his artist client and make him, to put it charitably, more sympathetic to the needs of the record company. In the pop-music business, the relationships that matter most are the ones that last longest. As one outspoken litigator put it, "Do you think lawyers fail to understand that artists come and go, but RCA is forever?"

The record industry has long been contemptuous of artist handlers who dared show independence. The pioneers of the rock business learned that the best defense against being sued by a wised-up artist was to hire his attorney to do corporate legal work. Some labels went one better, in fact, appointing an attorney or manager *for* the artist, someone completely under the company's control.

The seventies provided some classic horror stories from this scenario. When Teena Marie was signed to Motown in 1976 by founder Berry Gordy, she had no attorney at all. When she asked to take her contract home before signing it, she later testified, a Motown official admonished her: "Don't you trust us?" Motown assigned as her manager the common-law wife of Berry Gordy's brother. Result: Two of her albums made an estimated $2 million for Motown, while the label paid her about $100 a week for six and a half years. (Moral: Just like its white counterparts, black-run

Motown could operate on the plantation system; in the case of Teena Marie, the "slave" happened to be white.)

Today's major labels are only slightly more refined in their methods. There is scarcely one music lawyer of prominence who does not also do legal work for the labels, often on retainer. Conflicts of interest that would scandalize most businesses are commonplace in the music field. In fact, music attorneys willing to sue record labels have become so rare that two litigators have virtually the entire field to themselves. One is Leonard Marks in New York; the other is Don Engel, the Los Angeles lawyer of Boston and Teena Marie (Marks and Engel!).

Once Engel made a speech before the Copyright Council, not realizing it was a group of attorneys and executives on the staffs of record companies. "All of a sudden," he said, "they're *booing* me. So I said, Listen, you don't think your contracts are unfair and onerous? Well, you can boo and hiss all you want. But I've never had a judge who didn't agree with me on a record contract. It's the most onerous, impossible, unfair contract. Instead of booing and hissing, put one clause in for the benefit of the performer. Put *one* in. And maybe someday you'll enforce the contract. But you'll never enforce one against me as long as you keep the form you have."

The standard contract given out to new artists by today's biggest record companies *is* onerous—and the plainest evidence that the music bar is under the labels' thumb. The key to understanding why the contracts are so bad is the word "recoupable." In a standard agreement, most of the costs of making a record are to be repaid out of the artist's royalties rather than gross receipts. Items that are normally charged to the artists include manufacturing costs, recording-studio time, marketing, touring, packaging—in short, almost everything.

Under this system, only a superstar who sells millions of albums can make a reasonable return. For the 95 percent of artists who aren't multiplatinum sellers, the outlook isn't so good. The way contracts are structured, the record company can make a profit off an album while the artist's royalty account is still in the red. In fact, this is a frequent occurrence.

In 1985 *The Wall Street Journal* reported the case of Patty Smyth and her group, Scandal, a CBS act whose album *Warrior* did sell over a million copies, yet who nevertheless earned a paltry $100,000, less than ten cents an album. She and her group were not only charged for all production costs, but also the expenses of a promotional concert tour. "I haven't made a lot of money," Smyth said ruefully. "But I sure have spent a lot."

All this would be bad enough if the labels were good about paying the royalties due. But they aren't. "I would venture to say, except by accident, there isn't an honest royalty statement issued by any major recording company in the business today," Engel said recently. "That's my personal view, and I have a lot of evidence behind it. In one case, I deposed a man who had been audit manager for one of the biggest labels. I asked him, Did you ever in your career see an audit where there wasn't a shortfall to the performer? No. Did you ever see an audit where the performer was *overpaid*? Never. So these are not errors." No wonder the record business reveres men like Morris Levy.

■

Walter Yetnikoff was never one who liked independence in a lawyer. It caused headaches. Witness the cases of Paul Simon and Tom Scholz. There was not much Walter could do about Don Engel; making trouble was his stock-in-trade. But Michael Tannen, the man who had taken Paul Simon to Warner, was a different story. Long before the Boston affair reached the courts, Walter Yetnikoff had cashiered Mike Tannen.

By the early eighties, Tannen no longer represented Billy Joel or Bruce Springsteen, and he had lost most of his other top artist clients as well. (Tannen claimed he voluntarily gave up those clients, but acknowledged that it had become "increasingly difficult to deal with CBS.") Joel and Springsteen now belonged to a lawyer named Allen Grubman, a man Walter liked very much. Before long, Grubman was the biggest music attorney in the history of rock, and he represented over 30 percent of CBS Records' pop roster. He also did corporate legal work for David Geffen and Irving Azoff, who appeared to like him almost as much as Walter did.

It was no coincidence that as Mike Tannen faded from view, Allen Grubman's star rose higher and higher. In fact, it may have been the crowning achievement of Yetnikoff's career. Once a reporter mentioned to Walter that Grubman had an impressive practice. "I know," Yetnikoff shot back. "I *gave* it to him." He wasn't kidding.

8

GRUBMAN

■

WALTER Yetnikoff's first meeting with Allen Grubman took place in 1977, only a few months before the start of the Paul Simon debacle. He and Grubman had dinner at Sea Fare of the Aegean, a restaurant near the CBS building. The subject of the meeting was the third man at the table, artist manager Tommy Mottola, who handled Hall and Oates and some other acts. Mottola was Grubman's client and closest friend. He wanted a production deal under which he would bring acts to CBS, and Allen was on hand to help negotiate.

Grubman was a nobody then. True, he represented Hall and Oates, thanks to Tommy, and they had just had a number one hit with "Rich Girl." But after that, they were in for a long dry spell. Apart from Hall and Oates, Allen's top client was disco label T.K. Records, and a more typical one was K-tel, the company that sold Veg-O-Matics on late-night television.

Grubman yearned for a more prestigious practice. He had spent a lot of his life yearning. Allen grew up in Brooklyn without much money, and got his first taste of the high life as a boy soprano on the *Horn & Hardart Children's Hour*, a kiddie show on NBC television. Though he left the program at thirteen, when his voice broke, he never forgot the lifestyle he had briefly glimpsed. "Everyone in entertainment," he recalled, "rode around in big cars and could go to a restaurant and eat steak."

After getting his degree from Brooklyn Law School in 1967, Grubman made up his mind to go into entertainment law. He soon landed a job as a $125-a-week associate to music lawyer Walter Hofer, a short, slight man of German origin who had set up the Copyright Services Bureau to collect royalties for foreign music publishers. One Hofer client was Dick James Music in the UK, which published the Beatles' songs. By the early eighties, Hofer's practice was a shambles. Furious clients accused him of embezzling large sums from their accounts, and he was unable to pay them back. In 1983 Hofer suffered a heart attack and died, slumped over his desk.

By then, Grubman had long since left Hofer to open his own practice, in 1974. "I started with some clients from the Hofer firm," he recalled. "I had T.K. Records, I represented De-Lite. Then there was Bang Records [a holdover from the sixties, well past its prime]. Also, two record producers, Henri Belolo and Jacques Morali. They were Frenchmen. I started representing them in the early seventies, and a couple of years later, they came to New York. Henri Belolo sat down and said, *Alain*—French accent— we are going to do something very special in America someday, and you will be proud of us. I said, Great. I had no idea what he meant.

"Two or three years later, he said, We have an idea to put together a very special group, very American and very happy. I still didn't know what he was talking about. And they went into a studio and made a record, and they came out with 'Macho Man.' The group was the Village People. They said, we want this record to be with Neil Bogart on Casablanca Records. Because he was the disco king at that time. He had Donna Summer. So, I sent the record to Neil Bogart. He loved it. And we signed the Village People with Casablanca."

By the time Grubman sat down with Walter Yetnikoff at Sea Fare of the Aegean, he was making headway toward the lifestyle he coveted. He could not yet afford the fancy car of his dreams, a Rolls-Royce Corniche, but from the looks of him, he was eating a lot of steak. Allen Grubman was enormously fat. His pudgy face was almost like a baby's. He had not lost his full black hair, or his nasal Brooklyn accent (record came out "reckid," idea was "idear").

The accent suited him; Grubman was not a scholar. He admitted that he had finished near the bottom of his class at Brooklyn Law. One record executive said of him, "The only piece of paper I've seen him touch has been wrapped around something edible." Some industry people wondered how he had passed the bar—or even *if* he had passed. "Yeah," Grubman joked. "The Blarney

Stone, at Fifty-seventh and Third." On top of this, Grubman made no secret of the fact that he hated rock music.

None of these things mattered, though. Grubman's partner, Arthur Indursky, was a former tax lawyer and a first-rate draftsman of contracts. An aversion to rock never thwarted anyone in the music business. And whatever his abilities as a lawyer, Grubman had more important skills that would soon grease his way to the top. His talents as a dealmaker and *hondler* were superb. He had a quick mind and a warm, huggable personality. He was prepared to do anything to close a deal. He would bow, kneel, beg, prostrate himself, and literally furnish the shirt off his back. In a business of colossal egos, Grubman was able to submerge his own.

Grubman was bound to succeed, because he was a man for his time. In the early days of rock, the attorney was a mere scribe who drew up the contracts after the label and artist manager had agreed on the deal points. As the money became bigger and the deals more complex, the rock and roll lawyer gradually evolved into the equivalent of a Hollywood agent. Grubman was not a mere lawyer but a *packager*. He knew how to get people to work together and how to make them feel good about it. Best of all, he never, never sued. A profile of him in the B'nai B'rith gazette around this time described him as "part of a new wave of legal advisers that consider litigation a dirty word."

Tommy Mottola, meanwhile, had a lot in common with Grubman, including a love of food. He, too, had begun briefly as a performer. While studying voice and acting at New York's Hofstra University, not far from his hometown of New Rochelle, Mottola grew helmet sideburns and auditioned for Sal Mineo-type movie roles. He got his break as a singer when Epic Records gave him a recording contract in the late sixties. It was one signing for which Clive Davis would never claim credit.

As T. D. Valentine, Mottola recorded "Love Trap," "A Woman Without Love," and a few other songs. They were not hits. He sang well enough but lacked star quality. Mottola did his best to get good material, eagerly enlisting a young staff producer at Epic named Sandy Linzer to record him. Linzer was a songwriter with a number of hits to his credit, including "Let's Hang On" and "Dawn (Go Away)," written for the Four Seasons. Even Linzer could not make a star of T. D. Valentine.

Mottola left Hofstra with a bachelor's degree but no more recording contract. He wound up as a promotion man for Chappell Music, a leading publisher. Before long, Mottola befriended Daryl Hall and John Oates, who wrote songs for Chappell but were having difficulty getting them recorded. Mottola brought Hall and Oates to Sandy Linzer for an audition. He liked them, but Epic's head of A&R, Don Ellis, did not. In early 1972, Mottola helped get Hall and Oates a record deal on Atlantic. Three years later, Mottola quit Chappell to manage Hall and Oates full time, along with two other Chappell acts—Dr. Buzzard's Original Savannah Band and Odyssey—in partnership with Sandy Linzer. That same year Hall and Oates went from Atlantic to RCA.

Mottola had the image Walter Yetnikoff was cultivating for himself. "Tommy's a kick-ass little guy," said a man who knew him then. "He's a street Italian, and if there's anything this industry worships, it's the macho street kick-ass personality." As for Grubman, he spoke of the instant "natural rapport" he felt on meeting Walter. The two men had grown up not far from one another in Brooklyn with a similar "traditional Jewish upbringing."

In any case, the dinner went well. As Mottola remembered it, "We sat down to discuss the idea [of a label production deal] with Walter. I was talking, Allen was talking. We didn't even get a chance to finish our presentation. I'll never forget: Walter was drinking a glass of wine. He put the glass down, and before he even swallowed the wine, he said, I really like you, I want to make a deal with you. And that was it."

In September 1977, CBS announced a production agreement with Mottola's management company, Champion Entertainment. It never closed, however, because of objections from RCA Records. Champion's three big acts were all RCA recording artists at the time. Bob Summer, then RCA president, was upset that Mottola had not come to him first.

"Bob said, How can you do this to me?" Mottola recalled. "I sat down with Allen and said, What should we do? He said, Look, you're friends with Walter. Go talk to Walter like a friend, tell him this might damage your relationship with RCA, which is where all your clients are signed, and ask him what to do. I went in, sat down with Walter, and told him the situation. Walter shook my hand and said, Do what you have to do. No problem. Consequently, I went to RCA Records and made the production deal there. And from that point on, I knew the kind of guy that Walter was. If he was your friend, he was really and truly your friend."

■

148

Ten years after the Sea Fare dinner, on a spring morning, Allen Grubman arrived at his Madison Avenue office and phoned one of his many big clients, rock star John Cougar Mellencamp. His office was a veritable museum of *tchotchkes*: a slot machine, a miniature pink Cadillac, a miniature jukebox, a Sword in the Stone, a stuffed bear, a stuffed ape, a judge's gavel, an MTV gong, a model weight lifter, an old gramophone with a 78 on it ("When the Swallows Come Back to Capistrano"), a dart board. There were no law books.

Grubman was still overweight, but in less than a year he would shed fifty pounds on a crash diet, after divorcing his wife of two decades, Yvette, and being assured by client Raquel Welch that no woman would go to bed with him unless he glued his American Express card to his forehead.

Grubman looked a bit exasperated. Apparently, Mellencamp was holding up a contract over a disagreement about when to release his singles to Top 40 radio.

"John," Grubman said into the phone, "why are you busting my balls? You release a single in August—let's say the middle of August? And it's a hit? You're talking about twelve weeks. Okay? So you got September 15, October 15, November 15. That's if it's a *hit*. That's right. A hit single has a run of twelve weeks." Mellencamp didn't think so. "You wanna bet? Call anybody you know. Nobody releases singles between November 15 and January 1, because that's Christmas, and you don't get airplay. . . ."

Mellencamp wasn't buying it. "Look, John," Grubman said, his voice dropping down low, "we both have the same objective. You know why I want to get the deal done?" Now, his voice was a conspiratorial whisper. "Because the sooner the money's in our account, the sooner we *smile*."

Mellencamp had hired Grubman because he wanted the same lawyer as Bruce Springsteen. He first saw Grubman in action on a blistering summer night, without benefit of air-conditioning. "Allen has taken his shoes and socks off," Mellencamp recalled. "He's got his tie off. All he has on is his T-shirt with his big gut hanging out. He's sweating, and he's got his dirty, stinking feet up on the table. I said, *this* is the attorney I hired?"

Now, Mellencamp was giving him heartburn. The rock star had a wholesome public image—he helped organize "Farm Aid," a benefit concert for bankrupt American farmers—but in private he was a hard case. His former manager, Billy Gaff, once said of

149

him, not altogether unkindly, "John would murder his *mother* for a hit record."

Grubman had little to worry about, however. His practice had achieved a critical mass unprecedented in the rock era, and no one artist, however big, was central to his power. (This did not diminish his terror of losing a client.) Even as he and Mellencamp wrangled, Grubman's ever-growing list of clients included, or was soon to include: Bruce Springsteen, Billy Joel, George Michael, Madonna, Carly Simon, Hall and Oates, Bon Jovi, Cinderella, Luther Vandross, Sting, the Police, Debbie Gibson, Terence Trent D'Arby, Joan Jett, Barry Gibb, Stephanie Mills, the Beastie Boys—every one of them a platinum or multiplatinum act.* He also represented film star Robert De Niro and comics Jackie Mason and Rodney Dangerfield.

The performers told only half the story of his remarkable practice. The Grubman firm represented a passel of important label executives, managers, and producers. He did corporate work for Chrysalis, IRS Records, Def Jam, MTV, Tri-Star, and Disney, among others.

Most important, three powerful label bosses were steadfastly loyal to Allen Grubman, and vice versa. Grubman did all of Geffen Records' East Coast legal work. "He is my partner," said Geffen, "but he's called my attorney." He represented MCA Records on retainer and spoke almost daily to Irving Azoff. Above all, Grubman was close to Walter Yetnikoff.

Allen's law firm, Grubman, Indursky & Schindler, P.C., had a dozen young associates. (The third name partner, Paul Schindler, was another graduate of the Hofer firm.) No more was Grubman the lawyer for Veg-O-Matics. Now, label presidents leaped to the phone when he called. "Each lawyer hits his peak depending on the climate in the industry," said attorney Paul Marshall, who peaked in the sixties. "I'm combative. Allen comes at a time when there are only big companies, and the adversarial position is less popular. He's a marvelous agent-dealmaker, and that's the need of the moment."

For serving this need, Allen Grubman personally took home at least $3 million a year, according to *Forbes*, which ranked him

---

* In 1989 Billy Joel changed attorneys, marking the first time in a decade that Grubman lost a major client.

the fourth best-paid corporate lawyer in America. Unlike most of the lawyers he'd gone to school with, Grubman did not work on an hourly rate. He had a method he called "instinctive billing": At the end of a deal, he would sit down with a client and estimate what his services had been worth. Grubman's fees were the highest in the business. He loved money. A single deal Grubman negotiated for Billy Joel, for instance, netted the lawyer $750,000. Said Mottola, "He brags to all his old lawyer friends who thought he was basically a schmuck."

Mottola hadn't done badly himself. His Champion Entertainment now managed John Mellencamp and Carly Simon, in addition to Hall and Oates, who had broken big in 1981. These artists were all Grubman clients as well, which posed a conflict of interest. It is dangerous to represent both an artist and his manager, since artists often fire their managers. Moreover, Grubman faced the inherent conflict of working for artists and taking retainers from their labels, though this was commonplace in the record business. Grubman denied that conflicts were ever a problem.

In a 1984 lawsuit, however, Grubman was accused of favoring one client over another. The plaintiff was Sandy Linzer, who had been Tommy Mottola's partner in artist management. Linzer was one of Grubman's earliest clients, and even took credit for introducing Allen and Tommy. He apparently believed that Mottola had somehow deprived him of stock he should have had in Champion Entertainment, the company that managed Hall and Oates. His suit insinuated that, although Grubman represented both him and Mottola, Allen was more loyal to Tommy. Linzer alleged that Grubman admitted in a conversation with him that Mottola had defrauded Linzer, but said he was "unable to act in Linzer's behalf if Mottola directed otherwise." The defendants in the suit—Grubman, Mottola, and Arthur Indursky—denied all the charges. The suit was settled out of court, and the terms have not been disclosed.

In the decade since they had met, Tommy and Walter and Allen had become a tight threesome. Following Walter's lead, Mottola befriended Morris Levy and invested some of his and Daryl Hall's money in one of Morris's racehorses.* Allen, mean-

---

* At Morris's horse farm, Tommy also met Louis Gigante, the priest whose brother Vincent became head of the Genovese family in 1986. (Louis said Mot-

while, described his relationship with Walter as one of "great affection."

It was quite unlike the relationship Yetnikoff had had with Mike Tannen. One time, Mottola said, Allen was negotiating for Billy Joel. "Walter asked him to get on his knees and beg. And Allen, being the kind of person who would do anything to close a deal—and I mean *anything*—got on his knees. While Allen was begging for the final deal point, Walter ripped his shirt into shreds." Naturally, Mottola added, "Allen closed the deal."

On another occasion, Grubman and Walter were having an argument when, "all of a sudden," Allen said, "I see this plate fly past my head. *Pshew!* Breaks into a zillion pieces. I picked 'em up and said, Let's frame 'em or something and call it art." Once, Allen impatiently burst into Walter's private bathroom to pursue a deal point. "The next thing I know, I'm talking to him and he's sitting there," Grubman recalled. "Walter looks at me and says, I don't believe I'm talking to you while I'm making!"

One time Walter was having marital problems and needed a place to live. Grubman gave Yetnikoff the use of his Manhattan high-rise apartment for ten days, after which Walter moved into a hotel.

Walter was good to Grubman, too. He did not hesitate to steer clients in Grubman's direction. If a prospective client was thinking of hiring him, Grubman said, Walter "would always give me an endorsement." By 1987 the Grubman firm represented over 30 percent of all the artists on the CBS Records pop roster. He got them good deals. For Bruce Springsteen and Billy Joel, for example, Allen negotiated guarantees of $2 million an album and a 37 percent royalty. Given these stars' earning potential, however, it was hard to see how CBS could have granted them less. "Walter knows that he is only giving up as much as he wants to," said one leading attorney. "He can make Allen look good by making the deal quicker."

Walter also knew that Grubman was less of a troublemaker than certain other attorneys. One time, at a bar mitzvah party for the son of a record executive, Grubman lit into attorney David

---

tola knew Vincent as well.) Mottola and Father Gigante planned to produce a film biography of the priest, to star Al Pacino and be distributed by the Ladd Company. The project went through several scripts before Mottola and Gigante gave it up.

Braun, whose clients included a number of CBS recording stars. Braun, according to Grubman, had committed "the cardinal sin" by representing a client, United Artists, in a suit against CBS Records and Walter Yetnikoff. "How do you sue a record company, and the president of a record company personally?" Grubman recalled demanding of Braun. "What do you think you're accomplishing?" Grubman proceeded to give Braun his "nonconfrontational" philosophy of practicing law, which meant avoiding litigation. "The way *I* protect my clients," Grubman added, "is ingratiate myself and have the people I'm doing business with like me, respect me, and know that I'm not gonna kill 'em. That makes total logic to me."

Theoretically, Grubman had developed enough important supporters outside CBS to defy Walter and survive. But there was no reason for him to do this, and besides, Grubman was a bundle of anxieties. It might take a while, but the label boss that had made him could *un*make him. Walter certainly believed so. "Once I yelled at Allen," Yetnikoff laughed. "His wife told me he had to take three Valiums!"

Indeed, ever since Grubman's first meeting with Yetnikoff, Walter had played an active role in the development of his practice. Though the initial production deal for Tommy Mottola had fallen through, only two years later, in July 1979, Grubman worked out an agreement with Walter to sell T.K. Records to CBS for $17.5 million. T.K. was a disco label in Florida best known for K.C. and the Sunshine Band, which had four number one hits between 1975 and 1977 and contributed the song "Boogie Shoes" to the soundtrack of *Saturday Night Fever.*

T.K.'s owner and founder, Henry Stone, who in later years had a white goatee and resembled Colonel Sanders, was one of the early pioneers of rock and roll. A former trumpeter who played jazz with Sy Oliver in the forties, Stone entered the record business soon after World War II by selling records to jukebox operators from the trunk of his car. He eventually settled in Miami and became the biggest independent record distributor in the Southeast. He also founded a series of record labels and recorded R&B greats such as Ray Charles, James Brown, Betty Wright, and Sam and Dave.

"He's one of the great old-time record men, Henry Stone," said Grubman. "Like a legend. And somebody who is very, very responsible for my career. When I was thinking of going out on my own, I called up Henry. I was a kid, thirty-one years old. And I said, What do you think I should do? He said, Allen, if ever you want to be your own man, this is the time to do it. Don't wait until you're too old. He gave me great motivation, great strength. If somebody asked me who were the two or three people most instrumental in my career, Henry Stone would be one of them."

Stone was not universally beloved by the artists he recorded, however. Had you been sitting next to Allen Grubman in Stone's office in Hialeah on a summer day in 1974, you might have seen why. One of T.K. Records' artists, George McCrae, a black man from West Palm Beach, had the nation's number one hit, "Rock Your Baby." Pop historians would look back on "Rock Your Baby" as one of the finest records of the disco genre. It ultimately sold more than 6 million copies worldwide. Though the song was number one, McCrae apparently had not seen any money from it.

"Henry Stone ran his record company the way guys in the South ran plantations," said a man who was in the room that day. "Henry owed George about $110,000 in royalties. He hasn't gotten penny one, he can't pay his rent. George says to Henry, You don't pay me what you owe me, I'm gonna *cut* you. Henry doesn't bat an eyelash. George, he says to him, you really surprise me, today of all days. He reaches in his pocket and takes out a big thick roll. Maybe there's a few thousand dollars—how much can you stick in your pocket? Henry gives George the roll.

"But that isn't all, he says. Henry hands him a set of car keys and tells him, Look out that window. You see that Cadillac? It's yours, George. He says, I don't ever want you to come in this room and do that again. Meanwhile, Allen starts to make a funny gurgling kind of sound. I thought it was fear at first. But he was starting to laugh, he knew what was going to happen. At this point, George is ready to weep. I can't believe it, the guy is owed $110,000. Then he leaves. I said, Henry, how much did that Cadillac cost? He said, What cost? It's *rented*."*

Stone had given the old Cadillac trick of the fifties a diabolical new twist. At least early black rockers got to keep their cars. But if half the stories about Henry Stone were true, he made Morris Levy seem like Mister Chips.

None of this evidently mattered to CBS Records in July 1979,

---

* Stone said he could not remember the incident, but that it was "very, very possible."

when Walter had a $17.5 million check drawn up to buy T.K. What mattered was that CBS had not fully benefited from the disco boom because it was late to recognize the trend. Now, it seemed, Walter was late in recognizing that disco was dead. Retailers had already begun to ship back tons of unsold LPs, and the record industry was headed for its crash of '79. In just three months, CBS Inc.'s chief executive, John Backe, would install Dick Asher as deputy president to help cope with the mess.

Meanwhile, Backe was aware of all the store returns, even if Walter was not, and he put a stop to the T.K. deal at the last minute. This must have come as a blow to Allen Grubman, who had already celebrated the deal by splurging on a Rolls-Royce Corniche. Backe's move was lucky for CBS, however. By year-end, T.K. Records was insolvent and in the hands of Morris Levy, who specialized in taking over busted-out companies with valuable song catalogs. "It would have been the biggest fuck-up that CBS ever took in their lives if they went all the way," Morris laughed. "Because T.K. Records was bankrupt six, seven months later. I mean bankrupt. Ten million in debt."

The collapse of disco did nothing to improve Grubman's practice. His biggest successes to date had been T.K. and the two Frenchmen who produced the Village People. Hall and Oates would begin to have a string of number one hits in 1981 and become superstars, but for now they were in limbo. What Grubman needed most was to be hired by an established star.

In 1978 he had put in a bid for Billy Joel, whose recent album, *The Stranger,* was a monster hit. Joel's lawyer at the time was Ina Meibach, the only woman attorney of prominence in the entire record business (still true a decade later). Meibach was well regarded, and she appealed to Joel's manager-wife, Elizabeth Weber. But when Joel split with Weber following *The Stranger,* his new manager, Elizabeth's brother Frank, began shopping for another attorney.

Frank Weber chose Walter's archnemesis, Mike Tannen. By 1980 Walter and Weber had grown closer, and Joel's contract was up for renewal. According to knowledgeable sources, Yetnikoff let Weber know he was prepared to give Joel a better deal if someone other than Tannen did the negotiating. By then Grubman had Walter's full endorsement. In the meantime, Grubman had done some legal work for Weber's management company. Suddenly, Billy Joel fired Tannen and hired Grubman, Indursky & Schindler. From this point on, Tannen's practice began to go south, while Grubman's was perceived as the "hot" firm. Soon rock stars would want to hire him because he represented *other* rock stars.

Acquiring Billy Joel was the turning point in Grubman's quest for what he termed a "legitimate" practice. The same year Grubman completed his first deal for David Geffen, thanks, once again, to Walter Yetnikoff. Geffen Records had just opened its doors and, with Grubman handling the negotiations, Yetnikoff made a bid to have CBS Records distribute the label outside the United States. It was a slap at Warner Communications, which had bankrolled Geffen Records, and another shot fired in Walter's War. Like other CBS "victories" in the war, it lost the company money. Yetnikoff had to offer a guarantee so high that Warner would refuse to match it, and sources familiar with the CBS/Geffen deal said it was a financial disaster. Indeed, Dick Asher had done all he could to torpedo it. Though he failed, Geffen long harbored a grudge against him for trying. In the meantime, Geffen became a Grubman fan.

Having both Geffen and Walter in his corner helped Grubman win his next superstar client on CBS Records, Bruce Springsteen, in 1983. Springsteen's manager, Jon Landau, often referred to Geffen as his "rabbi," because Geffen had taught Landau, a former rock critic, some of the rudiments of the business. Geffen, who was stingy with praise, told Landau that Allen Grubman was a "genius," and that he should not do business at CBS without him. Landau took the advice and hired Grubman to represent Springsteen. Before long, Landau had grown enormously fond of Allen.

Just as Walter used Grubman to deal with Geffen, he needed him to transact business with the third member of the troika, Irving Azoff. Grubman was the attorney for Winterland, the nation's largest retailer of rock T-shirts and memorabilia. Winterland had also been a division of CBS Records since 1985, when Walter orchestrated its purchase from private shareholders.* Three years later, MCA Records wanted to buy Winterland from CBS. Enter Allen Grubman.

There were still bitter feelings and a lawsuit between CBS and MCA over Tom Scholz and Boston. This did not deter Grubman,

---

* Yetnikoff liked to brag that he had got William Paley, CBS's assimilated Jewish founder, "into the *schmatte* business"—that is, the rag trade.

who midwifed the deal and, in the process, collected fees totaling $1 million from MCA and Winterland. Allen acted not as a lawyer, he was later careful to say, but as an investment banker. All the legal work was handled by an outside tax lawyer who was paid a standard hourly rate. The deal almost fell apart when Grubman demanded his enormous fee; CBS insisted he get it or there would be no sale. When asked why he had sold Winterland to MCA, Walter gave two reasons. One, he said, "Irving understands that business better than we do." And two, "Allen needed the fee!"

■

Allen Grubman's ascent was roughly contemporaneous with that of the Network. Both were a means of control. Allen's non-confrontational style kept controversy at a minimum; the Network helped the labels control Top 40 radio. Unfortunately, the Network itself was going to prove harder to control than Allen Grubman.

The Network took root in about 1978, the peak year of disco. It was no coincidence. Disco created the climate that made the Network possible. The dance music breathed new life into the Top 40 format, after a decade of strength in album-oriented radio. More important, the disco phenomenon was fueled by hype, by the mistaken belief that hits are bought, not born. Of course, you *can* buy a hit, but not profitably. It was going to take the record industry a long time to figure this out.

PART
THREE

WHATEVER IT TAKES

CASABLANCA

∎

F you were cruising along Sunset Boulevard in the late seventies and saw what appeared to be an enormous Mercedes dealership, chances were good that you'd just stumbled upon the parking lot of Casablanca Records. Anyone who subscribed to the American Dream, California style, required a Mercedes convertible. Casablanca, the label of Donna Summer and Kiss and the Village People and synonymous with disco, embodied that dream.

The man who embodied Casablanca was Neil Bogart, a name that will forever conjure the worst excesses of the disco era. By the time he died at thirty-nine of cancer of the kidney and colon, possibly aggravated by drug abuse, Bogart had flogged the disco wagon up the mountain and seen it plummet down the other side. The result was the record industry's postdisco crash of '79.

This is not to say that Neil Bogart almost sank the industry single-handedly. He was not the only impresario of disco, and he was as much a symptom of his times as a cause. It *is* a fact, however, that Neil Bogart nearly wiped out one of the six major labels, PolyGram Records, which bought half of Casablanca in 1977 and the rest three years later. While Bogart made himself wealthy and launched many hit acts, he was not a model businessman. Said Art Kass, one of Bogart's earliest partners, "If it cost him three dollars to make two dollars, he would do it."

Today, there is no vestige of Casablanca's headquarters on Sunset, a Moroccan-style funhouse that rocked with disco and rolled with controlled substances. "No question about it," said Russ Regan, who ran Casablanca's Parachute label and was *not* a user. "If you were into drugs, man, you were in Camelot." The site of Casablanca has been cleared to make way for a mundane office complex. As for the hole that Casablanca left in the finances of PolyGram Records, it can only be guessed at, but the number is in the high tens of millions.

The story of Neil Bogart and Casablanca is essential toward understanding the pop music business of today. During the seventies, the dealmaker became the principal driving force in the business. A parallel event was the rise of the promotion man. The disco phenomenon lofted the promoter to new heights. He reached his pinnacle in the eighties with the power of the Network.

Men like Bogart made it possible. Casablanca was the first label composed entirely of promotion people. Its unofficial motto, "Whatever It Takes," became the industry's rallying cry. The idea took hold that *selling* the product was just as important—maybe more important—than the product itself. And it appeared to work. When Casablanca conquered the charts, it did not dawn on the industry, or even PolyGram at first, that the company was losing vast sums of money. Sales were great, but the cost of selling was greater. "Whatever It Takes" was a recipe for profitless prosperity, and that is what the entire record business suffered in the end.

Bogart, who died in 1982, is remembered fondly as one of the great Broadway characters. "I always referred to Neil as the Mike Todd of the music business," said Allen Grubman, who brought Bogart the Village People and later became his attorney. To Morris Levy, Bogart was like another Broadway producer: Flo Ziegfeld. "Neil was probably the biggest impresario type that ever hit the music business," Morris said. "Spend, parties, promotion, fly jockeys in, hire twenty-five promotion men. Whatever it took. He was a mover and shaker, there was nobody like Neil. God knows what could have happened with him had he stayed alive. No tellin'. He's the type that shoots for the moon and hits the stars."

In an industry where excess is a virtue, Bogart stories are told with awe. He launched Casablanca Records with a $45,000 party in the Century Plaza Hotel's grand ballroom, made over as the movie set of *Casablanca*, down to a Dooley Wilson lookalike playing cocktail piano. When the Village People released their hit "In the Navy," Bogart showed up at a record convention dressed as an admiral, with his entire staff in sailor uniforms. When Bogart brought Donna Summer from Germany to New York to promote her first hit album, *Love to Love You Baby*, he had Hansen's of

Los Angeles sculpt a life-size cake in her image. The cake was flown to New York in two first-class airline seats, met by a freezer ambulance, and taken to the Penta discotheque for Summer's performance there.

One night Bogart appeared on a late-night television talk show with Cher and presented her with a gold record for her new single, "Take Me Home." You must sell a million copies of a single for it to be certified gold (twice the number that it takes to have a gold album), but "Take Me Home" had sold only 700,000. Rick Bleiweiss, then vice-president of marketing at PolyGram, Casablanca's distributor, got a frantic call from Bogart's subordinates the next day. Rick, he recalled them saying, we can't make Neil a liar! At their insistence, PolyGram pressed and shipped another 300,000 copies of "Take Me Home," though there were no orders for them. Most of them were returned for full credit, and PolyGram took a sizable loss. "I'm talking about *excesses*," Bleiweiss said years later, shaking his head. "You didn't do it in *shoes*. I'll bet nobody ever had to blow out three hundred thousand brown loafers because Thom McCann said on the Carson show that he just went gold with a new shoe!"

∎

He was born Neil Bogatz, the son of a postal worker. His mother ran a foster home in the Brooklyn projects, where he grew up. Bogart went to the High School of the Performing Arts, made famous by *Fame*, and left with show business aspirations. He worked on Bermuda cruise ships and the Catskill circuit as a singer and adagio dancer. Bogart was curly-haired and cherub-faced. In 1961, all of eighteen years old, Bogart cut a few sides for Portrait Records under the name Neil Scott. One ballad, "Bobby," was a moderate hit, rising to number 58 on the charts in *Cash Box*, a trade magazine, and selling about 200,000 copies. Singing in an adenoidal tenor, Bogart told the story of a "lonely teenage girl" in a hospital, "unconscious in her bed," yet at the same time pining for her boyfriend—"oh Bobbee Bobbee"—who left town after the couple had a spat. Bobby returns in the nick of time to revive her.

Unable to duplicate the success of "Bobby" and needing work, Bogart landed a job at an employment agency. One day *Cash Box* asked him to send some applicants for ad salesman, and Bogart went down himself. He kept nagging the magazine to hire the man he had sent, and soon had his first job in the record industry. From *Cash Box*, Bogart moved to MGM Records as a promotion man, and then, in 1967, to Cameo Parkway Records in Philadelphia as vice-president and sales manager.

At Cameo Parkway, Bogart won the admiration of Morris Levy. Morris had made a tentative deal over the phone for the master of a new single by an unknown group, ? and the Mysterians. The song was the classic "96 Tears." Levy told one of his Roulette employees to wrap up the deal over the weekend, but his man assured him it could wait until Monday. "And over that weekend," Morris recalled, "Neil Bogart went down there and got the master and bought it. Which made me get respect for him. I said, Here's a kid that's a comer."

Unfortunately for Bogart, soon after he joined Cameo Parkway, the company was acquired by Allen Klein, a leading artist manager whose clients included the Rolling Stones, the Yardbirds, the Kinks, the Animals, and Donovan. None of them moved over to Cameo Parkway, however, and the label was not a success. Klein and Bogart feuded, and Bogart quit, joining a new label called Buddah. Bogart took several top Cameo employees with him, plus one of Cameo's few hot groups, the Five Stair Steps. Klein sued Bogart for $6 million, and Bogart countersued for $1.6 million, charging that his ex-boss had caused him "embarrassment" by refusing to pay expenses he had run up.

At MGM, Bogart had met a young accountant named Art Kass. While Bogart was at Cameo, Kass had left MGM to join three other men who had just started a new label, Kama Sutra, which featured the Lovin' Spoonful, best known for the archetypal sixties anthem "Do You Believe in Magic?" One of Kass's partners in Kama Sutra, Artie Ripp, would go on to become Billy Joel's first manager (and bind him to so oppressive a contract that industry wits suggested he inspired the word "rip-off"). The two other partners were Phil Steinberg and Hy Mizrahi.* Kass and company decided that Kama Sutra's distribution arrangement with MGM was shortchanging them, so they started a new label, Buddah. Remembering what a *kochleffl*—pot-stirrer—Neil Bogart had been at MGM, Kass persuaded his partners to hire him as Buddah's general manager. Bogart was twenty-four.

Within a year, *Time* magazine was hailing Bogart as the king of bubblegum, a reference to a new rock genre aimed at disenfran-

---

* Mobster Michael Franzese testified in a recent court case that his mafioso stepfather, Sonny Franzese, was a silent partner in Buddah.

chised eleven-year-olds. Bubblegum was a reaction against the socially conscious acid rock of groups like the Jefferson Airplane. Bogart told *Time*, "We are giving kids something to identify with that is clean, fresh, and happy."

Buddah's two biggest bubblegum groups, Ohio Express and the 1910 Fruitgum Company, were in reality some studio musicians assembled by the producing team of Jerry Kasenetz and Jeff Katz. Both "groups" had the same lead singer, Joey Levine. Some of the big Kasenetz-Katz hits included "Simon Says," which sold 1.7 million copies, "1-2-3 Red Light," and a song that opened with the words: "Yummy, yummy, yummy, I got love in my tummy, and I feel like a-lovin' you. . . ." Buddah's bubblegum roster also boasted the Brooklyn Bridge and the Lemon Pipers (Bogart's widow, Joyce, joked years later, "He was such a terrific salesman, he really *did* sell you the Brooklyn Bridge"). Buddah's estimated first-year sales: $5.8 million.

The success was short-lived, and for good reason. Since bubblegum was created in the studio by producers, it did not generate career artists. Once the fad died, so did Ohio Express and the 1910 Fruitgum Company. Bubblegum was a foreshadowing of disco, also a producer's medium, and it is no accident that disco yielded very few artists whose careers continued into the eighties. Bogart knew how to spot a trend and run with it, but he was *not* a record man. The only career acts on Buddah were Gladys Knight and the Pips, who had been lured from Motown, and Curtis Mayfield, who was signed not by Bogart but Art Kass.

Bogart's tenure at Buddah established him as a promotion maniac. His head of promotion, Buck Reingold, who was also his brother-in-law—nepotism was another Bogart trait—was equally driven. At the time, the most important Top 40 station was WABC-AM in New York, and its director of programming, Rick Sklar, was a hard sell.* Sklar said no most of the time, which was not a word that appealed to Bogart or Reingold. One time, Sklar recalled, Reingold ambushed him in WABC's men's room with a battery-powered phonograph playing the latest Buddah 45. Another time, as Sklar walked to work, Reingold trailed him in a rented limo, blaring a new single through a mounted loudspeaker.

In 1968, around the time Bogart appeared in *Time* magazine,

---

* He was also incorruptible, and under him WABC had the highest listener ratings in Top 40 history. One had a lot to do with the other.

a Long Island, New York, company called Viewlex acquired all the stock of Buddah. Viewlex made projectors and slides, largely for use in schools. Art Kass's three original partners took their cash windfall and left; he and Bogart remained. Soon it was just Art Kass.

Bogart approached Mo Ostin at Warner Bros. in 1973, the year Clive Davis was fired. They made a deal whereby Warner would bankroll and distribute a new Los Angeles label to be called Casablanca. In September of that year, Bogart quit Buddah to start anew as a Californian. "He always wanted to live that fast life," Kass said. "In New York, he was doing marijuana, but out there he could do coke and hang out with movie producers." Bogart and Kass did not part the best of friends. "Neil felt that *he* was Buddah," Kass said. "I think if he had a choice, Buddah had to go out of business if he left. That's what he really wanted."

If so, Bogart nearly got his wish. In 1976 Viewlex, Buddah's owner, went bankrupt, and Kass bought back the record label with $2.7 million in mostly borrowed money. By then Bogart had hit it big with Casablanca and grudgingly agreed to lend Kass $25,000; when Kass was late paying him back, Bogart fired off a petulant note. Kass borrowed more and more to keep Buddah running; he'd been an accountant and controller and had good credit. He kept assuring himself that the next record would be the monster hit that would bail him out. One day Kass missed a $250,000 interest payment and woke up to the awful truth: He was $10 million in debt. His bank summoned him. "I felt like maybe I was in jail," Kass said. "You're allowed one phone call. I called Morris." Morris Levy ran a hospital for record labels in financial trouble; he nicknamed his Roulette office "the Clinic."

At first Bogart planned to call his new Warner-financed label Emerald City, a reference to *The Wizard of Oz*. When he found out the name was taken, he settled for Casablanca, the title of a movie that had starred another Bogart. Casablanca began with fourteen employees, each with a Mercedes; Bogart's number two man was his cousin Larry Harris, who had a background in promotion. A short time later, Bogart brought in Bruce Bird, an independent promoter from Cleveland.

Casablanca's first year was distinguished by the signing of the rock band Kiss, a harbinger of the heavy metal groups of the eighties. Kiss's four members wore satanic costumes and makeup before there was MTV, and the visual appeal of a group was cru-

166

cial to its popularity. The band signed as managers the team of Joyce Biawitz and Bill Aucoin, mainly because they had produced a music television show in the early seventies. At the time, Kiss played bars in Queens and had no recording contract. Neil Bogart had been a guest on Biawitz's TV program, and she brought the group to his attention. He was fascinated by the theatrical aspect of Kiss and signed them immediately. In addition, Joyce Biawitz soon became the second Mrs. Neil Bogart.

Bogart wanted to carry Kiss's stage act even further. He and Joyce went to magic shops and loaded up on special effects. They hired Presto the Magician to come to the management office and demonstrate the art of fire breathing. When Gene Simmons of Kiss tried to duplicate the trick, Joyce Bogart recalled, everyone hid behind the couch; he sprayed her newly painted walls black. Neil kept some effects for his own use. He once went to a promotion meeting at Warner Bros. and announced, "Kiss is magic," sending a puff of smoke from his hand.

The Warner people weren't so sure. Not long after Casablanca signed Kiss, Warner threw a party at the Century Plaza Hotel and invited the group to perform. When Kiss came out in their rhinestone shirts and face makeup, said Neil's right-hand man, Larry Harris, "some of the Warner people were in shock." Little by little, Bogart began to resent that Warner did not share his enthusiasm for the band. The final straw for Bogart came when he intercepted a cable on Warner's promotion "hot line" that said, in effect, don't bother to promote Kiss, because radio isn't going to play them anyway. "He went crazy," a former employee recalled.

Bogart went back to Mo Ostin and asked that Warner release Casablanca from its distribution contract. Casablanca would use independent distribution and do its own promotion. Ostin understandably agreed; Casablanca hadn't come up with a hit in a year and a half. In September 1974, Bogart severed his ties with Warner.

Casablanca flirted with bankruptcy for a year. Its first post-Warner album was called *Here's Johnny: Magic Moments from the Tonight Show*. It was a compendium of comedy bits from Johnny Carson's program, featuring talents such as Bette Midler, Lenny Bruce, and Groucho Marx. Bogart promoted it so heavily that his independent distributors ordered massive quantities. The demand did not match the supply. Comedian Robert Klein took the occasion to coin what has become a standard industry joke: The record shipped gold and returned platinum. ("Not really," said Casablanca's Bruce Bird. "It shipped platinum and came back *double* platinum.") But because the distributors had put in for so many copies, Casablanca had the cash flow it needed to survive until its luck changed. It was symbolic. A gargantuan flop kept the company going.

A short time later, Bogart met Giorgio Moroder, an Italian record producer who had settled in Munich. There Moroder had found Donna Summer, a gospel singer from Boston married to an Austrian actor she met touring with the road company of *Hair*. After using her as a backup vocalist, Moroder gave her a solo called "Love to Love You Baby" in 1975. It was a novelty record—sort of a simulated orgasm. Moroder and his partner, Pete Bellotte, released the record on their Oasis label. Around that time, Moroder signed a deal for Casablanca to market Oasis in the United States; the two other acts that came with Donna Summer, Schloss and Eiselgeinger, did not make history. Bogart put out "Love to Love You Baby" in the United States, but initially it failed to arouse interest.

Then, one night, as legend has it, Bogart was at a party where people were dancing to the Summer single and asking that it be played over and over. Neil called Moroder in Germany and requested an extended version of "Love to Love You Baby." The new version clocked in at just under seventeen minutes. It became a favorite at New York discos, and then Frankie Crocker began to play it on WBLS. Donna Summer was suddenly very big, and her record had helped give rise to a fairly new format, the EP, or extended-play single, one of the most enduring vestiges of the disco era.

By 1976 Casablanca was hitting on all pistons. Donna Summer was hot. Kiss was hot. The funk group, Parliament, signed earlier, was hot. Meanwhile, Bogart enlarged his empire by merging his record label with a film company owned by Peter Guber to form Casablanca Record and FilmWorks. In 1977 PolyGram Records dished out a reported $10 million to become half-owner of Casablanca. That year Casablanca had gross revenues of $55 million. All in all, PolyGram thought its investment was the steal of the century. It was in for a surprise.

Bogart suddenly had a lot of money, and he was not at a loss how to spend it. Casablanca's original quarters on North Shelbourne were no longer big enough. The payroll had swelled from 14 to 175 employees, many of them Bogart relatives. The head count would reach two hundred before long. Bogart moved the company into three adjacent buildings in the 8200 block of Sunset Boulevard and bought the only two structures to the west for future expansion.

No one who set foot in Casablanca on Sunset ever forgot it. Asked to describe the ambience, Larry Harris said, "Loud. Real loud. You see these, these are *small* speakers." He pointed to a set that reached his navel. "We were *very* loud." The sonic assault wasn't only from the steady ta-TUM, ta-ta-TUM of booming disco music; Al DiNoble, the VP of pop promotion, struck an Oriental gong in his office whenever a Casablanca record scored a station. "Everything was at such a fevered fucking pitch," said PolyGram's Rick Bleiweiss. "You walked into Bruce Bird's office, music was blaring, twelve phones were ringing. You never could talk in that building. You had to shout. I think the average person walking in there would have been floored by the electricity and volume. Everything in that company was an exaggeration, a caricature."

The interior was patterned after Rick's Cafe in *Casablanca*. As you walked in the front door, you were greeted by a life-sized stuffed camel and a huge poster of Humphrey Bogart. There were ceiling fans, palm trees, thronelike chairs made of cane, Moroccan rugs and furniture. Joyce Bogart's mirrored office had fabric draped from the middle of the ceiling to all four corners, to suggest a tent. Neil's office had a fully stocked bar. Gold and platinum albums served as wallpaper. In addition to the exotic decor and head-splitting noise level, there was something else about Casablanca. Said Bruce Bird, "People were *happy*. It was probably one of the happiest record companies I've ever seen."

It was not happy for Danny Davis, however. He was a short, pudgy promotion veteran and former Borscht Belt comic. In the early sixties, Davis was the promotion man for producer Phil Spector, then worked at Screen Gems for another industry legend, Donny Kirshner, the impresario who invented the Monkees. After that he became national pop promotion director at Motown. Davis, who had won a number of awards, including *Billboard*'s promotion man of the year, was well qualified for a job at Casablanca in every respect but one. He did not do drugs.

"Motown was the best work experience of my career," he said. "I must score Casablanca as the worst. Absolutely. First of all, in

169

your own mind, you have to play out whether Neil Bogart was a great record man, or whether he was P. T. Barnum and Mike Todd. My evaluation is, he was P. T. Barnum and Mike Todd. I know the man died of cancer—*halevai sholem* and all of those kind phrases. But anybody that issues *Tonight Show* albums, and ships 'em gold, and takes 'em back platinum. . . . The man was a sensational crapshooter, I'll give him that.

"I believe that what happened to Casablanca Records was supposed to happen. With the abuses that were being perpetrated up there, and the things that were being done . . ." He shook his head. Davis had been fired from Casablanca in 1981, two years after the company collapsed and PolyGram was forced to slash its head count. His career had never quite recovered.

"Let me tell you, man. Twelve minutes after I started at Casablanca, almost by actual count, I called my wife and told her I had made the biggest mistake of my life. It's a true story. And I surely wanted to do good. First of all, I was getting more money. Second of all, they had given me a Mercedes 450 SEL.

"But what happened to Casablanca Records was supposed to happen. You can't *do* that twenty-four hours a day. At three o'clock in the afternoon, an adorable little girl would come up and take your *order* for the following day's *drug supply*. You understand what I'm telling you? It was the worst fucking experience of my life.

"On a Monday or Tuesday, I'd be looking for [a secretary], and I'd be calling her name. I'd look all over, and there she would be with a credit card in her hand, chopping, chopping the coke on the table.

"I would be on the phone with a program director, and a certain party would come in. And he would run around with a fucking golf club, squashing things off of my desk. And as I was on the phone, he would take a match and torch my desk. I would say into the phone, let's say to Jerry Rogers of [station] WSGA, Jerry, gonna have to hang up now, my desk is on *fire*.

"I would go into a meeting, and there on the desk would be maybe a gram and a half of a controlled substance. [An executive] would look at me and say, This shit isn't going to bother you, is it? And I would say no.

"So, we would sit there till maybe about seven-thirty, eight o'clock, when the gram and a half was gone. We've been in this meeting since five o'clock, not a fucking thing has been done. And now the substance is gone, and they would go into their desk and pull out the ludes. I've never taken a lude, so I can't tell you what it does for you, but I know it's great if you want to do an impression of Steppin Fetchit. Anyway, they got beer and the ludes. And they would pass out the ludes as if they were feeding elephants at a circus.

"Forget about it, man. It was absolutely the worst experience of my life. What happened to Casablanca was supposed to happen. It was *supposed* to go into the toilet."

■

It is difficult to imagine any record company more unlike Casablanca than PolyGram. Whatever else was wrong with Casablanca, no one would have called it bureaucratic or stodgy, or proposed that it had no discernible chain of command. But that was PolyGram throughout the seventies.

Given the company's origins, it was easy to see why it had turned out that way. PolyGram began as a European classical-music company in 1962 in an exchange of shares between two industrial giants: Siemens AG, a maker of electrical equipment, and Philips (full name: N. V. Philips Gloeilampenfabrieken), a manufacturer of audio hardware. Philips contributed its namesake classical label; Siemens had Deutsche Grammophon. But soon after its creation, PolyGram entered the U.S. pop market by purchasing Mercury Records in Chicago, whose pop roster had been built up by Mitch Miller before he joined Columbia. Meanwhile, PolyGram bankrolled a new label in New York, Spring Records, which recorded Millie Jackson.

In 1972 PolyGram Group was created as the holding company for all the Philips-Siemens labels. It had headquarters in Baarn, the Netherlands, and in Hamburg, West Germany. Then Poly-Gram went on a U.S. expansion binge, acquiring MGM Records, Verve, and the United Artists distribution system. With the latter purchase, the die was cast. PolyGram had to build its pop market share, because even its classical output, the biggest in the world, was not enough to keep a national distribution network running. In 1976 PolyGram bought 50 percent of RSO, the only disco label that could rival Casablanca. Meanwhile, it set up an American branch of Polydor, its homegrown European pop label.

To say that the Dutch and Germans running PolyGram did not understand the U.S. pop scene would be generous. It is always a mistake to try to buy into a market rapidly, before top management has learned that market. PolyGram assumed that its big acts on the Continent would play in the United States, even though few of them sang in English. Polydor's roster, for example, included a thirteen-year-old Dutch boy named Hein Tje who sold millions of records in Europe. America greeted him with stony indifference.

It was never entirely clear who was in charge of PolyGram, though there was a nine-member board of directors that answered to both Philips and Siemens. The best analogy for PolyGram was probably the Dutch guilds of the sixteenth century. Nobody at PolyGram was an *owner;* everyone worked for a salary and a retirement. At Philips and Siemens, you were an employee for life. PolyGram had no singular market vision, compared to, say, A&M or even CBS. Add to that the historic friction between the Dutch and Germans—nobody in Baarn was too young to remember what the Nazis had done to Holland—and you had a dangerous equation for a company about to enter the cutthroat U.S. market.

When PolyGram bought its initial stake in Casablanca in 1977, it became part of the ever-growing American arm of the company, which was run from Hamburg by a man named Werner Vogelsang. PolyGram's worldwide leader, Coen Solleveld, was a reserved Rotterdam native with a white handlebar mustache. Solleveld had been imprisoned by the Germans in World War II. He was the consummate company man: Four days after his wedding, Solleveld left Holland to become Philips's sales manager in Indonesia; his wife couldn't join him for a year. "I always wanted to get out of Holland, ever since I was a boy," he said. "If you press the accelerator, you're outside the country, so you may as well go."

The other top decision-makers at PolyGram Group were two Germans, Wolfgang Hix and Kurt Kinkele. Hix was short, Teutonic, soft-spoken, and a lawyer by training. Kinkele was more gregarious. Neil Bogart and the other Casablanca people liked Solleveld immediately. But, being Jewish, it was hard to suppress a dark thought when they met the Germans: Where was *he* during the war? With Kinkele, it was not necessary to ask. His favorite icebreaker on meeting an American was to brag that he had caught his first glimpse of the United States through the periscope of a U-boat he commanded. Kinkele thought this was simply hilarious.

■

The story of RSO paralleled that of Casablanca. But the crucial difference, perhaps, is that RSO's biggest successes—the movies *Saturday Night Fever* and *Grease* and their soundtrack albums —were so phenomenal that they covered RSO's losses. Though RSO was suffused with "Whatever It Takes," it managed to beat the house odds.

RSO was the creation of Robert Stigwood, an Australian who began as a gofer for Brian Epstein, the manager of the Beatles. Like Bogart, Stigwood was not a record man but rather an entertainment mogul. He had already made a mark in movies and Broadway shows as the producer of *Jesus Christ Superstar* before creating RSO. Stigwood was a visionary—he developed the idea for *Saturday Night Fever* after reading a magazine article about Brooklyn youths at a disco—but he was not interested in managing a company day-to-day. For that he recruited Al Coury, a top promotion executive who had just been passed over for the presidency of Capitol Records.

There are those who believe Al Coury was the greatest promotion man of all time. Promotion men are salesmen, and the salesman's job, essentially, is to motivate others. There were few motivators like Al Coury. He was not patient; one time, after waiting twenty minutes for an executive to conclude a phone call, he got the man's attention by urinating in his potted tree. "Al Coury must have broken more hits than anyone on earth," said Rick Bleiweiss. "He shouted great. He used to get *Billboard* printouts and read the riot act to his staff: WHY DID WE LOSE THREE POINTS IN PITTSBURGH ON THE BEE GEES? When things went well, he had a wonderful technique: I really want to thank you for a marvelous job, we went number one . . . BUT WE STILL HAVEN'T GOTTEN THERE WITH THE ANDY GIBB ALBUM! He inspired more fear than any human being in the industry. When Al Coury said jump, people not only went through hoops, they went through *flaming* hoops."

The quintessential Al Coury anecdote also said a great deal about the making of the *Billboard* charts in the disco era. *Billboard* had asked Coury to be on a panel at its convention in Venice in 1978. Coury at first resisted, but changed his mind when he learned that Bill Wardlow, who did the magazine's charts, would attend. As the late Michael Hutson, who had worked for Coury, told the story:

"There was a *Billboard* conference in Venice, and as the international person at RSO in the seventies, I went to wave the flag. To my astonishment, the day before I was planning to leave, I got a phone call from Al's secretary: He's coming. Now, this is a man who worked twenty-four hours a day, seven days a week, and would never waste time flying to a foreign country. There were no phones on an airplane. He was also a consummate American, not too sure about foreigners. And here he was, coming to Venice. I couldn't believe it.

"He gets off the plane with an elderly, white-haired gentleman. He looked very familiar, but I couldn't place him. He was introduced as Bill. We got on the boat, we went to the expensive hotel. Al was absolutely thrilled. I took him on a trip around Venice in a gondola. We'd been out to some hugely expensive dinner, and on the way back to the hotel, the elderly gentleman was sitting at the end of the boat, and Al and I were alone. He said, I'm finished here, I'm taking him home. I said, What do you mean? Who is this guy? Al said, this is Bill Wardlow. So I said, What the hell's the story? And Al said, It's my fucking Yvonne Elliman record! I've *got* to get it to number one somehow! Next week, Yvonne Elliman was number one."*

■

Success is sometimes a curse. In 1978 PolyGram tasted success beyond its dreams. It was an *annus mirabilis*—a year of miracles. RSO's *Saturday Night Fever* and *Grease* each grossed over $100 million at the box office; the latter film became the biggest movie musical of all time. The soundtrack albums of the two movies sold about 30 million copies apiece worldwide, an all-time record that would not be surpassed until Michael Jackson's *Thriller*. RSO began the year with five back-to-back number one hits, by Player, the Bee Gees, Andy Gibb, the Bee Gees again and, of course, Yvonne Elliman.

Casablanca tried to match RSO at the box office with a film about a riotous night at a discotheque, *Thank God It's Friday*. Neil Bogart came up with the story. The critics panned it, but it drew crowds and won a best-song Oscar for Donna Summer's "Last Dance." Meanwhile, Casablanca hit pay dirt with a Peter Guber film, *Midnight Express*. And Bogart's company sold millions of records by Donna Summer, Kiss, and the Village People.

When PolyGram Group totted up the year's sales in recorded music, it came to $1.2 billion. No record company had ever topped

---

* Wardlow was fired from *Billboard* in April 1983. The magazine was apparently unhappy with his handling of the charts.

a billion in annual revenues before. PolyGram was euphoric. During the year, Coen Solleveld had moved from Baarn to New York, an open declaration that PolyGram now considered itself a full-fledged American record company. The year-end results seemed to vindicate him. PolyGram's market share had jumped an astonishing fifteen points, from 5 percent to 20 percent. "All of a sudden," one PolyGram executive said, "we were right up there with CBS and Warner."

In mid-1979 PolyGram threw itself a huge bash in Palm Springs to celebrate, even hiring Henry Kissinger as an after-dinner speaker. Had the Dutch-German brass taken a closer look at the financial results, they would not have been toasting a victory. For all the money PolyGram was grossing, the profit margin was alarmingly slim. If you took away the two big soundtrack albums, the U.S. operation was barely profitable at all, in spite of all the other hit records. Though market share was way up, it was mostly a result of the two 30-million sellers, a feat that PolyGram could not expect to duplicate ever again, let alone every year.

Even in 1978, there were sure signs that Casablanca was out of control. Bogart issued four Kiss albums at once, each a solo effort by one of the group's members. "Neil ended up selling 600,000 or 700,000 of each guy, which would have been enormous," said a former PolyGram executive. "But he pressed so many that we were getting killed on the returns. We were already way behind in September, yet Neil persuaded everyone that Christmas would take care of it. So he pressed another quarter million and lost even more!"

There were danger signs at RSO as well. In 1978 Stigwood made a movie of the classic Beatle album *Sgt. Pepper's Lonely Hearts Club Band*. It starred the Bee Gees, Peter Frampton, and George Burns, and it bombed. The two-record set of music from the film was voted the worst album of the decade by *Rolling Stone*. Yet the Bee Gees were so popular that the record would have qualified as a monster hit had it not been overshipped. "It sold maybe 3 million records," said a PolyGram alum, "but we shipped out 8 million and got back 5." The millions of leftovers were finally sold to a cutout distributor for twenty-five cents apiece.

In its euphoria, PolyGram so misread what had happened that it imagined it *was* the equal of CBS and Warner. It began to build its distribution network to handle the volume of sales it had had in 1978. No one seemed to consider that movie soundtracks were the ultimate one-shot and should not be confused with hit careers. PolyGram opened huge automated depots in California, New Jersey, and Indianapolis. When 1979 came around and there was no *Saturday Night Fever* or *Grease*, the depots were hemorrhaging an estimated $7 million a *month*. Looking back, rueful PolyGram executives would often use a plumbing analogy. "We built a six-inch pipeline," one said, "to find out later that we could only fill it with two inches of product."

The crash of '79 was at first a retailing phenomenon. The record industry had never imposed limits on the number of records that stores could return. This meant, in effect, that retailers had no inventory risk. They could accept orders of any size, knowing they could return any unsold albums or singles for full credit. This was also true of the rackjobbers, the wholesaler middlemen who got rack space for records in department stores. It was quite a deal for the stores and jobbers, and PolyGram's Coen Solleveld, who was learning the American marketplace, was baffled by it. "If I were a wholesaler or retailer," he said, "I would laugh all day."

The laugh was on the entire record business, without a doubt. All the major labels had caught disco fever and were shipping vast quantities of dance and pop albums based more on egotism than demand. The retailers took them. Why not? In 1979 they started to come back by the steam-shovelful. The mistake made by PolyGram—and also CBS and Warner and the other majors—was shipping records and logging them as sales, never dreaming that the usual return estimates were way low.

Even though the market had shrunk in 1979, Casablanca and the other PolyGram labels continued to sign new acts by the score. Today, Casablanca's roster makes for an impressive list of "where are they now?" candidates: Phylicia Allen, Angel, Brenda and the Tabulations, Brooklyn Dreams, Bugs Tomorrow, Teri Desario, Eclipse, Alma Faye, Suzanne Fellini, Four on the Floor, the Godz, Leroy Gomez, Patrick Juvet, Lightning, Love and Kisses, Mizz, Munich Machine, Nightlife Unlimited, Paris Connection, Devin Payne, 707, Space, Starpoint, Trigger . . . and that wasn't the half of it. Before Bogart was through, Casablanca had a hundred pop acts under contract—more than CBS Records.

Consider that each signing cost $100,000 or so, *before* promotion. Add to that the expense of running the vast, automated distribution system that PolyGram had built in the United States to handle all the monster acts it was supposed to have. Almost from the start of its American excursion, PolyGram had made good money all over the world and given it back in the United States. Then, in 1978, it struck gold—for a year. After that, however, the profit drain became a sinkhole.

Casablanca began to lose tens of millions a year. It had two hundred employees on salary, and a large drug budget. In 1979 the Village People were played out, Kiss lost some popularity, and Donna Summer was about to leave Casablanca for Geffen. "Those things hurt," Larry Harris said. All the promotion in the world could not help the rest of the roster, but that did not stop Bogart from trying. Said one PolyGram alumnus, "Neil always spent everybody's money, and everyone always acted so surprised. Finally, the Germans woke up. Wait a minute! If he goes on like this, he'll bankrupt us! Well, of course!"

At long last, PolyGram Group decided to make one of its own people Casablanca's chief financial officer. It chose a young accountant from Polydor, David Shein, and sent him to Los Angeles. A short time later, a PolyGram executive visiting L.A. found Shein behind the wheel of a Mercedes convertible that Neil let him use. The accountant had become a Bogart ally. "Neil had a unique way of co-opting people," Shein admitted in retrospect. "It was real hard not to believe what Neil said."

Shein's replacement, Peter Woodward, did not work out for PolyGram, either. "I asked to see the guy, because he had overpaid some bills, and I wanted to know why," recalled a former executive at PolyGram's headquarters in New York. "In walked a guy with a necklace and chain around his neck, like some hip-looking Californian. When I asked him why certain things hadn't been done to regulate the payment of bills, because they had lost a fortune, he gave me some speech about how hard his team worked. And they were really tired—I remember his words—with 'assholes from central,' meaning *me*, coming in to criticize them!"

Bogart soon had troubles of his own. In October 1979 his mock-Tudor mansion burned to the ground. Then, in February 1980, Donna Summer filed a $10 million lawsuit against him, his wife, Joyce, and Casablanca, claiming she had been financially defrauded. When Neil brought Summer to the United States in late 1975, she did not have a manager, and in the best tradition of the record business, he provided one for her: Joyce Bogart. Summer alleged that every attorney who represented her was chosen by Neil or Joyce and did legal work for Casablanca.

When Summer at last decided to find a lawyer who had no ties to the label, she settled on California litigator Don Engel. "We developed evidence that Neil had tried to subvert Donna's previous attorneys," Engel said. "He even tried to subvert *me*. The first time I met with him as Donna's lawyer, he sidled up to me and said, I've heard you're a hotshot litigator. Our company spends a small fortune in legal fees, and we're going to start using you." For once, the ploy backfired. Engel asked Summer's co-counsel, John Mason, who had overheard the remark, to record it in an affidavit as evidence. "I had no malicious feelings toward Neil," Engel said. "He was merely doing to Donna what other companies do, what he was taught to do in the business."

The Bogarts denied Summer's charges and filed a cross-complaint, alleging that she had breached her recording pact. Neil died before the case could come to trial, and PolyGram settled with the singer. Summer was permitted to leave Casablanca for Geffen Records, but was required to deliver one last album to PolyGram, *She Works Hard for the Money*.

The same month that Summer filed her suit, PolyGram bought the 50 percent of Casablanca it didn't own and forced out Neil Bogart. It was not a bad way to be got rid of: Bogart was Casablanca's principal stockholder and received most of the buy-out price, a reported $15 million. He used some of the money to start a new label, Boardwalk. Casablanca FilmWorks was spun off and became the basis of the newly formed PolyGram Pictures, which went on to make several commercially unsuccessful movies, including *Missing* and *Endless Love*. Bruce Bird took Bogart's place as Casablanca president but only ten months later was terminated.

At last PolyGram decided its U.S. operations should be headed by a native American who knew the market, rather than Werner Vogelsang, who had been running things from Hamburg. The man Coen Solleveld chose, Harvey Schein, was American, all right, but by his own admission an administrator, and not a record man. Schein took over U.S. operations in May 1980. The same month, Solleveld was bumped up to the nine-man delegation that acted as PolyGram's board of directors, and Wolfgang Hix took over as chief of the worldwide group.

Harvey Schein was the man who brought Clive Davis to CBS and set up CBS Records International.* He quit CBS in 1972 to become president of Sony Corporation of America. Akio Morita, Sony's cofounder, got rid of Schein six years later, after the Sony Betamax lost the contest to become the predominant videocassette player in the United States. From Sony he went to Warner Communications and spent two years as a top executive. He was bought out of his Warner contract as well. Schein had negotiated contracts for himself with lucrative severance clauses. Sony reportedly paid him a six-figure annuity; his Warner severance pay was disclosed: $105,000 a year for fifteen years. Schein, whose annual salary at PolyGram was estimated at $500,000, was let go from that company in July 1982 and began collecting a third severance check. By the time he accepted a post at Rupert Murdoch's News America, Schein was receiving large sums from three major corporations *not* to show up for work.

Schein was probably destined to fail at PolyGram. He had a good grasp of corporate law and finance, but his people skills were abominable. He was prone to scream at subordinates at the top of his lungs. "Harvey was a very intelligent man, but he came with a whole set of emotional luggage," said one of his top aides. "He was wary of people who had charm. Harvey thought they were con men and that it was a weakness to be liked. He also believed that the way to run a big company was through fear. Love and nourishment for the people under you were nowhere to be found in his lexicon."

Schein looked back on his PolyGram experience with contempt. He scoffed at the European management for hiring Henry Kissinger as a convention speaker at the 1979 bash, before he arrived. "Record people are hardly literate," he said, "and they had Kissinger give his $15,000 Saturday night special." He also blamed management for understating the company's financial problems when he was hired. He reserved his greatest scorn, however, for his staff. At one early staff meeting, Schein was deeply sarcastic. "For the first time in the history of mathematics," he recalled

---

* Ironically, Schein was partly responsible for PolyGram having built an American branch in the first place. Until the early sixties, Philips was the European distributor for Columbia, but when Schein created CBS Records International, the Dutch company suddenly lost its American repertoire. Soon after that, PolyGram bought Mercury records in Chicago and began its American invasion.

saying, "each of you has told me you're doing a wonderful job, but it costs us $1.80 for every dollar of sales. The best thing for us to do is turn out the lights!"

Only a few months after taking charge, Schein recruited David Braun as his second in command. Braun was then one of the top lawyers in the music business. He represented Michael Jackson, whose first solo effort for Epic, *Off the Wall*, was one of the few monster hits of 1979. He was also the lawyer for Bob Dylan, Neil Diamond, Diana Ross, and George Harrison. Almost every powerful music lawyer has a secret hankering to be a label president; Braun's undoing was revealing it to a writer for *Rolling Stone*. Having read Braun's words, Schein offered to make him president of PolyGram. As chairman, Schein would concentrate on long-term strategy; Braun would run all the American labels day-to-day. Braun accepted.

It did not take Braun long to realize he had made a mistake. "There were things I did not know about running a big company, and Harvey was never there to help," he said in retrospect. "He was there to criticize." Schein was equally disappointed in Braun. "He didn't realize that [as a label boss] you have a lot of power, but also a lot of responsibility. David wasn't cut out for that. He wanted all the candy, not the spinach. And in corporate life, you've got to have spinach."

At a meeting attended by the European bosses, Schein and Braun had a fateful confrontation. Schein was screaming at two of Braun's people over an error in computation when Braun stopped him. "I said, Enough! This is not Nuremberg," Braun recalled. "Kurt Kinkele put his hands on my shoulders and said, Very nicely done. That set of German executives loved to see their senior executives fight with each other." Braun quit a short time later, in 1981, and went back into private practice; Schein was fired the following year.

■

Neil Bogart died of cancer in May 1982. Though still in litigation with his estate, Donna Summer sang at his funeral. Bogart's last label, Boardwalk, introduced rock singer Joan Jett and sold several million copies of her album *I Love Rock 'n' Roll*. Nonetheless, a year after Bogart's death, Boardwalk went under, which came as little surprise.

Bogart has passed into the annals of record industry legend. He is admired for having made a pile for himself and for living the life of a street hustler. It does not seem to matter that his legacy of great artists was far exceeded by his legacy of great losses. Poly-Gram did not return to profitability until 1985, at which point it had lost more than $220 million in the United States. Casablanca was responsible for a major chunk of the deficit. The exact amount has never been disclosed.

JOEY AND FREDDY

■

DANNY Davis, the Casablanca promotion executive who did not take drugs, became a victim of PolyGram retrenchment in 1981. He should have had no trouble getting a job, but by then he had some gray hairs. No one wanted him anymore.

Before long, Davis was feeling suicidal. One day he stood at the top of the stairs of his expensive home in Tarzana, California, and put a gun to his head. He would have pulled the trigger, but his wife chose that moment to come up the stairs. "I was fucking depressed beyond words," he said. "Every day I would drive over the canyon and pray that God would take my hand and send me over the side. My wall was solid with gold records, and here I was, struggling to make a living."

In Los Angeles at the same time, another promotion executive was earning enormous sums as an indie promo man. He was younger than Davis, in his mid-thirties, but unlike Danny, he had never won a single award. In fact, he showed no outward signs of being a good promoter. He was introverted, aloof, and rather humorless. Yet in 1981, the year Danny was discharged from Casablanca, Joe Isgro was one of the most powerful men in the record business.

Joe Isgro was no stranger to Danny Davis. In fact, Isgro's next-to-last job before becoming an indie, national director of pop promotion at Motown, had gone to Danny. Both men were Philadelphia natives who had worked for record outfits in their hometown in the sixties. But they did not know each other well until Danny arrived at Casablanca. Then Davis gave Joe Isgro his first major assignment as an indie promo man. It involved KFI, one of the biggest Top 40 stations in Los Angeles—one that refrained from playing Pink Floyd's "Another Brick in the Wall" in early 1980 until after indie promoters were hired to work the single.

"We had a record by Donna Summer toward the end of 1979 that [Casablanca general manager] Bruce Bird wanted on the playlist at KFI," Danny recalled. "I knew all around town who was tight with whom. When Bruce Bird came to me and said we must get the Donna Summer record on at KFI, I said, There's only one way. He said how, and I said Joe Isgro. Joe Isgro is extremely tight with John Rook [KFI's head programmer].

"Bruce said no. He said, I'll get the record on. I'll call John, John's a friend of mine. He called John Rook, had a very tremendous conversation, says it's on. Playlist came out, and when it didn't go on, I said to Bruce, You ought to put Joe Isgro on it. Nah, fuck Joe Isgro, I don't want to do anything with Joe Isgro. Second week came down, Bruce called John Rook again, thought for sure the record was going to go on. John Rook gave him a lot of pap. The record never went on.

"After the third week, I came to Bruce and I said, There's only one way to get the record on at KFI. He said to me, Okay, call Joe Isgro.* From that point forward, Joe Isgro has always acknowledged that it was I who gave him his presence in the independent promotion community by giving him his first pop account. After we gave him Casablanca, I was a steady client of his. He was very tight with some stations in the Northwest. He could always be counted on, if a Tuesday afternoon came, and you needed one more point to give you the bullet, or you needed another station to bring you home, so to speak, you could call Joe."

Apparently, Joe never forgot the favor Danny had done him. In 1983, after Danny had gone for two years without a job in the record industry, Isgro made him vice-president of business affairs for Larc Records, his custom label on MCA. It was a job for a lawyer, not a promotion man, but Danny wasn't about to turn it down. He enrolled in a course in entertainment law at the University of Southern California. Over time, however, Danny settled

* Rook, who was recently considered for FCC commissioner, could not recall Isgro promoting him on Donna Summer. He did acknowledge, however, that he and Isgro were briefly partners in Good Luck Broadcasting, a holding company for several radio stations.

into a job more appropriate to his skills. He became Joe Isgro's public relations man. "This kid," he said of Isgro, "saved me when I was on the balls of my ass."

Though Danny never admitted it, had he not been desperate for work he would have thought twice before joining Isgro Enterprises. He was quick to confess that he was "no choirboy"—what successful promotion man had never cut corners? But Danny's only involvement with payola—so he claimed under oath—occurred in the fifties when Big Top Records sent him to Philadelphia to give a twenty-five-dollar bribe to a disc jockey named Sir Lancelot. Danny tried to do it, all right, but he choked and was unable to get his hand in his pocket.

Joe Isgro had a different sort of reputation, and he knew it. He would be minding his business, enjoying a nice meal at Stefanino's, a restaurant he owned on Sunset Boulevard, and these investigators from the LAPD's Organized Crime Intelligence Division would show up and hand him their business cards. Isgro would refuse to talk to them. Or sometimes, he said, they might ask one of his cocktail waitresses to "send our favorite gangster over"—meaning *him*. Isgro always denied any mob involvement, though he did acknowledge a close friendship with Gambino family underboss Joe "Piney" Armone.

Danny did odd jobs for Joe Isgro. Among the first was to get him an audience with General William Westmoreland, commander of the American armed forces in Vietnam. Isgro, who enlisted in the marines after high school graduation and spent 1966 and 1967 in the Vietnamese jungles, seemed obsessed with his war experience. His military records disclose that he participated in operations "DeSoto," "Perry," and "Boone" in Chu Lai, for which he received the Republic of Vietnam Campaign Medal. He was also awarded the Purple Heart, the Vietnam Service Medal, and the National Defense Service Medal. Isgro came home with other mementos. He kept a box full of photographs of slaughtered Vietcong, all of whom he claimed to have killed; there were as many as forty or fifty pictures. "Un-fucking-believable," said one man who saw the photos. "Guys with their faces shot off. It would make your skin crawl."

Danny arranged a formal ceremony at the Century Plaza Hotel in Los Angeles, during which Westmoreland pinned Isgro's Purple Heart to his chest. It was a photo opportunity for Isgro— he had a snapshot of himself and the general enlarged to poster size—and a chance for Westmoreland to raise a donation for a veterans' charity. "After a security check in the hotel lobby, they let us up in the room," Davis recalled. "Joe and Westmoreland were engaged in conversation for forty-five to fifty minutes. And after Westmoreland mesmerized him, I said, Come on, Joe, let's go. And he whipped out a check and wrote *ten thousand*. I was absolutely fucking flabbergasted."

Not to belittle his generosity, but Joe Isgro was a wealthy man, and he liked to flaunt it. He drove a Rolls-Royce Corniche, wore custom-made suits and gold jewelry, and lived in a $1.4 million marble-floored mansion in the San Fernando Valley. His opulent office overlooked the Sunset Strip. Isgro put his yearly income from independent promotion at $10 million. To put this in context, Motown Records, the onetime "Hitsville" where Isgro had failed to distinguish himself as a staff promoter, grossed no more than $60 million the year he left. As an indie promoter, Isgro bragged he got far more money from Motown as just one account than the company had paid him in salary.

Isgro bore a strong resemblance to film star Burt Reynolds, and was pleased when anyone said so. He had a neatly trimmed black mustache and a perennial three-day beard. He greased back his thick hair. "Joey comes out of the limo looking like someone from *Miami Vice*," said one record executive.

The son of a carpenter, Joe Isgro was born August 10, 1947, one of six siblings. He completed high school in 1965, and promptly enrolled in the marine corps. A few months after his December 1967 discharge, he secured his first job in the record industry, as a local promotion man for Decca Records, in Camden, New Jersey. He made $135 a week. Isgro said he wound up at Decca because "I was dating a girl who worked at a radio station, and she said, You ought to go down and apply for the job." While at Decca, he met Fred DiSipio, then a roadie for singer Al Martino. Isgro subsequently held jobs at the two biggest independent distributors in the Philadelphia area, Universal Distributors and Schwartz Brothers. Until the major labels took away their accounts, Universal and Schwartz were powerful companies.

In the early seventies, Joe Isgro went to work for Morris Levy. He was Roulette Records' local promotion man in Philadelphia, then moved to New York and worked in the home office. Among Isgro's promotion projects for Roulette were records by Tommy James and the Shondells and the soul group Ecstasy, Passion, and

Pain. Levy recalled Isgro years later: "He was a good kid. I don't think he was that great, but he tried hard." Morris saw fit to add, "I think it's all bullshit with him, too. I don't think he's a mob guy. I don't think it exists."

When Isgro left Morris, he went back to Philadelphia to become a regional promoter for Motown, which had moved its corporate headquarters from Detroit to Los Angeles. By 1977 Isgro had settled in L.A. as Motown's national director of pop promotion. Motown was still in its glory days. How Isgro landed so high-powered a job, even after nine years of regional experience, is a bit mysterious. Barney Ales, Motown's president at the time, said Isgro was brought to Los Angeles by the company's national promotion VP, Paul Johnson, a former Washington DJ whose handle was "Fat Daddy." Ales said that when Johnson died suddenly in 1977, Isgro inherited his job.

Ales and Isgro did not see eye-to-eye. "I didn't get along with him," Isgro said. "I didn't agree with a lot of his business practices, and I'm sure he didn't agree with mine."

Isgro left Motown and spent an uneventful year at EMI. His fortunes took a dramatic turn after that, however, when he established himself as an independent promoter. Los Angeles was already home to two successful indie promo companies: MusicVision, run by Network man Dennis Lavinthal; and Scotti Brothers, named for Tony Scotti and his brother Ben. The Scottis had a number of prestige accounts, including all promotion work for Barbra Streisand. Isgro also faced competition from Fred Di-Sipio, who claimed some key L.A. stations from his base in Cherry Hill, New Jersey.

But Isgro had known DiSipio since his early days at Decca Records, and DiSipio seemed disposed to help his fellow Philadelphian get set up as an indie. At least, that is how Isgro told the story. It must have been the only time DiSipio assisted a competitor. Or were Isgro and DiSipio partners in some manner?

"I can assure you," Isgro said, "we were not partners. I can assure you we were competitors. I never worked with DiSipio in my life anywhere. I've known Fred DiSipio over twenty years, he's from my hometown. He's probably the elderly statesman in indie promotion. When you were starting in the business, he was the guy you would go to. My association was one of respect for his ability."

By 1981 Isgro was at the top of his newfound profession. The man with a high school education and a passel of confirmed kills had become one of the richest and most powerful people in the music business. He began to branch into other endeavors besides freelance promotion. Isgro formed ICE International, a management and production company, in the fall of 1981. Along the way, Isgro became friendly with Joseph Jackson, the stern father of the singing Jackson clan. La Toya Jackson soon became the top client of ICE.

In late 1982, Isgro launched Larc Records, a custom R&B label distributed by MCA Records. MCA's then-president, Mike Maitland, did the deal with Isgro. Larc made a good showing its first few months. In January 1983, it had three black singles on *Billboard*'s urban Top 40. But Larc failed to sell many records—proof, if ever it was needed, that even the most powerful indie promo man could not make a hit that wasn't "in the grooves." "We had a great measure of non-successes," recalled Danny Davis, who became Larc's vice-president of business affairs. "We had R.J.'s Latest Arrival, the Chi-lites, and a lot of acts that never accounted for anything. Joey went into the R&B business full tilt. We just didn't score the kind of successes that he would have liked."

Larc was barely half a year old when Irving Azoff became head of MCA Records. Irv Azoff and Joe Isgro never hit it off. Instead, Azoff was forming an alliance with Cleveland indie promo man Gary Bird and his brother Bruce, formerly of Casablanca. About six months later, Joe Isgro's Larc Records dissolved and reemerged at CBS as Private I. Walter Yetnikoff, evidently much fonder of Joe Isgro than was Irving Azoff, gave him the label, to be distributed by Epic. Private I soon became a client of attorney Allen Grubman. Meanwhile, Isgro was elected to the advisory board of the T. J. Martell Foundation, the record industry's top charity. His assimilation into the mainstream of the record business was complete.

Private I had the same roster as Larc, plus La Toya Jackson, who would put out two albums on Private I/Epic: *My Special Love* and *Imagination*. Both were stiffs, possibly the most unsuccessful albums by any of the Jackson clan. Perhaps it was symbolic of Isgro's lack of musical savvy. The other Jackson sister, Janet, inked a deal with A&M; her 1986 album *Control* sold 8 million copies. (Asked why CBS missed signing Janet Jackson, after its success with Michael, Yetnikoff replied frankly, "Because we were schmucks, that's why.")

Isgro had business interests outside of music. He invested some of the millions he was making as an indie promoter into Hawaii condos and other real estate ventures. It appeared his favorite investment was Stefanino's, a glitzy restaurant on Sunset Boulevard that once had been co-owned by Frank Sinatra. Isgro could be found holding court there almost every night.*

Isgro seemed more in his element as a restaurateur than as an indie promoter. In fact, he did little promotion work himself. In 1981 he hired a man named Ralph Tashjian to handle and supervise all contact with Top 40, and two years later created an urban radio division, headed by a promoter named Bill Craig (born William Craighead).

Both Tashjian and Craig had the promotion personalities that Isgro seemed to lack. Tashjian, dubbed "Tash the Flash" by one industry friend, was a glib, fast-talking man who once had his own indie promo firm in San Francisco. He briefly worked for Isgro at Motown and was a staff promoter at the post-Bogart Casablanca. Bill Craig also had detailed knowledge of the workings of radio; he could rattle off station call letters and describe their various markets as easily as reciting the alphabet. Craig had been a promotion executive at ABC and then CBS Records. Tashjian and Craig each had several promoters working under them. By the mid-eighties, between his promotion company and other music ventures, Joe Isgro employed about forty people, including clerical help and bodyguards.

Isgro said that his job was to drum up new business and maintain contact with his record company clients. Sometimes this meant entertaining promotion VPs at the labels. Though not by nature a glad-hander, Isgro performed this job gamely. He entertained label executives in Las Vegas, paying for their food and lodging and often carrying more than $100,000 in cash. David Michael Smith, one of Isgro's two bodyguards, joined in these sorties.

Isgro kept Tashjian and Craig on retainer, rather than making them full employees, even though they worked out of his offices. Asked under oath whether he considered them key people in his operation, Isgro replied, "Absolutely." Both Tashjian and Craig

* In a rare display of humor, Isgro once explained why he did not invite Frank Sinatra to a gala party he threw at Stefanino's on becoming its owner. "Are you kidding?" he said, mock-horrified. "You know the kind of people he hangs around with?"

resorted to payola to promote records. On one occasion, Tashjian sent a program director a Federal Express package of cocaine. Craig dispensed close to $100,000 in bribes to stations in Jacksonville and Memphis.

Isgro repeatedly denied any charges of impropriety and bristled at any mention of drugs as a payoff. "If anybody in this business knows me," he said, "the one thing they know about me is that I *appall* drugs. I'll walk out of a party if somebody's using drugs. Anybody in this business that you talk to, one thing they'll tell you, Joe Isgro would never use drugs. To me, that's a disgrace. Accuse me of something, don't accuse me of that kind of shit. That's ridiculous."

It seemed to rankle Isgro even more that LAPD officers and other authorities kept appearing at Stefanino's, asking him about his supposed mob ties. One of Isgro's favorite themes was that he was being harassed because he was an Italian-American who had come from the streets and made a lot of money. "Guy's name ends with a vowel, big problem," he said. "I want you to know, I've never been in a police station in my life. I'm like any other street guy. I accomplished the American dream. In this country, forget about it. Nothing worse than being from back East, Italian, and successful.

"I've been accused of being in the Mafia because I wear a black shirt. There was an organized crime intelligence sergeant, I said to him, What *is* all this shit? Why are you following me around? What is it I do? He said, You're always in a black shirt. He was stone serious. I've been told by everybody, Joe, you're an Italian driving a Rolls-Royce, you're looking for trouble. Fucking sad state of affairs in this country that I should be afraid to drive a Rolls. I've been a renegade all my goddamn life. I'll be fucked if I'm going to sell that car."

But surely, the Rolls and the black shirts had less to do with Isgro's image than the two huge bodyguards who dogged his steps. They went by the names of David Michael Smith and Bruce Pond, both English. Smith, a former amateur boxer with a mean disposition, stood 6'2" and weighed 195 pounds. Bruce Pond was equal to Smith in stature but a less saturnine personality. Isgro told authorities that he had met Smith at Stefanino's, and Smith had introduced him to Pond. He said he initially hired them as limo drivers, having owned a company called Blackjack Limousine.

When asked why a tough ex-marine needed two bodyguards, Isgro looked exasperated. "Once and for all, the bodyguards were *not* bodyguards. They were security guards." What was the distinction? "A security guard is there to protect my office, the personnel in my office, and property in my office. A bodyguard is around with you protecting you personally. When I went on a date, I didn't have a bodyguard. If I had a client with me, I chose to have Bruce Pond walk behind me. What's the crime, so what? I defy one person in the music business to say they were threatened by one of my security people. I'll be fucked if someone says I shouldn't have a security man. I was attacked in front of my home, driving home from work. My home has been broken into and robbed. So yes, I have security guards. Perhaps if John Lennon had one, he'd be alive today."

Police records confirmed that Isgro was attacked near his Encino home under mysterious circumstances. He was pulled from his Rolls-Royce by several men and clubbed, yet nothing was stolen. But Isgro's assertion that his security guards were "perfect gentlemen" was far from true, at least as far as David Smith was concerned. Even Danny Davis, Isgro's valued employee, kept a respectful distance from Smith. "Dave is the kind of guy—this is really the truth, not meant to elicit laughter—he likes to beat people up," Danny said. "He gets a kick out of it. He used to come in with his face all aglow, and feinting punches, and say to me, Pshew, Danny, I'd *love* to kick the shit out of somebody today!"

January 17, 1986, was one of those prized days, if Renee Michelle Gordon, Smith's then-girlfriend, was telling the truth in a complaint she filed against him with the LAPD. The complaint read, in part:

> Defendant [Smith] with his closed fists hit Plaintiff [Gordon] about the head and other parts of her body numerous times; choked her; pulled her hair and kicked her several times. Defendant also kicked Plaintiff's car, causing damage to car. From October 1985 to January 17, 1986, on approximately twelve to fifteen occasions, Defendant has threatened to kill Plaintiff and her dog. . . . As a result of the beating on January 17, 1986, Plaintiff had to receive medical treatment. . . .

Gordon was granted a temporary restraining order against Smith. But at a February 5 hearing on the charges, he showed up and she didn't, and the matter was dropped.

Even the need for bodyguards did not reflect so sinisterly on Isgro as did his own ambiguous associations with another man. Since the mid-eighties, the FBI had linked Isgro with Joseph Armone, who in 1987 was convicted by a Brooklyn jury of being a top boss in the Gambino crime family. Asked shortly before the conviction whether he denied his friendship with Armone, Isgro was visibly angered.

"I *never* denied my friendship with Joe Armone, and I won't. He's like family to me, and will always be. If I go to New York tomorrow, I will meet Joe Armone and his wife and children and have a plate of linguine with them, like I always do. If you're telling me that a man I've known thirteen years, I can't have a linguine dinner with him—hey, I *fought* for those rights. I do not deny my friends. I deny any criminal or illegal activity."

Isgro explained that he had met Armone at Vesuvio's, a restaurant owned by his uncle, since deceased. Located on West Forty-eighth Street in Manhattan, Vesuvio's was a well-known mob hangout, the virtual headquarters of Mafia boss Russell Buffalino. "When I worked for Roulette, I used to have dinner there with my uncle. We'd shoot the shit about baseball. Joe Armone was in there all the time. It was like I'd known him for years. He'd take me out for linguine dinners. I'm still going to have linguine with Joe Armone. If I gotta go to jail for twenty years for that, so be it."

The man Isgro called friend and, in a deposition, "Uncle Joe," was not the sort of person most Americans would want for a friend, relation, or, for that matter, neighbor. Joseph Armone was a short, wiry man with iron-gray hair, thick glasses, and a nasty disposition. Before he was old enough to vote, Armone had been arrested on charges of larceny and possession of firearms. His body carried the scars of five slugs fired at point-blank range in a 1964 shootout in a Second Avenue bar—bullets that miraculously failed to kill him.

Born in Brooklyn in 1917, Joe Armone had been a "made" man, or member of the Gambino crime family, since the fifties. The Gambino family is the largest of New York's five Mafia families; only the Genovese family can compare in size and influence. Supposedly, Armone's loyalty oath had been administered by the family patriarch, Carlo Gambino himself. Somewhere along the way, Armone acquired the nickname "Joe Piney," and no one was sure why, although columnist Jimmy Breslin claimed it was because Armone forced people to buy Christmas trees in July.

Isgro, who loathed drugs, was apparently willing to overlook that "Uncle Joe" was convicted of dealing heroin in 1965 and served eight years of a fifteen-year sentence. A professed friend of Armone's and former Playboy bunny, Patricia De Alesandro, drew five years for attempting to bribe a juror.

Though Armone did hard time, he was lucky in a sense. Don Carlo Gambino prohibited his people from dealing narcotics, not on principle, but because the stiff jail sentences in drug convictions increased the likelihood of a man turning informant. He need never have worried about Armone, however; Piney would not even identify the man who had shot him at close range. Eventually, the family made it a crime punishable by death to deal in drugs. But Armone had transgressed before this stern edict came down, so he escaped with his life.

In a strange twist of fate, the antidrug rule paved the way for Armone's rise in the family. When Carlo Gambino died in 1976, he left his son-in-law "Big Paul" Castellano in charge. Castellano had trouble winning the respect of his men because he had become boss through nepotism. One of the twenty or so captains under Castellano was an up-and-comer named John Gotti. By 1985 Gotti had reason to be wary of Castellano. Two members of his crew, one of them his brother, Gene Gotti, had been indicted for selling large amounts of heroin, which put them on the endangered list. Meanwhile, Castellano passed up John Gotti for promotion and made an underboss of his chauffeur, Thomas Bilotti.

Sitting in a favorite social club in Queens in June 1985 and secretly bugged by the FBI, Gotti was heard to say, "We ain't gonna get nothing. You know what we're gonna do then? Tommy and the other guy will get popped." On December 16, 1985, Paul Castellano and Tommy Bilotti were gunned down in front of Spark's Steakhouse in Manhattan.

John Gotti was now the head of the Gambino family. But the following April, *his* new underboss, Frankie DeCicco, was blown to bits by a car bomb—evidence of angry Castellano loyalists in the family.

To help mend fences, Gotti appointed a new underboss, a man loyal to him but respected by the older family members. That man was Joseph Armone. (Piney found himself acting boss a few months later when Gotti went to jail, awaiting trial for racketeering. But in a surprise verdict, Gotti was acquitted on all counts, and Armone returned to second in command.)

Armone's luck ran out around this time when he and four other Gambino family members were indicted in Brooklyn on numerous counts of extortion, robbery, loan-sharking, and bribery. The trial ran several months, during which lawyers for Armone and the other defendants inveighed against the government for asserting that such a thing as the Mafia existed—it was a fantasy, one attorney said, born of watching *The Godfather* too many times. The jury was not moved by these arguments. On December 22, 1987, Armone and the others were convicted of, among other things, belonging to a Mafia family. Piney got fifteen years. Three months later, George Yudzevich, the principal government witness who helped convict Armone, was shot dead in a parking lot in Irvine, California.

Armone's trial revealed his interest in diverse ventures such as printing, coin-operated video machines, and labor unions. His involvement in the music business was not explored, nor is the full extent of it known. But a portion of an FBI wiretap made public during the trial caught Armone, in his own words, "talking about records." The bugged conversation occurred on April 2, 1983, at approximately 9:45 A.M. at the Staten Island home of Paul Castellano, the doomed head of the Gambino family.

Armone:	That kid in California came in to see me, said . . . they gave him fifty thousand to a hundred thousand to push a record. The company, they *pay* you, just to make a record on the air, you know. . . . There is a lot can be done.
Castellano:	*Big* figures.
Armone:	Over here they give you a hundred thousand just for pushing a record.
Castellano:	That's good, you know. Promotional work.
Armone:	Promotional work.

Still referring to the unnamed "kid," Piney said something half-audible about "when he was out with Levy, with records . . ." Joe Isgro had befriended Armone while working for Morris Levy at Roulette in New York. But nowhere in the conversation is Isgro's name mentioned. Isgro denied to a reporter that he was the "kid from California."

Armone had two other known links to the music business. According to an FBI agent who did some of the field work that helped convict Piney, the manager of a reggae artist had persuaded Armone to take an interest in concert promotion. The FBI also believed that Piney's nephew, Steve Armone, also known as "Steve Charles," had a hand in the concert promotion business. A music industry veteran who said he had done business with Steve Armone claimed that the nephew worked as an indie promoter and lived in a mobile home equipped with a recording studio. Papers filed in a civil lawsuit state that Joe Isgro employed Steve Armone and paid him $48,000. Steve Armone has never been charged with belonging to a crime family.

■

Though it is unclear what role the Gambino family might have played in indie promotion, one knowledgeable source said its job was to mediate border wars. Or perhaps the family provided muscle to one or two Network promoters and enabled them to head off territorial disputes. Turf battles were fairly common among the leading promoters, often because a radio station had changed its personnel and was suddenly considered fair game.

A spectacular fight erupted, for example, between promotion men Gary and Bruce Bird of Cleveland and Ben and Tony Scotti of Santa Monica, California, over one of south Florida's two big Top 40 stations, Y-100. In this instance, mob involvement was nowhere in evidence; the Birds and the Scottis appeared to settle the matter themselves.

Gary Bird was the younger brother of Bruce Bird, the Casablanca Records executive. Bruce had begun as a Cleveland-based independent promoter; when he moved to Los Angeles to work for Neil Bogart, Gary took over his territory. In 1980 *Billboard* identified Gary as a member of the Network. "In the business of independent promotion, Gary was a kingpin," Danny Davis said. "He could deliver a primary station in Cleveland almost, as we say, on demand." Bird also claimed stations outside the Midwest, including five in the Carolinas.

Gary Bird's career seemed in danger of derailing in February 1983 when he was indicted in Cleveland for rape, gross sexual imposition, kidnapping, and possession of cocaine, marijuana, and hashish. The woman he attacked required medical treatment. Bird pleaded guilty to gross sexual imposition and drug abuse. The judge, Ralph McAllister, fined Gary Bird $1,000 and gave him a year's probation, then released him from that after only six months. At the sentencing, McAllister reminded Bird that probation "requires that you live an exemplary life, be a good citizen. But I note that you do; you are successful in your business."

In the business of indie promotion, Bird was indeed a success, more so than the Scotti brothers, who appeared to operate outside the Network. When Tony and Ben founded Scotti Brothers in 1974, it was mainly an indie promo company, but their prominence in the field diminished as the Network rose to power. Since then Scotti Brothers had become an independent label, first distributed by Atlantic, then CBS—one of its stars was "Weird Al" Yankovic—and a movie production company. But the Scottis never left the indie promo business entirely, and well into the eighties they took fees from record companies to promote songs to Y-100 in Miami. The brothers were friendly with Bill Tanner, vice-president of Metroplex Communications, the chain that owned the station. In late 1984, however, Tanner left his post.

Then, well-placed sources said, Gary Bird decided the station belonged in his territory. But the Scottis were not easy people to push around. Both brothers were former football stars for the University of Maryland, and Ben had gone on to play for the Washington Redskins (he was MVP in 1960). What's more, the Scottis employed Rick Caseras, a former fullback for the Chicago Bears, as a bodyguard. Ben Scotti liked to introduce Caseras—6'3" and 230 pounds—as the company's "secretary of defense."

On the afternoon of February 27, 1985, Bruce and Gary Bird had a sitdown with Ben and Tony Scotti on the second floor of the Scotti Brothers headquarters on Pico Boulevard in Santa Monica. A musician on the ground floor heard a violent scuffle upstairs, went to investigate, and saw Bruce Bird under attack. He called the police, who found Bird at the top of the stairs with his left leg broken. Tony Scotti told the police that Bird had had an accident, and no one else present admitted seeing Bird get injured. Bird insisted he had taken one step down the stairs, slipped, and fallen backward. But at the Santa Monica Emergency Hospital, Bird decided to change his statement and press charges. He said he was leaving the office when Ben Scotti punched him in the face. The two men wrestled on the ground until secretary of defense Rick Caseras grabbed Bird's leg, twisting it until it broke.

No sooner did Bird relay this information to police officer M. Beautz than Gary entered the hospital room.

"Bruce," Gary said, "I called him and everything's all right. Don't press charges."

Beautz asked Bruce if he wished to file a complaint. Bruce looked to Gary.

"No," Gary insisted. "This will end up all over the record industry."

A few months later, Jay McDaniel, a former disc jockey from North Carolina, unwittingly found himself in a turf dispute with the Network. In June 1985, McDaniel launched Musicstream, an independent promotion firm, in partnership with Barrie Bergman, head of Record Bar, a large retail chain in the Southeast. McDaniel reasoned that some of the millions being spent by the labels on indie promotion could better be used to sponsor radio station contests ("Name this tune and win a free trip to Bermuda!"). McDaniel and Bergman believed this would be a perfectly legal way to promote a record, and a lot more productive than payola, which was not legal. Record Bar would provide the contest prizes initially, but Bergman hoped to get other major retailers to do the same. If Musicstream were successful, it could pose a real threat to the Network.

From the start, McDaniel was warned that the Network would take exception to his plan. Shortly before the official launch of Musicstream, McDaniel called on a pop station in the Southeast and explained the idea. The owner said he would be happy to run the contests and allow Musicstream to claim his station. McDaniel was delighted, but then senior promotion executives at two big labels told him to forget it. "They said, That station belongs to [a Network promoter]," McDaniel recalled. "You can't have it unless you settle it with him."

Nevertheless, by the time Musicstream opened for business in June 1985, McDaniel had lined up the station and a number of others supposedly claimed by various Network indies. At a Top 40 convention in Atlanta that month, people began to warn McDaniel of serious repercussions. A promotion executive from one major label told him "how one guy tried to go against [a Network indie], and [the promoter and his retinue] had hung him off the rooftop of a hotel by his toes. And he changed his mind."

McDaniel did not know whether to believe such stories. But

he continued to hear that a number of indies—one in particular—were "upset" over Musicstream. Finally, he called on a label president who knew the Network promoter most strongly opposed to Musicstream and asked him to arrange a conference. "He calls me in about a week and says, Okay, I talked to [the promoter], but you'd better get ready to take your lumps. I've never seen him so mad," McDaniel remembered. At the end of July, McDaniel phoned the Network indie, using a private number provided by the label president.

It was a disturbing conversation. The promoter warned that another indie was planning to sue Musicstream for antitrust. He also professed to have the presidents of all the major record companies "in my pocket," and concluded with a threat McDaniel would never forget: "We could have your face rearranged. We do things like that."

After McDaniel discussed the incident with Barrie Bergman of Record Bar and some of the retailer's attorneys, Bergman decided to fold Musicstream.

■

When it came to protecting his own territory, people often said that Fred DiSipio was a tough competitor. Not that he looked tough; DiSipio was about 5'7" and scrawny, and spoke in a nasal tenor. But then there was his bodyguard, Big Mike, who made Isgro's security people seem like bantamweights. "It takes him a while to come around the corner, that guy," said one record label president. "Unbelievable." A popular joke about Big Mike was that when he walked into a restaurant, they did not give him a menu—he got an *estimate*.

"One time," said a record industry publicist, "I was in Patsy's [a Manhattan restaurant] having lunch. Fred DiSipio saw me and came over. He brought with him a great white ape. Looked just like a person. And DiSipio says to me, Gee, I haven't seen you in a long time, how have you been doing? I said, You're catching me at a moment I'm a bit down—I'm owed a lot of money. So Freddy said, Don't worry, I'll loan [Big Mike] to you—you'll collect."

Like Joe Isgro, Alfred DiSipio was a decorated war hero. Born in 1927, he dropped out of South Philadelphia High School at seventeen to join the navy. During World War II, DiSipio was stationed aboard the USS *Gambier Bay* in the Leyte Gulf. The aircraft carrier was sunk by Japanese shells in one of the fiercest battles of the war. About 120 of the 1,000 men on board were killed. DiSipio had his ribs fractured and took shrapnel in the head, neck, shoulder, and back.

Two decades later, DiSipio was working in the music business. He told people he managed Mike Douglas, a Philadelphia singer and, later, host of a nationally syndicated TV talk show. A man who wrote a hit single for Douglas recalled DiSipio: "He was taking care of things here and there. Maybe he was sort of an errand guy for Mike Douglas. That's what it looked like." Before the decade was out, DiSipio had become the road manager for singer Al Martino, perhaps best known for his portrayal of Johnny Fontane in the movie *The Godfather.*

DiSipio's career as an independent promoter began in the early seventies. He was a willing pupil of Kal Rudman, publisher of *The Friday Morning Quarterback.* By the mid-eighties, Fred DiSipio was perhaps the most successful of all the Network men, collecting bonuses whenever records were added by an estimated ninety stations in the *Radio & Records* survey. DiSipio owned, among other things, a stable of racehorses. One time, Danny Davis asked Al Martino what he thought DiSipio was worth. "I said, What do you figure he's got, Al?" Davis recalled. "I said, Joe tells me he's got $17 million. Al Martino says, Danny, add *ten* to it."

Though Isgro said DiSipio helped him become an indie promoter, it is not clear whether the men were friends or enemies. Apparently, they were a little of both. "When I was vice-president of promotion at Motown," said Danny Davis, "Fred DiSipio called and ordered me *not* to use Joe Isgro. There was a tremendous beef between Joe and Freddy. Freddy didn't want Joe to be in the business."

Sometime after that, however, it appeared the men had patched up their differences, because DiSipio loaned Isgro his bodyguard. When he was in New York with La Toya Jackson, Isgro used Big Mike for her protection. Big Mike also turned up at Isgro's Los Angeles office. For one brief but terrifying period in Danny Davis's hitch with Isgro Enterprises, Joe suspected Danny —wrongly, it turned out—of taking some money.

"Big Mike walked into my office," Danny said. "I had already had this little showdown with Joe where he absolutely believed that I had taken a kickback, which was just the furthest thing from the truth. Anyway, he sent Big Mike in, and Big Mike has the capacity to intimidate. And I said, Mike, you know, I didn't do this. He said, Geez, Danny, I don't know whether you did or not. But if you did, *I can't help you.* Meaning—forget about it!"

DiSipio believed that Isgro's flamboyant lifestyle was the cause of his problems with law enforcement people, and he resented it. If Joe Isgro went down, DiSipio reasoned, he could bring down the whole house.

"One time," Danny Davis said, "Freddy was in my kitchen for an hour and twenty minutes, complaining about Joe. He says to me, Danny, how do I look? I says, You look fine, Freddy. He says, Do you see this sweater? Eighty dollars at Diamond Brothers on South Street in Philadelphia. You like the pants? A hundred and a quarter at Krass Brothers on South Street. You see the shoes? Florsheims, $95. You understand, Danny? I don't need to go to Bijan for $2,000 suits. You know what I'm driving? A three-year-old Mercedes. I don't need a Rolls-Royce Corniche.

"He says, Your guy—he always refers to Joe as my guy—needs all that shit. That's what makes him happy. But I don't need that, Danny. Now, let me ask you a question: Are your shirttails clean? Geez, Freddy, I think so. With that, he reaches over and takes my shirt out of my pants. And he says to me, Danny, would you want to bet that your shirttails are clean? You understand what I'm telling you? He says, Danny, I don't want anybody taking *my* shirttails out!"

THE DEPUTY AND THE PRESIDENT

...CONTINUED

THE BOYCOTT

O N May 8, 1980, about seven months after he had appointed Dick Asher deputy president, John Backe was fired as head of CBS Inc. Backe had promised Asher that he would mediate any dispute between Dick and Walter Yetnikoff. If tempers began to get out of hand, he said, he would be there to restore calm, and without a doubt, he meant it. But Backe had forgotten to take into account the capriciousness of William Paley.

The business world was unprepared for Backe's dismissal. In his four years as CBS chief, Backe had presided over sharp increases in both revenues and earnings, and had led the network back to first place in the coveted prime-time ratings. If Backe's job should ever have been secure, it was in the spring of 1980. The newspapers were filled with barbs for Paley. An unnamed former executive of CBS told *The New York Times,* "We should have known. Just two months ago everybody including Paley was saying what a godsend Backe was for CBS. He said exactly the same thing two months before firing Arthur Taylor."

Paley was stung by the criticism, and six months later tried to justify his actions in a magazine interview. "I think Backe wasn't secure enough. He felt he didn't have the authority with me there. You need to feel secure to grow in a job. I'd hoped I could mold Backe, bring him around. I'd chosen him because he had done well running our publishing division and because I didn't want to go outside the company again, as I had for Taylor.

"But after Backe had been president for a couple of years, I began to question whether he was the right person to lead the company on his own and I decided we should do a reexamination.

I thought it was the only prudent thing to do. I wanted to be goddamn sure the company was left in good hands, that it was guided in the future as well as it had been in the past, in all immodesty. The evaluation wasn't complete, and we hadn't decided anything, but when Backe found out about it, he took offense and demanded the showdown. We probably handled the Backe thing wrong. We should have said more, but how much do you say, where do you stop? I'll tell you that it hurt to read all those things written about me during that period."

On taking the president's job, Backe had insisted on the additional title of chief executive officer, which Taylor had lacked. But even the CEO handle was insufficient armor against the whims of Chairman Paley. Whoever replaced Backe would have to secure Paley's title as well—it was the only sure way to survive. Backe's successor would do just that, only not right away.

On June 2, 1980, the board named Thomas Wyman to replace Backe. Like Arthur Taylor, he came from outside CBS, with no broadcasting—or for that matter, entertainment—experience. Wyman had been a top executive at Polaroid and, most recently, vice-chairman of Pillsbury, the food company, where he had run the successful Green Giant frozen food division. He was the very picture of a Paley chief executive, a tall, handsome WASP in a forty-two extra-long. Yetnikoff had many pet names for him: "the Pillsbury Dough Boy," "Tom Tom," "Super Goy"—sometimes just "the goy upstairs." Whatever his personal feelings for Tom Wyman, the goy's appointment would mark a distinct change in the fortunes of Walter Yetnikoff.

Dick Asher's growing rift with Walter was not his only problem as he brought financial order to the CBS labels. He was finding it difficult to rein in the recalcitrant staff of Epic Records. Once an impoverished label compared to Columbia, Epic was now home to Michael Jackson, Cheap Trick, Ted Nugent, Meat Loaf, and Adam Ant. Despite this, Epic still harbored an inferiority complex about being the number two label. In these economically trying times, Epic felt more defensive than usual. To Epic, Dick Asher seemed not only a nonadvocate but an antagonist. Before long, some Epic staffers were concealing buttons behind their lapels that read: DEPUTY DICK MUST GO!

Asher had little use for the head of Epic, Don Dempsey, who had replaced Ron Alexenburg shortly before Dick became deputy. Dempsey learned, however, that a no from Asher could be

204

trumped by a yes from Yetnikoff. One time at a meeting with the Epic staff, Dick began to lash out at Dempsey for defying a direct order. But Dempsey had the perfect comeback: Walter said it was okay. "Walter had never even talked to me," Dick said later. "To have this come up at a public meeting, that makes you this high."

Still, Asher believed that Dempsey was weak and therefore controllable. Dick was far more wary of a man two levels down, Epic's head of promotion, Frank Dileo. Asher began to think that Dileo was really running the show at Epic, a view shared by others.

"Frank had that sense of unbelievable confidence," said Susan Blond, Epic's former director of publicity. "Like, everything's okay, I'll take care of it. No one could intimidate Frank. He could answer any question. He walked into a meeting when he wanted to. They always thought he was working for them, but if they had even looked at all, he was running the whole thing."

Frank Dileo was a human cannonball: 5'2", over 200 pounds. He wore sweatpants and sneakers around the office. He also sported a pinkie ring and smoked big cigars. Though Walter had little to do with Dileo being hired at Epic in 1979, the two men began to grow close over the next year or two. One time, Dileo recalled, Walter summoned him to his office, literally for a show of strength. Yetnikoff, who drifted in and out of shape, had lately been lifting weights. "I appeared in the door," Dileo said, "and Walter says, I'm gonna show you how good my arm is. And he ran from his desk and went into me like a football player. Well, he hit me hard, but he bounced off. I didn't budge. See, when you're short, you've got better gravity."

Dileo enjoyed no such easy camaraderie with Dick Asher. As vice-president of promotion, Dileo was a staunch advocate of indie promo men. The more Asher challenged the merits of freelance record-pluggers, the more Dileo defended them, and an enmity was born.

The hard feelings intensified when Asher began to suspect that Dileo was allowing himself to be unduly influenced by artists and their managers. He found no logical pattern to the songs that Dileo chose to work the hardest. "Artists and managers were constantly trying to change our people's priorities," Dick said. "They'd take 'em to dinner, they'd buy 'em little gifts. It's wrong, because the artist wants favors that give him preference over other artists."

Dileo said his choices seemed strange to Dick only because Asher had no ears for a hit record. "I had so many crazy conversations with Dick," said Dileo. "I remember when I first brought him 'Do You Really Want to Hurt Me?,' by Culture Club. I said, Dick, I've got this tape here, and I've asked Epic to pick up the option. I really believe this can be a number one record. I played it for him twice, and he looked at me and said, I really think you're off your rocker, and I don't know what you're into anymore. And I said, Well, Dick, thanks, but I really believe this is going to be big. He said, Good luck.

"So then I said, I gotta find somebody that likes it. So I played it for Walter. He says, You really think this is going to be big? I said, Yeah, I really do. Well, I don't know, he says. You promotion guys exaggerate so much, who really knows? But that was his attitude: If you believe it, I'm with you. The other guy was, I don't like it, I think it's wrong. And, needless to say, it did go to number 1.* And the album did sell four and a half million copies in America."

But by this time, Asher's suspicions about Dileo seemingly had been confirmed. A little while after he became deputy, Asher began to notice that Dileo was wearing a gold Rolex, then worth at least $8,000. At the time, Asher recalled, that was a fifth or sixth of Dileo's yearly salary. Dileo was enormously fond of the watch. "Once I told him he couldn't wear his gold Rolex with his pinkie ring," said an Epic employee, "but he didn't listen to me. Frank's into power, and a gold Rolex did mean power. And what he liked was that he could wear a sweat suit and sneakers, but the watch would show a head waiter that he was someone important."

The watch had been a gift of the band REO Speedwagon; Dileo was one of three executives at Epic to receive a Rolex from the group. There was nothing illegal about it, but Asher became incensed soon afterward to discover that Dileo was heavily touting REO's new album—a record Dick found mediocre—and all but ignoring an album by the Clash, a critically acclaimed band from London. Dick decided to make a public issue of Dileo's choice of priorities.

"It wouldn't have bothered me so much if the REO album had been a real good album," Asher said. "But it just wasn't. The Clash had a super album, and it was not getting any support. And I was at a meeting with [the heads of Epic], and I said, I don't hear anything about the Clash. And they said, Well, we're working this

---

* It peaked at number 2 in *Billboard*.

REO album, it's much more important. And I said, Anybody want to bet me that the Clash album sells more ultimately than REO's album does?

"I mean, you can't fire people on your suspicions. So if you're the boss, all you can do is let them know that you're paying attention. Which very often at least curtails their activities. They stay away from the more outrageous things, anyway. Dileo, who is not stupid, knew why he was getting so much attention from me, and why I was continually questioning, very often publicly, what he was doing."

Asher did one other thing about Dileo. He complained to Yetnikoff. Dick did not realize at the time that Walter and Frank were becoming social friends. Dileo had endeared himself to attorney Nat Weiss, a member of Walter's elite inner circle, whose Nemperor label was then distributed by CBS Records. "One day, I took Dileo to Walter by the arm and created the relationship between him and Walter," Weiss said. "Walter likes him very much."

When Dick began to complain about what he thought were "inconsistencies" in Dileo's choices, Walter pressed him for hard evidence. Having none, Dick found his objections overruled.

Around the same time, Dick raised his suspicions about indie promotion to Walter, which also seemed to fall on deaf ears. Asher was beginning to grow paranoid about the promoters. He learned that every time he spoke out against independent promotion in a private meeting at CBS, word leaked to the record-pluggers within a few hours. Maybe, Dick began to tell himself, I should let somebody else take on the indies.

Suddenly, in late 1980, somebody else did. David Horowitz was not a record industry figure per se. As a member of Warner Communications' three-man office of the president, Horowitz was a notch below Warner chairman Steve Ross on the corporate totem pole. He had oversight of all the Warner labels, plus music publishing and record manufacturing and distribution. Mo Ostin, chairman of Warner Bros. Records, oversaw the records group from his outpost in Los Angeles; Horowitz, based in New York, was Ostin's boss.

For the most part, Horowitz, a lawyer by training, let the record divisions run themselves. "We respected the autonomy of the divisions," he said. "They were all well run. My task, really, was to achieve through diplomacy the goals of the corporation, such as avoiding ruinous competition between the divisions. I tried to get them to work together when they should. Most important, I tried to establish an esprit within the group so that all divisions would feel pride in being part of Warner, even while competing with each other."

Needless to say, Horowitz was less apt to interfere with the record labels when times were good. But Warner Bros., Elektra, and Atlantic, like CBS and the industry as a whole, had suffered in the postdisco crash. Though the chief reason for the collapse was probably boring music, it was popular to blame the current video game craze for the record industry's woes. Every quarter dropped in the slot was one less that might have been spent on music.

Though it was a flawed theory, Warner Communications was prepared to accept it, because Warner happened to own Atari, the leading purveyor of video games. In 1980 the Atari unit grossed $513 million, almost twice as much as the year before, while sales for the records group increased only 11 percent, to $806 million. And the Atari unit hadn't even existed five years previous. Overnight success breeds shortsightedness, and Warner Communications began to believe that video games were a better business than records. Warner would learn otherwise in 1983, when the bottom fell out of Atari, never to recover fully, and the company watched its stock price plummet 33 percent in one day.

But by late 1980, it appeared that maybe video games would burgeon and records would never bounce back. So David Horowitz began to scrutinize the labels' budgets. He found that expenditures on independent promotion had reached several million dollars.

Horowitz knew what indie promotion was. He had heard rumors of wrongdoing, which disturbed him, because Horowitz was an ethical man. But when he decided to suspend Warner's use of indie promoters, it was not on moral or legal grounds. "I feared there was impropriety, but we were unable to pinpoint it," he said. "So the decision was primarily a financial one."

It was not a popular decision. Horowitz said he consulted all the label heads—including Joe Smith, Ahmet Ertegun, David Geffen, and Mo Ostin—but implied that he had to persuade some of them. Ostin never commented publicly about independent promotion, but people close to him said he was *not* one of its supporters. "Mo hates it," said lawyer Paul Marshall, who did business with Warner Bros. "He fumes when the subject comes up."

The news that Warner was unilaterally dropping its indie promoters began to circulate in the late fall of 1980. In its November 8 edition, *Billboard* made the Warner boycott its lead story and said the move had been under discussion for three months. An unnamed record executive was quoted as saying, "The reason independents have not been dropped before now is because each company wanted the next company to do it first. The lead had to be taken by the Warner Communications labels or CBS." *Billboard* also reported that the Atlantic label might be undercutting the boycott. There were "whispers in promotion circles," it said, "that while freelance promotion is out at the three labels, Atlantic still has funds for independents."

The key question was whether other record companies, particularly CBS, would join in the boycott. *Billboard* made this the subject of follow-up articles. An unnamed CBS spokesman, probably PR head Bob Altshuler, said he had "absolutely no comment," adding that "we do not follow the lead of Warner Bros. or any other label." *Billboard* found that MCA was considering a ban of independent promoters; the company would decide against it, however. Other executives were adamant in their support of indie promotion. The most outspoken was Bruce Wendell, vice-president of promotion at Capitol. "There's no reason in the world why I should drop indie promo men," Wendell said. "Why should I give up one of my strengths because somebody else does?"

At last, Dick Asher thought, at last. It was exactly what he'd hoped for. Everyone knew independent promotion had got out of hand and become too expensive, too powerful. No one wanted to be first to drop out, for fear that his company would be left hanging, that the other labels would take advantage. Now, Warner had taken that big step, knowing full well it could not hold out on its own. But if Warner *and* CBS, the two biggest companies, boycotted the indies, that was something else. The other companies would fall in line, and the scourge of the Network would end.

Dick would have to sell Walter Yetnikoff and Bruce Lundvall on the idea of a CBS boycott. With Backe gone, Asher's influence with Walter had begun to wane. Lundvall was no problem, however, since he reported to Dick; he would do what he was told. But persuading Walter and Bruce to go along with a boycott was not enough. They had to be resolute about *maintaining* the ban, whatever the pressure. And the pressure would be tremendous, no doubt about that. Artists and their managers were bound to start torturing them. They had to be firm. Walter, Dick, and Bruce were the only men with authority to disburse funds for indie promotion. If one of them gave in, the CBS boycott would fall apart.

The decision was made in Yetnikoff's office. Asher recalled his pitch: "We weren't making money, sales were shrinking. Independent promotion remained a huge expense. And all of sudden, Warner announces they're going out. Warner is looking at the same financial information that we are. It's not the same, but it *is* the same. They're having problems because the market is in bad shape. They're trying to figure out how to reduce expenses so they can make a profit. They see this as a major expense item.

"So, instead of hanging back and letting them take all the shit, and playing the usual games, let's support them immediately by also announcing that we're going out. Because probably if we and Warner do something, the other companies are looking at the same things, they're gonna follow suit also." The argument was irrefutable. By early 1981, the CBS boycott of independent promotion was official.

The Network did not take kindly to the joint CBS-Warner boycott. It moved to retaliate against both companies.

In Asher's mind, the CBS ban fell just as squarely on the shoulders of Yetnikoff and Lundvall as it did on his own. It was too important a decision to be made by one man, but the Network did not seem to see it that way. Word had got to the promoters that Asher had been the driving force behind CBS's decision to boycott them. If they were going to send a message to CBS, what better way than to vent their wrath on an act associated with Dick Asher?

The Network found the perfect victim, a Canadian hard rock band called Loverboy. The group had been signed by CBS Canada when Dick was still head of International. It had just released its first album, eponymously titled *Loverboy*, on the Columbia label. CBS had high hopes for the group. The first Loverboy single released by Columbia, "Turn Me Loose," seemed to be catching on with Top 40 radio. The week ending January 31, 1981, "Turn Me Loose" broke into *Billboard*'s Hot 100 at 87. Next to the title was a star, awarded, the magazine said, to records "showing greatest airplay and sales strength."

Over the next seven weeks, the Loverboy single made a rapid ascent up the Hot 100 charts, climbing to 77, then 68, then 57, then 52, then 48, then 44, and finally 38, the week ending March 28. Each week it had a star. The week following, "Turn Me Loose" had moved up to 37, but the star was gone. Like a jet plane whose engines have sputtered out, the song hung suspended in the mid-30s on the *Billboard* Hot 100 for two more weeks. Then it went into free-fall: 46, 51, 74, 97. The week ending May 30, "Turn Me Loose" had vanished from the Hot 100.

"The indie promoters chose to wipe our noses in it, and I was the target," Asher said. "My interest in international acts was well known. And Loverboy, being Canadian, was one of those acts. Their single was beginning to break at the time our ban went in. If I remember right, the ban didn't take effect immediately. We'd finish out the records that already had independent promotion coverage, and then no new records would be given coverage. The records in the middle of their lives, so to speak, would be played out to the end. And so the ban shouldn't have affected Loverboy that way. But it affected Loverboy that way because they wanted to give me a message.

"All of a sudden, it just came off the air. It's one thing to keep something off the air to begin with; it's another thing to take something that's obviously doing pretty well and just take it off the air. Despite the fact that the stations might have been playing it, the listeners might have been liking it, they actually could reach back and pull it off. That was pretty impressive.

"Eventually, thank goodness, Loverboy became successful anyway. But I must tell you something: The group's managers sort of skirted me after that. I had been quite friendly with them before Loverboy was released in the United States, when I was still in International. But now they had a record out in the States, and apparently, they had investigated why they had suffered this horrible fate. From that time on, they almost didn't talk to me. Whatever business they conducted, they did so mainly through others."

Around the same time Loverboy rose and fell on the charts, Warner Bros. was getting an even more dramatic lesson in the power of the Network. It was one thing to bump a baby act like Loverboy; it was quite another to knock a rock and roll legend off the air. But it happened. The song was "You Better You Bet," from the Who's critically acclaimed 1981 album, *Face Dances*.

"You Better You Bet" got off to an auspicious start. It entered the *Billboard* Hot 100 the week ending March 21 at 63. It boasted not merely a star but a superstar, signifying records with the "greatest upward movement." A few days earlier, "You Better You Bet" went breaker in *Radio & Records* with an astonishing seventy-eight adds. *R&R* gave the song a bullet, its equivalent of *Billboard*'s superstar.

The Who single rose in *Billboard* to 48, then 35, then 28, then 26, 24, 21. The week ending May 9, it peaked at 18, with a star. For two more weeks, it hovered at 18. Then, like the Loverboy song, it went into free-fall: 31, 36, 73, 90, 100, gone. Its descent in *R&R* was comparably swift.

Fred Haayen, then an executive at Warner and a close friend of Who lead singer Roger Daltrey, could not believe it. "It was *at least* a top five record," he said. "It was shooting up the charts, then bang, it was stopped." The Who's album *Face Dances* failed commercially.

Asher assumed that Warner artists were complaining bitterly about the boycott and its effect on their songs' airplay. He certainly knew where his own artists and their representatives stood. Almost from day one, he felt tremendous pressure from them. One man who came in to protest was attorney Paul Marshall. To Dick, that was a hard blow, because he and Paul Marshall were close. Asher's father had been a friend of Marshall's for many years, and Dick had got his start as Marshall's law clerk.

Marshall complained on behalf of two clients. One was an Irish group on Columbia called the Boomtown Rats, whose lead singer, Bob Geldof, was later knighted for organizing Live Aid, a 1985 rock concert to raise funds for African famine relief. The other client was Adam Ant, a punk rocker, also on Columbia. His single "Ant Music" suffered because of the boycott, according to Marshall.

It did not surprise Asher that Geldof, who achieved almost saintly status for his role in Live Aid, should disagree with the CBS boycott. "Bob Geldof is a lovely guy, very bright, very articulate," Asher said. "And very interested in independent promotion. When he was with the Boomtown Rats, he was all over CBS that we didn't use enough of it." But Asher did not accept that the indie boycott had anything to do with the commercial failure of the Boomtown Rats. "If you really examine it," he said, "Geldof has never sold records. It's hard to get an artist to admit a record didn't have it. Quite frankly, any time an artist is unsuccessful, they blame the record company." As for Adam Ant, Asher recalled the record wasn't promoted because the album had already broken big without a hit single.

Whatever the case, Marshall found he had a philosophical difference with Asher. "Dick," he said, "did not believe in the use of independent promotion men as a moral issue. And I represent clients; I believe in hits. My kids were getting injured, and I thought Dick was wrong. I thought he was right morally, assuming there was the moral issue, because I never knew of payola. But you cannot ride a white horse when the artists who are giving you your job are the ones suffering the lance. Lousy metaphor. But that was Dick's mistake. That is high-mindedness. The fact that the victim of the high-mindedness was the artist, when the artist is dependent on him, I thought he was wrong. The position Dick took is laudable in so many objective areas until you say, Wait, are we gonna take these artists and put them back pumping gas the rest of their lives?"

Asher was pained to learn of Marshall's opinion. "It wasn't a moral judgment," Dick insisted. "I know it was painted that way. I really do have fairly strong moral feelings about it, but the ban was justified in several other ways. Number one, the company was losing money. You know, people were getting fired. Number two, there was this dismaying by-product [of independent promotion] that certain people who supposedly worked for you had other loyalties. Their priorities were coming from elsewhere. Third of all, we had a responsibility to CBS, whose major asset was its federal licenses, which could have been jeopardized if any part of CBS was caught in serious lawbreaking activities. That's not a moral judgment. Bribery is illegal."

Marshall found, however, that neither Walter Yetnikoff nor Bruce Lundvall really supported the boycott. "Bruce never agreed with it," he said. "If Bruce did agree, it was an internal passive agreement. He understood the plight of the artist. Dick didn't deal much with the artist. Bruce would talk to artists and hear them pleading for what's actually a short-term career." Marshall said he and Lundvall "worked out a method where the artist was going to hire some of the major promotion people himself," but "Dick shot it down."

Because the pressure from artists was so great, and because only Asher believed in the indie ban, the CBS boycott was doomed. Though officially the CBS ban continued throughout

1981, it really lasted only a matter of weeks. Asher could not pinpoint the exact date he knew it was over, but it was not long before he discovered that Walter Yetnikoff and Bruce Lundvall were paying advances to artists on Columbia, who were then spending them on independent promotion. At Epic, which abandoned the boycott even sooner than Columbia—perhaps from day one—the money for freelance promotion was doled out under the guise of "tour support."

Asher was devastated. "I don't think Epic ever [observed the boycott]. Within a few weeks, I noticed Epic had tremendous tour-support expenses. They just started giving tour support to the artist, and [Frank] Dileo told them how to pay it, and it stayed the same. I think in the beginning, the first week or two, Walter and Bruce kept faith, but the pressure was unbelievable. I had major artists in my office, complaining. Soon, I realized that Columbia artists were getting money, and they were using it for independents." It was obvious, he said, that Walter and Bruce were giving advances to artists.

"And then you have that sinking feeling that you've been had. Because Walter and Bruce and I had recognized that if any one of us broke down, the pressure on the holdouts would be impossible. It would be making the other guys look bad. Nobody wants to be the bad guy." When it was all over, Dick said, he was painted as anti-artist. "I was Dr. No, because the major artists were getting it from the other two a different way, but getting it."

The industry knew that CBS was not firmly in the boycott, that Warner would have to face it alone. It seemed certain that the ban would not last, so why not take advantage? As Warner and CBS product got knocked off the air, the other labels began to dominate Top 40 airplay as never before. Warner's sales dropped, and it suffered a decline in U.S. market share. By 1982 Warner had resumed its use of the independents, at prices higher than ever before.

David Horowitz recalled why Warner gave up: "Columbia initially followed us, the other companies did not. And then Columbia fell out, and we were left alone. The heads of our record companies felt strongly that we were suffering, that we were not getting our records played. If you look at sales during that period, there was a bit of a falloff. I never totally believed the situation was as serious as they said, but they were on the line, and it was the essence of the Warner system that they had the authority to go with their responsibility."

Every story has a moment of truth. In the story of the Network's rise to supremacy, that moment came when Walter Yetnikoff undercut the CBS boycott. Had he held firm, the rest of the record industry would have had at least a strong incentive to fall in line. No one can say for sure that Walter's fortitude would have led to the abolition of the Network in 1981. But his failure to keep faith made any such hopes impossible.

Dick Asher now felt truly isolated. First the Pink Floyd experiment, now the abortive boycott. He had taken a stand twice and lost twice. His point of greatest despair came when he asked a key question of a major artist and got the answer he expected but hoped not to hear.

Maurice White was the leader of the R&B band Earth, Wind and Fire. The son of a Memphis doctor, White had put the band together in the early seventies with Chicago slum kids. He wrote the songs, sang them, and played percussion. Earth, Wind and Fire fused rock, jazz, and gospel, and had enormous appeal. To Dick Asher, Maurice White was a god.

"I never detach myself totally from being a fan," Asher said. "I like music, and some of these guys, I do business with them, but I sort of idolize them at the same time.

"When we first went off indies, Maurice White came into my office. He made the rounds and found out this [boycott] comes from Asher. We had a long conversation. He was saying he had to have independents. I said, We're just not doing it, Maurice. I said, Maurice, you're the greatest artist in the world, you're such a huge talent. Isn't it demeaning to you that some guy with an Italian name has to get paid off to get your records played on the air? You know?

"He said, Look, man, I only have one career. So don't make me your crusade."

12

THRILLER

■

WITH the boycott over, it was business as usual for the Network. For Dick Asher, there would never be such a thing again, at least not at CBS. His relations with Walter Yetnikoff were coming to a boil, and John Backe was no longer there to clamp down the lid. Backe had created the deputy job for Dick and had a lot invested in making it work. The man who had replaced him, Tom Wyman, did not.

Dick soon discovered that he and Wyman were not destined to be friends. Asher found his messages did not always filter through to Wyman. To make matters much worse for Dick, a short time after Wyman arrived at Black Rock, he took the CBS/Fox home video operation away from Walter. Backe had given the film unit to Yetnikoff to mollify him when Dick became deputy. Movies had diverted Walter's attention from records, giving Dick more breathing space. But Wyman believed the film unit should be run by the television people. "All of a sudden," Dick said, "Walter's responsibilities boiled down to me and the Columbia Record Club. It was a one-over-one situation."

Yetnikoff made fun of Wyman and called him "Super Goy" but was more on the CEO's wavelength than Asher. Though Wyman presented a cool corporate exterior, he was a lot less buttoned down than his predecessors, and seemed genuinely amused by Walter's antics. Perhaps Wyman understood that Walter needed to prove he was too wild, too ethnic, too powerful for any white-bread corporate executive to rein in. "He always had to be the big *starker*," said Debbie Federoff, his former secretary. "Walter doesn't take orders from the goyim."

Walter rebelled against Wyman in a number of ways, some subtle, some less so. Subtle for Walter was wearing his standard outfit—a loud sports jacket and an open collar—to a somber corporate ceremony, like CBS Inc.'s panel for the Wall Street analysts. At one such panel, after Walter made an optimistic forecast for the record division, Tom Wyman interjected that if it came true, "none of us will wear ties for next year's meeting." Walter shot back, "Is that a promise?"

Other times, he was not subtle. His loud voice would fill the thirty-fifth floor of Black Rock, the corporate enclave, in a crescendo of anger and wounded pride. His favorite threat was that he would quit, and the artists would march out after him, Pied Piper fashion. It was ridiculous, though Walter bristled when any of his peers said so. Not one major artist had a "key man" clause in his contract pegged to Walter, and you didn't get to be a rock star in the first place by putting loyalty ahead of ambition. Arthur Taylor had hesitated before firing Davis for fear that Clive might raid the pantry, yet no hit act had followed him to Arista. "Clive can't take artists," Walter agreed. "*I* can take artists."

When Walter threatened, the CBS brass did not laugh. Ever since Clive had shifted the pop roster from Eydie Gorme and Ray Conniff to the likes of Janis Joplin and Moby Grape, the suits upstairs had acted bewildered and put off by the music division. It was safer to devote time and attention to TV programming; anyone could have an opinion why a show succeeded or failed. But who was Meat Loaf, and why would 5 million adolescents buy his records? Clive resented CBS corporate's fear and loathing of rock, but he also exploited it. Walter was no different. "As many times as you try to explain the record business to CBS, it doesn't seem to get through," Walter once said, smiling mischievously. "Wyman introduced me to one of his dear friends, saying, This is Walter Yetnikoff; he's that witch doctor who utters this strange melange of voodoo that no one can understand."

By the time Tom Wyman stepped in, Yetnikoff was on his fourth CBS president.* They came and went; Walter endured. Yetnikoff twitted Wyman in ways he probably would not have dared attempt with John Backe or Arthur Taylor. One time Wyman summoned Yetnikoff and other CBS executives to a con-

---

* Five if you counted Chick Ireland, who served between Frank Stanton and Arthur Taylor but died of a heart attack after only a few months in office.

ference in the Dominican Republic. Walter ambled in late to one of the sessions, covered with blood, casually explaining that he had rented a motor scooter and crashed into a wall.

Yetnikoff's bursts of *machismo* were not only for the benefit of his bosses. He liked to brag about how he had ordered CBS security guards to bounce *Rolling Stone* publisher Jann Wenner from Black Rock. "I never liked Jann Wenner," Yetnikoff said. "A fat, grasping little guy." Some years later, when Walter granted the magazine an interview, he issued Wenner a warning in person. As Walter recounted, "I ran into him and threatened to hit him. He's a little afraid of me, anyhow. I poked him in the back of the head and said if I don't like the article, I'm gonna punch him in the belly. This is my new way of handling the press. I've been squeezing my Bullworker [body-building kit], I have giant muscles."

Walter's physique was actually that of a Lower East Side deli clerk, though he seemed to believe himself irresistible to women. To hear him talk, he'd been born with an extra Y chromosome. Though he wed college sweetheart June Horowitz and had two grown sons, the marriage didn't last, and Walter cultivated a group of gentile girlfriends—his "shiksa farm"—who tended to be submissive and beneath him intellectually. "Those women represent Walter Yetnikoff's low opinion of himself," said one of his friends. "You're not going to find Walter pursuing Dina Merrill's daughter or the Count de Floury's niece. He's only comfortable with women who are extremely grateful to be in his presence."

There did seem to be a lot of them. "Puppy one, puppy two, puppy three—I know them all," said his friend Nat Weiss. Walter made a game out of juggling his women. "I've seen some real cliff-hangers," Weiss said. "He's picking this one up at the airport while getting the other one out of town." Weiss laughed. "Walter thinks it's all based on physical attraction, on him being macho man, that it has nothing to do with the fact that he runs CBS Records, or is a man of power and money. He equates himself with Tom Cruise."

Unfortunately, even the head of a record company was no competition for rock stars. A writer for *Esquire* shared lunch one afternoon with Yetnikoff, Mick Jagger, Daryl Hall, and Dave Stewart of the Eurythmics. Young women thronged the table, and Walter eyed them appreciatively, to no effect. "It's hard to hang out with these guys," he sighed afterward. "For one thing, the girls don't pay any attention to you when they're around."

Dick Asher, for his part, was amazed at the spectacle of Walter turning into, as he put it, "the Playboy of the Western World." Not because Walter was having affairs, but because he seemed bent on wrecking his marriage. To Dick, that was unthinkable. Asher always believed he and Yetnikoff had similar values, but he didn't recognize Walter any more. Dick, like Walter, had married his college girlfriend, Sheila Siegel, and they had three grown children. Asher bragged that their union would set an industry record for longevity.

Walter's marriage began to come apart in late 1981, when June learned he was having an affair with his secretary, Debra Federoff. Federoff, who talked good Yiddish, was nonetheless a gentile. She had gone to work for Walter in 1978. "It was between me and another girl," she said. "I was bending over and he liked my buns, so I got the job. I didn't type, I had long nails. But he never sent memos, he hated paper. Walter is brilliant, the funniest person I ever met in my life. He has a vile temper, he's also crazy. I fell in love with Walter." She saw fit to add, "Not for his looks."

By the time June learned about Debbie, the affair was already in trouble. "Walter couldn't control me," Federoff explained. She was not intimidated by him. On one occasion, Walter came back from a board meeting in a rage and shattered a glass against the wall. Everyone in the vicinity cowered except Debra, who walked into Walter's office with a tray full of glasses. Another time she had his private number changed without his knowledge because "some broad had it."

One night Walter called Federoff and said his wife had found out about them. "I had, like, a breakdown," Federoff said. "I got smashed and called him at home. I said, I want to talk to June. He got *nuts*. Finally, he said, Here, talk to her. I talked to her. I said, It's true, I'm sorry, and I'm quitting. The next day, I went in and quit. Walter said, You're out of your mind, let me put you into a different division. I said, Fuck you, fuck CBS. I wouldn't take his phone calls for *months*."

A short time later, the Yetnikoffs were separated. Walter, according to Federoff, could not stand to live alone, and she was not, so she said, about to move in with him. But soon Walter was preoccupied with another shiksa, one who would have a strong influence on him. Her advent would signal Walter's passage to a newer, crazier stage of life, auguring the dramatic events to come at CBS Records.

Her name was Lynda Emon, but she was known as "Boom-Boom." Walter was introduced to her by Norman Winter, his personal publicist on the West Coast, who got to know Emon in 1981 when she married a prominent Beverly Hills pediatrician. The couple had a splashy wedding ceremony in Acapulco; Winter was hired to do the publicity. "It was the biggest wedding of the year," Emon said. "And probably the shortest marriage in the history of the world."

With Lynda and Walter each newly separated, Winter saw a chance to play matchmaker. She seemed perfect for Yetnikoff: blond, *zoftig*, and a gentile—though in preparation for marriage, she had converted to Judaism and gone to the *mikva*, an Orthodox bathing ritual. At thirty-one, she was seventeen years younger than Yetnikoff. She liked him. "The real Walter is a teddy bear," Lynda concluded, "who happens to have a real big mouth."

Before long, they moved in together, first in guest quarters at the palatial East Side brownstone of attorney Eric Kronfeld, later in an apartment on Riverside Drive. Lynda was quite a departure from June Yetnikoff, who, like her ex-husband when she married him, was shy and unostentatious, only, unlike him, had not changed. Asher, who was fond of June, could not believe Walter would throw away twenty-five years of marriage for someone he described as "almost a caricature of the wrong woman."

Around CBS Records, people had to be nice to Lynda for fear of offending Yetnikoff. She knew she was not popular. "Everyone hated my guts," she said. "I don't know why. Maybe it was my image." Norio Ohga, chief of the CBS/Sony joint venture in Japan, once exhorted Dick Asher, Please do not let Walter bring her to Tokyo! Lynda did enjoy the friendship of Frank Dileo, Epic's vice-president of promotion—Dick Asher's bête noire. By coincidence, she had known Dileo since the late sixties; Frank had dated her sister. This served to tighten further the social bond between Dileo and Yetnikoff. By another remarkable coincidence, a man on Frank Dileo's promotion staff was a former lover of Lynda's who had jilted her when she was twenty—which gave her an idea.

"I'm in New York a week, and I am now the queen of the world, right?" she recalled. "I go prancing into Frank Dileo's of-

220

fice. Frank, I want you to do me a favor. I want you to fire this
guy and say it's for me. All these years later. Frank is sitting there,
and he says, I can't do that, Lynda. Are you fucking *nuts*? Frank
threatened him a little, though. He says, Guess who's in New York
now? But this guy's still working there, making tons of money,
with a very nice life and the same girlfriend he left me for. The
bottom line: Women have nothing to say in this business. It
doesn't matter who you're sleeping with."

Lynda, who hailed from Minneapolis—"a farm girl with hay-
seed in my hair"—had a history in the record business. At twenty-
one, she became a receptionist for a local record distributor. By
1972 she was working for United Artists in Cleveland as a promoter, only to be fired a year later. As an act of "revenge," she
became "the first woman in America to do independent record
promotion."

She was good at it, she said, and landed some big accounts,
including MGM and Polydor. The latter held a contest to see who
could get the most airplay for a new single, "Gudbuy T'Jane," by
Slade. Lynda's approach was innovative. "I found a model and got
an artist to paint her naked body with the name of the group. Big
letters everywhere. Then I'd take her to program directors at radio
stations. They'd put the record on, she'd take her coat off." When
the model posed for photos with radio personnel, Lynda said, she
was a bit more demure. "She put 45s over her boobs."

By the time Walter met her, Lynda had formed a company
called Prodisco to program dance music at roller rinks. She had
got the idea from Buck Reingold, Neil Bogart's brother-in-law and
promotion man. After she moved in with Walter, an ad in *Billboard* listed her as "vice-president, East Coast," of Norman Winter
Associates, Yetnikoff's West Coast PR firm.

Back in Minneapolis, Lynda had been impressed by two local
artist managers, Owen Husney and Ron Soskin. Now that she
shared a Manhattan co-op with the most powerful man in the
music business, she figured—why not?—she'd get them a production deal. Lynda presented them to Walter, who structured an
agreement in about an hour. The managers subsequently brought
a Minneapolis act to CBS, Brian McDonald. Their custom label,
distributed by Columbia, was named after their company, American Artists Management. For brokering the deal, Husney said,
Lynda was given an override, meaning she would share in any
record royalties. Unfortunately for her, there were none; the

McDonald album was a stiff, and the custom label was disbanded. ("So much for my career in production," Lynda said.) Still, the prospect of his live-in mistress earning royalties on a CBS Records artist did not appear to offend Walter Yetnikoff.

■

By the middle of 1981, Bruce Lundvall, the head of CBS Records U.S. and the Columbia label, had grown disgusted with his job. It was bad enough to have two bosses, but even worse that Dick and Walter were always feuding. He had never recovered from the two massive rounds of firings he had been forced to carry out in 1979. Lundvall knew another purge was coming, probably the worst yet. He had little time to devote to A&R, his passion. Dick had him working on a project to construct a new cassette plant in Carrollton, Georgia, and he was bored. In early 1982, Lundvall quit CBS to open the New York office of Warner Communications' Elektra label.

The news that Lundvall was leaving CBS electrified Alvin Teller, a young man on Asher's Posse. Teller was that rarest of animals in the record industry, a Harvard MBA. He began at CBS Records in 1968 as Clive Davis's assistant but left a short time later to become corporate development director for Playboy Enterprises in Chicago. The job did not work out well. Teller came back to CBS in the fall of 1971, "begging forgiveness." He went to work for Bruce Lundvall, and learned marketing and merchandising.

In 1974, at twenty-nine, Al Teller was named president of United Artists Records, only to experience what he called "the worst of corporate nonsense" from UA's owner, TransAmerica. He quit in 1978, and for the next three years dwelled in record industry purgatory. Teller worked as a consultant and, for a while, helped run Windsong, a short-lived label partly owned by John Denver. About the most successful project Teller worked on as a free agent was a novelty album handed out at the track, *Thoroughbred Racing's Greatest Hits*.

Then, in 1981, Al Teller got a call from Dick Asher. There was a spot open on Asher's Posse, in manufacturing—not very glamorous for someone who had left a higher post at CBS six years earlier to run a record company. Teller swallowed his pride and accepted, praying for a promotion. Dick, meanwhile, took a lot of heat for taking Teller back to CBS a third time; in his two previous stints, he had made a lot of enemies.

Teller had barely settled in when Lundvall announced he was

leaving. Asher decided he would assume Lundvall's post as president of CBS Records U.S., a layer of management that no longer seemed necessary. But he would need a new general manager of Columbia. It was exactly what Teller craved.

"Teller was very anxious to get the job," Posse member Bob Jamieson said. "He was always in the office, interested in rumors, what did you hear? I said, Al, you're eminently qualified. Why don't you just say, Dick, I want the job? At least you'll know where you stand."

Teller soon found out where he stood. Dick wanted him to have the job; Walter did not. "Walter very much opposed Teller," Dick said. "He wanted [business affairs head] Myron Roth, who is a great guy, and somebody I like very much. I didn't think he was the right guy for that job. And I had suggested Al almost immediately, and Walter just kept saying no no no no no. And eventually he said no enough that the job was offered to someone else—to Rick Blackburn, who's head of the country division. That was the compromise candidate because I couldn't get Walter's approval of Teller. And then Rick Blackburn turned it down. He didn't want to move to New York from Nashville. Throughout all this, Teller was in my office every day. Won't he back down? Won't he let me have the job? Because Teller's an ambitious guy. And then, finally, Walter came around.

"Al used to say to me, Listen, I owe my life to you, you gave me a chance again. He was ostracized, he was on the outs. Here was a bright guy, a capable guy, who made waves. And they could afford to get rid of the people who made waves, and keep 'em away.

"Anyway, Teller took over the Columbia label. And after six months or so, it became apparent that Al was doing a pretty good job. He had gotten Columbia together, it was beginning to become much more effective. And one day Walter said to me, Teller's doing a pretty good job. And I said, Yeah, I'm glad you agree. And Walter said, I just gave him a $50,000 raise.

"Now this was something he had done without consulting me. He had called Al in and told him, You've got a $50,000 raise. I was Al's boss. As a matter of courtesy, before you give someone a raise, you talk to his boss. Especially a raise of that magnitude. That was a big, big raise for Al. I guess Walter wanted Al to know where the sugar came from."

■

On August 13, 1982—a Friday, no less—CBS Records fired three hundred employees and closed nine of its nineteen sales branches around the country. It was the biggest one-day purge at any record company since the industry downturn had begun three years earlier. Among those let go were nine vice-presidents. About 15 percent of all nonhourly employees were axed. An entire layer of management in sales and promotion was eliminated.

Just as he had done in 1979, Yetnikoff distanced himself from the firings, and Dick Asher made an effective lightning rod. He was not well liked to begin with; now, his standing in the popularity polls dropped further. Never mind that a restructuring of this magnitude could only have been made in consultation with Yetnikoff and Tom Wyman. Never mind, too, that the failed boycott of independent promoters meant that CBS Records had returned to spending at least $10 million a year on the service, equal to three hundred salaries at an average of $33,000 per employee.

Friends of Dick Asher insisted that Yetnikoff had set him up to take the blame, and that he was traumatized by the firings. "Of course Dick was set up," said attorney Eric Kronfeld. "When all those people had to be let go, that was at the corporation's insistence, and Walter's insistence."

The resentment against Dick Asher lingered at CBS for years. Looking back, a CBS man said recently, "Asher came in and rather ruthlessly cut the place down to size. He didn't have any concept of the company, so he just went clip, clip, clip. They're gone. I think he approached the cutting back in a purely arithmetical way. He did it without any real finesse."

Two days before the "Friday Massacre," Walter Yetnikoff turned forty-nine. Attorney Nat Weiss and Lynda Emon threw him a surprise birthday bash. Among the gifts was a blood-pressure gauge to "hold his blood pressure down and his bottom line up." Parties, often riotous ones, were becoming a mainstay for Walter. Lynda enjoyed socializing, and particularly liked rubbing shoulders with CBS recording stars.

Some months later, Lynda unwittingly became part of a controversy between Walter and CBS News. In early 1982, Steve Glauber, a producer for CBS-TV's weekly news program 60 Minutes, had admitted that he and Mike Wallace, one of the show's stars, were working on a story about indie promo men. "We're looking into the role of the independent and corporate promotion representative," Glauber told Billboard, "and why certain records get played. That's the angle." On top of that, Yetnikoff recalled, "there was an article in the *Detroit Free Press* to the effect that if [CBS chairman] Bill Paley knew what Mike Wallace knew about WY's operation, BP would do to WY what he did to Clive Davis!"

Then, on November 16 of that year, Paley was guest of honor at the black-tie Family of Man dinner at the Waldorf. Walter took Lynda, and they found themselves at a table with Mike Wallace. When Wallace was introduced to Yetnikoff, he cracked, "You mean, this is the man who is helping CBS on its way to bankruptcy?" Walter, who harbored a grudge against CBS News to begin with, was furious. The prearranged seating at the banquet table left Lynda next to Wallace, with Walter several places away. During the course of the dinner, Wallace asked the waiter for napkins, and placed one on the lap of the woman to his left, Marilyn Berger (wife of *60 Minutes* executive producer Don Hewitt) and to his right, Lynda Emon.

The next day, Wallace and Hewitt got a frantic phone call from David Fuchs, an executive in the CBS broadcast group. "He says, Listen, we've got big trouble over here," Hewitt recalled. "Yetnikoff has just announced to [CBS chief Tom] Wyman that this company is not big enough for Walter Yetnikoff and Mike Wallace—and one of them has to go!" Walter, it seemed, was convinced that Mike Wallace had put his hand under Lynda's dress. Fuchs asked Wallace to write Yetnikoff a letter of apology, and, a day later, Wallace complied. In the letter, Wallace apologized for what he called his "bad joke" about Walter leading CBS into bankruptcy and debunked the statements in the *Detroit Free Press* article, but made no mention of Lynda. *60 Minutes* never did a story on independent promotion; Wallace said the idea was abandoned because his news team was unable to get enough good information.

Years later, Yetnikoff bragged to a reporter about how he had bested Wallace. He remembered the events leading up to the letter somewhat differently. "I contacted Don Hewitt and said, I'm going to investigate *you*. So I got an apology letter from Mike Wallace. This is after extensive investigation which everyone knew he was doing—and he's supposed to be real good at what he does, although we could disagree about that. It applies specifically to [CBS Records] because he's not going to apologize to the whole world. . . . It says: 'If Bill Paley knew what I know, he'd know nothing.' Then, as soon as I got this, I called up corporate affairs and said,

I'm releasing this [letter] to the *Times*. And they said, Don't do that!"

Wallace's wisecrack had stung because it was certain that 1982 would prove an even worse year for CBS Records than 1981. The company was cold. Boston's Tom Scholz still hadn't delivered his third album, and never would—not to CBS, anyway. Columbia had a hit with Paul McCartney's *Tug of War*, but little else to brag about.

When the full year's results were tallied, the numbers were depressing. Profits sank to a paltry $22 million on sales of just over $1 billion. The company had not earned so little in a year since 1971, and the dollar was worth a lot more then. The profit margin for 1982, about two cents on the dollar, was appalling—a testament to far too many unsuccessful albums and the continuing ill effects of economic recession. Moreover, CBS was back to spending over $10 million a year on indie promotion.

Viewed in another light, however, the 1982 results were not quite as bad as they looked. For one thing, earnings would have been higher but for a number of big write-offs, including the two factories that had been closed. CBS also amortized a large capital investment in its new, more efficient plant in Carrollton, Georgia. Then there was a big, onetime hit against earnings in severance pay for those who had been laid off. Under Dick Asher's day-to-day management, CBS Records had swallowed some bitter medicine. But if the economy improved—and the music, too—CBS Records was now poised for a dramatic turnaround.

Toward the end of 1982, two hit albums were released by CBS. The first of them entailed a bit of irony. It was a record that Dick Asher championed over the objections of Epic, whose staff often criticized his musical savvy. Earlier in the year, CBS Records International signed the Australian band Men at Work to an overseas, non-U.S. deal. The group promptly delivered its first album, *Business as Usual*, which sold 200,000 copies in Australia, an unheard-of feat. Asher was convinced that the record would do well in the United States, but he could not get Epic to distribute it. Finally, he demanded that either Epic head Don Dempsey or Columbia's Al Teller option the album. Teller at last agreed. "We put it out just to shut Dick up," a Columbia man later confessed, sheepishly. The album yielded two number one singles—"Who Can It Be Now?" and "Down Under"—and sold 6 million copies.

The second album, released in November 1982 by Epic, was

a monster of unprecedented proportions. It would ultimately sell 38.5 million copies worldwide, spend thirty-seven weeks at number one on the *Billboard* album chart, and spawn seven hit singles. *The Guinness Book of World Records* would proclaim it the biggest album of all time. Most important, it would earn at least $60 million for CBS Records, restoring to full strength the company's bottom line—and Walter Yetnikoff's power.

The album was Michael Jackson's long-awaited *Thriller*. CBS had been desperate for it, and the pressure Epic put on Jackson and his producer, Quincy Jones, to complete it in time for Christmas was palpable. Jones was busy with a Donna Summer album, and Jackson faced a number of distractions as well, not the least of which was his parents' divorce. Finally, Jackson wrote in his autobiography, *Moonwalk*,* CBS "said it had to be ready on a certain date, do or die." He and Jones found they had three months to record the album, during which time they also had to produce *The E.T. Storybook*, a children's record, in a one-shot deal with MCA.

The deadline crunch took its toll when it came to mixing the dozens of vocal and instrumental tracks for the album. "When we finally listened to the tracks we were going to hand in," Jackson wrote, "*Thriller* sounded so crappy to me that tears came to my eyes." Jackson put his foot down. He would not release the record. There was "yelling and screaming" from CBS, he wrote, but he and Jones took another month to remix the album. Handed over at last, *Thriller* was put on a crash production schedule, and Epic began shipping it just before Thanksgiving.

Few expected *Thriller* to surpass the sales record previously set by *Saturday Night Fever*, but no one was surprised that it was an instant smash. Jackson had been at the top of his profession ever since November 1969, when Motown released "I Want You Back," a Jackson Five single on which he sang lead. It sold 2 million copies in six weeks and went to number one. Michael Jackson was eleven years old. The next three Jackson Five singles were also number-one records.

In 1975 Michael Jackson and all but one of his brothers moved over to Epic. Four years later, Jackson cut his first solo album for Epic, *Off the Wall*, also produced by Quincy Jones. Jackson wrote the words and music to two songs and coauthored a third. One of

* Ghostwritten, without credit, by Stephen Davis.

his solo compositions, "Don't Stop Till You Get Enough," went to number one. The album sold 8 million copies, making it the biggest hit of a bad year.

So though there was a precedent for *Thriller*, the magnitude of its success was staggering. The United States alone accounted for 20 million units sold, which meant the record landed in one of every 4.25 American households. A number of factors conspired to make the album the monster it was, aside from its undisputed merits. For starters, seven of *Thriller*'s nine cuts went top ten; "Billie Jean," a Jackson composition, stayed at number one for seven weeks. Meanwhile, MTV's ratings were at an all-time high, and videos of three of the album's songs were aired incessantly.

One other factor played a key role in *Thriller*'s success. On May 16, 1983, the NBC television network aired a special, *Motown 25: Yesterday, Today, and Forever*, seen by an estimated 50 million Americans. It featured nearly all of Motown's greatest stars, most of whom had by then left the label. At the time of the show's taping, "Billie Jean" was the nation's number one single. Donning a black jacket and a Fedora, Jackson lip-synched "Billie Jean" and went into a dance routine that left the audience agog. He took the occasion to debut a new step, the "Moonwalk," in which he appeared to defy gravity.

Though the public made him out to be living on the edge of fantasy, Michael Jackson was an ambitious man with extensive knowledge of the record industry's workings. "I consider myself a musician who is incidentally a businessman," he wrote. Jackson was ecstatic over the success of *Thriller*, and he believed Frank Dileo in particular had a lot to do with it.

"Frank was responsible for turning my dream for *Thriller* into a reality," Jackson wrote. "His brilliant understanding of the recording industry proved invaluable. For instance, we released 'Beat It' as a single while 'Billie Jean' was still at number one. CBS screamed, You're crazy, this will kill 'Billie Jean.' But Frank told them not to worry, that both songs would be number one and both would be in the top ten at the same time. They were."

Frank Dileo was a heavy user of independent promotion and a personal friend of Joe Isgro. It is hard to imagine that any Top 40 station needed to be persuaded by an indie promo man to play the singles from *Thriller*. Yet one Epic man admitted, "That campaign cost about $100,000 and change for each single in independent promotion."

Jackson soon showed just how deeply he appreciated Frank Dileo. For eight months, he had been without a personal manager, having dismissed the team of Ron Weisner and Freddy DeMann, and during that time it was the most coveted spot in the music industry. Whoever occupied it would become entitled to a kingly salary, if not a percentage of Jackson's gross income. Jackson, who seemed deeply fond of Dileo—he called him "Uncle Tookie"—gave him the job in March 1984, three months before he was to embark on the nationwide "Victory" tour with his brothers. Walter Yetnikoff was delighted, and probably had played a hand in Jackson's decision.

Whether Jackson understood the role performed by the Network and Frank Dileo's relationship with the indie community was something he alone could say. He was certainly not naive about promotion. Yetnikoff said of Jackson, "He has made observations to me about things like promotion which indicate he would be totally qualified to run a record company if he so desired." Frank Dileo's appeal as a manager obviously had to do with his abilities as a record promoter. Apart from that, Jackson seemed capable of managing his own career.

No one would ever again question how Frank Dileo managed to own a gold Rolex. "Everyone turned fucking green when Frank pulled that one off," said an acquaintance. "I was talking to him on the phone about six months after he became Michael's manager. He said, You know, I can't believe what a different world I'm in versus the one I left. I just concluded a clothing deal for Michael this morning. It took me half an hour and I'm a millionaire, just today. I said, Frank, I'm getting tired of this conversation."

In September 1984, Dileo bought a handsome six-bedroom house on three quarters of an acre of land in Encino, about five minutes from Jackson's home and not far from Joe Isgro. He got it for $825,000, all cash, and spent another half a million in improvements. Parked out in front was a black Rolls-Royce sedan, license plate THANXMJJ—a gift of Michael J. Jackson.

Alongside the house was a poolside cabana complete with pinball machines and Michael memorabilia. Among the latter were photographs of Dileo and Jackson with Ronald Reagan at the White House, a shot of Frank kissing Pope John Paul II's ring, and a pair of Jackson's sequined white socks. It was there on a recent summer afternoon that Dileo expounded on the secrets of his success, gesturing with a gold pen in one hand and his trademark unlit cigar in the other. His thinning brown hair had been pulled back and braided in a rather incongruous ponytail.

Dileo said he began as a $120-a-week flunky for a rackjobber in Pittsburgh, his hometown. By 1968 he had moved to Cleveland as a local promotion man for Epic, then was promoted to the Chicago office. Before the decade was out, RCA "came and snatched me away," bringing him to New York as head of the pop promotion department. He was twenty-one. "I was so young that American Express wouldn't give me a card." From RCA he went to Bell Records, but a year later, at twenty-eight, Dileo "retired" and moved back to Pittsburgh. "After so many years, you just get to the point where you don't give a shit."

Dileo did not explain how he spent his retirement. In point of fact, he was a bookie for college basketball games, a misdemeanor offense for which he was twice convicted and fined, in 1977 and 1978. Dileo had the foresight to record his bets on rice paper, which dissolves in water, but hadn't the alacrity to dispose of the sheets before the police nabbed him. He did explain, however, why his retirement abruptly ended in 1979. "I had a tragedy. I was at a funeral for my wife's grandmother, which was in Ohio. And my house had an electrical fire and destroyed everything we owned." Again, Dileo omitted a telling detail: His insurance carrier refused to pay.

He continued, "At that point, I had to make a decision. All I had left was a Cadillac, and I sold it for $2,000. I bought two blue suits and three white shirts and a plane ticket to New York. And I ran into a friend of mine, Gordon Anderson [marketing vice-president of Epic], in Gallagher's Restaurant. He said, Geez, you know, we've been looking for you, we need some grass-roots people."

From 1979 until Michael Jackson hired him in 1984, Dileo was Epic's promotion director. During that period, Epic did the unthinkable for two years running: It outperformed Columbia. And it wasn't only because of Michael Jackson. There was Quiet Riot, there was REO Speedwagon's *Hi-Infidelity* album, there were Meat Loaf and Cyndi Lauper and Culture Club. Frank Dileo promoted them all.

What was his secret? "The secret of doing it?" Dileo said, jabbing his still-unlit cigar. "I hate to even tell you, because it gives it away to everybody else. But the thing you have to do, I go by what Vince Lombardi said one time. He said, When my team's winning, I kick 'em in the ass. When they're losing, I gotta hug 'em and pat 'em on the back. It's much like when you're running a staff of thirty or forty people. You have to make them believe they can accomplish things they never thought they could.

"And once you can get a little roll going, to keep pressing them. Because it's normal for anybody to be negative. Or satisfied. I got two records on this week, and I did my job. No, man, that ain't it. If you're a baseball player, and you're getting paid a million dollars a year to play center field, and the ball's hit, and you jump up and hit the wall and catch the ball, you did your job. It's nothing extraordinary 'cause you ran into a wall. What the hell are they paying you a million dollars for? Now, if you jump up and catch the ball, fall over the wall, and roll three times and still held on, I'll give you a hand. Now you did something. You gotta make those guys realize that. If you had four records that deserved to be on there, get the four on. When you're satisfied, you're over and out."

Dileo was an outspoken fan of independent promotion. "It takes some of the burden off of you. I think it helps you concentrate on certain records." As for all the accusations floating around about indie promo men—payola, kickbacks, organized crime—Dileo had nothing but disdain. "No, there's not anything dishonest going on. Yeah, there could be one or two dishonest situations. But, you know, it's like, if you're in a restaurant, right? And you order a steak, and it comes and it's bad, you don't quit eating meat. It's one bad steak. And organized crime? That's bullshit. There ain't been organized crime since Capone died."

Dileo could not help but muse on the remarkable turn his life had taken. "If you coulda gone back twenty years ago and said, What are the odds of Frank Dileo ever managing the biggest act in the world, it probably would have been two trillion to one. To the general public. To me, I knew that I would do something, or handle somebody big, or be in some big entertainment position, because that's what I imagined my whole life. I had no intentions of ever being a manager. My intentions were to be president of CBS. But I knew that some time, some way, somebody would recognize the talents that I have."

■

If Walter Yetnikoff was pleased to see such a close ally become manager of his biggest act, he must have been doubly pleased with the act's attorney, John Branca. As with Dileo's appointment, Walter's good fortune in seeing Jackson become Branca's client was not altogether a coincidence. Up until 1980 Jackson had been a client of attorney David Braun, a man Walter considered an enemy. Braun had had the chutzpah to represent United Artists in a lawsuit against CBS and Yetnikoff. Then, in October 1980, Braun abandoned his practice to begin his brief, disastrous stint as president of PolyGram. John Branca, a former tax lawyer who was then one of Braun's young associates, wound up with Jackson. Branca was twenty-nine at the time.

When Braun's reign at PolyGram ended a year later, he attempted to regain Jackson, without success. Walter, according to Dick Asher, helped John Branca hold on. Yetnikoff found in Branca an attorney more to his taste, a man not unlike Allen Grubman. A member of the music bar quoted in *The American Lawyer* summed up the Branca credo: "Controversy is bad. It loses you clients."

Though Branca had come out of nowhere, after *Thriller* he was one of the top people in the music business. Said attorney Eric Kronfeld, "John is a power broker because he makes most of Michael's decisions. People will come to him because they want a piece of Michael."

One man who came to Branca for a piece of Michael, and got it, was MCA Records head Irving Azoff. Branca made Azoff a "consultant" to the Victory tour. Though Azoff still owned Front-Line, his old management company, his "consulting" amounted to little. But as one professional on the tour put it, "Michael Jackson is the biggest star in the world, and Irving knows the simple rule of the power junkie: If there is something that has power, acquire it. You will become the master lodestone to which all things are attracted."

Azoff threw some of his big Front-Line clients Branca's way in a seeming show of gratitude: Stevie Nicks, Dan Fogelberg, Tommy Shaw, David Lee Roth, and ZZ Top. When Azoff offered a joint-venture record and video deal to MTV cofounder Robert Pittman, Branca did the legal work and captured Pittman's company as a client. "I have been accused, rightfully, of trying to steer business to John," Azoff said. But he only did it, he added, because "John's very capable, competent, one of the best."

Branca failed to form a relationship with the third troika member, David Geffen. But between Azoff and Walter, Branca soon built a practice second only to Grubman's. "The only attorneys Walter deals with are Allen and me at this point," Branca said in 1987. "In the last four or five years, he and I have gotten all the new business that's come up. The competition," he added with a grin, "has really shrunk."

THE FIRING

∎

E VEN before Frank Dileo became Jackson's manager as a reward for *Thriller's* success, the album paid huge dividends to Walter Yetnikoff. In the first quarter of 1983, the long-awaited turnaround in CBS Records' financial fortunes had come home at last. A month before the results were tallied in April, Walter proclaimed the recovery at a forum for Wall Street stock analysts who rated CBS. Yetnikoff credited *Thriller,* but also the Men at Work album that Dick Asher had forced the company to put out. There was no mention of Asher, however. Yetnikoff also cited a third act that he felt had great promise, Culture Club, whose lead singer, Boy George, was getting a lot of press coverage over the question of his gender. Walter said the band represented a new idiom: "transvestite rock." When the laughter subsided, he added, "Don't knock it if it sells."

CBS chief Tom Wyman stood by beaming as Walter addressed the analysts. He was no longer smiling toward the end of the month, however, when Walter dropped a bombshell: He said he was weighing an offer to move to Los Angeles and become the new president of MCA Records. It was hard to believe Walter meant it. He had been with CBS since his twenties. But MCA was offering a substantial raise. Yetnikoff's contract with CBS, set to expire at year-end 1984, provided an annual base salary of $275,000. In any given year, however, he made much more than that. In 1982, for instance, he received a bonus of $284,052, despite the layoffs and poor earnings, plus another $19,804 for serving on the CBS board of directors, making his 1982 total $578,471. MCA's offer was higher.

The news that Walter was mulling a switch came to light in the March 26, 1983, edition of *The New York Times*, a Saturday. But between then and the following Monday, March 28, he made up his mind to stay at CBS. In a statement issued that day, Walter declared, "CBS Records is enjoying enormous success at this time, on a worldwide basis, and prospects for the balance of the year are tremendous. I am very pleased with the decision to stay where I am. I'd be crazy to leave."

The job Walter turned down soon went to Irving Azoff. Meanwhile, the CBS board raised Walter's salary as an incentive for him to stay. Given what was to occur in less than a month's time at CBS Records, Tom Wyman may have granted Walter another concession.

■

For the first time since he took the deputy job, Dick Asher began to feel good about the shape the company was in. As he liked to put it, using a favored football analogy, it was a lot more fun to play offense than defense. He knew that when the first-quarter earnings were tabulated and released in mid-April, they would be much larger than 1982's profits through March. Just as important, the profit *margin*—earnings as a percentage of sales— would be substantially improved, thanks to his cost-cutting.

He proved right on both counts. First-quarter sales were $296.6 million, a mere $500,000 higher than in 1982. But profits had zoomed to $39.4 million against $19.6 million the year before. Not only had earnings doubled, they were the best first-quarter figures in the company's history. The profit margin had risen to an admirable thirteen cents on the dollar from less than seven cents.

Asher was elated. About the only thing dampening his high spirits was the unrelenting tension between him and Walter. It seemed to have got worse. All the same, Dick still believed the rift between him and Walter was manageable.

"Walter and I had been friends for a long time," Dick said. "I thought we were friends. I mean, yeah, he'd play his little shticks. And I realized he had a bruised ego. The company was turning around, it published its best first quarter ever, and people were beginning to say that I did that. I knew that was annoying him. He was very happy to let me be identified with all the unpopular things, but even though they were unpopular, in the end things really began to turn around, and people began to attribute it to me. And I realized that piqued his ego a little bit, so I tried to be conscious of that. We could sort of take jabs at each other. But we were friends. We never really hurt one another."

In early April, Dick flew to Australia with Columbia president Al Teller and Allen Davis, the head of CBS Records International. The trip reunited Dick with one of his closest friends in the company, Bob Jamieson, promoted the previous fall from Asher's Posse to managing director of CBS Records Australia.

Jamieson was happy to see Dick but disturbed by a rumor. "Just before Dick arrived," Jamieson said, "I got a call from my dad. He's a professional golfer, belongs to a club. And there was another club member who worked for RCA Records. My dad says to me, God, the rumors about your boss, Dick Asher, are unbelievable. I hear he's going to get fired. I said, Dad, those rumors have been around forever. He said, Well, they're savage now. I said, I can't believe it. He's on a plane, on his way down. If he's fired, no one's told him. I picked Dick up the next day, we went to all the different branches. I said to him, Dick, the rumors are unbelievable. He said, Nah, Walter and I always have disagreements. But I think we'll be okay."

On Monday, April 18, 1983, a few days after the release of first-quarter earnings, Dick was in Walter's corner office on the eleventh floor of Black Rock. They were discussing a business matter when Walter suddenly announced that he had some bad news. Tom Wyman, he said, had "problems" with Asher and did not want to pick up his option when it expired in October. Dick was flabbergasted. He barely had any dealings with Wyman, and besides, the record company had turned around. Why did Wyman suddenly have problems with him? What sort of problems? Walter grew increasingly uncomfortable. "I kept saying why, why, and I was questioning him," Dick recalled. "And he said, Look, this is very difficult for me to discuss. And I said, Walter, I'm sorry if it's uncomfortable for you, but it's my *life*. I've been here seventeen years. What's happening?"

Without replying, Yetnikoff got up and left the room. Dick sat there, stunned. He assumed Walter had gone to the bathroom and would return in a few minutes. But after half an hour ticked by, Dick realized that Walter had gone home, unable to continue the conversation. Walter had never fired anyone in his life. Now, he was attempting to fire Asher, but so awkwardly that Asher had no idea he was being fired.

Dick didn't know what to think. "All he told me was that

Wyman didn't want to pick up my option in October. What did that mean? Did it mean that I stayed at CBS but didn't have a contract anymore? Did it mean I had to leave CBS? I didn't know. It certainly didn't mean anything was happening tomorrow."

The next day, Tuesday, April 19, Asher came to work as usual. All that morning, he looked in vain for Walter. That afternoon a lunch was scheduled in Bill Paley's dining room for all group heads. When Asher was made deputy, his contract stipulated that he would enjoy all the prerogatives of group president, so both he and Walter were asked to represent the records group at the luncheon.

"I go to this luncheon, and Walter comes in at the very last second, before everyone sits down, so I never have a chance to talk to him. I wanted to continue the conversation, but he hadn't been in that morning. So I quietly said to Wyman at the luncheon, I'd like to talk to you if I could, privately, for a few minutes after lunch. He said, Fine, come to the office.

"So I went into Wyman's office after the lunch, and I said, Walter tells me I have terrible problems with you, that you don't want to pick up my option, and I don't understand why. Wyman says, You don't have any problems with me. You have problems with Walter. I said, Well, I've worked for the man for twelve years, and I've never had a problem I couldn't discuss with him. You mean if I can sit down and talk this out with Walter that I stay at CBS after October? He said sure. I said, Well, gee, that's great.

"Look, I said, last night he ran out on me; you know, he just left. And he wasn't there all this morning. I may have a little trouble talking to Walter about this. I may need your help a little bit, just to sit down with Walter. He said sure. Look, he said, we've got to go to the stockholders' meeting in an hour or so, and I've got a lot to do. But sure, I'll help. And he put his arm around me —literally, put his arm around me—and walked me out of his office, patting me on the back. Everything's wonderful.

"So I immediately ran downstairs to look for Walter. Walter's not in his office. I subsequently found out he was hiding in Allen Davis's office, who had been my replacement in International. But I just couldn't find him. I spent an hour trying like hell to find out where he was.

"An hour later, Walter was on the corporate plane, on his way to the stockholders' meeting. The next morning, Wednesday, I had my usual staff meeting. And my staff meetings were always early. The guys would have to come in at nine o'clock for those meetings. I get to the office, and there's a memo from Walter: Mr. Wyman and I have decided to cancel today's staff meeting. It has gone to all the members of my staff. Then I got a call from one of the [CBS corporate] lawyers, and they told me to contact Wyman's secretary, to make an appointment to meet with Walter and Wyman on Friday.

"I really wasn't sure what was going on Friday morning. The meeting was in Walter's conference room, so I thought maybe I would just be sitting down with him and Wyman. I walked in, early in the morning, and there were Wyman and Walter and a bunch of lawyers. And Wyman and Walter had a press statement, like one line, saying Dick Asher has left CBS, and some papers which they asked me to sign.

"I said, Wait a second. What's happened? What did I do? They said, We acknowledge it's without cause. I said, Look, then why am I getting this announcement, this one-line announcement, which sounds to all the world as if I got caught with my hand in the cookie jar? They said, We're not gonna negotiate with you. I kept saying why, why? They said, We aren't gonna respond. We acknowledge it's without cause. I said, Well, I'm not signing the papers. I should consult an attorney first. You guys obviously have your attorneys. They said, You can bring in your attorney; our attorneys will be happy to explain the agreement; they won't change one line. That's exactly what they said. So I said, Well, I've got to talk to my attorney. The meeting broke up.

"So my attorney came in from New Jersey. I say 'my attorney,' it was a friend and neighbor of mine by the name of Herman Ziegler. He's not a show-biz attorney. A friend calls you up and says, I've got a problem, please come. He was there within an hour. The CBS attorneys just said, Look, we won't negotiate, and that was the position they maintained. I tried to call Walter, tried to call Wyman. They refused to talk to me."

Dick left with his lawyer. Asher wanted to litigate; Ziegler was determined to talk him out of it. "He said, Look, you're gonna become obsessed with this, it will consume you," Dick recalled. "To them, it costs them nothing. They'll just turn it over to their batteries of lawyers and spend the corporation's money. Even if you win, you might not recover what you've spent, and for two years your life will be obsessive. You've got to get on with your life."

Reluctantly, Dick agreed it was sound advice. He would not

sue. Getting on with his life and not allowing his termination to obsess him was another matter.

"I really couldn't take it quite that easily, because I spent too many years there, and put too much of my life into that place, and accomplished too much there. I never thought anything like that would happen. I never was disloyal. No one's ever accused me of that. If Walter said he wanted me to do something, I never played a double game.

"And—this is my *mishegoss*—I was the guy who lost all the sleep when we had to let people go. A lot of other people thought it was just part of the game; I couldn't treat it that way. It just made me crazy. It just hurt a lot."

Many industry people found it hard to believe that Asher never saw it coming. But in some fundamental way, Dick was naive. Perhaps it was his military training that made him think the institution would always protect him if he was loyal. Three years earlier, before Harvey Schein had offered the presidency of PolyGram to David Braun, he had approached Asher. "Dick would only consider it," Schein recalled, "if we were prepared to hire him for life. I said, Are you sure you'll be at CBS the rest of your life?"

Evidently, he was. "Dick had a very naive attitude for an executive in the entertainment business," David Braun said, "which is that the main thing was to do a good job for the company, and the company would take care of you. Dick assumed if he worked hard and didn't ask for anything, they would reward him. Instead, they canned him."

The news of Asher's firing was greeted warmly within CBS. People at Epic threw a champagne party. Among those who raised a glass was promotion vice-president Frank Dileo, who in less than a year would have something even bigger to toast to. "When he was fired, it took an awful lot of burden off everybody's back," Dileo said, chuckling quietly. "And I believe there were a few corks popped that night, yeah."

Billboard ran three short paragraphs on Asher's dismissal, under a one-column headline, in its April 30 edition. The industry's cold-shoulder treatment toward one of its fallen soldiers had just begun.

■

Not long after Walter fired Dick Asher, he began intense negotiations to win the Rolling Stones from Atlantic. By then the group was not merely old; it was hoary. The youngest original member of the group, Keith Richards, was forty. The band had not toured in two years.* Boston comedian Steven Wright made jokes about the group's age: "The Stones, I love the Stones, can't believe they're still doin' it after all these years. I watch 'em whenever I can. Fred and Barney . . ."

Whether it was the *Thriller* phenomenon or euphoria over the departure of Dick Asher, Walter must have been feeling his oats when he bid for the Stones. His offer, which included some of the Stones' back catalog and the right to Mick Jagger's solo career, came to $28 million. The band took it. Atlantic's Ahmet Ertegun, who had outbid Clive for the group a decade earlier, was stunned by Walter's bid, which was twice his own. If there was ever hope that the deal might break even, it died with Jagger's second solo album, *Primitive Cool*, one of 1987's most embarrassing stiffs.

Aside from the Network, getting the Stones was Yetnikoff's biggest loss-leader deal. Considering what it had cost, the prestige of landing them was even of questionable value. If Walter wanted to hang out with Mick Jagger, however, he certainly got what he paid for.

The two men did seem well matched. Walter described for *Esquire* a memorable moment in the negotiations: "So we're in the Ritz hotel in Paris; we'd moved over from London. Mick is there on one side of the table, Keith is there, Prince Rupert [Lowenstein]—I don't know what he's prince *of*—the Stones' financial adviser, and we get to a point about the Stones having the right to select singles from their album product. We're disagreeing over the numbers. Suddenly Jagger explodes: 'You fat fucking record executives!' he screams. 'What do you know?' He jumps up. *I* jump up. 'Fuck you!' I scream back. I'm pretty sure I can take him, but I don't want to get into a real fistfight. He backs down. I think he has to try you—it's part of his personality—but *nobody* outgeschreis me. . . ."

■

August 11, 1983, was Walter Yetnikoff's fiftieth birthday. For two months, Lynda Emon planned a surprise party for August 10, to be held in the presidential suite of the New York Hilton. She raised $20,000 in guest donations to cater the event. On the ap-

* And would not do so again until 1989.

pointed day, surprise guests flew in from all over the country. Walter's friends were there: Allen Grubman, Tommy Mottola, Fred DiSipio, Nat Weiss, Morris Levy. Publicist Norman Winter and *Billboard* staffer Tom Noonan printed up a mock front page of the magazine to commemorate the occasion. A banner across the top read, SPECIAL ISSUE! SHIKSA FARM DEBUTS IN PHILLY.

The only problem was how to get Walter to the hotel without tipping him off. For that, Lynda enlisted Mick Jagger, who was still in negotiations with CBS. Mick called Walter and said the two of them had to go to the Hilton so that Yetnikoff could meet guitarist Keith Richards. "And as Mick and Walter are driving to the Hilton," Lynda recalled, "Mick is saying, This fucking Keith, look at all the money he spends, staying at these big hotels."

Two years later, most of the same players, including Mick Jagger and Fred DiSipio, would return to the same hotel suite for Lynda Emon's thirty-fifth birthday party. This time, however, there was a special guest: Thomas Wyman. According to one attendee, Wyman's presence did not stop some people from using cocaine in one of the bathrooms, though the CBS chief may have been unaware of it. One spectacle Wyman probably did not miss was the evening's highlight. Walter hired two male strippers to do a bump and grind for Lynda's benefit. One of them stuffed a "Happy Birthday" telegram from Billy Joel's manager in his jockstrap. Lynda retrieved it with her teeth.

■

As 1983 drew to a close, CBS Records appeared certain to post its highest profits ever. At the end of the first three quarters, profits were up *600 percent* over 1982, on a mere 6 percent increase in sales. This meant, quite simply, that the profit margin had improved a hundredfold. In large measure, it was a tribute to Dick Asher's cost-cutting.

In November Walter hosted a special meeting for the Wall Street analysts who rated CBS stock. This meeting would be devoted solely to the records group. When Walter gave the two percentages, 600 versus 6, and wryly pointed out that they indicated "a nice increase in margins," the room rocked with laughter. Walter waited a beat, then another beat, and remarked, "Tom Wyman didn't laugh when I said that." More guffaws.

Walter had never been in better form before the analysts. He brought with him two sets of glasses, one clear and the other tinted. Depending on whether he was asked a question about business or music, he would flip on the appropriate pair of specs. "I can't see out of either one of them," he deadpanned, "so it doesn't matter."

Just as Clive Davis had been "Stalinized"—had ceased to exist in CBS Records' corporate history after being fired—so was Dick Asher now a nonperson. Not one of the highly paid analysts had the gumption to ask Walter why he had fired Asher, assuming they knew who he was. (Nor did they ask a single question about indie promotion, still the largest variable cost on the ledger books.) Walter went on explaining the CBS Records recovery, citing the Men at Work album, deflecting a question about Mick Jagger's age— "you try to keep up with him; I had a tough time"—and appearing to take credit for the cost-cutting exercise: "We took the opportunity to write off a number of things. Actually, anything that moved."

Soon after the analyst meeting, *Thriller* was nominated for eight Grammys, including best album. On February 28, 1984, it won in every category for which it was nominated, save song of the year, which went to "Every Breath You Take" by the Police. Jackson kept his frequent trips to the podium brief and low-key, only once lifting his sunglasses. But as he rose to accept one of his last few trophies, he grabbed Walter Yetnikoff by the arm and brought him along. Walter was more than pleased. "That's unheard of," Walter said. "You don't bring record executives up at the Grammys, 'cause no one's interested. I went back to CBS and said, Give me another $2 million for that!" Though Walter had little to do with signing Michael to CBS and even less with resigning him in 1980—Dick Asher negotiated the contract—he had evolved into Michael's rabbi. "Michael Jackson would ask Walter for advice on most anything," said Yetnikoff's attorney, Stanley Schlesinger. At the moment, nothing could make Walter more valuable to CBS.

Two months after the Grammys, almost a year to the day after firing Dick Asher, Walter was honored at the New York Hilton as the T. J. Martell Foundation's "Humanitarian of the Year." He had never been more powerful. CBS profits for 1983 had zoomed to $109.4 million, an all-time high, from $22.2 million the year before.

The industry did not know that Walter Yetnikoff was at that very moment negotiating to leave CBS for Warner Bros. The last time Walter had threatened to leave, for MCA, he had got a big raise. This time, to prevent what was probably an even emptier threat, considering Walter had been at war with Warner for eight years, CBS offered him an unprecedented employment contract. Just for setting his name to the October 31, 1984, agreement, Walter got a $250,000 signing bonus. His base salary was raised to $475,000, and he was granted stock and participation in a bonus plan that could bring him hundreds of thousands more. Best of all, Walter won a provision almost unthinkable at Bill Paley's tight-reined CBS. He could devote "not more than ten percent" of his time "in the independent production of theatrical films." Soon that clause would literally be worth millions.

■

Dick Asher had gone back into private practice. Though he had grudgingly taken his lawyer's advice to get on with his life, it was proving far more difficult than he had imagined. "I remember being with one of the more famous headhunters, who knew me well from my time at CBS," Dick said. "And I said, Everything I've done has been successful. CBS kept taking me from one bad situation to another, and I'd turn it around. How come I am not flooded with offers? And he said, You're over fifty. It's going to be very tough. And he was right."

On top of that, when Dick was fired, his severance pay was, in his opinion, "less than generous." He did walk off with a large sum, but most of it was his own savings. Dick had deferred thirty-five percent of his bonus money into a corporate savings plan for fourteen years, and in all that time, the cash hoard had accumulated interest as well. After the firing, PR head Bob Altshuler liberally quoted the figure Asher had received upon departure as proof that he had been well taken care of, never bothering to explain that only a small percentage of it was his actual severance. "He made it sound to all the world as if CBS had been so wonderful to me, and there was nothing personal in it, and they were such nice people, and it was just a difference of opinion. Altshuler even ran into a member of my family at a social function and had the gall to tell him, Oh, when Dick left, he got so much money from us."

Worse, Dick had trouble getting the money out of CBS, because no one at any level of responsibility would take his phone call. "They absolutely refused to talk to me. I had to deal with somebody on the lowest rung of the personnel ladder."

Dick also felt he had unfinished business with Tom Wyman.

He had never been able to talk to the CBS chief during his ordeal, and now he was determined to get an audience. Finally, after five months, Wyman agreed and invited Dick up to his office.

"I still wanted to know why this had happened. I said, You told me you would help me meet with Walter, at least try to talk it out. He said it had gone too far, he had to let Walter do what he wanted. It was his group, you know? So I said, A one-line press announcement, and the silencing of the press, and all of these humiliations, and things like that. I thought this place had a lot more class than that. He got very angry as I said that. It was a funny thing. I was watching him, and his eyes began to flash fire. And he suddenly realized that he was no longer in a position to squash me like a bug. He had done as much as he could have done to me."

Only months after Dick's firing, the music division of the United Jewish Appeal gave its annual dinner. Against all odds, Walter Yetnikoff managed to persuade Barbra Streisand, who rarely made public appearances, to be the honoree. Two weeks before the dinner, Dick called one of the UJA board members to ask whether he would be on the dais, as he had been the past several years. Out of work or not, Dick said, he was as good a Jew as anybody. The board member said he would check; he called Yetnikoff. Walter made his position plain: If Dick Asher was on the dais, he said, he would not come to the dinner. Dick was not invited.

Adding to Asher's despair, most of the people who had been his loyal soldiers at CBS were being politically executed. One victim, Bill Fox, who had been Asher's financial operations man, was also in his fifties. "Bill was a fine accountant and he'd been with CBS twenty years," Dick said. "CBS has so many accountants, they could always use another one. All of a sudden, after twenty years, he was thrown out. There was no room for him. His only fault was that he had been loyal to me and worked for me." A similar fate befell Posse member Stephen Reed and staff attorney Eliot Loshak, one of Dick's boyhood friends.

The climate of fear created by these political sacrifices meant that almost no one at CBS dared speak to Dick in public. When he went to a social function, former employees walked by him as though he were not there. One man who shunned Asher in this way was Al Teller, the head of Columbia, whom Dick had rescued from oblivion when he was putting together compilation albums

of racetrack announcers. This was hard to stomach. On one occasion, Dick simply refused to let such an insult pass. It was from
a man who could not possibly be perceived an Asher loyalist: Don
Dempsey, the head of Epic. Recalled an eyewitness, "Dick walked
over to Dempsey at this party and said hello, and Dempsey turned
away. So Dick said, Don, you're going to say hello and shake my
hand like a gentleman or I'm going to knock the *shit* out of you.
Dick was an officer in the marine corps. Dempsey turned around
and sheepishly said, Hello, Dick."

CLIVE REDUX

■

N April 1983, the same month Dick Asher got fired, Clive Davis signed to Arista Records a nineteen-year-old named Whitney Houston. She would soon become the most successful female recording star in history, earning Clive a secure place in the annals of great record men, not to mention millions as her executive producer. She single-handedly would make Arista one of the three top-grossing independent labels in the country. Coming a decade after Clive himself was let go from CBS, the Houston signing marked the final stage of his resurrection.

Clive said he had never doubted for a moment that he would return to the record business after his downfall at CBS. After taking time out to write his memoirs, he mulled over job offers from rock impresarios Chris Blackwell and Robert Stigwood. Clive settled on an invitation from Columbia Pictures president Alan Hirschfield to take charge of Bell Records, a subsidiary of the movie studio. Bell was until then a middling label celebrated for singles rather than albums. Clive liked Hirschfield, and he liked the incentive that came with the job: 20 percent of the stock of Bell. "I felt that if I was going to be signing artists primarily from scratch," Clive said, "it would be nice to have a sizable equity stake."

Bell was soon rechristened Arista (rhymes with "barrister"), the name of the New York City school system's honor society, of which Clive had been a perennial member. In its first year of operation, Arista struck gold with Barry Manilow, one of the few . acts Clive inherited that he chose to keep. As far as Clive was concerned, he was singularly responsible for Manilow's overnight superstardom in early 1975. Manilow didn't argue. Clive found him a minor hit from three years previous called "Brandy." When Manilow recorded it as "Mandy," it shot to number one. Arista also did well with Melissa Manchester and the Outlaws. The rapid growth delighted Clive. "His ambition," said Elliot Goldman, then executive vice-president of Arista, "was to create another CBS."

By the middle of 1979, Alan Hirschfield had been fired from Columbia Pictures, and the movie company was in turmoil. Columbia's board decided it wanted to divest Arista. This was an agreeable prospect to Clive, who stood to make perhaps $4–5 million from the sale of his stock to the acquiring company. Before long, Columbia had worked out a deal to sell Arista to Bertelsmann A.G., a West German media and entertainment consortium.

The sale upset Elliot Goldman, who believed he was instrumental in Arista's success and entitled to some of the payoff. Before long, he quit Arista and joined Warner Communications as a senior vice-president.

After Goldman left the company, Clive depended more and more on his two senior vice-presidents to handle the administrative chores. One of them, Richard Dobbis, a zoologist turned label executive, had an unsentimental view of the record business, perhaps shaped by his knowledge of the animal kingdom. "It's a mean industry," he said. "Especially when you're on the outs."

Dobbis, who had joined Arista its first full year as a product manager, learned this firsthand after Clive fired him in 1983. Dobbis never denied that Clive was enormously talented and one of the hardest-working people he had ever met. "He had tremendous conviction about the music and was willing to go to the mat for it," Dobbis said. "I was very impressed by that. And he could be a warm and caring person."

But by 1983, Dobbis had reached the conclusion that Clive was seriously weird, and his distaste for the man was obvious. One afternoon, Dobbis was called to Clive's office and, when he arrived, found it vacant. Moments later, Clive swept out of the adjoining private bathroom. Rick, he intoned, our long-rumored parting of the ways is finally at hand.

Dobbis never disputed that the firing was justified. "Getting fired was not a big deal," he said. "I have a firm belief that employers should be able to relieve employees of their duties because they feel it would be best overall. It's a question of how they treat those people after they've departed." Dobbis discovered after leaving

Arista that his ability to make a living was virtually nil. Clive was impeding him from getting work—or so Dobbis alleged in a $3 million defamation suit he filed in August 1984 against Clive and Clive's personal attorney, Paul Marshall.

According to the suit, Clive Calder, the owner of Jive Records, a label distributed by Arista, had planned to hire Dobbis as a part-time consultant for $5,000 a month and free office space. Davis allegedly persuaded Calder not to hire Rick Dobbis by telling Calder that Dobbis was "evil."

The suit also alleged that in June 1984 Paul Marshall told Elliot Goldman that Dobbis had implicated Goldman in an illegal scheme. Goldman, by then an officer at Warner, had given Dobbis some consulting work.

(Goldman said later that he confronted Dobbis, who was flabbergasted and denied implicating anyone. It did not take Goldman long to reach the opinion that Dobbis was telling the truth. "When Clive was down and out," Goldman said, "he was subject to the same kind of whispering, innuendo campaign. And he was so irate about it, so outspoken. He kept saying, Why don't people stand up for me? For him to turn around and do the same thing to somebody else—I found that appalling." Dobbis had the same reaction. "After Clive was fired from CBS," he said, "I thought he was subject to vicious, mean, and unfair rumors. I thought it was crap, and I resented it and felt bad for him. And I just thought that a person who had suffered that kind of distasteful behavior would be careful not to repeat it. But that was not the case.")

Both Clive and Paul Marshall denied all the allegations in Dobbis's suit. Recently, Clive insisted that he had never attempted to prevent Dobbis from getting employment. "You don't gratuitously knock people. There is sensitivity for the downtrodden. I do have that. That's why for Arista's fifteenth anniversary, all the proceeds are going to fight AIDS."

To defend himself from the suit, Clive hired the high-powered law firm of Weil, Gotshal & Manges. Dobbis figured Clive's strategy was to grind him down: He had no job, so how could he afford a good attorney? But Dobbis was lucky: He had the free legal services of his brother-in-law, Jeffrey Bernbach, a top labor lawyer.

The suit was settled out of court in September 1985, when Dobbis went to work for RCA Records, which by then had bought 50 percent of Arista from Bertelsmann. Marshall called the settlement "amicable," and said he did not pay anything. Clive also denied making any payment to Dobbis. He said RCA gave Dobbis some money to end the litigation, but did not know how much.

Dobbis would not discuss the settlement. He said the whole affair had been a grim experience, aside from one moment of comic relief at the outset of the suit, when all the parties were summoned to Weil Gotshal's enormous conference room in the General Motors Building on Fifth Avenue.

"We all sat at this gigantic round table that you could have had ten couples dancing on," Dobbis said. "Clive was asked a question. He started talking, and he talked for about forty-five minutes, during the course of which he said many things, including how wonderful I was, and how talented I was, and how much our relationship had meant to him, and how good he was to me. It sounded like we should have gotten married. Clive worked himself into a frenzy. Eventually, he just said, This is too much. And he got up and left the room. It was a great performance."

Dobbis's brother-in-law thought so, too. "Jeffrey turned to me and said, I can't wait to get this guy on the stand. The man's out of his *mind*."

■

By early 1983, Clive's status as Arista's chief was at low ebb. Ever since Bertelsmann had bought Arista in 1979, the label had failed to make a good profit. Barry Manilow had fallen from the charts, and Arista had not come up with anyone nearly as big to replace him. In March 1983, RCA Records acquired 50 percent of the company from Bertelsmann and became Arista's distributor.

A month earlier, on the advice of Arista A&R executive Gerry Griffith, Clive had gone to Sweetwaters, a New York supper club, to hear nineteen-year-old singer and fashion model Whitney Houston. She was first cousin to Dionne Warwick and the daughter of Cissy Houston, a gospel singer who had done background vocals for Aretha Franklin. Both Warwick and Franklin had recently signed with Arista and had their flagging careers "rejuvenated," as Clive put it, under his supervision. The night Clive saw her, Whitney and Cissy were billed as a duo. Whitney was building a following of her own but did not yet have a record deal.

Whitney's lawyer, Paul Marshall, was weighing an offer from Bruce Lundvall, the former head of Columbia who had become president of Elektra. Unfortunately, Lundvall was in a losing power struggle with Elektra's chairman, Bob Krasnow. "If Bruce had been the undisputed head of that company," Marshall said,

"Whitney would have been on Elektra." CBS Records was considering Houston as well, but with less enthusiasm.

"Then Clive called," Marshall said. "From the moment he went down to Sweetwaters and heard her, he was relentless. And yet, interestingly, he did not make the high bid. Elektra kept upping their offer. And I finally recommended that she sign with Clive for less money." But, Marshall said, as a tradeoff for the lower bid, he had to have a key-man clause in her contract, an almost unheard-of provision in the record industry. If Clive left Arista for any reason, Whitney would become a free agent. Obviously, Clive was delighted with the idea; the board of RCA Corporation was not. Nonetheless, RCA approved the clause.

Clive had set a $175,000 recording budget for the first album, to be called *Whitney Houston*. But as it neared completion, toward the end of 1984, the cost had climbed to nearly $300,000. "It came higher because she was growing and I was supervising," Clive said. "I knew she was capable of giving stronger performances. She was gaining mike technique. I believed we were on to something special. I felt good that we would have hits."

At this point, the story becomes fuzzy because Clive has been revising it ever since. The official account is that from the moment Clive heard Houston perform at Sweetwaters, he saw a chance to create a full-blown pop diva from scratch. There is no question that Clive made all the key artistic decisions for Houston—that she was, as one former Arista man put it, "a totally contrived artist" and "a reflection of what Clive sees in music." But it is simply untrue that he foresaw her monstrous success or imagined that she would become a pop diva at all.

"When the record came in, no one, including Clive, thought it would be a major smash," said Dennis Fine, Arista's publicity director at the time. "Clive was hopeful she could sell 100,000 or 150,000 copies, so she'd have a base to build from. And he did not think there were any pop hits on the album."

In fact, the first single Clive released from the album, on Valentine's Day, 1985, "You Give Good Love," was promoted to black radio, not Top 40. It gradually moved up the charts on the black stations and managed to cross over. Clive repeated the strategy six months later with "Saving All My Love for You," which not only crossed over but hit number one on the pop charts the week of October 21, 1985. The next two singles, "How Will I Know?" and "The Greatest Love of All," were released to pop and urban stations simultaneously. Both reached number one on pop radio, but, interestingly, failed to top the black charts.

Whitney Houston went on to sell close to 20 million copies, making it far and away the most successful debut album in history. Her follow-up album, *Whitney*, would do nearly as well. But A&R man Gerry Griffith did not stick around to bask in the success. In the summer of 1985, Griffith opened up a consumer magazine and saw a publicity photograph taken when Houston was signed to Arista. Though he had been at the photo session, he was not in the picture—only Clive and Whitney were. Griffith had not only discovered Whitney Houston for Arista, but had chosen "How Will I Know?" for her first album and picked the song's producer. If Clive won't give me credit now, Griffith told himself, he never will. "I made up my mind at that point to leave the company," Griffith told *Manhattan, inc.* magazine. He went to work for Bruce Lundvall, who had become head of Manhattan Records.

When Clive read Griffith's words in *Manhattan, inc.,* "I couldn't believe it," he said. "He didn't want to leave. He was very, very happy here. The reason he left Arista Records was that he got double the salary. His conclusion [about the photograph] was totally incorrect. It was a consumer magazine which felt that, where I'm a noteworthy figure, the picture would be somewhat diminished by an unknown A&R man being in it. Consumers never heard of Gerry Griffith. I will always say Gerry was the first one that tipped me off to her. But he had nothing to do with her thereafter. She gravitated toward me. I became the person who chose every song on the album, picked every producer, took over the entire career, other than that original tip, for which I think I've given gracious enough credit. . . ."

DICK REDUX

■

W HEN Elliot Goldman landed at Warner Communications in
1982, chairman Steve Ross gave him the lofty title of senior vice-
president but no real portfolio. Goldman was in essence a full-time
consultant. He worked on various projects related to records.
Some of the label heads took to him more than others. Ahmet
Ertegun had little time for him. At one round-table meeting Goldman asked Ertegun to spell out Atlantic's strategy for increasing
its profits. Ertegun answered like a true record man: By having
more hits!

Before long, however, Goldman was at work on a deal that, if
successful, would change the shape of Warner for years to come.
He had persuaded his Warner superiors and the owners of Poly-
Gram that the two record companies should merge. Though
PolyGram had never fully recovered from its misadventure with
Neil Bogart and was still deeply in the red, it had two strengths
that Warner lacked: a powerful overseas presence and a rich clas-
sical-music catalog. Warner, meanwhile, had a vaunted U.S. dis-
tribution system that in terms of overhead was twice as efficient as
PolyGram's. The merger seemed to make sense for both parties.

Goldman had come up with the merger idea in late 1982 after
flying to Hamburg with Elektra founder Jac Holzman, then a consultant to Warner, to discuss a different matter with PolyGram.
Philips, the half-owner of PolyGram, had introduced in 1979 a
new format called the compact disc. There was only one CD plant
extant, in Hanover, and it belonged to PolyGram. Warner believed
the compact disc had a future and wanted to negotiate a licensing
agreement under which PolyGram would manufacture its CDs.

Goldman and Holzman talked it over with Jan Timmer, who had taken charge of PolyGram International toward the end of 1981. Goldman had learned to be wary of PolyGram's European management. He had repeatedly turned down the head job at PolyGram U.S. after meeting the multinational's brain trust from Baarn and Hamburg. He found that Coen Solleveld "wasn't too bad." But Wolfgang Hix and Kurt Kinkele—*oy vay!* Much to his surprise, Goldman discovered that Jan Timmer was very different. "I was totally impressed with Timmer. He's very pragmatic. He kept saying, We've got to do things the American way in America."

Timmer was indeed a departure from his predecessors at PolyGram. A native of Holland, he was bald and solidly built and looked like a villain from a James Bond movie. Timmer was a company man. He joined Philips in 1952 as a twenty-seven-year-old accountant, and his last position before taking charge of PolyGram was chairman and chief executive of Philips South Africa. When Timmer was called in to replace Wolfgang Hix at the end of 1981 by an increasingly desperate Philips board of directors, PolyGram was in its third year of heavy losses in the United States. Though Timmer fancied himself a turnaround artist, PolyGram was quite a challenge.

Timmer was the furthest thing in the world from a record man, yet precisely what PolyGram needed. He was a professional manager who knew how to select strong people, when to delegate authority, and when not to. Financially speaking, he ran a tight ship. "You will always find, if you look at a company in trouble," he said in his clipped English, "that its control systems are not adequate. That's the reason very often why they got in trouble in the first place. I think that was a true assessment of PolyGram."

PolyGram's earnings would not return to the plus column until 1985. Even as the losses continued, Timmer approved large investments in compact disc technology. The CD was a priority for its inventor, Philips, which viewed the record business as the software supplier for its all-important stereo hardware. Had PolyGram not been a means to help introduce the CD, it is questionable whether Philips would have borne the financial losses as long as it did. Siemens, the German industrial giant that owned the other 50 percent of PolyGram, did not make stereos, and its impatience with the money-losing unit had reached a breaking point. Soon it would unload all but 10 percent of its PolyGram stock on Philips.

The CD became Timmer's pet project, and he believed in it when, as he put it, "many executives in the record industry saw it as yet another gimmick." Timmer deserves credit for the successful launch of the CD. Though an industry outsider, he contributed more to the music business in the eighties than many of his flashy counterparts at other companies. The CD, more than any factor aside from good music, would lift the industry's profits to new heights after years of stagnation.

After PolyGram, Warner was the label most enthusiastic about the compact disc. David Horowitz, who oversaw the Warner record division, had one of the first CD players, and he was convinced the format would catch on. So he was pleased to learn that Goldman and Holzman had worked out the CD licensing agreement with Timmer. While negotiating the deal, however, it had dawned on Goldman that a merger of Warner and PolyGram might make sense. The fit was self-evident, but such a deal would have been unthinkable with PolyGram's old, befuddled management. Timmer, however, seemed firmly in control.

After Warner Communications chairman Steve Ross approved the merger plan, Goldman and Horowitz became the point men for Warner. The negotiations were arduous, because the deal called for melding two large operations in the United States and two abroad. In addition, there was the issue of which Warner and PolyGram people would wear the cardinal hats in the merged company. Warner believed it should control the domestic operation, but there was never any doubt that Jan Timmer would be the head man overall.

The deal was formally announced on June 29, 1983. After working on the merger for six months, Goldman suggested early the following year that the Warner labels could use a high-level consultant to assist with the deal and other projects. Goldman had just the man in mind, someone he had once worked for who had broad knowledge of the record industry, but who was currently out of a job. Dick Asher.

Steve Ross was amenable to the idea, but asked Goldman to take a straw poll of the Warner label heads to see what they thought. On January 25, 1984, Goldman turned in his findings:

> Mo Ostin thinks that the idea of a consultant for this area is an excellent one and Dick Asher is an excellent choice for that role.

Ahmet Ertegun has high regard for Asher as a knowledgeable record business executive, but doesn't have a strong opinion one way or the other on his being used in this role. His only negative comment was that Yetnikoff told him that Asher had done "nothing" at CBS Records. Hardly a surprising comment, since Asher and Yetnikoff never got along. . . .

I haven't spoken to David Geffen . . . [but] I know that Geffen will be highly negative and critical of Asher on two counts. The first is that Dick was not a big supporter of [Yetnikoff's bid to have CBS distribute Geffen Records abroad], opposed a number of . . . extra-contractual advances made to Geffen by CBS, and was violently opposed to any five-year, $50 million new deal with Geffen. Asher is not viewed as a "creative" person by Geffen. While I would prefer that Geffen were a supporter of Asher, none of his negatives really are relevant to the consultancy role I am suggesting for Asher.

Goldman not only got Dick the consulting job, he tried to go one step further, suggesting to Jan Timmer that he hire Asher as an officer of Warner/PolyGram as soon as the merger closed. Timmer did not like the proposal. "He became furious," Goldman said. "I guess he had heard bad stories about Dick. There was absolutely no way, he would never consider it. And if I continued to raise the point, he was going to cancel the whole deal."

Since Asher was evidently not about to land a job working for Timmer, Goldman began to prevail on Steve Ross to hire Asher at Warner full time. It took a while, but in November 1984, Dick Asher was named senior vice-president of Warner Communications, reporting to Elliot Goldman. As SVP, Dick was, like Goldman, a glorified consultant with no real authority. He, Goldman, and former Columbia head Bruce Lundvall were now the highest-ranking CBS Records alumni to work for Yetnikoff's enemy. Dick found the experience eye-opening. "I saw a lot of things that they did differently than CBS," he said. The main thing: "Warner almost never fought with their artists."

Though Timmer evidently thought little of Asher, he was high on Goldman and assumed he would run the U.S. operation of the merged company. Goldman had applied himself diligently to the technical problems of combining two far-flung companies. Each time there were obstacles, Goldman came up with solutions, some of them ingenious. The deal was structured to create two joint ventures, one in the United States to be owned 80 percent by Warner, and one abroad, with ownership to be split down the middle.

But there was a hazard that no one, including Goldman, had foreseen: the all-out assault on the deal by Walter Yetnikoff. Its very suggestion made Walter seethe. His bitter feelings toward Warner were well known, and he didn't much care for PolyGram either, because of its part-German ownership. For some reason, Walter insisted on calling the company Polydor, the name of one of its labels. Once someone corrected him. "PolyGram, Polydor," Walter snapped. "Nazis all look the same to me."

If the merger succeeded, CBS Records would cease to be the largest and most powerful record company. Warner/PolyGram would have a U.S. market share of 26 percent, a full six or seven points above CBS. There was no way Walter would allow it. He began his attack on June 30, 1983, the day after the merger plans were announced. The deal was "patently illegal," he told *Billboard*, and would be scuttled on antitrust grounds. If the deal went through, however, CBS Records would counter by acquiring one of the other major labels. "I can't see how the government will permit this," Walter said. "But if the government does permit it, they're giving me the green light to set up an auction block and say, Who wants to sell?"

Warner knew it had to clear some antitrust hurdles. But, said David Horowitz, "we were more concerned about [the Cartel Office] in Germany. We didn't think that under current concepts of antitrust that the deal would run afoul of U.S. antitrust law." Horowitz, Timmer, and other advocates of the deal traveled to Berlin to testify before the German Cartel Office. Walter Yetnikoff went as well to argue against the deal, but the proponents won the day.

As Horowitz pointed out, it was hard to imagine that the U.S. Federal Trade Commission would object to the merger. Under President Reagan, the FTC had approved one megadeal after another. Besides, PolyGram was in such parlous condition that it could go out of business, which would be far more disruptive to the marketplace than a marriage with Warner.

But Yetnikoff had done a good job of marshaling the record industry against the merger. CBS hired attorneys to complain to the FTC, and a number of major wholesalers and rackjobbers, probably at Walter's instigation, joined in the fight. Yetnikoff went to Washington to argue the case in person.* And much to the surprise of Warner and PolyGram, the Federal Trade Commission filed suit in district court to stop the deal. "My guess," said attorney Eric Kronfeld, "is that absent CBS filing its petition, the FTC would not have given a damn." The FTC lost the first round in district court. But then the ninth circuit court of appeals overruled the decision and the merger was blocked, pending an FTC administrative trial.

Warner and PolyGram were simply stunned. Their high-powered law firms showered the appellate court with briefs and petitions. Experts were brought in to testify that the merger made sense, including economist Alan Greenspan, future chairman of the Federal Reserve, and Clive Davis. The briefs made public for the first time the extent of PolyGram's U.S. losses: $200 million between 1979 and 1982 alone. In 1983 PolyGram lost $6 million despite two huge hits: the soundtrack of *Flashdance* and Def Leppard's *Pyromania*. It expected to lose $15 million in 1984. "[PolyGram's] financial condition is now such that it can no longer compete effectively on its own," the company testified.

All the same, in October 1984, the ninth circuit upheld the FTC. "That was the kiss of death," said William Willis, PolyGram's antitrust counsel. Carrying on the legal fight would be at least a two-year battle, and no deal could survive that. Deeply disappointed, Jan Timmer railed against "the twisted logic of the American judicial system." The merger was finished. So was Elliot Goldman, who found life at Warner increasingly uncomfortable in the wake of the failed merger. After being "sliced up" politically, he quit in May 1985.

∎

Jan Timmer soon had a different problem on his hands. Should he appoint a new president of PolyGram's U.S. operation? When David Braun quit the job in 1981, he recommended that the presidency go to Guenter Hensler, the head of PolyGram's classical music division. Timmer agreed. Less than a year later, Timmer fired Harvey Schein, the hot-tempered former CBS man who chaired PolyGram Records. Schein was not replaced. This left Guenter Hensler in charge.

Hensler was an odd choice to run one of America's six major

---

* Walter reputedly told the chief attorney he planned to testify in Yiddish and demanded an interpreter. The FTC attorney thought he was serious.

pop companies. Though PolyGram owned three of the top classical music labels—Philips, London, and Deutsche Grammophon—the combined sales of Def Leppard, the Scorpions, and a few other hard rock acts on PolyGram outsold all the classics put together. This was where Hensler had to focus his attention, yet it was hard to believe he could listen to Def Leppard without wincing. Straight and slim, with curly blond hair, Hensler had studied to be a concert pianist, and as a record executive he hobnobbed with all the lions of the symphony hall.

Hensler never denied that hard rock, let alone pop music, was not his field. "It was not my youthful dream to be president of a pop music company in the United States," he said. "I consider myself a semi-expert on the classical side, but there was a phase of my life of almost fifteen years when I didn't listen to anything pop. I had an opportunity to hear the Beatles at Shea Stadium and I didn't go. I was just not interested."

In some ways, though, Hensler was a logical choice. PolyGram Records was numb from years of losses, and demoralized by the abrasive management style of Harvey Schein. Hensler was a soft-spoken gentleman. "I picked Guenter because he was a classy guy," David Braun said. Hensler held the German equivalent of an MBA and had a good grasp of accounting and finance. Furthermore, PolyGram Records did not need to add to its artist roster at the time—just the opposite.

But because Hensler lacked knowledge about the American pop market, and because he was a consensus manager, the people under him began to jockey for power. The biggest feud occurred between marketing head Harry Anger and promotion vice-president John Betancourt. Before long, Betancourt emerged as the clear winner. He was widely thought of as abrasive, abusive, arrogant, and angry—and those were just the a's—but Betancourt was also a talented promotion man. He got adds and bullets as PolyGram had never got them before. To the outside world, it often looked as though Betancourt, not Hensler, was running PolyGram.

It fell upon Hensler, however, to make the painful but necessary cutbacks. He trimmed the artist roster to about 80 acts from the company's peak of 250, shut warehouses in California and New Jersey, slashed the number of regional sales offices, and let go about 30 middle managers. He also sold Chappell Music, Poly-

Gram's prized publishing company, for about $100 million. It was bitter medicine, but it worked. By the third quarter of 1985, it looked as though PolyGram Records would squeak back into the black for the first time since 1978. It helped that PolyGram had a number one album, Tears for Fears' *Songs from the Big Chair*, and that John Cougar Mellencamp, on the company's Riva label, had become a big star with *Scarecrow*.

Despite the first faint signs of a financial turnaround, by the autumn of 1985 there were loud rumors in the industry that Timmer was planning to remove Hensler from his post. On October 16, Hensler got the news: He would go back to running the classical division, with some new duties in the audiovisual field.

Timmer explained afterward that Hensler had understood that his role as head of the pop company was temporary. Hensler confirmed this but was clearly stunned by the timing of his removal. After all, he had turned the company around. "I feel it is a good thing to make a change when things are going well, not when they are bad," Timmer said.

For twenty-four hours, the name of Hensler's replacement was a closely guarded secret. Everyone in the industry had a short list. Surely, Timmer would choose an American, and someone with experience running a pop label. It seemed the most likely candidate was the currently unemployed Elliot Goldman. The other name that surfaced was Al Teller, the head of Columbia.

On October 17, PolyGram Records put out a press release naming the new head of the company. Dick Asher.

Timmer, who had been so negative about Asher in early 1984, had changed his assessment. There were reasons for this. First of all, Timmer had subsequently seen Dick at work on the merger as a consultant and been impressed. More important, perhaps, Timmer had recently hired two former CBS people who were loyal to Asher. In 1984 he tapped Alain Levy, the head of CBS France, to run PolyGram France. Levy, a Wharton MBA, had been Dick's assistant in International. And in summer 1985, Maurice Oberstein was forcibly retired from CBS Records UK, and Timmer brought him over to run PolyGram in the UK. Insiders said Oberstein all but insisted that Dick Asher get Hensler's job.

Timmer had apparently soured on Elliot Goldman because of the merger debacle. In any case, in December 1985 Goldman was named the new president of RCA Records. "I was never offered PolyGram, but I should have been," Goldman said, a short time after landing at RCA. "Anyway, this is a better job."

It wasn't, though. RCA did not possess the fundamental—though long-hidden—strengths of PolyGram. The company had had two great assets: Elvis Presley and one of the nation's best-loved logos, Nipper the dog, cocking his head to the sound of "his master's voice." Elvis was dead and, inexplicably, Nipper was no longer in use. Lately, RCA didn't have much else to brag about, at least not in the pop field. Its one superstar pop act, Hall and Oates, had contracted to leave the label for Arista. Goldman's predecessor, Robert Summer, made overpriced deals for pop stars such as Diana Ross and Kenny Rogers. When Goldman joined, RCA was running a deficit. In 1986 RCA had to take back $25 million in unsold albums. For the fiscal year ending June 1987, the company lost $35 million.

Even worse, from Goldman's standpoint, was that General Electric acquired RCA Corporation, the parent company, in December 1985, the month he signed on. To help finance the take-over, GE immediately agreed to sell RCA Records and RCA's fifty percent stake in Arista to Bertelsmann. Goldman had worked for Bertelsmann once before, after the company bought Arista, and hadn't liked it. Now, the German owners were back.

Goldman did well by the company anyway. He brought in two executives who proved more than capable. The first was Rick Dobbis, the man who had sued Clive for slander, whom Goldman hired as executive vice-president. Then Goldman named Robert Buziak, a former artist manager, as head of RCA Records U.S. Buziak cut down the roster from forty acts to eleven and began to rebuild, concentrating on baby acts. Soon the company broke Bruce Hornsby and the Range, Rick Astley, and a number of rap artists. Buziak also authorized a $200,000 investment in the soundtrack album of *Dirty Dancing*, which, along with its sequel, sold more than 20 million copies worldwide. The financial results for the 1987-88 fiscal year showed a marked improvement: RCA made a $65 million profit.

Unfortunately, Goldman never got on with Michael Dornemann, the president of Bertelsmann Music Group. Dornemann felt he could do Goldman's job, and the pilot's seat could not accommodate them both. On September 10, 1987, Goldman was forced out. In a press statement, he said he "resigned" over "differences in management and operational philosophy." Fortunately for Goldman, he had a severance clause in his contract worth at least $1 million.

While Goldman was expendable, Clive Davis was not. His employment contract at Arista came up for renewal by Bertelsmann just as Whitney Houston became a smash, and she had a key-man clause pegged to Clive in *her* contract. "Clive, God bless him," Goldman said. "His timing is unbelievable."

Though Goldman had not been offered the PolyGram job, the rumor mill had correctly guessed the name of another contender, Columbia head Al Teller, whom Dick had rescued from oblivion and who subsequently shunned Asher in public after Walter fired him. The same month Dick took over PolyGram, October 1985, Teller was promoted to president of CBS Records U.S. It was a high-profile job with a lot of power.

Teller may have used PolyGram's prospective offer as leverage with CBS chief Thomas Wyman to get himself promoted. Walter did not like Teller. He had not wanted him in the first place; Al was Asher's man. Now, Teller, who was very ambitious, was starting to pose a threat to Walter, just as Dick had, and for the same reason. The suits upstairs appreciated Teller. He had an MBA, he kept regular hours, and he was far more corporate than Walter. Conscious of Walter's wariness, Teller made his moves in measured steps.

There was no disputing that Teller was highly competent—or that the rank and file of CBS Records hated his guts. Though deferential to Walter, Teller was tough on the rest of the company. "If you are a fierce competitor," he said of himself, "you want to beat the brains out of the other guy, because that's what you love doing." It was not lost on at least one staffer that Teller was the name of the man who invented the hydrogen bomb.

Meanwhile, having taken the PolyGram job, Dick Asher was on his way to reemerging as one of the record industry's top power brokers. His timing was exceptionally good. A little more than a year after he took over, PolyGram had the top album in the country, *Slippery When Wet*, by the hard rock group Bon Jovi. Though the band had been kicking around for a few years, no one had foreseen its sudden breakthrough to monster status. Though Dick later said he spotted the group's potential early in his reign, the industry did not take his word for it. At a charity dinner, emcee Joe Smith got a hearty laugh when he introduced Asher: "Truth be known, six months ago Dick thought Bon Jovi was a red Italian wine."

They could laugh all they wanted. Bon Jovi's album sold 8 million units. Dick had once said, "After you've finished being smart in the record business, you also have to be lucky." He had been both. Anyway, Bon Jovi was not the whole story of Poly-Gram's good fortune. Partly because of MTV, hard rock and heavy metal bands were enjoying a renaissance. With groups like Def Leppard, the Scorpions, and Rush, PolyGram was *the* heavy metal company.*

Meanwhile, the music-buying public had begun to go compact-disc crazy. It did not hurt that PolyGram had the world's richest classical catalog, since devotees of serious music were among the most ardent CD customers. The demand was amazing. A vinyl LP of, say, a Strauss tone poem that you could not sell for $3.99 retail flew off the racks as a CD costing four times that amount.

Dick had taken over PolyGram expecting to find a company shallow in executive talent but tight in structure. He found the opposite. "I was amazed at the lack of organization," he said. The most competent people were "running around trying to do everything." No one seemed to be able to define his job. Dick claimed he reorganized the company and made it more efficient. He also raided so many top people from CBS that PolyGram was soon dubbed "Columbia West." He brought in former Posse member Bob Jamieson as general manager and tapped Columbia's Dick Wingate to run PolyGram's A&R department. Dick said his greatest joy was giving a top finance job to Bill Fox, the twenty-year accounting veteran of CBS whom the company had fired, apparently for being an Asher loyalist.

Dick had come to PolyGram with a secret goal he called "three in three." He wanted PolyGram to finish a solid third in the United States, behind CBS and Warner, in three years. Largely because of Bon Jovi, he would achieve his goal a year early.

Ironically, had Walter Yetnikoff not torpedoed the merger of Warner and PolyGram, Dick would probably not have resurfaced

---

* It was no coincidence that the heavy metal band in the film spoof *This Is Spinal Tap* recorded for a fictitious company called "Polymer" Records.

as a label president. Walter was not pleased to see Dick back on top. "You know what I did the other day?" he told a reporter for *Rolling Stone*. "I decided I was mad at Polydor. Dickie Doo was bothering me. Nothing important, but annoying me. So I have an agenda item in the RIAA [Recording Industry Association of America]. . . . I want Polydor expelled!"

THE BOARD MEETING

■

THE abortive merger of Warner and PolyGram gave the record industry a lot to talk about. But a year later, in 1985, the power of the Network was the topic that dominated the corridor conversation.

The cost of independent promotion had become suffocating. After the industry blew its chance to abolish the Network in 1981, the promoters grew more powerful than ever, and their tabs went up accordingly. "The record industry has created a bastard child they can't control anymore," one artist manager said in late 1985. "It's gotten greedier and greedier, until even the big companies can't afford it."

At the time of the 1981 boycott, the Network was still affordable to all the majors and big independents and a means to keep small companies off the charts. By 1985 it was a game for only the highest of the high rollers: CBS Records. Perhaps Warner's flagship label had enough volume to afford the stakes as well. But Mo Ostin had become increasingly opposed to the use of indie promo men; his senior vice-president of promotion, Russ Thyret, used them sparingly. In 1985 Warner Bros. spent $6 million on indie promotion. Walter Yetnikoff said CBS's tab was $12.8 million, more than double. *Rolling Stone* estimated that CBS in fact spent closer to $17 million in 1985.

Even if $12.8 million was correct, it is inconceivable that CBS Records earned back anywhere near that amount through the use of indie promotion. The figure was almost 10 percent of CBS Records' total pretax profits. But it gave Walter power over his peers, and that seemed to justify the cost. If Walter needed another motive to remain a supporter of independent promotion, one could not discount his personal relationship with Fred Di-Sipio.

With the stakes at an all-time high, the indies were a weapon that Walter could wield over his two biggest rivals for power, David Geffen and Irving Azoff. Geffen had used independent promotion heavily when he began Geffen Records; Joe Isgro bragged that he had helped break the Geffen group Quarterflash in 1981. But lately, according to sources close to him, Geffen had found the Network too powerful and too expensive.

Irving Azoff, president of MCA Records, had become publicly critical of indie promotion. In the summer of 1985, Azoff yanked MCA's advertisements from *Radio & Records*, complaining, among other things, that the magazine had just added twenty new Top 40 stations to its survey. According to Azoff, this proved that *R&R* "condones the independent promotion system" because "the more stations that report to *R&R*, the more stations that can be under the sway of independent promotion, so the more money it costs record companies to break a new record." It was a fatuous remark. *R&R* publisher Bob Wilson deplored the Network and wished he could alter his charts without ruining their legitimate usefulness. If anyone appeared to condone indie promotion, it was Irv Azoff. MCA spent nearly $9 million on the service in 1985, the biggest outlay of any company after CBS. Even as Azoff attacked the Network promoters, he was using them heavily.

Azoff knew, however, that MCA could not afford to spend that kind of money for long; only CBS could. At least twice he accused Walter Yetnikoff of deliberately supporting the indie system for anticompetitive reasons—once in *Esquire* and once under oath. The magazine reported: "Irving Azoff . . . charges that Yetnikoff tried to 'corner the market' on indies by hiking fees to the point where smaller labels wouldn't be able to afford them." In a pretrial deposition, Azoff said that Walter "once told me that one reason CBS supported the indie system was that he felt it made the cost of entry for, shall we say, new upstart labels [too] high to get into the record business."

If so, Walter was not the only one to support the system for this reason. Companies such as Irving Azoff's MCA were equally happy to "corner the market" at the expense of smaller labels. It only became insupportable for them when they, too, were bid out of the auction. Now resolved to do away with the Network, or at least reduce its cost, the labels faced a dilemma. If the heads of the companies got together and mutually agreed to stop using the indies, the promoters would have grounds for an antitrust suit. Of course, the record companies could drop them for violating the payola statute—but the labels were not supposed to know this was happening. Meanwhile, each label was afraid to initiate a boycott in a unilateral move, mindful of what had happened to Warner in 1981.

One possible solution was a government probe. In 1984 it appeared that one or more disgruntled labels tried to provoke a Congressional investigation into the Network. The House Subcommittee on Oversight and Investigations, headed by Michigan Democrat John Dingell, began a preliminary investigation. It went nowhere and was soon dropped. Tennessee Democrat Albert Gore was a member of that subcommittee. He told the press that the investigation had failed because of a "conspiracy of silence" among label executives, and said he believed some potential witnesses feared physical harm.

By the late fall of 1985, the grumbling over the cost of indies echoed throughout the record business. On October 1, the Recording Industry Association of America discussed the problem at its regularly scheduled board meeting. Evidently, at least three record companies—MCA, Motown, and Arista—suggested that the RIAA conduct an investigation into whether indies were engaged in payola. This might provide an out. If the RIAA came up with evidence of misconduct, all the record companies could feign surprise and outrage and suspend use of indie promotion without being susceptible to an antitrust suit. Though the essence of hypocrisy, the plan was a shrewd one.

The RIAA was a trade group for record companies only; no retailers, no radio stations. Its main function was certifying records gold and platinum and issuing the awards that papered the industry's walls. The RIAA board consisted of two full-time officials— chairman Stanley Gortikov, a past president of Capitol Records, and general counsel Joel Schoenfeld—along with twenty-four label heads.

At the October 1, 1985, board meeting, the RIAA passed the following resolution:

> The RIAA should fund and, through its general counsel [Schoenfeld], direct a private investigation to determine

whether or not the conduct of independent promotion involves or results in criminal violations or other violations of federal regulations or law.

The vote was twenty-three to three. One of the nay votes came from CBS. Walter Yetnikoff was not present; his most trusted aide, executive vice-president Seymour Gartenberg, stood in for him. Two days before the meeting, at Yetnikoff's request, Gartenberg had drafted a file memo laying out several reasons why CBS would oppose an investigation. Gartenberg voiced these reasons at the meeting. Later, *The Wall Street Journal*, which had obtained the confidential RIAA minutes, paraphrased what Gartenberg had said: He "strenuously objected to the investigation, contending that CBS's internal reviews had disclosed no improprieties and that any industrywide examination of the promoters might in itself constitute an illegal group boycott in violation of the antitrust laws."

When the resolution passed anyway, Yetnikoff fumed. He said he was upset because Gartenberg came back and complained that the RIAA had changed its voting procedures at the last minute from an open ballot to a secret ballot. "You know I have a temper. . . . [Seymour] came back and said, they changed the vote, [and] I said, Fuck 'em all." Walter also said he doubted the sincerity of the resolution. "I was pretty sure that the motivation was *not* illegality," but rather that "the independents were charging too much, some of the smaller companies couldn't pay, and they'll try to find a way to lower the prices that the independent promoters charge."

Walter disparaged the way the RIAA passed resolutions in any case. He said it reminded him of the Israeli parliament. "It's a little bit like the Knesset, where one guy says, [Yiddish accent] Fuck you, I knew your father in Russia, he's a dirty bum. And one guy's wearing a yarmulke, this guy wears a tallith. He's a dirty bum then, he's a dirty bum now. And the prime minister says, Will you guys shut up, we got work to do. That's what an RIAA meeting sounds like."

All the same, Walter said, in a few days his anger had subsided. By mid-October Walter had a talk with RIAA chairman Stan Gortikov and RCA Records chief Bob Summer. Gortikov supported the investigation; Summer's position is not known. As Walter recounted the meeting: "So I said, You know what? I got over my momentary spurt of anger. Let's go ahead with it. It would be the wrong thing to stop it. But I want all these issues addressed: Who's gonna do it; how are you gonna do it? I'm not gonna go along with Watergate break-ins." Walter said he recommended that the investigation be guided by the RIAA's legal committee, on which he served.

On November 4, RIAA general counsel Joel Schoenfeld sent a memo to all members of the legal committee, which would convene three days later at MCA Records' New York office. Schoenfeld wrote that "a number" of label executives had recommended that the legal committee run the investigation, and that he had "accepted this advice." Schoenfeld had done some research to identify the specific crimes of which independent promoters might conceivably be guilty. These included payola, wire fraud, mail fraud, racketeering, extortion, and blackmail. Schoenfeld said he would personally collect information from each company on its indie promotion practices. He promised that all data would be kept confidential and said he could assert attorney-client privilege should anyone attempt to subpoena his findings. The RIAA board, he added, would use the data "to determine whether or not there is a need for civil litigation or the filing of complaints with appropriate government agencies."

Schoenfeld made another proposal that was more controversial. He said he expected to hire "outside investigators to conduct discreet inquiries into the relationship between independent promoters, radio station personnel, and trade publication staff." He listed four private eye firms the committee might wish to choose from, including Wells Fargo and Pinkerton.

The idea was shot down at the meeting. Walter was one who voiced opposition. "They were going to use all sorts of sleazy tactics," he later complained. "Sting operations, parabolic listening devices, gumshoes—you know, private detectives." Another proposal made at the November 7 meeting *was* adopted: For the investigation to proceed, all the companies had to agree to participate. There would be a vote at the next executive board meeting, scheduled for January 23, 1986.

Dick Asher did not attend the November 7 legal committee meeting; he was not a member. Asher had been president of PolyGram for less than three weeks, and had not been to any RIAA meeting since his firing from CBS. Now, Dick would fill Guenter Hensler's spot on the RIAA executive board, which was made up of all the label presidents. Dick had already been made aware that Guenter had agreed to support the October resolution to investigate the indie promoters. Despite Asher's long crusade against the indies, one of his first acts was to have PolyGram's lawyers tell the RIAA that the record company did *not* want to participate.

RIAA chief Stan Gortikov was no doubt surprised that Dick, of all people, should oppose the resolution. The whole industry knew where Asher stood on indie promotion. But ever since the failed boycott, Dick had become exceedingly paranoid about the Network. In particular, he could not get out of his mind that the promoters had knocked the Loverboy single "Turn Me Loose" off the air, which he had interpreted as a personal message. Both of his confrontations with the Network, first with Pink Floyd, then the boycott, had ended in his being publicly humiliated. Dick had come to believe that maybe the Network was omnipotent.

When Gortikov dropped by Dick's office to find out why he did not support the investigation, Asher gave him his reasons. As he recalled the meeting: "I said, Look, Stan, the RIAA is not an investigatory body. If the government is willing to do it, wonderful. It's not something we can do well. And even more than that, on a personal level, I got a pretty bloody nose the last time around. I'm walking into a company that's not terribly healthy, and I sort of figure [the promoters are] watching me. And I have better things to do than pick a fight with somebody who could bury us very quickly. It could be a recipe for a funeral."

Dick went on to explain why he believed the RIAA could not conduct a successful investigation. "I don't think we can maintain any kind of security," he told Gortikov. "Whatever we discuss gets to those guys in five minutes." Gortikov had to agree. He told Dick that someone on the legal committee—no one knew who it was— had given Fred DiSipio the confidential November 7 memo, listing the private eye firms the RIAA might consider hiring. That clinched it for Dick Asher: The idea of an RIAA investigation was "ludicrous." *

So Asher went to the January 23 board meeting expecting to vote against the investigation. He was aware that the vote had to be unanimous, and he had told Gortikov that if PolyGram were

---

* Gortikov did not explain how he knew DiSipio had the memo. But a few months later, Joe Isgro described its contents to *Billboard*. The publication noted that Isgro "declin[ed] to reveal how he obtained the proposal."

the one holdout, he would change his stance. It turned out not to be necessary. Jerry Moss, the chairman of A&M Records, voted against the proposal, and so did Jack Craigo, the president of Chrysalis Records, which was distributed by CBS. A reliable source on the RIAA board claimed that Craigo initially had voted in favor of the investigation, but had changed his mind under "CBS pressure." Craigo denied this. The source also claimed that the details of the January meeting were "known by Fred DiSipio within hours of its conclusion."

When a reporter subsequently asked Yetnikoff whether the rumor was true that he had stopped the investigation, Walter accurately described what had happened at the meeting. PolyGram, A&M, and Chrysalis had voted it down. "And since three companies refused to join in the unanimous requirement," he explained, "the thing fell of its own accord. And I said, I am still voting for it. Now, does that sound like I stopped it?"

At the time the RIAA was considering an investigation of the Network, Walter Yetnikoff was having papers drawn up to give Fred DiSipio a custom label on CBS. It was to be called Empire Records, and DiSipio would own the label with manager Tommy Mottola. Naturally, Allen Grubman would represent Empire. Mottola was Allen Grubman's closest friend, one of Walter's inner circle, and the manager of Hall and Oates, John Mellencamp, and Carly Simon. The manager had long been a close friend of Fred DiSipio's. Danny Davis described Mottola and DiSipio as "the hand inside the glove."

That Allen Grubman, the industry's most powerful attorney, was planning to become the lawyer for Fred DiSipio was not common knowledge. One man who did know about it, however, was Jon Landau, the manager of Bruce Springsteen.

Landau, a former rock critic, had selected Grubman to represent Springsteen in 1983, partly on the advice of his "rabbi," David Geffen. Landau had left journalism to manage Springsteen in 1973. One of his final articles, for *Rolling Stone*, was an essay on industry ethics, written in the wake of Clive Davis's dismissal from CBS. Landau wrote, in part:

> Not only is payola a crime, it taints everyone associated with it, inevitably inviting the participation of organized crime and the dispensing of money and goods. Payola laws should thus be strengthened and rigorously enforced, and

record companies should recognize the practice as a blight on the industry.

By 1985 Landau had a good idea who Fred DiSipio was, having met him on a number of occasions. He was not pleased with the idea of Springsteen's lawyer brokering a label deal for DiSipio, but he was prepared to live with it. Asked recently whether he should have demanded that Grubman drop the Empire project, Landau sounded stung by the implied criticism. "First of all," Landau said, "I don't have a general inclination to tell [Grubman] who his clients should be. I don't see that as my particular role in life. What I'm concerned with is, how's he doing for us. But it so happens that in this particular case, I absolutely told him that it was a crazy thing to do, to take his friend Mottola and put him in business with DiSipio and Yetnikoff. That combination just did not sound healthy. . . . But I don't see that it was my job to make a decision to fire him for that particular reason."

As it turned out, however, the Empire deal did not close anyway. In February 1986, shortly before the papers were to be signed, Fred DiSipio became the brunt of some very bad publicity.

271

THE EVENING NEWS

■

"THIS block on First Avenue on the Lower East Side of New York is a stronghold of the Gambino Mafia family. . . ."

With these words, TV journalist Brian Ross kicked off a story on *NBC Nightly News* entitled "The New Payola." It was February 24, 1986, one month after the RIAA probe of independent promoters had flickered out. Now, any such probe was pointless. Ross and his producer, Ira Silverman, had uncovered the ugly secrets of indie promotion on their own, and were presenting them to a national television audience.

Ross and Silverman had been one of the top investigative news teams in television since 1980, when they broke the ABSCAM story, about an FBI sting operation to expose corrupt congressmen. Since then, they had won a sheaf of awards. They were also responsible for the biggest libel judgment in history: $19.2 million awarded by a Las Vegas jury to singer Wayne Newton, later reduced to a still-record $5.3 million. The jury found that NBC News had falsely implied that Newton bought a Las Vegas hotel with mob money, even though the story by Ross and Silverman contained no such assertion. (The verdict is currently on appeal.)

The payola story originated with some sketchy leads from law enforcement sources and an unfamiliar name. The Los Angeles Police Department had its eye on Joseph Isgro and discovered that he spoke regularly to a certain "Piney," someone important. Who was he? Gradually, the LAPD figured out that Piney was Joseph Armone, an underboss in the Gambino family. With that information, Ross and Silverman knew they were on to a big story.

There were FBI photos of Armone but no film footage. So Silverman holed up in an unmarked van in front of one of Armone's favorite hangouts, the DeRobertis pastry shop on lower First Avenue, squinting through a viewfinder, waiting. Ross stationed himself across the street, in an apartment belonging to gypsies. At the end of a long day, they had the shots of Armone that opened the news segment.

> . . . According to the FBI and New York City police [Ross's narration continued], the Mafia *capo* who runs things on this block and in places far from this block is Joseph Armone. . . . For months now, the activities of Armone and others have been watched closely by the FBI and police as far away as Los Angeles as part of an investigation of corrupt practices in the rock music business and what appears to be the reemergence of payola. . . .

From the gritty Lower East Side, the story moved to the luxurious Waldorf-Astoria hotel on Park Avenue. It was January 23. Earlier that day, the RIAA board had convened and decided to drop the indie probe. That night in the grand ballroom of the Waldorf, the top names of the record industry gathered for the first annual Rock and Roll Hall of Fame dinner. The music business, in one of its fits of self-aggrandizement, planned to construct a Hall of Fame Museum in Cleveland to commemorate rock stars and industry legends. This evening, the first inductees—including Ray Charles, Jerry Lee Lewis, and the late Elvis Presley—would be honored. The NBC lens zoomed in. . . .

> . . . among the guests, two of the most powerful and feared men in the rock music business: Joseph Isgro, who, authorities say, has described Mafia *capo* Armone as his partner; and Isgro's close associate, Fred DiSipio, who rarely does business without *his* associate, Mike, by his side. . . .

There, large as life in a sea of dinner jackets, were Isgro and DiSipio—and, larger than life, Big Mike, the bodyguard, in what appeared to be a size-seventy tux.

> . . . DiSipio and Isgro, each with his own company, are top men in what is called the Network . . . independent record

promoters who, industry executives say, are getting millions
of dollars a year from record companies. . . .

Though for months industry people supplied information to
Ross and Silverman, the newsmen were unable to persuade any of
them to go on camera. At last they found a willing subject in Don
Cox, a popular disc jockey at WINZ in Miami, also known as I-95.
Cox had been arrested in 1980 for selling cocaine to an undercover
cop and convicted a year later. He had since donated his services
to drug outreach programs. With cameras rolling, Ross asked Cox
how indie promoters had tempted him with cash and cocaine, and
the DJ reenacted a meeting:

> Cox: Here, take this ounce . . . of cocaine. Couple of
> thousand dollars. . . . And I'll give you a call Tues-
> day.
> Ross: And what happens Tuesday?
> Cox: They call you and go, How was that? By the way, I
> got this record I want you to hear. Now, if you take
> it, you gotta answer the phone.
> Ross: They cozy up and they corrupt?
> Cox [with a laugh]:   It's their *job*.

About seventy-two hours after the broadcast, Don Cox was
leaving the radio station when he was jumped by four men wield-
ing sawed-off baseball bats, razor blades, and a pistol. He went
back on the air on March 4 from a hospital bed, assuring listeners
that "the reports of my demise have been greatly exaggerated."
Cox told *Rolling Stone* that he was savagely beaten and that one
of the assailants said he "shouldn't have such a big mouth on TV."
Brian Ross was fairly certain, however, that Cox's mugging was
not related to indie promotion.

Neither Fred DiSipio nor Joe Isgro was interviewed for the
February 24 story, but viewers were treated to pictures taken of
them *sub rosa*. DiSipio was shown locking up his Mercedes in the
parking lot beside his Cherry Hill, New Jersey, office suite. Isgro
was filmed driving his cream-colored Rolls-Royce along a Los Angeles freeway, a cigarette dangling from his lips, seated beside
bodyguard Bruce Pond.

The NBC camera crew then followed Isgro as he strolled with

Walter Lee, vice-president of promotion at Capitol Records.* The two men were en route to a Hollywood restaurant, Simply Blues, for a private business lunch. Trailing them, with a blank expression, was big, beefy Bruce Pond.

. . . Isgro, shown here with a record company executive, is well known in the music business, and so is his bodyguard [the lens zoomed in on Pond]. But of ten record company presidents contacted by NBC News, including the heads of such major labels as CBS, Warner, RCA, MCA, none would agree to talk on camera about Isgro or DiSipio, or the network of independent promoters, some saying they feared repercussions. . . .

Next, Ross interviewed Jay McDaniel, the former disc jockey who had been menaced by a Network promoter when he attempted to create an indie promo company.

Ross: Were there threats of violence against you?
McDaniel: Yes.
Ross: What was said to you?
McDaniel: It basically came out that I could have my face rearranged.

The final segment of the story was the most dramatic, and the result of an incredible stroke of luck. On January 23, the night of the Hall of Fame dinner, Ross and Silverman attempted to locate Joe Isgro. They assumed he would fly to New York for the black-tie gala and stay at a deluxe hotel. So they phoned around asking for Isgro and located him at the Helmsley Palace, just two blocks from the Waldorf. Coincidentally, Ira Silverman, who worked out of the NBC bureau in Washington, D.C., was also staying at the Helmsley.

Early that evening, Silverman was in his room at the hotel, and Ross was waiting for him in the lobby. Suddenly, Ross was startled to see the new Gambino family boss, John Gotti, heading

* Walter Lee would leave Capitol in March 1987 after being sued for battery by Bill Bartlett, one of his staffers. Bartlett alleged that on four occasions, Lee shocked and burned him with an electric cattle prod, declaring, "You're dog meat; go back to your stall," and "If you don't get airplay . . . you'll get more of this."

his way. Gotti circled the bank of elevators and shook hands with a little old man Ross recognized as Joseph N. Gallo, the Gambino *consigliere*.* Ross phoned Silverman and told him to get down to the lobby, pronto.

Ross began to move toward Gotti through the crowded lobby. Presently, the two mafiosi were joined by Gotti's doomed underboss, Frank DeCicco, who in three months would be blown to bits by a car bomb. Within earshot of Ross, Gallo said to Gotti, Joe's got a suite upstairs you can use. Joe who? Ross wondered as the three Gambino men went up in the penthouse elevator.

Moments later, Ross received another jolt. Two more men with familiar faces left the Helmsley bar and entered the lobby, deep in conversation: Joe Armone and Joe Isgro. Right behind them were Isgro's two bodyguards, David Michael Smith and Bruce Pond. The foursome went up the same penthouse elevator taken by Gotti, Gallo, and DeCicco.

By this time, Silverman had joined Ross in the lobby, and the two journalists stood there, dumbfounded. They had a camera crew waiting in a van outside, ready to accompany them to the Hall of Fame dinner at the Waldorf. Had they known what would unfold before their eyes, they would have arranged a hidden camera in the lobby. Scrambling to make up for a lost opportunity, the newsmen phoned for two extra camera crews to rush to the hotel.

Fortunately, the Helmsley drama was not over. Minutes after Isgro and Armone went upstairs, Isgro came back down with his bodyguards. Then a stretch limo pulled up to the door, and out stepped Fred DiSipio and three associates: promoters Ron Kyle and Matty "the Humdinger" Singer, and Big Mike. With them were some young women, possibly their dinner dates. Isgro and DiSipio greeted one another, and the three bodyguards, Mike, Bruce, and Dave, hugged and kissed.

Isgro went over to the hotel phone, and Ross trailed him. The promoter had never set eyes on Brian Ross before, and did not notice him eavesdropping. Isgro phoned his employee Ralph Tashjian, who also had a room at the Helmsley. Come down and join us, Isgro told Tashjian. It'll be good for you. Tashjian did as

---

* Not to be confused with Profaci family soldier "Crazy Joe" Gallo, who was executed mob-style in a Manhattan clam house in 1972.

told. In about ten minutes, Gambino underboss Frank DeCicco returned to the lobby and gathered up the promotion group: Isgro, DiSipio, Tashjian, Kyle, and the bodyguards. Matty Singer was left behind with the women. DeCicco, a huge man, packed the promoters and their big bodyguards into the elevator. Ross, who had a reputation for fearlessness, chose not to follow them. "It didn't seem healthy," he said later.

By then, the extra camera crews had begun arriving, in time to get shots of DiSipio entering the hotel. In about forty-five minutes, DiSipio and his entourage left the Helmsley for the rock and roll dinner, and the cameras captured them again. Meanwhile, Isgro returned to the lobby with David Michael Smith, the bodyguard, and went to the hotel safe deposit. He extracted a brown paper parcel the approximate length and breadth of U.S. paper currency, then went back upstairs.

Some minutes later, Gotti, Armone, DeCicco, and Gallo returned to the lobby. Seizing his chance, Ross directed a camera crew to film the four mobsters through the plate-glass window. When the Helmsley doorman objected, Ross barked at him, Do you know who you have in there? It's John Gotti! The doorman retreated.

Around this time, the hotel drama became something of a Keystone Cops comedy. Though Ross and Silverman did not know John Gotti would show up at the Helmsley, the FBI and the New York State Organized Crime Task Force apparently did. Acting at cross purposes, both agencies had sent an undercover cop to the hotel. The agents quickly recognized one another, then found themselves dodging an NBC camera crew to avoid appearing on the evening news. Within minutes, Frank DeCicco spied the agents and the camera; it may have dawned on him that he was participating in the least secret mob meeting in history.

Meanwhile, the Hall of Fame dinner was in progress, and Ira Silverman had followed DiSipio to the Waldorf with a camera crew. Ross waited for Isgro to leave the Helmsley. With the additional film of the promoters at the rock dinner, the newsmen had more than enough footage for their story. The shots of John Gotti and his soldiers, taken through window glass, were of poor quality, but the men were identifiable. Ross and Silverman had missed filming Frank DeCicco gathering the promotion men and Isgro and Armone together. Still, Ross had *seen* the events transpire; he could now state unequivocally in his story that Isgro and DiSipio had met mobsters.*

> ... Just how important the rock music business is to the Mafia became clear last month at this New York City hotel. Joseph Armone, the man from the pastry shop, arranged an unusual meeting with the top three men in the Gambino Mafia family, including the Gambino family boss, John Gotti —in the view of the FBI, a mob summit meeting. Also observed here: Joseph Isgro . . . and Fred DiSipio. . . . One hour after meeting top people in the American Mafia, Isgro and DiSipio were at the Waldorf, taking their places among the top people in the American music business.

With that, Brian Ross signed off. The story had run just under seven minutes, an eternity by evening news standards.

Though stunned by the unprecedented frankness of the NBC story, and publicly outraged, much of the record industry rejoiced in private. Ross and Silverman had done the business an incalculable favor. Now, it had the best of both worlds. The industry could unleash a paroxysm of righteous indignation—how *dare* NBC suggest the rock business was corrupt to the core!—yet use the controversy to drive a stake through the heart of the indie promo monster it had created.

At first, Walter Yetnikoff appeared to regard the NBC story as a joke. He and other top executives of the business gathered in Los Angeles on February 25, one day after the telecast, for the Grammy Awards. Late that evening, following the ceremony, Joe Isgro was a guest at the CBS Records party. When he entered the room, on Walter's instructions, the band struck up the theme to *The Godfather.* Two days later, a federal grand jury in New York, under the direction of U.S. Attorney Rudolph Giuliani, began to subpoena documents related to indie promotion, first from the RIAA, then from the labels. No one had any doubt that the grand jury inquiry had been spurred by the NBC telecast. It wasn't funny anymore.

Because the Grammys brought all the label heads together,

* Further evidence that the promoters conferred with Gotti surfaced after the NBC story aired. The FBI had bugged Gotti's social club in Queens a few days after the Helmsley meeting and heard him discuss the record business.

the RIAA had scheduled a board meeting for the morning after, Wednesday, February 26. The topic on everyone's mind was the NBC broadcast. Originally, the meeting had been set for 10:00 A.M., but because the post-Grammy parties dragged on till the small hours, it was rescheduled for noon. Unfortunately, no one had bothered to tell Dick Asher about the time change; he was booked on an early flight out of Los Angeles and was able to attend only the first few minutes.

As Asher recalled, RIAA chairman Stan Gortikov said he was being bombarded with phone calls from the press demanding comment on the NBC story. What should he say? Almost on cue, Elliot Goldman, the new president of RCA Records, whipped out a statement he had prepared for his own company and read it aloud. Other board members began to suggest changes in the wording. "Whereupon," Asher recalled, "I said, I'm sorry fellas, I have to leave. Whatever you work out, just send me a copy in New York, and if it's okay, I'll let you know."

Asher never had a chance to give his approval, however, for the next morning, the RIAA issued its official statement. If the release bore Elliot Goldman's handiwork, it was not one of his finer moments. Goldman, after all, once rebuked the record industry in a keynote convention speech for pouring "$50 million or $60 million a year into a marketing technique [indie promotion] that doesn't pass the smell test." Yet the RIAA statement read, in full:

> We have no knowledge that any firm or individual with whom our companies do business is engaged in any illegal activity, contrary to reports in recent televised network broadcasts. If law enforcement agencies were to inform us that such individuals or firms are engaged in any illegal activities, we will [sic] take immediate and decisive corrective action. Until such time, we find it unjustified and distressing that the recording industry is so indiscriminately maligned by insidious innuendo. Such broad and unspecific charges unfairly taint the innocent. They also detract from the monumental contributions of the industry to American and international humanitarian and charitable causes.

Despite the "insidious innuendo," a phrase worthy of Spiro Agnew, Capitol and MCA Records announced the same day that they would drop all use of indie promoters immediately. Early the following week, the Warner labels, RCA, and Arista did the same. This left PolyGram, Chrysalis, and A&M—the three companies that had voted against the RIAA investigation—and CBS. On March 5, the remaining four labels announced they, too, were no longer using indie promo men. The ban was complete.

■

"Cocksuckers!"

Joe Isgro was not taking it well. As one record label after another terminated his services, he saw his multimillion-dollar company going down the drain. Isgro spoke to several reporters in the dark days following the NBC broadcast. To one, he said, "I'm destroyed. My whole business was ruined by insidious innuendo." To another, he kept repeating, "Where is my crime?" He seemed genuinely baffled. He had built up his company using lawyers, accountants, independent contractors—everything a legitimate businessman was supposed to do. To one observer, Isgro was Jay Gatsby. "In his own mind," he said, "Isgro was doing things the American way."

"I've worked twenty years to build this," Isgro said. "I started from the bottom of the fucking pile here. I got out of Vietnam, I fucking got into this business, I've worked hard all my life, never been arrested in my entire fucking life. I've acquired the American Dream here. And by one guy [Brian Ross] coming on, not saying anything, he destroys my entire business. Absolutely *devastates* my fucking business.

"This is Elliot Goldman's statement, and I quote: 'We know of no wrongdoing in the activities of the independent promotion firms we retain. However, as a major distributor of recorded music, we are concerned about the perception of our industry by the public.'

"Okay. Well, you know, this is really nice. The *perception* is that Isgro and DiSipio and the other indie promoters are little Italian guys sitting in a phone booth collecting hundred-dollar bills all day. I got thirty people over here, which I got to leave go twenty fucking people tomorrow because of this. Why? What have I done wrong? Where's my fucking crime? Somebody tell me what my fucking crime is here.

"You know what? Me, I don't care for me. I don't give a *fuck*. I'm a tough kid from the streets, I've been in Vietnam. It's the pregnant girl working on the switchboard. And it's the people that have worked here hard all their fucking lives are gonna be out of fucking jobs here. You know what I mean? For what?

"This is a major, major *smear* campaign. They show a mobster meeting held where nowhere in the picture am I at. And don't show pictures of me going to lunch with Walter Lee! For chrissake, what's my job? What's *his* job? Where is the sin? What have I done? Don't put my fucking picture on television, marching around, 'most feared man in the music business.' Most feared man! Call a lot of people. I could give you five hundred people to call. Call 'em up, ask them how *feared* I am. Ask how many people I've *helped* in this goddamn business.

"How do you think that makes my family feel? What effect does that have on my fucking family? You talk about organized crime in this country, let me tell you who the organized criminals in this fucking country are. It's the fucking press! I'm gonna tell you—right now go on record with you—they're rotten no-good cocksuckers. They're the criminals. That's organized crime in this fucking country, I'm gonna tell you that right there."

Joe Isgro had problems apart from the loss of business. Around the time of the NBC report, a prosecutor with the Los Angeles Organized Crime Strike Force, Marvin Rudnick, began the early stages of a payola investigation that would include Isgro as a target. Isgro believed it was no coincidence that the strike force and the news media had developed an interest in indie promotion at the same time. He had a theory that a certain top label executive was a behind-the-scenes player in both the NBC story and the government investigation. That man, he insisted, was MCA Records chief Irving Azoff.

Isgro's theory was not as outlandish as it might sound. Azoff had two distinct motives to do as Isgro suggested. The first was common to all companies but CBS—the Network game had become too expensive to play. The second motive was to divert attention from MCA Records to the indie promo men. For at that very moment, Azoff and MCA had problems with both the L.A. strike force and the news media as a result of another mob-related scandal—the one that would send Morris Levy to jail.

It began in 1983 when an alleged Gambino family soldier from New York, Salvatore "Sal the Swindler" Pisello, left his job as consultant to a frozen-pizza company and began working out of the offices of MCA Records in Los Angeles. How he wound up at the record company is not known; what he did for MCA *is* known.

THE DEPUTY AND THE PRESIDENT...CONTINUED

In 1984, for example, Pisello took a $100,000 consulting fee to test-market break-dancing mats. The venture bombed.

Around the same time, Pisello orchestrated the sale of almost 5 million MCA cutout records and tapes to a Philadelphia wholesaler, John LaMonte, using Morris Levy as a middleman. The shipment was supposed to include albums by former MCA stars, including the Who and Elton John, but someone—probably Levy and Pisello—skimmed the cream, leaving LaMonte with truckloads of *schlock* by unknown artists. When LaMonte refused to pay for the shipment, Levy's partner, Gaetano "the Big Guy" Vastola, smashed his face. Levy and Vastola were tried and convicted on extortion charges in Newark. The cutout deal, according to the prosecutor in the Levy case, was "an organized crime concept from day one," though it was never clear how all the mob figures involved were going to profit from the transaction.

Pisello was not charged in the LaMonte beating, but he had other legal problems. In 1980 he was a suspect in an alleged scheme to import heroin from Italy in live lobster tanks. The drug shipment never came off, but the government wound up with evidence to nail Pisello for tax fraud. The case fell to Marvin Rudnick, the L.A. strike force prosecutor, who happened to be a tax specialist. Rudnick won a conviction in 1985. Pisello drew a two-year sentence, though he stayed out of jail on appeal and continued working for MCA Records. As soon as Rudnick learned that Pisello had a consulting job at MCA, his hackles were raised. Pisello had no experience in the music business. What was he doing at a major record company?

Rudnick considered several theories. Pisello was a career con man—he wasn't called "Sal the Swindler" for nothing—and might have duped MCA. There was another possibility. Irv Azoff had called upon Morris Levy to help MCA obtain some important rock acts and a catalog of vintage rock and roll masters. Was there a *quid pro quo*, a verbal agreement between Irving and Morris to install Sal Pisello at MCA? Did Azoff realize that the MCA cutouts handled by Pisello would be used in a racketeering scheme? These were provocative questions that could leave MCA itself vulnerable to racketeering charges.

Rudnick was determined to find answers, and in November 1985, he got the green light from the Justice Department to convene a grand jury in L.A. Pisello was a target, but so was Azoff. The grand jury began investigating Azoff's finances in a search for "potential criminal tax and other related violations," according to an IRS memorandum.

Rudnick had no sooner begun his MCA/Pisello probe when two organized crime specialists from the Los Angeles Police Department made an appointment to see him to discuss payola. They may well have been the same LAPD officers who tipped off Ross and Silverman. Rudnick discovered that the two officers had been made aware of indie promotion by an LAPD cop named John St. John, whose former partner was the head of security at MCA.*

It could easily have been a coincidence, but it made Rudnick suspicious. Here he had just launched his first music-related investigation, and people were urging him to embark on a second one. A prosecutor's first instinct, he told himself, should be to remember what road you're on. Rudnick wondered whether the payola charges were a diversionary tactic. He was more interested in Pisello and MCA, and he had more to go on. The payola information was scant; good enough for a congressional hearing, perhaps, but not a criminal inquiry. Nevertheless, Rudnick figured, for good measure, he could take one obvious target and at least run down his tax records. He picked Joe Isgro.

Isgro had thought himself persecuted by the government and the news media before, but nothing had prepared him for this. He felt Brian Ross, especially, was hounding him to death. Ross had gone directly to the Grammys in Los Angeles the night after the payola story to get additional film of him and Fred DiSipio. When Ross spotted DiSipio, he yelled, "Freddy, hey! Come on over!" DiSipio smiled and waved—then wilted as he recognized the newsman. Ross's attempts to draw a comment from Isgro at the Grammys were more persistent but equally fruitless. As Isgro related the scene: "Cameras, boom mikes hanging over my fucking head, in my face, they're walking with me for an entire city block. Screaming things at me. They didn't choose to show that. You know why? Because it would look like harassment—exactly what it was. Why, Mr. Brian Ross? Why didn't you show that on television?"

A few days later, Isgro was in New York to close a business

---

* If Azoff was helping the NBC newsmen, with or without their knowledge, he was not getting favored treatment. This became clear in March at a record convention in Los Angeles. Brian Ross sent an NBC camera crew to get footage for a second installment of "The New Payola." As the crew prepared to shoot Irving Azoff entering the convention hall, his close aide and public relations man, Larry Solters, tackled the cameraman.

deal unrelated to music with some Wall Street investors—"very *nice* Wall Street people," Isgro pointed out, "not Boesky types." Isgro was paranoid; the last thing he wanted was Brian Ross with cameras in his face. So he registered at the Helmsley under an alias and took his Wall Street guests to lunch at a different hotel, the Parker-Meridien. Constantly looking over his shoulder, Isgro led the way in serpentine fashion, going up one side street and down another. When he and his guests reached the hotel restaurant and took their seats, Isgro at last began to breathe easily. He went to the men's room, came out by the bank of telephones, and found himself face-to-face with Brian Ross.

It was a coincidence. Ross had gone to the hotel to interview a record industry source. Having finished, he was phoning the office. Each man said the other was rattled by the chance meeting. "Ross turned purple to see me," Isgro said. "Isgro gulped and walked on fast," Ross related.

Not one to pass up a good opportunity, Ross called for a camera crew. "He had them there in four minutes," Isgro marveled. When Isgro left the Parker-Meridien, he said, an NBC camera and boom mike trailed him for two blocks. Then the cameraman accidentally hit an old woman and knocked her to the ground. Isgro got the woman's name and had his attorney write her a letter encouraging her to sue NBC. The woman did not take the advice.

Ross and Silverman had other fish to fry besides Joe Isgro. Sources told them that Walter Yetnikoff had sandbagged the RIAA investigation of indies. They felt this information was reliable enough to include in their next payola report, which would run Monday, March 31.

The week before the broadcast, Ross made two attempts to elicit a comment from Walter Yetnikoff. Both times he was intercepted by Walter's PR man, Bob Altshuler, who wrote a memo to Yetnikoff reconstructing the phone calls from memory. The first conversation took place March 26.

> Ross: I understand that Walter voted against the RIAA proposal to investigate independent promotion men.
>
> Altshuler: No one can know that. My understanding is that voting procedures of the RIAA call for secret balloting.

Ross: Two presidents of record companies have confirmed to me that Walter voted against the proposal and that he called some other label heads
on how they should vote.

Altshuler: Since presidents cast secret ballots, how would
they know how anyone else voted?

Ross: I am planning to do another piece on the record
industry. Do you think Walter would want to be
on it?

Altshuler: I don't think so.

Ross: Has your company received a subpoena from the
grand jury?

Altshuler: No.

They spoke again the next day.

Ross: Haven't you now received a subpoena from the
grand jury?

Altshuler: No. And I am sure I would know if we had.

Ross: The record company presidents I have talked to
insist it was CBS who opposed the RIAA proposal
to investigate independent promotion men.

Altshuler: I do not know who opposed it. Why do you keep
insisting it was CBS? There are other players in
the RIAA as well as CBS. My understanding is
they did not achieve unanimity on this issue for
a number of reasons.

Ross: I have heard that Walter thinks there is a drug
problem at NBC News.

Altshuler: I have never heard of that. Good-bye.

Having learned of Ross's interest in him from Altshuler, Walter must not have been looking forward to the payola update that
ran on *NBC Nightly News* on March 31.

The segment began with film recycled from episode one, of
Fred DiSipio locking up his car, and a recap of the NBC allegations about indie promotion. Then it cut to the Waldorf for
vignettes from the Hall of Fame dinner that had not been used in
the first installment. There was DiSipio hugging Chubby Checker,
another Philadelphia native. Next, there was DiSipio hugging
Tommy Mottola.

Walter had been negotiating with Allen Grubman to give Mottola and DiSipio the Empire Records label on CBS. Immediately after the first payola story, the deal was scotched. Now, the wisdom of that decision was all the more evident.* Oddly, Mottola later denied that he ever appeared in the NBC story. He denounced the NBC coverage all the same, because "it made most people in this business look like a bunch of criminals, which is absolute bullshit. I think it was a stupid and unwarranted form of yellow journalism."

Mottola vanished from the screen. Now, DiSipio stood beside John Fagot, Columbia's vice-president of promotion. DiSipio did not appear to mind being filmed; he must have thought NBC was doing a puff piece on the Hall of Fame dinner. Off screen, Ira Silverman asked what it took to have a hit record, and DiSipio's answer became the next "sound bite" of the broadcast: "You need a lyric . . . you need the artist, company behind it—and you need me!" Fagot threw back his head and laughed: "You need Freddy!"

If that gave Walter *tsuris*, he was in for much worse at the end of the segment. Ross set it up by interviewing Leonard Marks, an outspoken litigator in the music business.

> Marks: The independent promoters are close personal friends of many of the heads of the record companies that we've been talking about. And it's also no secret in the industry that there are several heads of record companies who are major abusers of drugs, particularly cocaine. There's a relationship going on in this industry, and it really has to be fully uncovered.

The very next shot showed Brian Ross standing in front of Black Rock.

> Ross: The biggest company in the record business is CBS, and top industry executives say CBS Records did the

---

* Luckily for Walter, Joe Isgro's Private I label—a company represented by Allen Grubman—was no longer distributed by Epic. The deal had lapsed in October 1985 and not been renewed. However, two Private I/Epic singles were on the black charts after the first NBC expose: "Sugar Free," by Juicy, and "He's a Pretender," by La Toya Jackson. "There are still a couple of records that dribbled out after the deal was terminated," Bob Altshuler explained to *Rolling Stone*. "You don't just turn it off like a faucet."

> most business with the independent promoters now under investigation. [The camera slowly zoomed in on a still photograph of Yetnikoff.] CBS Records president Walter Yetnikoff has now curtailed the use of independent promoters at CBS. But industry executives say it was Yetnikoff who had a lot to do with stopping an investigation by the [RIAA] earlier this year, an investigation of independent promoters. A spokesman for CBS said Yetnikoff was not the only record company president who opposed the investigation.

The next morning, April Fool's Day, Walter went screaming to CBS chief Tom Wyman. He demanded that Wyman strike back at NBC. Though it was unusual for the head of a television network to attack a competitor, Wyman did so later that day in a memo to all CBS officers, department heads, and record personnel. The memo was made available to the press. In it, Wyman branded the NBC story "a second-class example of broadcast journalism," stated that CBS and its record group shared "a well-earned reputation for honesty and integrity," and expressed unhappiness that the broadcast shed "unfavorable light" on Yetnikoff's "distinguished career." He added, "You may be sure that he has our one-hundred-percent confidence, admiration, and support."

That appeased Walter somewhat, but he was still fuming to a reporter later that week. "What did they prove?" he demanded. "*Nothing!* What have they got? That I'm a dope addict? Never use the stuff. . . .

"If I took that NBC program, and I sent it to the Columbia School of Journalism, I think that they would all get an F. How come people believe it? Because it's on television? I always love these kind of journalist statements that talk about an undisclosed source close to the business. Somebody's girlfriend? I don't know what that means. I choose not to believe anonymous people.

"You know the lawyer they had on? A guy named Marks. I don't know who he is. I do not know him. How close can he be to the record business? * He makes some sort of statement that many

---

* Leonard Marks was one of the foremost litigators in the business. His clients included the three surviving Beatles and David Bowie.

of the heads of record companies are heavily into cocaine. How that is relevant to what they're investigating, I have no idea. I probably drink a little too much, I don't know what that means in terms of organized crime. But leave that alone. How the fuck did this guy know that many heads of record companies are heavily into cocaine? Is he a *dealer*? How does he know this? I don't know what my colleagues do. How can anybody take a statement like that and broadcast it?

"In a week filled with airplane crashes, Gorbachev is not sure about Aquino, or whatever her *name* is, giving aid to Honduras, blah blah blah. I mean, the world is full of real, terrible news. Planes were blowing up. NBC ran what? Five, seven minutes on this? I haven't timed it. Out of what? Five or six stories? This is one of the five or six stories most important to the world?

"I happen to be very patriotic. The First Amendment is very important. But the privilege carries with it some sense of responsibility. I could start talking about [a top executive of NBC] and call him 'Gram-of-Coke.' Hey, I could make this his nickname, if I talk long enough. That's irresponsible. Well, so are they fucking irresponsible.

"I am told that Brian Ross has a lousy reputation. When I see some of the stuff that he's done—for example, Isgro walking over to Gotti. I know for an absolute fact—I know it from confidential police sources, okay? And I'm not bullshitting. He just walked over because he wanted to be a big shot. He was not supposed to be there. He had no association with Gotti. I am told that Gotti turned to one of his people and said, Who the fuck is that, and why is he over here? Poor Freddy DiSipio saw two people talking, they happened to be in the same hotel. And walked over. I'm telling you I hear this from confidential police sources, which I respect. DiSipio saw two guys talking, walked over, Hey, Freddy, say hello. That is the meeting of the Gambino family that Brian Ross broadcast. Now, that is shoddy journalism. He knows these facts."

As Yetnikoff complained bitterly about the indie promotion scandal, over at PolyGram, Dick Asher was smiling. The Network, he had discovered, was not invincible after all.

"The outside pressure is what cleaned it up," he concluded. "The system was so pernicious, it was almost impossible to clean up from the inside. On the day before the NBC story broke, there was not one record on a parallel-one station that was not 'paid for,' in the sense that an indie charged a record company for it being on the playlist.

"Now, it will be clean, at least for a while. But I'd like to see investigations. If they uncover some stuff, it may finally scare people in the business enough to see this isn't fun and games time."

The scandal was rattling even an industry kingpin like Allen Grubman. A short time after Dick became president of PolyGram, Grubman had asked him to have breakfast with Joe Isgro. "He feels he doesn't know you," Asher recalled Grubman telling him. "I said, Well, he can deal with the promotion people. So Grubman said, He likes to know the heads of companies. Please, do me a favor and see him. I said, Why, what's the big deal? Just take my advice, I'm trying to help you."

So Asher made an appointment for a 9:00 A.M. breakfast meeting with Joe Isgro at the Helmsley Palace, soon to be the site of the notorious mob meeting. By nine-thirty Dick was still waiting for Isgro to show. Finally, he rang Isgro's suite and woke him. Isgro had thought the breakfast was a day later. By the time he got dressed and came down, it was nearly ten o'clock, and Asher had only a few minutes to spend with him. "It was sort of a nonconversation," Dick recalled. "I took it as a social event. Maybe he was angling for a label deal or something.

"A month later, this whole NBC thing broke, and I was on the phone with Allen. And I made some remark like, Who do you want me to have breakfast with *next* week—Adolf Hitler? And he said, Isgro wasn't my client! I was just doing him a favor! He wasn't a client of mine! Obviously, Allen was trying to disassociate himself as far as he could, as quickly as he could. He must have thought the phone was tapped or something."

■

Senator Albert Gore, Jr., of Tennessee called a press conference on April 2 to declare a Senate probe of the "new payola." It would be conducted by the Government Affairs Committee, on which he served. Gore's wife, Tipper, had made waves in the music industry the previous year when she went on a tear about obscene rock lyrics and formed the Parents Music Resource Center to push for warning stickers on album jackets.

Gore was asked why he believed a Senate payola probe would succeed when the House investigation of 1984, in which he played a part, came up empty. "Some people," Gore explained, over the sound of popping flashbulbs, "didn't come forward, in some cases, because of threats of being physically hurt." Now, he said, industry people wanted to talk. Had Gore already been approached by record executives? He sidestepped the question but remarked that "the record companies are the ones, I would say, who are most anxious about stamping this out."

■

MANAGERS IRATE OVER INDIES: CLAIM PROMO SERVICES ESSENTIAL.

The story ran on the front page of *Billboard*. Managers were angry, all right, and so were their artist clients. Artists wanted to have hits, not crusade for justice—Maurice White of Earth, Wind and Fire had made that plain to Asher in 1981. Who cared whether some indies were bagmen? The artist never had to pay for them out of his own pocket, and they got the job done. "Independent promotion has to be there," insisted Steve Machat, president of the company that managed New Edition. "Anybody who says it doesn't is either a liar or a fool who doesn't understand the realities of the industry."

The most irate manager quoted in *Billboard* was Frank Dileo, whose client, Michael Jackson, should never have needed indie promotion in the first place. "What they did to Joe Isgro is a crying shame," Dileo said. "He happened to be a nice, hardworking guy. He does have a flamboyant lifestyle, but he works for the money, and the way he chooses to spend it is his business. If I was Joe, I'd not only sue NBC, I'd sue every fucking record company. I'd sue them for antitrust, for getting together and boycotting him."

Joe Isgro did not sue NBC, but on April 30 he took the second half of Frank Dileo's free legal advice, filing a $75 million lawsuit against the record labels that had once employed him. He cited sections 1 and 2 of the Sherman Antitrust Act and sections 4 and 16 of the Clayton Antitrust Act. Isgro characterized the indie boycott as an attempt by the record industry to stifle competition and fix prices for promotion services. The defendants in the suit were A&M, Arista, Atlantic, Capitol, Chrysalis, Elektra, Geffen, MCA, Motown, PolyGram, RCA, Warner Bros., and the RIAA. One name was conspicuously absent from the suit. CBS.

While Joe Isgro remained in the public eye, Fred DiSipio all but disappeared. When the defendants in Isgro's antitrust suit tried to compel DiSipio to testify, they were unable to locate him to serve the subpoena. DiSipio did make one splashy public appearance in September 1987, however. He turned up in Port Everglades, Florida, for the christening of a navy battleship named after the USS *Leyte Gulf*, the aircraft carrier on which he had served in World War II. DiSipio accepted a citation from Ronald Hayes, the navy's highest ranking admiral, and recited from Psalm 107.

DiSipio & Associates was no longer listed in the Cherry Hill directory. It had not folded, however. Now, it was based in nearby Medford, New Jersey, under two names: Intercontinental Promotion and MidAtlantic Marketing. Ostensibly, the companies were run by DiSipio associate Ronny Kyle.

Indeed, the indies had no intention of playing dead. Immediately after the ban went into effect, the Network flexed its muscles by getting pop airplay for Profile Records, a small label not distributed by any of the majors, best known for the rap group Run-D.M.C. The Network had been a tool to prevent such labels from getting Top 40 exposure, having been made too expensive through competitive bidding. Now, it was both affordable and available to Profile, and the label's president, Cory Robbins, was grateful. By April 1986, "I Wanna Be a Cowboy," by Profile group Boys Don't Cry, was all over the Top 40 airwaves.

"This is like a gift the major labels gave to me," Robbins told *Rolling Stone*. "It's like the old days are back where independents can have pop hits again like they did in the fifties and sixties and even to some extent in the seventies. . . . This record has been out six months, and if this whole . . . thing hadn't happened, by now this record would be dead." Robbins said he had hired "the Network guys," including Gary Bird, Jerry Meyers, and associates of DiSipio, Isgro, and Jerry Brenner. "I'm pretty much using all the famous guys. I feel like the independents are good people. They're doing really great things for me at a very fair price. Right now they're my heroes."

The indies must not have been thrilled with nickel-and-dime jobs like Profile, however. A few of them expressed their pique. *Billboard* reported in the early days of the ban that "reliable sources indicate that some indies are making calls to pull [program directors] *off* records."

One year after the indie boycott went into effect, Isgro said he was still in business, but his tabs were one tenth of before. He was handling projects for $2,000 that would have brought him $20,000 in his heyday. "Am I doing anything different?" he asked. "In method of promotion, no; in enthusiasm, yes."

Isgro now dealt directly with artist managers. Through them, he was paid to work records for some of the biggest names in the business, including Duran Duran, Billy Idol, Lionel Richie, Journey, Kenny G, Luther Vandross, and Anita Baker. All of these artists recorded for labels that officially did not use indies. Isgro said the labels were aware that he was working their records. In fact, several vice-presidents of promotion "have called us and have told us the managers would be sending us the project and told us to correlate all the information through them."

Sometimes the promoters were paid directly out of artists' pockets. "Very often, I'm asked directly [for indie promotion funds], and I just say no," Dick Asher said in 1987. "We're not doing it. But some of our artists are doing it regardless of the fact, with their own money. The heaviest users seem to be successful artists, because they have the money, and because they want any edge they can get."

Two British labels had never taken part in the ban and continued to hire Isgro and other indies out in the open: Island and Virgin. Both were distributed by Atlantic Records, a Warner label. The Network worked heavily on "Addicted to Love," a record by Island artist Robert Palmer, after the boycott took effect. Virgin hired Isgro and other indies to promote new singles by T'Pau, Johnny Hates Jazz, and Cutting Crew.

Other labels found ways to disburse funds for freelance promotion, in violation of the ban. The money might come in the form of an artist "advance" or ostensibly for tour support.

But however it was paid out, the allotment was charged against the artist's royalties. Indie promotion was at long last a "recoupable" expense. The implications of this were shattering. The record industry had not only solved the indie crisis in the most hypocritical manner, it had gone one better. The labels still had indie promotion, but now the artists had to pay for it.

For all of Dick Asher's evident pleasure over the indie boycott, soon after the ban took effect, he made a surprising staff appointment. Asher hired a man named Fred Deane as PolyGram's new head of album-oriented rock promotion. Before Deane changed his name, it was Fred DiSipio, Jr. His album promotion firm, Hot Trax, had operated from the same Cherry Hill office suite as DiSipio & Associates.

PolyGram already employed a man who once had worked for Fred DiSipio, Sr., the company's national director of pop promotion, David Leach. But Leach had been with PolyGram since 1977; the connection with DiSipio was too old to have meaning. Fred Deane was a different matter. Yet Dick got angry when people insinuated that Deane was unsuitable because of his father.

"Do I impute the sins of the father to the son?" Dick said a short time after Deane was hired. "People tell me he changed his last name because he and his father never got along. He's considered one of the best [album promotion] people going, and album promotion was never a contaminated area. I've never heard a bad word about Fred Deane."

Deane stayed at PolyGram only a few months, long enough to help break Cinderella, a hard rock band. Then he quit and went to work for Kal Rudman, the tipsheet publisher in Cherry Hill who had close ties to Fred DiSipio. Asher believed he had been taken, and one person he suspected of misleading him was John Betancourt, PolyGram's senior vice-president of promotion. "John assured me Fred Deane and the father had no connection," Dick protested.

The Deane affair did nothing to improve relations between Asher and Betancourt, which had grown increasingly tense. Dick fired him in early 1988, and Betancourt sued PolyGram for breaching his employment contract. Later he tacked on an added charge of slander, claiming that company officials told people he was a drug addict. PolyGram charged that Betancourt had breached his own contract by misappropriating company property.

■

Despite the apparent willingness of artists to pay for indie promotion, it might not have made such a rapid comeback had the government, in its various incarnations, carried out its threatened crackdown. But the federal investigation into the "new" payola was rapidly becoming the latest chapter in a long history of ineptitude, bad luck, and missed opportunities.

The first setback was the collapse of the much-ballyhooed Senate probe in the Government Affairs Committee. By the end of 1986, Albert Gore had moved over to the Armed Services Committee. Without him, the investigation died of neglect. Gore had not even stuck with it long enough to hold a hearing.

The grand jury in New York that had subpoenaed data from the RIAA and several labels disbanded without handing down an indictment. Perhaps the office of U.S. Attorney Rudolph Giuliani was too busy prosecuting mafiosi and Wall Street insider traders to persevere in a complex payola case. Another grand jury had convened in Philadelphia, but no indictments came forth.

This left Marvin Rudnick, the strike force prosecutor in Los Angeles, to carry on his investigation of Joe Isgro. Rudnick was assigned a number of IRS agents to help gather evidence. The investigation got off to a somewhat rocky start, however, because Rudnick and the IRS people did not always see eye to eye.

Early on, Rudnick decided he should subpoena David Michael Smith, the more homicidal of Isgro's two bodyguards. When people like Joe Isgro employed security men, he reasoned, it was usually because they carried large sums of cash. In a tax case, you always wanted to drop a subpoena on the bodyguard. But Rudnick was unable to persuade the IRS to haul Smith in for questioning. Finally, in frustration, he called on the Immigration Service to write the summons, on the grounds that Smith might be an undesirable alien. No sooner was Smith served, in early 1987, than he fled to England and went into hiding.

In the meantime, Rudnick had broadened his investigation to include Ralph Tashjian, the indie promoter who ran Joe Isgro's Top 40 operation. He did not go after William Craig, Tashjian's counterpart in black radio, but the IRS did. Before long, the strike force believed it had strong evidence of tax irregularities against Tashjian and Craig.

As Rudnick's payola probe went forward, so did the matter of Sal Pisello and MCA Records. If the indie promoters' tax statements looked out of line, Pisello's were a joke. Between 1983 and 1985, Pisello failed to report more than $375,000 in income earned as a consultant to MCA. It was not difficult for Rudnick to secure an indictment against Pisello, and one was handed down on July 9, 1987. This was the second time in three years that Pisello had been charged with a tax felony. No one following the case had any doubt that Rudnick hoped to get a stiff sentence for Pisello, sixty-four, as a two-time offender. This might compel Pisello to cooperate in an investigation of MCA. The press release handed out by the Los Angeles U.S. Attorney's office on July 9 was headed: CENTRAL FIGURE IN MCA RECORDS PROBE INDICTED. The headline infuriated MCA.

The same day, Rudnick called his first witness before the payola grand jury: John Dantzer, program director of KIKX in Colorado. Ross and Silverman of NBC had an update of "The New Payola" in the can, centered around the confessions of a program director, filmed in silhouette, who admitted taking over $100,000 in bribes from an independent promoter. Ross got a tip that Dantzer would testify and thought it would make a good tag for the story, which aired the next evening. He rushed to the courthouse, caught Dantzer on the way in, and asked the radio man if he had any comment to make. He did. "Buddy," Dantzer said to Ross, "you could use a good dandruff shampoo."

■

Danny Davis had been Joe Isgro's loyal sideman for four years. But now Isgro was a target of a grand jury investigation, and NBC News was still on his trail. Danny wanted to quit his job, but he hesitated. Then he got word from Allen Grubman via David Chackler, who had been president of the Private I label. Grubman's message: What the fuck's wrong with Danny? Does he want to put himself out of business? Tell him to get *out* of there. So Danny quit Joe Isgro Enterprises. "The truth is," Danny said, "I stayed too long at the fair."

Joe Isgro was a bitter man. His antitrust suit against the record labels had become highly personal. It was inconceivable to Isgro that the record companies that had embraced him would cast him away just because some TV reporter said he'd met John Gotti. He was right. The record industry could have ignored the NBC allegations. It had shrugged in the seventies when mobster Patsy Falcone infiltrated CBS Records, and was still shrugging in the eighties after alleged mobster Sal Pisello infiltrated MCA Records. How did they get in the door? Who knew? Who cared?

In fact, on April 11, 1987, a year into the suspension of indie promoters and smack in the middle of the Sal Pisello scandal, MCA chief Irving Azoff was honored by the T. J. Martell Foundation for Leukemia and Cancer Research, the top music industry charity, as "Humanitarian of the Year." It seemed there were no limits to the insincerity of the record business. Even setting aside the mob scandal, Azoff, the man who once sent a live snake as a party favor, was not most people's idea of a humanitarian.*

Isgro was not fooled. The industry was sorry it had bid up the price of indie promotion so high, and NBC was just an excuse for the record companies to undo what they had done. "I applaud

---

* As if to prove the point, Azoff made an impassioned acceptance speech about the importance of the charity, then refused to pay his pledge in an argument over the color of the tablecloths.

them for it," he said. "The figures of what they were spending on indie promotion, between $50 million and $80 million, I assume they were in the ballpark. What the labels wanted to do was move the cost of indie promotion to the artist. That's what they're doing. The companies funnel money through management and tour support, and it gets paid to us with their full knowledge and direction. They have deferred that cost, charging it back to artist royalties. I think it was a brilliant move."

Moreover, Isgro pointed out, it was only days after the indie suspension that this new system began. "Two days later, the labels are back in the independent business. Two days later. If they thought everybody was so tainted, why are they back?

"And I got no problem, really. I understand what they did, I understand why they did it. But they're gonna *pay* me for the damage they did to my business. My billing has been devastated; it's less than a tenth of what it was. I didn't file an antitrust suit because I woke up one morning with a hard-on for the industry. I'm not looking to make a big hoopla out of it. Just pay me for the twenty years it took me to build my business. The record industry has no trouble forgiving Clive Davis for committing a felony. I'm not looking for their fucking forgiveness, I want the *money*, I'm looking for *damages*. I didn't *do* anything to be forgiven."

Isgro's failure to include CBS Records in his lawsuit had both relieved and embarrassed the record company. ("He thought he was doing us a *favor*," Yetnikoff said, smacking his forehead.) It implied that Isgro supported the theory that Yetnikoff had tried to quash the RIAA investigation. In fact, he did. "I did not sue CBS," he said, "because I have conclusive evidence at this point in time that CBS was adamantly opposed to any of these investigations the RIAA wanted to run."

Isgro believed he had a strong case, and that under normal circumstances the record companies would have rushed to settle it out of court. But everyone knew he was the target of a grand jury investigation. "This would all be settled right now, but they're banking on the fact I'm gonna get indicted. They're banking on it. If I don't get indicted, they got a big, major problem."

Did he believe he would *not* be indicted? "From your mouth to God's ears," he said. "They can indict a ham sandwich. I've had friends that were indicted on absolutely nothing. And me, they'd love to indict. There'd be a lot of press, let's face it. They've spent millions, untold millions, on this investigation. So somebody's got to take a fall; there's no two ways about it. Whether they have the balls to go after MCA, I have serious doubts about. I think that's gonna be a tough road. And I will be the prime candidate because I'm a gangster and every other fucking name they come up with."

Isgro's words about MCA proved prophetic. In December 1987, L.A. prosecutor Marvin Rudnick was called before his Justice Department superiors in Washington, David Margolis and Michael DeFeo. They told him he could continue to pursue a tax case against Sal Pisello, but he must not go after MCA or any of its executives. Rudnick was stunned.

The turnabout at Justice appeared to stem from a courtroom incident two months previous. While arguing a legal motion, Rudnick said in open court that two MCA executives had invoked their Fifth Amendment right against self-incrimination. MCA immediately went on the warpath, demanding that Rudnick be removed from the case for breaching grand jury secrecy. Around this time, the strike force got a new head man—appropriately named John Newcomer—who immediately clashed with Rudnick. In October he wrote MCA a letter calling its complaint against Rudnick "a matter of the highest priority," and promised that "neither MCA nor any of its executives or employees are targets" of the investigation.

Rudnick did, at last, get to prosecute Sal Pisello in a nonjury trial in August 1988. He had no trouble winning a conviction; this time Pisello drew a four-year sentence. But Rudnick was reined in by his "cocounsel," John Newcomer, every time he attempted to steer the questioning toward the conduct of MCA. As Rudnick cross-examined one defense witness, Newcomer passed him a testy note: "Marvin—This does nothing for our case. Pls wrap it up. . . ."

The apparent quashing of the MCA probe drew a lot of press, nearly all of it sympathetic to Rudnick. The conspiracy theorists pointed out the close ties between MCA and Ronald Reagan. MCA chairman Lew Wasserman was Reagan's former talent agent; in 1986 Wasserman donated over half a million dollars toward a Reagan library. Still, it was a farfetched explanation for what had happened. Taking on a bedrock, Fortune 500 company is a psychologically difficult move for the Justice Department under the best of circumstances. Perhaps men less intrepid than Rudnick had exploited his courtroom slip to sidestep the whole issue. As *The American Lawyer* pointed out, Rudnick's slip did not sound like serious misconduct, and even if it were, "it stands to reason that Justice would have replaced or fired him" rather than narrow the investigation to a simple tax case.

The other odd thing is that in August 1987, a month before his ill-fated remarks in court about MCA, Marvin Rudnick was removed from the payola case. This has never been explained, either.

The timing was inopportune. Rudnick's payola grand jury had voted to indict Ralph Tashjian and William Craig, Isgro's top men, on charges of tax evasion and payola. Tashjian's wife, Valerie, was also fingered as an accomplice on the tax charges. The recommendation had gone to Justice in Washington and been approved. It was sitting on Rudnick's desk when he was suspended from the case, and it tumbled into the lap of acting strike force chief Richard Small, who had announced plans to leave in four months. When Newcomer replaced Small, he assigned payola to federal prosecutor Richard Stavin. Unfortunately, Stavin already had an enormous caseload. Rudnick, meanwhile, refused to quit and was relegated to handling Freedom of Information Act requests. In July 1989, Rudnick got his termination notice and went into private practice.

By this time, the eternally pessimistic Joe Isgro began to conclude that he would not be indicted after all. If he was right, it was one of the few things that had gone Isgro's way since NBC did its first story on him. His antitrust suit had been a disaster.

For over a year, the suit had consumed Joe Isgro. He was subjected to five grueling days of depositions. And when Isgro produced the one industry figure who agreed to testify on his behalf, Michael Jackson manager Frank Dileo,* the defense attorneys bared their claws.

Isgro sat in on the first of two Dileo sessions, both of which went badly. Said a lawyer present, "Isgro thought he was thumbing his nose at the record companies by bringing in Dileo. Here's the most powerful manager of the most powerful act in the business. I think Dileo expected to come in, say a few provocative things, and leave. But after two full days of depositions, he was contradicting himself.† He got his ass in a sling. Finally he said, I don't

---

* On Valentine's Day, 1989, Jackson split with Dileo. No explanation was given.
† This could not be confirmed by a reading of the depositions. Except for a few stray passages, all pretrial testimony was sealed and remains so to this day.

want to be deposed anymore. Well, that's too bad. We haven't questioned him yet." Dileo was called a third time, but before he could testify, federal agents showed up and led him away to answer questions before the grand jury.

The deposing of Danny Davis provided some of the few lighter moments. As Davis recalled one episode: "They said to me, Do you know John Gotti? Yes. Who is Mr. Gotti, Mr. Davis? Mr. Gotti is an alleged organized crime figure. Is he the head of any family? Yes, I believe he is head of the Gambino family. Did you and Mr. Isgro ever discuss John Gotti? I said yes, we did. And what did you talk about? We both commented on what a magnificent *dresser* he is."

By the late fall of 1987, after the grand jury had failed to produce its first indictment, the record labels began to settle. Capitol had led the way by settling with Isgro the previous May for an undisclosed sum. Next in line was Motown, in October. Later that month, PolyGram, the only company that had countersued Isgro, dropped its charges in return for Isgro dropping his. In November, RCA and Arista settled, followed by Chrysalis and A&M in December.

This left the Warner labels, MCA, and the RIAA. The two labels finally counterattacked, filing racketeering suits against Joe Isgro. The antitrust litigation, after dragging on for more than two years, came to an abrupt end on August 22, 1988, when the judge, Constance Marshall, in a stunning reversal of her previous rulings, threw out Isgro's charges on grounds of insufficiency. Warner and MCA promptly withdrew their countersuits. The case was closed.

In the end, the lawsuit took its toll financially. By one estimate, Isgro spent over $1 million on the litigation. The settlements were mostly small change, in some cases merely payment of outstanding bills owed Isgro by the labels. By the end of 1988, Isgro had moved to North Hollywood in what he described to a friend as a "charming little house." He also sold his beloved restaurant on Sunset Boulevard, Stefanino's. After living the high life for ten years, Joseph Isgro was busted out.

THE BIG SCORE

■

T HE independent promotion crisis appeared to be over, and the record industry seemed to have learned not a single lesson from it—except, perhaps, that winning is everything. The industry also discovered that the power of Walter Yetnikoff was not absolute.

In fact, whether Walter's power would remain undiminished into the nineties was an open question. Though by the end of the decade, most of the indies would again be exacting payment for all records added at stations in the *Radio & Records* survey, their influence would never be the same. Walter, whose power was dependent on the strength of CBS in the marketplace, could no longer use the Network to buy market share.

The change in the indie system was not the biggest potential blow to Yetnikoff's clout. He had done a poor job of providing A&R leadership, and by the late eighties it was beginning to weaken the company. CBS's sales and earnings were still way up, but if you analyzed the numbers, there was a hidden problem.

Every company in a fad-sensitive business must ask a key question: What percentage of earnings comes from products that did not exist five years before? In the record business, baby acts are the equivalent of new "products." Though CBS did not break out the numbers, it was easy to see that most of its profits were derived from catalog and from new recordings by artists who had been around a lot longer than five years. In 1987, for example, the biggest items were a Bruce Springsteen concert album and *Bad*, Michael Jackson's follow-up to *Thriller*. The Warner labels, meanwhile, were minting gold with relative newcomers such as Madonna and Anita Baker.

But CBS Records' A&R problem had yet to hit home, and in the wake of the indie suspension, Walter Yetnikoff was still the foremost man in the business. And as the indie matter drew to an unhappy conclusion for Walter, he had something else to be upset about. His compensation.

"I am probably the most powerful record executive," Walter said around that time. "Why I am not the richest by far, I don't know." By the standards of most working stiffs, Yetnikoff was making out all right. According to his attorney, Stanley Schlesinger, Walter's net worth then exceeded $4 million. His base salary was up to $550,000, CBS had given him an interest-free loan of $1.25 million, and his annual bonuses usually came close to half a million. It was true that David Geffen and Irving Azoff had a much higher net worth than Walter. But both of them were entrepreneurs who had gambled their own money to create record labels and artist management companies. Walter had never risked a dime.

Still, Walter took up Clive Davis's old lament—that CBS was cheap. Yetnikoff talked and dreamed of making "the Big Score," a windfall that would put him in league with Azoff and Geffen. "I hope he does make his big score," said Walter's friend Nat Weiss. "That's all he seems to care about." "Every time I talk to Walter," said his old girlfriend Debbie Federoff, "he says, I want to get rich. I keep telling him, You're rich enough. He says, I want to get *richer*. I don't know why. He doesn't spend money."

It was true. For years Walter lived in a modest suburban ranch house and bought his clothes off the rack at Dapper Dan's. Perhaps he wanted more millions than he already had as a way of keeping score with his business rivals. Or perhaps he gave away the real reason in explaining why attorney Allen Grubman was so money-hungry. "It's the immigrant fear," Walter said. "He's a poor boy, and I think he has the impression, as do I, that something's going to go wrong and we're all going to go back and live under the subway tracks in Brooklyn." Rational or not, Walter's desire for the big score had become an obsession.

Fortunately, Walter's 1984 employment contract with CBS contained an unusual provision allowing him to produce movies on the side. Never before had CBS permitted a division head to moonlight. But Walter had shrewdly used his job offer from Warner Communications as leverage to get the movie clause. He did not wait long to take advantage of it. Yetnikoff became one of three executive producers of the 1986 Disney film *Ruthless People*. Aside from overseeing the CBS home video division for a few years, Walter did not know the movie business. He did know Billy Joel, Bruce Springsteen, and Mick Jagger, however, all of whom contributed songs to the soundtrack.

CBS wound up with the soundtrack album. It was supposed to have been released on Empire Records, the ill-fated label Walter had planned to give Tommy Mottola and Fred DiSipio, but there was a compensation prize for Mottola. He was listed in the film credits as "music supervisor." One of his top management clients, Daryl Hall of Hall and Oates, also recorded a song for the soundtrack. It is not known how much Mottola was paid for this; for Walter's efforts, Disney agreed to give him $2 million—not bad for a bit of schmoozing. It was not the big score, but it helped. Shortly before *Ruthless People* came out, Walter told a reporter why he had insisted on the movie clause in his contract: "The goy upstairs won't let me make any money."

Lately, the goy had his own troubles. Thomas Wyman believed he had more job security than his predecessors, Arthur Taylor and John Backe, because he had persuaded the CBS board in 1983 to give him Bill Paley's title of chairman. Paley remained a board member and a large shareholder, with 8 percent of the company, but officially no more than that.

What Wyman had not foreseen was a takeover threat to CBS from Ted Turner, the founder of cable TV's Turner Broadcasting. Such an attempt by Turner, whose roughneck style earned him the nickname "Captain Outrageous," would have been laughed off a few years earlier. CBS was a $5 billion colossus, well out of Turner's league. But this was the era of junk bonds, a financing tool that enabled private investors to raise unprecedented sums of cash. Despite this, Wall Street was skeptical that Turner could come up with the money. Yet Wyman took the threat seriously.

Wyman's critics felt he had left CBS vulnerable to a takeover, if not by Turner, then someone else. His diversification moves into theatrical films, toys, and computer software had failed. Meanwhile, the all-important television network fell in ratings from first to second, and earnings dropped accordingly. Paley urged the board to get rid of Wyman, and for once he may have been right, but now Wyman had more loyalists on the board than he.

In April 1985, Turner offered $5.4 billion for CBS—all in flimsy debt securities—and Wyman committed the first of three serious blunders that would cost him his job. Panicking over Turner's ambitious bid, he made a counteroffer: CBS would buy up to 20 percent of its own stock at $150 a share.

Wyman's offer flashed across the Quotron terminal of Daniel Tisch, the head of risk arbitrage at Salomon Brothers. He called his father, Laurence Tisch, with the news. At sixty-three, Larry Tisch was one of the world's great financiers. He had taken over the family business, a small summer camp in New Jersey, and parlayed it into Loews Corporation. Loews comprised a large insurance company, a cigarette manufacturer, and a chain of movie theaters and hotels, including the upscale Regency Hotel in New York. It also boasted a $13.5 billion investment portfolio.

Tisch was the kind of investor that Wall Street calls a "bottom fisher." He looked for companies or properties selling at bargain prices because others were blind to their hidden worth. A classic Tisch deal was his purchase of five oil tankers for $5 million, less money than their scrap value. From a lifetime of such hard-nosed deals, Tisch had made himself a billionaire, yet he was so unimpressed with his wealth that he drove around in an old station wagon.

A high-profile company like CBS was normally of little interest to Tisch. You rarely found a hidden bargain in a stock the whole world was watching. But Danny Tisch figured that, using Salomon's trading capability, he could buy CBS shares for Loews at an average price far below $150, then quickly sell them at a nice profit. It was exactly the type of investment Larry Tisch loved, one with no apparent downside. Tisch told Danny to go ahead.

But sometime during the next few months, Tisch changed his investment strategy. The whole point of arbitrage is to sell—and he didn't. Instead, in April 1986, real estate moguls Lawrence and Zachary Fischer put one million CBS shares up for sale, and Tisch bought them. Before long, Loews owned 25 percent of CBS. People who thought they knew Larry Tisch were amazed. Was he starstruck?

Not altogether. Tisch had come to regard network broadcasting as a hedge against bad times. A confirmed pessimist, Tisch always believed an economic catastrophe was lurking just around the corner. At the same time, Tisch *did* appear to be growing starry-eyed at the prospect of owning an American institution like CBS. He began to speak of CBS as a "legacy" for his sons. Tisch's 25 percent holding bought him a seat on the board, and Loews had the wherewithal to up the ante to majority control if necessary.

Tom Wyman tried to put the best face on Larry Tisch's investment, which at least ended the Turner threat. Publicly, he called Tisch a "white knight"; privately, he fretted that Tisch could become a worse nemesis than Turner. Then Wyman made blunder number two, asking Tisch to sign a pledge that Loews would purchase no more CBS stock. Tisch indignantly refused. From that point on, the two men were enemies.

At a CBS board meeting on September 10, 1986, Wyman committed blunder number three, his worst yet. The day's events would be remembered as one of the year's biggest boardroom dramas—not to mention one of the great coups of Larry Tisch's career.

Wyman announced that he had been holding secret talks with the Coca-Cola Company. Coke, he said, had expressed an interest in buying CBS at a handsome premium. Tisch pounced. He would not sell his stock, he insisted, at *any* price. And what did Wyman think he was doing? When Ted Turner made his pass at CBS, Wyman had delivered fiery speeches about the importance of the network's independence. Now, he would sell CBS to a soda-pop manufacturer?

The stunned board members asked Wyman, Tisch, and Paley to leave the room. After an hour, the board had reached a decision. Wyman was out. Tisch was appointed "interim" president and chief executive. Bill Paley, eighty-five, was again chairman. Within a few months, the "interim" had fallen from Tisch's title. He was firmly in charge, without ever having had to raise his 25 percent stake. Paley could not control Tisch; chairman or not, he would prove a mere figurehead.

One look at Larry Tisch showed he was not Paley's kind of man. Taylor, Backe, and Wyman were tall and elegant; Tisch was short and almost entirely bald. He was not only the first Jewish CBS president but a militant Jew at that. Tisch wore a Magen David in his lapel and invited a Talmud scholar to teach scripture at Loews once a week. He served as president of the Greater New York United Jewish Appeal. His wife, Wilma, was the first woman

304

president of the Federation of Jewish Philanthropies. The welfare of the state of Israel was his most passionate cause. When Moshe Dayan died, Tisch gave his widow $1 million for Dayan's collection of biblical relics and donated them to Israel anonymously, lest they wind up in the hands of foreigners.

Walter Yetnikoff should have been delighted with Tisch. At first he was. He told Tisch to call him "Velvo," Yiddish for Walter. But before long, Walter did not like Tisch so much, and soon after that, he hated him more than he ever hated a CBS president. By 1987 Walter was calling him a "*pisch*," and "Tischburg," and "the evil dwarf," and even "the kike upstairs."

Tisch was more than a match for Walter Yetnikoff. He was tough and unsentimental and exceedingly frugal. Like Clive before him, Walter complained that Warner provided a corporate jet to ferry rock stars around the world, and begged CBS to do the same. Instead, Tisch eliminated *Paley's* jet. He also closed off Walter's private kitchen and dining room. "Ha! A major cost saving," Walter said, showing the room once to a visitor. "Not exactly the Taj Mahal."

Walter had been able to throw past presidents off guard with his ethnic bluster. Tisch came from Flatbush, near where Yetnikoff grew up; he knew Walter's shtick inside and out and was not amused. He also had firm ideas about the decorum with which Jewish businessmen should conduct themselves. Walter's tantrums left him cold. Tisch did not laugh when Walter threatened to leave the company and raid the talent, or when he screamed allegations about drug use in the CBS news division.

The rift between Tisch and Walter may have begun with a profile of Yetnikoff in the November 1986 issue of *Esquire*. It hit the stands the previous month, just as Tisch took over CBS, and he found it appalling. In the article, Walter made his "goy upstairs" remark, referred to Fred DiSipio as a "friend" and the indie promoters in general as "mensches," and volunteered that he owned a racehorse with Morris Levy. He was profane, as usual. In one section, Walter complained about a grilling he had just received from CBS general counsel George Vradenburg III. "Vradenburg, for Christ's sake, wanted to know if I could *prove* that I hadn't given or taken kickbacks. . . . How the hell is a man supposed to prove a thing like that? Do you put your pecker on the desk and swear an oath?"

A few days after the article appeared, Tisch gave an interview to *Channels* magazine. The CBS chief did not like to talk to the press, and when he did, candor was not his long suit.

Tisch dismissed Walter's remark about DiSipio as inconsequential. "There's no big scandal over independent promotion," he insisted. "That was examined very carefully by the law department and outside counsel for CBS over the years. There was never anything done knowingly wrong here.

"All I know is, Walter Yetnikoff is a lawyer, he's a respected member of the bar, he's a very intelligent and honorable man. And I've never heard anybody say anything about Walter Yetnikoff that in the least way disparaged his integrity. He's a very, very honorable fellow. The *Esquire* article didn't capture Walter Yetnikoff. He may walk around without a tie, but underneath it all, he's a very conservative businessman. Don't go by the fact that he's not wearing a tie and has a beard. Walter is a very conservative lawyer and businessman and a very capable executive. And Walter is too smart to do anything that would jeopardize the company or himself. I have great faith in Walter Yetnikoff."

But what about the NBC allegations that this "friend" of Yetnikoff had attended a Mafia meeting? "What do you want me to say?" Tisch snapped, angrily. "I wasn't there, I don't know anything about it. You know, people being spotted at meetings with other people, I don't condemn people for that. To me that gets to the point of irresponsibility. Maybe somebody could say that *I* was at an affair with somebody who was unsavory. Being spotted in a room with somebody, God forbid that was a sign of guilt in America, we'd all be in trouble."

Tisch's point was well taken. At an affair the following March, he *was* spotted with two notorious people: Fred DiSipio and Morris Levy. Morris had been indicted on extortion charges seven months earlier. The occasion was Walter Yetnikoff's wedding to Cynthia Slamar, the latest in his line of blond, gentile girlfriends. Other guests included Bruce Springsteen, Barbra Streisand, and Mick Jagger. The wedding was held at the Plaza Hotel, the site of Clive Davis's infamous bar mitzvah reception.

Walter's marriage to Slamar signaled to friends that he was cleaning up his act. Lynda Emon, according to her best friend and lawyer, Sandy Katz, worked out a "divorce" settlement with Walter. She went home to Minneapolis and became a sales representative for *Billboard*. Later, she moved to Nashville. No longer Walter's woman, she discovered that most of her former industry friends ignored her phone calls. "I feel like the beheaded queen," she said.

For all of Walter's growing dislike of Tisch, the financier presented an opportunity for Yetnikoff's big score. If CBS were to sell its record division, Walter would almost certainly be paid a huge signing bonus by the buyer to remain at the helm. He might even get equity in CBS Records. Though Tisch insisted repeatedly that CBS Records was "not for sale," his word was not his bond. His first full day as president, he wrote a memo expressing "complete confidence" in CBS publishing head Peter Derow, then eliminated his job a month later.

In fact, Tisch was known for his willingness to sell anything at the right price. He even sold his mother's residence, the Americana Hotel in Florida. When Tisch took over a company, he had a habit of whittling it down to its core business, divesting all extraneous parts. The record unit interacted very little with the rest of CBS. Tisch had bought CBS because he believed in the future of network television, not recorded music. Sure, CBS Records was making good money now, but it had earned nothing in the early eighties. Who was to say the cycle wouldn't swing back?

Walter fueled these fears, pointing out to Tisch and other board members that records were indeed cyclical. And despite Tisch's assurances that he feared no indie promo scandal, he later admitted this was not so. "Our licenses come from the Federal Communications Commission," he said, "and there are always questions raised about relationships within the record business."

Walter began discussing a possible sale of CBS Records with Tisch almost from the moment he replaced Wyman. Yetnikoff thought he had Tisch's word that no sale would be negotiated without his knowledge. If Tisch had made such a promise, it was another he promptly broke. In October 1986, weeks after taking over CBS, Tisch got a call from Nelson Peltz, the head of Triangle Industries. Triangle made packaging goods, but Peltz had turned the company into a conglomerate, with interests in vending machines and wire and cable. Why not music? Tisch told Peltz that CBS Records was indeed for sale, if he was willing to pay $1.25 billion. This was 16 times CBS Records' average earnings over the previous five years. Peltz thought the price sounded high but said he'd think it over.

When Walter learned of the Peltz bidding through an investment banker friend, he was enraged. "I screamed and yelled a bit," he said. Tisch calmed Walter by welcoming him to make his own deal to sell CBS Records, provided he could find someone willing to pay $1.25 billion in cash. Also, for tax reasons, the deal had to close before the end of the year.

The next weeks were among the most hectic of Walter's life. First he attempted to organize a leveraged buyout, that is, purchase of the company by its own management with borrowed funds. He found it rough going; Wall Street had never felt comfortable with the rock and roll business. Meanwhile, Disney expressed interest in buying CBS Records, but balked at the price.

Finally, two days before CBS's November board meeting, Walter left an urgent message for Michael Schulhof, vice-chairman of Sony U.S.A. Walter was a known quantity to Sony. As a young lawyer in 1967, he had done the legal work to create CBS/Sony, a joint-venture record company in Japan. CBS/Sony was an enormous success; from start-up capital of $2 million, it had grown to produce more than $100 million in yearly earnings. Walter had remained on warm terms with Norio Ohga, Sony's president in Japan. "It's an unusual relationship between an Easterner and an American," Walter said. "We talk about how people should develop their character, and what life's all about."

Walter told Schulhof that CBS Records was for sale and laid out his terms. He wanted a $1.25 billion bid within two days, in time for the board meeting, plus a guaranteed bonus pool of $50 million for him and "the *mishpocheh*"—his management team. Within twenty minutes, Schulhof had spoken to Ohga and Sony chairman Akio Morita, and he had an answer for Walter. Yes.

The big score appeared at hand. "The sign-on bonus was a *lot* of money," Walter said. "Plus the equity participation. It was a chance to be an owner of—my God!—CBS Records. I started off working here as a lawyer three from the *bottom* or something. Now, I was gonna be a big equity player in a deal worth a billion, two hundred and fifty million dollars? A kid from Brooklyn? You know, it's not bad."

Early the next morning, Walter met with Schulhof and three Sony representatives at his apartment on East Fifty-sixth Street. By nine-thirty, still in his bathrobe, Walter had concluded the side deal for himself and his management team. He would personally get an upfront cash bonus of $10 million plus equity and other compensation worth at least the same amount. Walter then phoned Tisch, but as they spoke, Yetnikoff's heart sank. Tisch had mentioned to board members the idea of selling the record division and found more resistance than he had expected. It was possible that the board would veto the proposal when it came up at the next day's meeting.

That night, Walter was unable to sleep. "I had like twenty-two brandies," he said. He attempted to sit through the board meeting the next day, but "they threw me out. I wasn't there at the vote." The vote was no; Paley was especially vocal in his opposition. Walter was crushed. In his mind, he said, "I already had my own record company and half the south of France."

A month later, the first hints of Walter's disdain for Larry Tisch surfaced in a *Wall Street Journal* article. The newspaper suggested that Walter blamed Tisch for the board's refusal to sell CBS Records, which was possible, since Tisch was powerful enough to have overridden the veto. Walter denied the story, however. "It's crazy, because Tisch was a proponent of the deal. I *was* upset at CBS. I was a little emotional about it. But Larry Tisch was the guy who was trying to fulfill all my dreams—or at least all my *business* dreams."

Though the deal had fallen through for now, it was not dead. Walter was determined to try again, and so was Sony. The Japanese company hungered for CBS Records, and the reason was no mystery. It stemmed from Sony's failure in the home video market.

In the late seventies, Sony took the lead in home video by introducing the first videocassette player, the Betamax. Philips and other competitors countered with VHS-format machines, which used tapes of larger size. Though the Betamax was considered technologically superior to the VHS machines, what mattered to consumers was that there were more movies available in VHS. To Sony's shock, the Betamax bombed and VHS became the universal format.

The effect of a gigantic flop on a corporation's psyche is comparable to that of a nation defeated in war. Another such defeat must be prevented at any cost. Sony, cofounded and run by a scientist, Akio Morita, had believed that the best technology would prevail. Now, the company realized, too late, that it could have won with the Betamax had it owned a movie studio with a large catalog of popular films. Then it could have flooded the market with Betamax-format movies.

Around the time CBS Records became available, a new technology was in the offing. It was called digital audio tape, or DAT, the tape equivalent of the compact disc. DAT cassettes could record and reproduce music with no tape hiss whatsoever. Given the success of the CD, few doubted that DAT machines could become the next big thing in stereo hardware. The machines could be made ready for mass consumption by the early nineties. If Sony owned CBS Records, it would have access to the richest catalog in recorded music. It could manufacture DAT machines and virtually dictate the format.

Yetnikoff had been a vocal critic of DAT ever since the technology surfaced in 1986. Like other industry figures, Walter railed against home taping, which, though not illegal, he denounced as "stealing." Walter insisted that DAT would increase the incidence of home taping. CBS had led unsuccessful lobbying efforts to get Congress to impose a tax on standard blank audiotape. Meanwhile, the company said it would refuse to make digital cassettes unless the DAT machines of the future came equipped with "spoilers." These were microchips that would make recording impossible and therefore greatly diminish the appeal of DAT. No stereo manufacturer in its right mind, Sony included, would willingly adopt the spoiler.

The record industry did not miss the irony in Walter's eagerness to sell CBS Records to Sony. If he were successful, he would be all but ensuring the success of spoiler-free DAT machines.

By the fall of 1987, relations between Walter and Tisch had gone from bad to terrible. Walter insulted Tisch to his face, sometimes at high decibels. To some people in the company, it almost seemed as if Walter were defying Tisch to fire him. More likely, Walter was trying to give Tisch another good reason to sell CBS Records—it would rid the corporation of an enormous pest. Not that the animus wasn't genuine. Tisch treated Walter as just another division head, and his ego could not take it.

Tisch wanted to sell the records, but he was too obstinate a businessman to be rushed into a deal that did not meet all his terms. Now that it was 1987 and the new federal tax code was in force, the original sale price of $1.25 billion was nowhere near as attractive as it would have been the previous year. CBS would have to pay a much higher tax on capital gains. Tisch believed a better plan would be to sell all or part of CBS Records to the public in a stock offering. This approach would leave Walter's bonus dependent on Larry Tisch's largess, a word that applied to him as a philanthropist but not as a businessman. If Sony or another company wanted to buy the record group, Tisch insisted, the price tag was now $2 billion.

The price hike, more than 60 percent in only nine months, turned off every interested suitor but Sony. Over the same time period, the yen had risen slightly against the dollar, which for Sony took some of the bite out of the price increase. Still, Sony's willingness to consider paying $2 billion showed just how badly it lusted after CBS Records.

In September, Sony put its offer on the table. Tisch assured Michael Schulhof of Sony that this time he could override the objections of Paley and the board. But after that month's board meeting, Tisch backed off, saying the board wanted to hire a consulting firm to assess the value of CBS Records. One day around that time a CBS executive overheard someone screaming at the top of his lungs in Tisch's office on the floor below. Pressing his ear to the floor, he recognized the voice of Walter Yetnikoff.

Tisch still wanted to consider a public stock offering for CBS Records. This plan became impractical on October 19, however, when the stock market crashed. Moreover, the crash brought out the pessimist in Larry Tisch. This is it, he told himself, the first throes of economic calamity. At such times, one wants to be as liquid as possible. If he could still get $2 billion cash from Sony, no protest from the CBS board would stop the sale. Schulhof asked Tisch to make that promise in writing. Tisch did so.

Still, the talks almost fell apart over the issue of CBS Records' fourth-quarter earnings. Tisch wanted CBS to have those earnings. Sony held out for them, certain that Tisch would not bust a $2 billion deal. Then, on November 17, CBS drafted a statement, to be released the next day, saying that the agreement was off. Sony gave in on November 18. Both sides shook hands, and the deal was done. "Larry, bless his soul, didn't budge an inch, and they couldn't believe it," said someone close to the talks.

The crash, which impoverished so many, brought Walter his big score at last. Since Walter did not play the market, he lost none of his preexisting wealth. Now, he had a deal that would bring him more than $20 million. There was another $30 million in bonus money to be spread around, and it trickled down to hundreds of employees around the world. Walter had never been more popular at CBS Records.

Walter immediately took a shot at Tisch in a November 18

memo to the records staff, saying it was "nice to be wanted again." Now, Tisch was off his back and his new bosses were 6,757 miles away. The next day, disc jockey Don Imus made some cracks about the Sony deal on his popular morning program. If you thought Walter Yetnikoff was out of control before, he said, just wait.

As if to prove Imus's point, Walter began to set the stage for the removal of CBS Records U.S. head Al Teller. In many ways, it would be a replay of his political execution of Dick Asher. Teller had been foisted on Walter by Dick, just as Dick had been foisted on him by John Backe. Now that Walter had bosses who supported him in the fullest, he could dump Teller and replace him with someone more to his liking.

The rumors of Teller's demise were fierce by late March 1988. On April 1, they surfaced in print, on the gossip page of *New York Newsday*. It's possible that Teller would already have been gone, were it not for an event that had been in the works for many months. Teller was designated to receive the 1988 T. J. Martell award as "Humanitarian of the Year." It would be painfully embarrassing for CBS to hand the record industry an unemployed honoree. Teller's firing would have to wait until after the April 16 dinner.

The Teller dinner went smoothly, but if anything it was even more surreal than Azoff's the year before. Though none of the half-dozen speakers so much as dropped a hint that Teller was on his way out, his fate was common knowledge throughout the industry.

On Tuesday, April 19, the second business day after the dinner, CBS Records issued a press release announcing Al Teller's departure. No reason was given, though Teller was quoted saying he was leaving to explore "new challenges and opportunities which have been made available." If he had a job lined up, it was not spelled out in the release. Six days later, CBS Records made another announcement, naming Teller's replacement. The new president of CBS Records U.S. was Tommy Mottola.

It may well have been Walter's ultimate display of chutzpah. Apart from being one of Walter's closest friends in the business, Mottola had few apparent qualifications to run the largest American record company. It was true that David Geffen and Irving Azoff had also begun as artist managers, but no one put Mottola in their intellectual league. Even Walter noted, somewhat ambiguously, "I think one of the more interesting facts about Tommy is that he's extremely smart. He's hidden that from the world until recently."

On top of this, the apparent conflicts of interest were acute. For starters, Mottola had no intention of selling Champion, which managed an act on Columbia, John Eddie. Worse, Mottola was a client of attorney Allen Grubman, who represented 30 percent of the CBS Records pop roster. One could not fault Mottola for accepting the job, however. He had barely been on the job a few months when Walter arranged for him to get $3 million in incentive-plan bonus money—based on financial results that had occurred under Al Teller.

Around the time he hired Mottola, Walter had the satisfaction of seeing Tisch take a beating in the press. Treated with reverence when he replaced Tom Wyman, Tisch was now haunted by his repeated false statements to the news media. He had said he was "not touching" the news division, yet he let 215 people go there and then attempted to pin the cutback on division head Howard Stringer. He had repeatedly said the record division was "not for sale," then sold it. Before that, Tisch had spun off CBS's magazine group, which included *Woman's Day* and *Yachting*, and its publishing unit, which included Holt, Rinehart & Winston. Critics charged that Tisch was dismantling CBS exactly as Ted Turner would have done it.

Walter happily voiced these same criticisms in interviews. Though he had got all that he wanted, his hatred of Larry Tisch would not die. His ego was still bruised, and he took to avenging it at every opportunity. Walter was an active fund-raiser for the United Jewish Appeal, but he told the UJA he would pull out unless it dumped Tisch. Yetnikoff insisted he could raise more money, which was preposterous; Tisch's circle included some of the richest people in America. Twice in front of a reporter for *Rolling Stone*, Walter called Manhattan D.A. Robert Morgenthau to demand a gun permit in return for chairing a Police Athletic League benefit concert. Taking the bait, the reporter asked Walter why he wanted a gun. Walter snapped, "Larry Tisch!"

Walter began to regale people with stories of how he had bested Tisch. He told *The New York Times Magazine* that at a fancy restaurant one evening with his wife, Cynthia, and the Tisches, he ordered a $50 glass of cognac just to watch Larry's consternation when he got the bill. Walter told friends how he arranged for Frank Dileo, Michael Jackson's manager, to call Tisch and describe Yetnikoff as a "key man," though Dileo knew there was no key-man clause in Jackson's contract.

These episodes were relatively harmless, but before long, Walter and Larry Tisch found themselves on opposite sides of a nasty lawsuit. It began in February 1988, when two employees of CBS Records, Ralph Colin, Jr., and Robert Kennedy, sued CBS Inc. and Larry Tisch. It was a class-action suit, filed on behalf of the plaintiffs and others "similarly situated." The lawsuit alleged that CBS had broken a promise to pay profit-sharing bonuses for 1987 to employees of CBS Records (this included Walter). The profit-sharing money would have supplemented the bonuses from Sony. Colin and Kennedy used the law firm of Stanley Schlesinger, Walter's personal attorney and best friend. That Larry Tisch was named as a defendant showed the depth of animosity on the part of the plaintiffs.

In May, CBS Inc. counterclaimed against Colin and Kennedy, as well as Walter Yetnikoff, his right-hand man, Seymour Gartenberg, and other unnamed CBS Records employees. CBS Inc. alleged that they had "improperly depressed" profits of the records group in the fourth quarter of 1987 by, among other things, making "unjustified and improper payments." These alleged payments apparently included big advances to artists who hadn't had a hit in years, and unused vacation pay for Gartenberg dating back to 1972.

That month CBS held its annual shareholders' meeting in the Titus Theater at the Museum of Modern Art. In response to a question, CBS general counsel George Vradenburg made public the existence of the suit against Yetnikoff and Gartenberg, accusing them of "mismanagement." Both Walter and Seymour were in the audience. Short, pixieish, hearing aid in ear, Seymour lashed out at Vradenburg after the meeting. The suit hadn't been served on him yet, he said, but he had seen the papers, and the word "mismanagement" was not in them. Therefore, Vradenburg was an "asshole" to use the term in his remarks. "George Vradenburg must be the dumbest lawyer in the world!"

Walter sat silently through the early part of the meeting, listening with obvious contentment as Tisch was heckled by stockholders. The first to attack him were John Gilbert and Evelyn Davis, two notorious kooks who seemed to own a few shares of every blue-chip company in New York in order to browbeat management once a year. Then Ralph Colin took the floor and recited a self-righteous speech, denouncing Tisch for "greed and stinginess," and for turning a "Tiffany" company into junk jewelry. Colin failed to mention his lawsuit against Tisch and CBS.*

A few minutes later, in the middle of remarks by Tisch, Walter stood up, strode down the aisle, passed in front of the press gallery, and collected most of the reporters who had come to cover the meeting. Just outside in the hall, Walter gave an unscheduled press conference. Nearby stood a large man Walter identified as Barney, a bodyguard hired, he said, to intercept anyone attempting to serve him or Seymour Gartenberg with the CBS lawsuit. Wearing a loud sports jacket and an open collar and chain-smoking Sherman cigarettes, Walter looked enormously pleased with himself. It delighted him that he had taken most of the press coverage away from Tisch. "Isn't this more interesting than *that* bullshit?" he asked more than once, gesturing in the direction of the auditorium.

"Does anybody disagree with what Ralph Colin said about CBS, which I also used to regard as a Tiffany company?" Walter demanded. Sony would prove a far better owner for CBS Records. "They're interested in people, they want to build, they want to do. This guy just wants to *sell* everything."

Several reporters asked Walter about the lawsuit against him. What was the story?

"It's no big deal. It's a relatively small matter. Larry Tisch thinks that everyone is a bellhop at the Regency Hotel. And I'm *not*. And I wasn't when I worked for him. He thinks he can push you around and say, [whining voice] My lawyers'll sue ya, my lawyers'll sue ya, my lawyers'll sue ya. He thinks people are afraid of him. And none of the other guys that he's trying to cheat are bellhops at the Regency. He would like us to be.

"If Mr. Tisch thinks I am afraid of him, he's wrong. If Mr. Tisch thinks Sony is afraid of him, he's even wronger. And he can't go around threatening people. He once said to me, when we were getting into a dispute, I'll sue you, and I'll make your life miserable. All right? An interesting threat. So far, my life is great, compared to what it was. And you know what? He's not going to

---

* The speech also compared Tisch unfavorably to Paley, which was surprising. Colin's father had been Bill Paley's personal attorney for forty years until the CBS founder fired him over a petty argument concerning, of all things, the Museum of Modern Art.

make my life miserable. I can afford as many lawyers as he can afford. And if he wants to have a fight, we'll have a fight. And if he wants to sue me personally, I'll sue him back personally. He doesn't scare me."

Didn't Walter also threaten to ruin people? asked a reporter familiar with the Paul Simon and Boston cases. Walter nodded. "But *I* do it for theatrical purposes."

Why did Vradenburg say Walter had mismanaged the company?

"You want my real comment? He's full of shit."

Walter proceeded to explain how he had made Tisch promise the bonuses that became the subject of the Colin suit. As Walter told the story, he was prepared to bust the whole deal with Sony if his "boys" did not share in the 1987 profits of CBS Records. Considering what Walter had gone through to make the deal happen, this claim defied belief.

"Up until the day of the contract signing, Tisch doesn't call me. If I don't sign off, Sony doesn't sign off. I'm a party to the deal. They're not signing without management, and I represent management. I'm the union leader. So he waits. So I wait. So he waits. Normally, I'm not a very patient guy, as some of you may know.

"Finally, on the day of the signing, Walter, do you want to come to my office? Walter, let's talk about your contract. I said, Larry, I don't have as much money as you, I don't need that kind of money. I don't keep score with my life for how much cash I have. I like it. But it's not totally necessary, and I have some money. And I can go to Istanbul and meet Ahmet Ertegun, and you'll have to pay me.

"I said, I want to talk about what the other guys are going to get. You had a great year, right? So he says, What do you mean? What do you mean? He says, They're supposed to work! They're paid to work! I said, What are you running, a sweatshop, circa 1904? So we get into a discussion. We are apart a million and a half dollars. This has nothing to do with me. Or very little to do with me. I don't need all that money to sit on. In fact, it's a pain in the ass sometimes. So I said, Larry, if we don't work out a deal for the boys, I won't sign. He says, You're holding me up! You're holding me up! I said, Then call me Jesse James.

"So he starts to scream at me. He's sitting behind his desk, and he says, You're a fucking prick! Now, I hate to be scatological

[sic], but those were his words. He says, You're a fucking prick, and I'm gonna tell the whole *world* you're a fucking prick. And I started to laugh at him. And I said, Why bother, Larry? The whole world knows this. And I'm gonna tell the whole world that you are a *cheap* fucking prick. But why should I bother, Larry? The . . . whole . . . world . . . knows . . . this! Right?

"So he starts screaming at me, and the top of his head is getting red. He's standing behind his desk, and I'm sitting in front of it. And I don't have to listen to this garbage anymore. You know, in the springtime, life blooms, and the flowers grow, and the grass is green, but dwarfs die in the light of the sun. And it's sort of early spring. That's a dream I had. It's not relevant to anything.

"Anyway, he's screaming, screaming, screaming like a maniac. This is the head of CBS, screaming at me. The head is shining, right? And finally, I had enough of this. So I get up, and I said to him, Listen, you! Your yelling at me doesn't mean *shit*! I'm generally a classy, cultured guy, but calling me a prick? The head of CBS? So I said, Your yelling doesn't mean shit, but I have to warn you: If I lose my temper, I . . . COULD . . . GET . . . PHYSICAL! I slam my fist, *boom*, on the table. And he says, [meek voice] Let's go to the next point.

"And that's what the employee lawsuit is about. The exact subject matter of that meeting. That's all I'm going to say about it."

Someone asked Walter whether CBS Records lost money in fourth quarter 1987.

"How do I know? Have you seen the CBS numbers? I can't figure them out. A little on the bottom, a little on the top, a spin on the *tochis*. Read the year-end statement, tell me if you can figure out what CBS made. I thought the reason for corporate accounting was openness and honesty. I don't know what we made."

Tisch found out about Walter's press conference a short time later. He was no longer describing Walter to the press as a "very, very honorable fellow." "Disgraceful," Tisch said. "Walter is an animal."

For all the histrionics, the most significant aspect of Walter's feud with Larry Tisch was that it had hastened, if not caused, the sale of CBS Records to Sony. Digital audiotape was surely just around the corner, even though the industry continued to fight it.

Since the industry had also resisted the LP, the cassette, and the compact disc, chances were good that DAT would prove a boon to business. Foresight is not one of the record industry's strengths.

CBS Records had always been autonomous, and Sony planned to keep it that way. The change of hands was not likely to have as profound an effect on the record industry as, say, the failed Warner and PolyGram merger would have had. But it did have symbolic significance when placed beside Bertelsmann's purchase of RCA Records in December 1986. Now, four of the six major U.S. labels were foreign owned.

Much more important than what Sony was likely to do to CBS Records was what Yetnikoff had done to it by the time of the takeover. As the decade came to an end, Walter's A&R shortcomings at last took their toll.

In 1989 Warner's share of the top pop albums in *Billboard* exceeded 40 percent, versus 16 percent for CBS. "Astounding and a little bit scary," said the head of one big retail chain. The longer CBS's shortfall continued, the harder it would be for the label ever to reclaim its past prominence.

Warner was hitting hard with new acts like Guns N' Roses, Debbie Gibson, and Anita Baker. CBS had no big hits by baby acts in the first half of 1989 (though in the latter half CBS did a commendable job of breaking a group called New Kids on the Block). "We need more A&R people," Yetnikoff admitted to *The New York Times*. He then went on to blame Tom Wyman and Larry Tisch for not giving him funds to build the A&R department—a shameless remark from a man who had willingly spent over $12 million a year on indie promotion.

By the middle of 1989, people who saw Walter Yetnikoff agreed that he looked terrible. His two-year-old marriage to Cynthia Slamar was in trouble. He had begun to drink heavily. Finally, in August, he checked into the Hazelden Foundation, a clinic for drug and alcohol abuse in Minnesota. When he emerged in mid-September, his PR man, Bob Altshuler, pronounced him in "superb fighting condition."

The Sony brass did not seem worried about Yetnikoff's drinking problem, or even that the thirty-year market leadership of CBS Records had come to a decisive end under him. Sony was at the moment preoccupied with its recent $3.4 billion purchase of Columbia Pictures. Walter had no sooner returned from Hazelden when Sony asked him to recruit two of his old friends, Peter Guber

318

and Jon Peters, to run the studio. Guber was the movie man who had once been a partner of Neil Bogart's; Peters had made his entrée to Hollywood as Barbra Streisand's hairdresser. As independent producers, Guber and Peters's credits included box office smashes such as *Batman* and *Rain Man*, but also bombs like *Clan of the Cave Bear* and *Who's That Girl?*

The compensation package that Walter negotiated for Guber and Peters was outrageous even by Hollywood standards. Sony agreed to pay $200 million, a large premium over market value, for Guber–Peters Inc., which produced TV game shows. Guber and Peters owned 28 percent of that company. They also got yearly salaries of $2.7 million apiece, $50 million in deferred compensation, and an 8.08 percent share of Columbia's equity appreciation. ("Why 8.08 percent?" Guber reportedly asked at one point. "So you'll remember me when this is over," said Yetnikoff.)

The deal soon became even more expensive for Sony. Guber and Peters had just signed a five-year contract to have their films released through Warner Communications. On discovering that the two producers had turned around and agreed to run Columbia Pictures, Warner filed a $1 billion suit for breach of contract. The defendants in the suit were Sony, Guber–Peters, Walter Yetnikoff, and Sony U.S.A. vice-chairman Michael Schulhof, who had played a role in the negotiations. Sony and Guber–Peters countersued Warner for trying to block the deal. The litigation was dropped when Warner agreed to release Guber and Peters from their contract, and Sony gave up, among other things, 50 percent of CBS's lucrative record club. As Lisa Gubernick of *Forbes* put it, "Sony chairman Akio Morita must be wondering whether he ought to let Walter Yetnikoff do any more negotiating for him."

Despite all this, Sony continued to indulge Yetnikoff. The Japanese company fulfilled one of his dreams by getting CBS Records a corporate jet. It also agreed to name Yetnikoff chairman of a new entertainment committee that would oversee both CBS Records and Columbia Pictures. At long last, Walter had the dual influence over movies and records that had enhanced the power of his chief rivals, David Geffen and Irving Azoff.

Oddly enough, the latter two prepared for the nineties by switching employers. In late 1989 Azoff quit as head of MCA Records—his job went to Al Teller—and launched a new label under Warner's auspices. Then, in March 1990, Geffen agreed to sell his company to MCA for $545 million in stock, nudging his personal net worth toward the billion-dollar mark. To the naked eye, it seemed like a vastly overpriced deal, since Geffen Records was only ten years old and had a rather skimpy catalog. In mid-1988, Motown Records, which possessed some of the most beloved master recordings in pop music, though few current stars, was acquired by MCA and some outside investors for a mere $61 million.

The purchase of Geffen Records occurred only months after PolyGram agreed to buy two other big independent labels, A&M and Island, for a total of $732 million. The nineties will bear witness to an even more concentrated record business; there are few large independents left.

Unfortunately for Dick Asher, PolyGram's acquisition of A&M and Island marked the beginning of the end of his presidency. He did not participate in the negotiations, and he did not agree with the brain trust in Europe that the mergers made sense at the prices being paid. Meanwhile, there was growing tension between Asher and the PolyGram board over his compensation. On taking the PolyGram job in 1985, Asher had complained that sixteen years of loyal service at CBS had left him without much money. So the board granted him a bonus plan pegged to the U.S. division's earnings but, to its subsequent regret, forgot to put a ceiling on the amount Asher could be awarded. The Dutch company had lost money year after year in the United States; in 1985 it made a measly $3 million. Under Asher—thanks in large measure to the success of Bon Jovi and the heavy-metal craze—the company began to earn $15–20 million a year. Asher suddenly found his annual compensation in the "healthy seven figures," more than the chairman of PolyGram's owner, N. V. Philips, was making.

Asher was forced to resign in November 1989 because, he said, the board could not resolve the compensation dilemma any other way. PolyGram head David Fine, who had replaced Jan Timmer, gave *Billboard* a different account of the divorce. The bonus issue "never even arose," he said. "It was purely a question of chemistry and performance." Considering that PolyGram's profits had soared in five years under Asher, the gripe about performance was hard to figure. The problem of bad chemistry, however, was not a new one for Dick.

As a survivor, Dick had proven once and for all that he was not the equal of Walter Yetnikoff, who appeared indestructible. But at least Asher's fall was cushioned by his newfound wealth, and he accepted the loss of his job with equanimity. Quite by accident, Asher had made a big score of his own. "I have ideas of teaching," he said a short time after leaving PolyGram. "That's what I wanted to do before my folks persuaded me to go to law school. I'd like to lead a less structured life. Maybe," he added with a sigh, "it's all for the best."

THE RECKONING

■

SONY'S purchase of CBS Records overshadowed all other news in the music business for almost a year. The industry had ceased talking or worrying about the payola investigation in Los Angeles. It appeared to be a lost cause, the final episode in the government's long history of bumbling on the payola front. Word was spreading that Marvin Rudnick, the strike force attorney who had initiated the probe, was off the case and soon to be out of a job. There were rumors that forces within the Justice Department were inexplicably trying to kill the investigation altogether.

Yet even with Rudnick out of the picture, and the apparent adverse pressure from Washington, the investigation went on. It had gathered too much momentum within the IRS and the strike force to die quietly. The effort was given a lift in early 1988 when David Michael Smith, the former bodyguard for Joe Isgro who had fled to England to avoid a grand jury subpoena, came out of hiding and returned to Los Angeles. Apparently, Smith had decided to seek a movie or book option on his life story. He began to talk. "The evidence I've got," he warned, "is going to dramatically change the music industry."

The record business was jolted awake on February 26, 1988, less than two months after the Sony deal closed. That day, the payola grand jury returned its first four indictments. Ralph Tashjian, who for years had been Joe Isgro's chief liaison to Top 40, was charged with bribing men at three pop stations with cash and cocaine, distributing the drug, tax evasion, and obstruction of justice. His wife, Valerie, was accused of abetting the tax fraud. William Craig, Isgro's black-radio specialist, was charged with tax evasion and bribing men at four urban stations with cash. Lastly, the grand jury returned an indictment for failure to file tax returns against George Wilson Crowell, the former general manager of KIQQ in Los Angeles, a traditional Isgro station.

No other radio man besides Crowell was charged with a crime, although the indictment papers named seven alleged recipients of the gifts tendered by Tashjian and Craig. Supposedly, Tashjian had given $40,000 and "various quantities of cocaine" to Johnny Lee Walker, the program director of KYNO in Fresno and cochairman of the local "Just Say No" program. (Walker said the assertion that he received drugs was "ridiculous.") The other six alleged recipients, whose combined take was put at more than $230,000 in cash and an unspecified amount of coke, were employees of stations in El Paso, Cincinnati, Kansas City, Atlanta, Fresno again, and Jacksonville.

Hours after the indictments were unsealed, Ralph and Valerie Tashjian were arrested at their home in San Mateo and led away, handcuffed, in separate cars. The couple's children witnessed the scene. Ralph Tashjian's lawyer, Anthony Brooklier, complained bitterly about the "heavy-handed" arrest of his client. Obviously, he said, the indictment of Valerie was an attempt to coerce Ralph to cooperate with the government. "A triple play," he said. "From Valerie to Ralph to Isgro is what the government is trying to do."

If so, the strategy at first appeared to be working. Faced with up to ten years in prison, Valerie was given the opportunity to plea-bargain a suspended sentence if her husband would also plead guilty and become a witness in the ongoing payola case. And on February 14, 1989, almost a full year after the indictments, the couple appeared in district court to do just that. But then Valerie broke down crying and said that while she did list personal receipts as business expenses, as charged, "I just figured the tax accountant would sort it out at the end of the year. . . . I was very busy taking care of our children." Hearing that, District Judge Pamela Rymer threw out the plea agreement and scheduled a trial. She also ruled that the indictment against Ralph Tashjian was not specific enough.

In April 1989, the government filed a new, 175-count indictment against Ralph Tashjian. Almost every count was for a specific record he had allegedly bribed radio stations to play. Among the records were songs by Bruce Springsteen, Cyndi Lauper, Prince, Hall and Oates, Phil Collins, and Paul McCartney.

Then, on May 15, Judge Rymer accepted a defense motion to throw out the charges against Valerie Tashjian, on the grounds that the government had tried to force her to plead guilty to save her husband from more serious charges. Rymer accused the prosecutors of "reprehensible" behavior, "well below the standard of conduct expected of government prosecutors."

Nevertheless, one week later Ralph Tashjian pleaded guilty to one payola charge, a misdemeanor, and to filing a false tax return and obstruction of justice, both felonies. He admitted sending a Federal Express package of cocaine to an employee of Fresno station KMGX. And on October 17, 1989, the government extracted a guilty plea from William Craig. He confessed to payola and the preparation of fraudulent tax returns.

By this time, Joe Isgro knew he was in trouble. He continued to run his independent promotion company, though he was no longer much of a factor in the business, perhaps because he had lost the services of Tashjian and Craig, or as a consequence of having sued the labels for antitrust. Other past members of the Network, including Fred DiSipio, were back making large sums of money in record promotion. Isgro had renamed his company The Music Group, but his activities seemed to be centered around movies. He represented Robin Moore, author of *The French Connection*, and owned the rights to a Moore screenplay, *The Jimmy Hoffa Story*. Toward the end of 1989, Isgro was optimistic that 20th Century–Fox would agree to make the film.

That was perhaps the last good news the decade would hold for Joseph Isgro. On November 30, 1989, almost four years after NBC News had brought him national notoriety, the payola grand jury voted to indict him on fifty-one counts of payola, drug trafficking, racketeering, obstruction of justice, and tax fraud.

Two other men were indicted with Isgro. One of them, a convicted drug offender named Jeffrey Monka, was little known in the record business. Monka was accused of conspiring with Isgro to defraud the IRS by creating a sham corporation, Star Promotions, through which Isgro allegedly exchanged corporate checks for cash. The indictment charged Isgro with using this cash to bribe radio station employees and pay kickbacks to record company executives.

The other man indicted with Isgro, on charges of receiving kickbacks from him, was well known in the record business. He was Ray Anderson, the former head of Epic Records. Before taking that job, Anderson had been head of promotion for Columbia, where he oversaw campaigns to get radio airplay for acts such as Bruce Springsteen and Billy Joel. Anderson had moved up to the Epic job at the behest of Al Teller, the president of CBS Records U.S., a man Walter Yetnikoff never liked. When Yetnikoff got rid of Teller in April 1988, Anderson became a political sacrifice, ending up as an artist manager in Los Angeles. Now, Anderson stood accused of taking at least $70,000 in kickbacks from Isgro when he was promotion VP for Columbia.

As soon as the grand jury delivered its indictment, IRS agents set out to arrest Isgro and Monka. (Anderson, it was decided, would be allowed to turn himself in.) Monka was quickly pulled off the freeway, but for several tense hours, agents tried to locate Joe Isgro. They went to his home in Glendale and his office in Universal City. There was no sign of him. Finally, at about 3:30 P.M., they received word that he was at the courthouse in downtown Los Angeles, ready to give himself up.

Isgro did not look as sharp as usual as agents handcuffed him and led him across the plaza to the Federal Building. He wore chinos and an oversize white chemise that flared at the biceps. His face was puffy, and he was sweating profusely. As the agents escorted him down the fifth-floor hallway, he found himself face to face with television cameras and his old nemesis Ira Silverman of NBC. The newsman shouted questions at Isgro but got no reaction. So Silverman decided to goad him a little. "Have you been in touch with Walter Yetnikoff?" he asked. Isgro's temples began to pulse rapidly. "How about John Gotti?" The pulsing accelerated.

After Isgro was fingerprinted, the agents bundled him into a car and took him back to the courthouse for a bail hearing. Magistrate Volney Brown set bail at $500,000, and for the first time in his life, Joe Isgro spent the night in jail.

The following day, Isgro appeared before the magistrate in prison-issue blue shirt and pants to ask for a reduction in bail to $100,000. He was accompanied by his attorney, Donald Re, a top white-collar lawyer who had helped defend John DeLorean. Strike force prosecutor Drew Pitt argued that bail should not be reduced because Isgro, he alleged, was "threatening to harm" his former bodyguard, David Michael Smith, now a cooperating witness.* Such threats should be taken seriously, Pitt said, because Isgro had "influence with people in organized crime." Pitt charged that Isgro shared a $1 million money-laundering operation with convicted mafioso Joe "Piney" Armone. Don Re mocked these assertions, and Magistrate Brown did reduce Isgro's bail, but only to $300,000. Isgro was nonetheless able to post bond that evening. He subsequently entered a plea of not guilty; so did Anderson and Monka.

Free for the time being, Isgro faced up to two hundred years in jail and $1.5 million in fines if he lost his case. Unlike Tashjian and Craig, Isgro had been hit with RICO, the tough racketeering statute that had been used successfully against mobsters and Wall Street miscreants. And if he stood trial, Tashjian and Craig, not to mention his ex-bodyguard, could probably be counted on to testify against him.

Indeed, both Tashjian and Craig were given light sentences after federal prosecutors refrained from recommending jail terms, a sign that the two men had agreed to help nail Isgro. Craig drew five years' probation, a $60,000 fine, and one hundred hours of community service. Tashjian was sentenced to sixty days in a halfway house, three years' probation, a $100,000 fine, and five hundred hours of community service. Judge Rymer said she had planned stiffer punishment for Tashjian but was moved by his tearful seven-minute plea, in which he claimed to have overcome an addiction to alcohol and cocaine. "Since my indictment," Tashjian said, "even though my wife and I have gone through hell, I can honestly say these have been the best years of my life because of my change in spirituality."

While all this was occurring, the payola investigation spread to Memphis, where a grand jury charged a local promotion man, Howard Goodman, with fourteen counts of mail fraud and payola. Goodman pleaded not guilty.

The independent promotion crisis was not over after all. The service had ceased to be a financial albatross but had provoked a full-scale crackdown. The indictment of Ray Anderson showed that the government was willing to go after a top industry executive, albeit a former one. The indictment of Howard Goodman in

---

* At the moment, Smith was stewing in state prison. He had got in a barroom brawl the previous August.

Memphis suggested that the investigation was spreading. And above all, the case against Joe Isgro posed grave consequences for the record industry.

Isgro had fallen a long way since 1985, his peak year, when the labels paid him $10 million to promote their records, even as some of them lost money. When the industry that created Isgro tried to discard him, he was bitter enough to file suit against the labels. Now, the question remained: How much further was Isgro willing to fall without turning on the industry that had betrayed him? As this book went to press, the trial was scheduled to begin in mid-1990. For the time being, he was defiant. "I will defend my innocence vigorously," he said, "and I don't plan to do that by pointing a finger at somebody else."

Perhaps Isgro would remain, as he liked to phrase it, a "stand-up guy" to the end. But Marvin Rudnick, the former strike force prosecutor who had started the investigation, was not so sure it would end with Isgro. "I can't wait for the trial," he said. "It's going to be great to hear how Joe Isgro fooled the whole record industry into paying him so much money."

DEBTS AND SOURCES

I can't say this book wouldn't exist without Ruth Fecych, but it would not have been the same book. She has been a great friend and collaborator—editor is too weak a term to describe her contribution. Though I take full responsibility for its contents, I feel this book is hers as much as mine.

My deepest gratitude to two people who have since left Times Books: Elisabeth Scharlatt and Jonathan Segal. Many thanks to Beth Pearson, production editor, and Joan Marlow, copy editor, for a great job. Thanks also to Marge Anderson, Sandee Brawarsky, Susan Luke, Lesley Oelsner, Della Smith, Jenny Vandeventer, and Steve Wasserman.

I'm extremely grateful to all my sources, but one bears special mention. Less than a month after I interviewed Michael Hutson of Gaia Records, he died in a drowning accident. Michael was one of the most charming and straightforward people I met in the record business. His death is a terrible loss.

The greatest side benefit of working on this book was that through it I met a number of fine journalists, many of whom have become personal friends. Susan Adams, Fred Goodman, Bruce Haring, John Lombardi, Chris Mills, Jeff Ressner, Jeff Rutledge, and Adam White all gave me valuable assistance. Special thanks, as well, to Michael Gillard of the London *Observer* and Bill Bastone of *The Village Voice*.

Other journalists, some friends as well, provided assistance: David Breskin, John Campbell, Jim Carnegie, Michael Caruso, Pat Clawson, John Cooney, Hal Davis, Claudia Deutsch, Barbara Donnelly, Steve Dupler, Gene Ely, Stephen Fried, Michael Goldberg, Jill Jonnes, Neal Koch, Janet Lewis, Andrew Marton, Libby Mosier, Michael Orey, Ginnie Sidaris, Marty Spaninger, Stu Stogel, and Ken Terry. Finally, I must single out William Knoedelseder of the *Los Angeles Times*, who came to my aid even though he was writing a book of his own—truly a statesmanlike act. Bill's articles, many of which are cited in the source notes, have added immeasurably to the public record on the music business.

I received help from numerous law enforcement people, including Andy Baxter, Douglas Grover, Andy Kurins, Ed McDonald, Fred Rayano, Brian Waldron, and many others I cannot name. None of these sources, I might add, ever overstepped the bounds of propriety in discussing a criminal matter.

Harry Gossett of Rowan Associates in Alexandria, Virginia, is a superb private investigator and, I'm happy to say, a friend. Harry helped me obtain declassified police reports and other documents, and generously refused to accept payment aside from expenses. Thanks, also, to Barbara Rowan.

A few people provided paid assistance. John Rosenberg of On-Line Resources in Arlington, Virginia, ran a number of computer searches for me and turned up valuable news items. Andy Kivel of Data Center in Oakland, California, found other useful clips. Two Los Angeles-based reporters, Jeff Gottlieb and Geanne Perlman, obtained court documents for me. Thanks also to Geanne for covering Sal Pisello's arraignment in my absence.

Many thanks to the following PR and investor relations people: Dick Auletta, Sue Binford, Andrew Freedman, Richard Gersh, Gershon Kekst, Dan Klores, Barry Kluger, Ann Morfogen, Diane Millett, Jerri Perkovich, Doris Robin, Sue Satriano, Gerald Vukas, and Susan Zampolino.

I am grateful to those people who helped me obtain or gain access to useful books, articles, recordings, and documents: Mikie Harris, Lee Hasin, Bob Hyde, Carol Hyun, Mary Kate Leming, Marty London, Tina McCarthy, Richard Perry, Sarah Prown, Marian Russell, William Thomas, Chris Washington, and David Wheeler.

For hospitality and other assistance, thanks to: Bob Braunschweig, David Cudaback, Chel Dong, Steve Futterman, Peter Landau, Carole and Harry Schachter, Rita Stollman, and Gail and Diva Zappa.

Most of my library research was conducted at the Elmer Holmes Bobst Library of New York University, my alma mater. My thanks to all the helpful librarians there, and at the Lincoln Center Library for the Performing Arts.

This book was written in XyWrite III-Plus. I'm grateful to XYQUEST Inc. for creating this excellent word-processing software.

I want to single out two close friends who were instrumental in the life of this project. Fiammetta Rocco introduced me to Ruth Fecych and provided valuable advice on the subject of book writing. Edward Baker gave me the idea to do this book.

Very special thanks to L.B.S.

Last on my list but foremost in my appreciation, I would like to thank my parents, whose encouragement and support made this book possible.

1 The Education of Dick Asher

[Estimates of dollar volume of record business for various years and number of units sold of specific records provided by RIAA or data base assembled by *Billboard*'s Adam White, unless otherwise noted. Corporate sales and earnings and executive compensation figures from annual reports, 10-K forms, and proxy statements, unless otherwise noted. AI is an abbreviation for author's interview.]

pp. 3–4. Depiction of the Wall tour: *Pink Floyd* (New York: Delilah/Putnam, 1980); "Pink Floyd to Play Two Cities," *Rolling Stone*, Jan. 24, 1980; "Talent in

Action," *Billboard*, Feb. 23, 1980; "Pink Floyd: The Wall Tour," *Rolling Stone*, June 4, 1987.

p. 3. "This is very tough stuff": "Pink Floyd: Up Against 'The Wall,' " *Rolling Stone*, Feb. 7, 1980.

pp. 4–11. Asher's thoughts and quotes: AIs with Asher, Oct. 22, 1985; Jan. 6, 1986; June 3, 1987; June 29, 1987; Sept. 29, 1987.

p. 5. CBS Records outspent all others: AI with Asher, Jan. 6, 1986. Also confirmed by CBS Records for the year 1985 in *Joseph Isgro* v. *Recording Industry Association of America*, Case No. 2740 (1986), Central District of California.

p. 6. Backe's thoughts on Asher and Yetnikoff: AI with Backe, Aug. 11, 1987.

p. 11. The Network: *Billboard* first reported the term in "WCI Cos. Drop Indie Promo Reps," Nov. 8, 1980, and named some of its key members in "MCA Studies Its Independent Promoters' Expenditures," Nov. 15, 1980. The term received wider currency in "Unease over Clout of the Promoters," *Los Angeles Times*, Oct. 21, 1983.

    Golf shirt story: AI with RCA executive vice-president Richard Dobbis, Apr. 30, 1987.

    Subcontracting arrangement: Joe Isgro testified to this effect in his deposition of Apr. 22, 1987, in *Isgro* v. *RIAA*. He said he had been given projects to work by Jerry Meyers and Jerry Brenner that they in turn had got from artist managers.

p. 12. DiSipio's ninety stations: "The New Payola," *NBC Nightly News*, June 10, 1987.

p. 12. DiSipio and Isgro territories: DiSipio stations reported in "A Few Promoters Dominate Record Business," *The Wall Street Journal*, Apr. 18, 1986. Isgro stations alleged to have accepted payola from his top employees, Ralph Tashjian and William Craig, in *United States* v. *Ralph Tashjian*, Case No. 124(B) (1988), U.S. District Court, Central District of California; and *United States* v. *William Craig*, Case No. 125 (1988), U.S. District Court, Central District of California.

p. 12. Descriptions of Isgro and DiSipio: See Chapter Ten: Joey and Freddy.

p. 12. "Freddy could open the shul": AI with *NBC Nightly News* producer Ira Silverman, June 22, 1987.

p. 14. Payola as the "price" of airplay: Professor Ronald Coase of the University of Chicago Law School has argued, correctly, that payola is another name for advertising. Radio play is the main means to advertise a new record. This advertising is rightly free. Coase, however, believes it should not be free and that payola should be legalized. This is absurd. Radio already receives a payment in the free use of the records. Without music, pop radio would have no listeners—and no revenues. One could as easily argue that radio should pay the labels for music. Indeed, MTV, the music video channel, pays record companies for the use of film clips.

    But perhaps the professor should not be blamed for his flawed conclusion. In a Sept. 16, 1986, letter to Stanford Law's J. Gregory Sidak, Coase complained that "one problem in dealing with this industry is that it is very difficult to get reliable information. . . . It soon became apparent that much of what I was told consisted of lies."

p. 14. Law journal study: "The 'New Payola' and the American Record Industry: Transactions Costs and Precautionary Ignorance in Contracts for Illicit Services," *Harvard Journal of Law & Public Policy*, Summer 1987.

p. 14. Confessions of California PD: "The New Payola," NBC *Nightly News*, July 10, 1987. See also: "Ross Plans New Payola Probe," *Radio & Records*, June 26, 1987.

p. 14. Methods of paying bribes:

Cassette boxes and record sleeves: "Inside the Payola Scandal," *Rolling Stone*, Jan. 14, 1988.

"There are programmers": AI with Fred Haayen, June 18, 1987.

pp. 14. The cost of using indies: In *Isgro* v. *RIAA*, CBS, Warner Bros., MCA, and A&M disclosed their indie expenditures for 1985. The combined total for just these four companies was $30 million. It's hard to imagine that the entire industry could have spent less than twice that amount. The $60 million estimate was cited to the author in a number of interviews, including one conducted on Oct. 23, 1987, with Jack Craigo, former president of Chrysalis Records. Others thought a more likely figure was $80 million.

p. 15. "There was . . . a suspicion": Quoted in "Payola: The Record-Label Connection," *Rolling Stone*, Apr. 21, 1988.

p. 16. " 'Jesse' is legendary": AI with RCA's Rick Dobbis, Apr. 30, 1987.

p. 16. "it wasn't payola": AI with Asher, Apr. 17, 1986.

p. 16. "You got the feeling": AI with Goldman, July 21, 1986.

p. 16. "I call them claim jumpers": AI with Gallis, June 27, 1987.

p. 16. "The line about Freddy": AI with Danny Davis, Feb. 29, 1988. He was referring to when he was vice-president of pop promotion at Motown in the late seventies.

p. 17. The Network contract and R&R: A perfect illustration of the Network-R&R symbiosis could be found in the contract given Joe Isgro by MCA Records on January 1, 1986, for his promotion services. Under the heading COMPENSA-TION, the contract read, in part, "You will be eligible to receive a bonus payment when your promotion and exploitation activities for a Recording in the Territory result in that Recording being broadcast on so-called 'P1,' 'P2' and 'P3' . . . class radio stations in the Territory. . . . Your bonus payment . . . shall be $2,500 for each P1 station, $750 for each P2 station and $500 for each P3 station . . . unless you and we have mutually agreed upon a *greater or lesser* amount [emphasis added]." (A promotion contract given to Isgro by Warner Bros. Records on July 1, 1983, had identical wording, except the bonus for a P1 was $1,500. Of course, this was three years earlier.)

R&R had created and was the sole user of the designations P1, P2, and P3 (the "P" stands for "parallel"). These were specific stations ranked by descending size order—P1s had the most listeners—that R&R judged to be leaders in their respective regions. R&R's charts were calculated solely from the playlists of these stations. As Isgro's contract makes clear, the Network promoter was being paid, above all else, to get a record a good chart position in R&R.

p. 17. Paper adds: AIs with Bob Wilson, July 28, 1987 and Mar. 15, 1988. Also explained in detail to author on same date by Danny Davis, ex-employee of

Isgro Enterprises. See also: "Record Firms Don't Always Get the Radio Play They Pay For," *Los Angeles Times*, Mar. 19, 1984.

2 Dick and Walter

p. 18. "king of the grooves": "The King of Records at CBS," *The New York Times*, Jan. 22, 1984.

p. 18. "Nobody out-*geschreis* me" and depiction of tantrums: "King of the Schmooze," *Esquire*, Nov. 1986.

pp. 18–19. Yetnikoff's tone-deafness: AI with Yetnikoff's ex-secretary, Debra Federoff, on Apr. 9, 1987. She said, "He can't hear shit. When they'd play him a new cut, it was a joke. He doesn't know one from the other."

   "I mean I can't *sing*": Unpublished comment made to *Rolling Stone*'s Fred Goodman in May 26, 1988, interview.

p. 19. "moth among butterflies": Quoted in "Asher Beats His PolyGram 'Secret' Goal by a Year," *Radio & Records*, Oct. 23, 1987.

p. 19. "Think about what it takes": AI with Asher, Oct. 22, 1985.

p. 19. Asher and the artists:

   "I'm not sure": AI with Asher, Apr. 21, 1987.

   Asher and Iglesias: AI on Oct. 2, 1987, with Susan Blond, who represented Iglesias as his freelance publicist; and AI on June 4, 1987, with former CBS employee Stephen Reed.

   Asher and Zappa: AI with Zappa, July 6, 1987.

   Asher and Jackson, Diamond, and Joel: AI on July 21, 1987, with artist attorney John Branca.

pp. 19–20. Romeo on Asher: AIs with Romeo, Feb. 26, 1987, and Mar. 14, 1988.

p. 20. Asher's football aspirations: AIs with Asher, Feb. 15, 1987, and Sept. 29, 1987.

p. 20. Shulman story and quote: AI with CBS alum Bob Jamieson, Sept. 3, 1987. Shulman declined to comment on the incident.

pp. 20–21. Braun on Asher: AI with Braun, July 14, 1987.

p. 21. "Four hours was nothing": Interview notes of John Lombardi for article on Yetnikoff, "King of the Schmooze," *Esquire*, Nov. 1986. Hereafter: Lombardi notes.

p. 21. You know what your punishment is?: AI with Braun, June 15, 1986.

p. 21. "You never knew": AI with Blond, Oct. 2, 1987.

pp. 21–22. Yetnikoff's tantrums and crudeness:

   "Walter worked himself into a fury": Confidential source.

   "When he has a fit": AI with ex-CBS France head Alain Levy, Dec. 18, 1986.

   Beach Boys story: AI with Branca, July 21, 1987.

p. 22. Yetnikoff's father and grandfather:

   Little affection for father: AI with Federoff, Apr. 9, 1987.

   Grandfather story: Lombardi notes.

p. 22. Yetnikoff and Paley:

   Paley's ambivalence about his religion: Robert Metz, *CBS: Reflections in a*

Bloodshot Eye (New York: Signet/New American Library, 1976), p. 10; and David Halberstam, *The Powers That Be* (New York: Alfred A. Knopf, 1979), pp. 31–32.

"I tried to get Paley": Lombardi notes.

Aren't the goyim boring!: AI with Yetnikoff's attorney, Stanley Schlesinger, Sept. 9, 1987.

pp. 22–23. Yetnikoff's Jewish militancy:

Dorchester ban: AI with Romeo, June 22, 1987.

Sheik of Qatar story: AI with Alexenburg, Feb. 10, 1987.

"It's nothing more": AI with Arthur Taylor, Apr. 28, 1987.

Preference for shiksas: AIs with Yetnikoff confidants Debra Federoff, Apr. 9, 1987, and Nat Weiss, Mar. 5, 1987; "shiksa farm" expression cited to author by Yetnikoff's personal publicist, Norman Winter, on July 30, 1987.

p. 23. Yetnikoff's brilliance: AI with Blond, Oct. 2, 1987; AI with Braun, June 15, 1986.

p. 23. "You have to be sensitive": Goodman's interview with Yetnikoff, May 26, 1988.

p. 23. "Sometimes I can't believe": "The King of Records at CBS."

p. 23. "We had a big fight": "Walter Yetnikoff: The Most Powerful Man in the Record Business," *Rolling Stone*, Dec. 15-29, 1988.

p. 23. "My wife had an uncle": AI with Braun, July 14, 1987.

p. 24. Yetnikoff as mensch:

No softer touch: AI with Schlesinger, Sept. 2, 1987.

Employee with back injury: AI with the employee, Alexenburg, Feb. 10, 1987.

"You know what my problem is?": Lombardi notes.

p. 24. "Walter had to have the personnel man": AI with Backe, Aug. 11, 1987.

p. 24. "I was very naive": AI with Asher, Sept. 29, 1987.

p. 25. "They divided the floor off": AI with Braun, July 14, 1987.

p. 25. "I had it put in": AI with Federoff, Apr. 9, 1987.

p. 25. "It never got personal": AI with Jamieson, Sept. 3, 1987.

pp. 25–26. Asher vs. Yetnikoff on indies:

Common justifications for payola: This is based on numerous interviews by the author.

Yetnikoff himself used the lobbying analogy in a 1986 interview with John Lombardi (the exact date is not in Lombardi's notes; probably March or April). Speaking of the indies, Yetnikoff said, "Why do people use lobbyists in Washington? In the disc business, they call it payola; in Washington, they call it lobbying."

Brazil story; Asher's fears about billing system: AI with Asher, June 29, 1987.

"They get results": "King of the Schmooze."

3 Lullaby of Gangland

p. 31. Lubinsky's failure to pay royalties: AI with former Savoy A&R man Lee Magid, Mar. 29, 1990. Magid said, "Nobody ever got what they should have got" from Lubinsky. Even Fred Mendelsohn, Lubinsky's successor as Savoy president and a diehard apologist for him, had to admit that his late boss rarely paid royalties. AI with Mendelsohn Mar. 27, 1990. Mendelsohn said that artists were charged for all the costs of recording, which more than wiped out their share of the proceeds. Of course, today's standard contracts are not much better than Savoy's (see pp. 143–44).

p. 31. "We were all characters": This and all subsequent Levy quotes, unless noted, from AIs on Feb. 24, 1987; Apr. 29, 1987; May 27, 1987; and July 30, 1988.

p. 32. "Octopus" and "Godfather": On Oct. 30, 1957, *Variety* ran an item entitled "Big Wheel and New Disk Deals (Morris Levy, Music Octopus)." It was a reprint of observations made the previous week by noted jazz critic Ralph Gleason in his column for the *San Francisco Chronicle*. Gleason described Levy as a "lean, muscular New Yorker who . . . heads a music empire of staggering proportions." In an interview on Apr. 29, 1987, Morris complained about the "Octopus" moniker. "That didn't help me, as time went by," he said. NBC-TV's Brian Ross used the "Godfather" handle in an interview with Levy on *Today*, NBC News, Sept. 24, 1986.

p. 32. "It's always pennies": "Frankie Lymon: A Lover's Legacy," *West 57th*, CBS News, July 9, 1986.

pp. 32–33. Levy's personal finances:

$75 million net worth: Author's estimate, not disputed by Levy.

Number of Big Seven copyrights: "Morris Levy: Big Clout in Record Industry: His Behind-the-Scenes Influence Is Felt Throughout the Industry," *Los Angeles Times*, July 20, 1986.

Sunnyview's value: Stated by Levy for purpose of securing bail in *United States* v. *Morris Levy, Dominick Canterino, and Howard Fisher*, Case No. 301 (1986), Camden, New Jersey.

Strawberries bid: AI with Levy's eldest son, Adam, Apr. 8, 1988.

p. 33. "That don't make me a Catholic": Relayed to author by attorney Freddie Gershon, Mar. 16, 1988.

p. 33. Irving Levy's death: This is a classic example of how legend becomes fact. At least a half-dozen different sources assured the author that Irving was bumped off by the mob, and that Morris was the real target. This false assertion also turns up in an exhaustive but hardly infallible FBI document concerning Levy: "Affidavit in Support of Orders Authorizing the Interception of Wire Communications," Lawrence Ferreira, Special Agent, Federal Bureau of Investigation, Aug. 1985; *United States* v. *Biaggi and Esposito*, Case No. 151 (1987), U.S. District Court, Eastern District of New York. The rumor appears in even more distorted form in Marc Eliot's *Rockonomics* (New York: Franklin Watts, 1989), which states on p. 48 that Irving was "gunned down" by "purported gangland rivals who mistook him for Morris."

In fact, the killer, Lee Schlesinger, was convicted of manslaughter and went to jail for the murder. Schlesinger had arrived at Birdland on Jan. 31, 1959, in the early morning hours, with his wife, Betty, a prostitute. Irving ordered her from the club, and a scuffle ensued between him and Schlesinger. The two men carried the fight outside; presently, Irving staggered back into the club, mortally wounded with a knife. No one actually witnessed the stabbing. Schlesinger's lawyer, Herbert Lippman, told the author on Mar. 23, 1990, that his client was "one of the boys. He worked for the mob [as] a collector for shylocks." But, Lippman added, this was a personal dispute, not a mob killing. And, clearly, Morris was not the target.

See also: "Couple Is Refused Bail in Slaying at Birdland," *(New York) Herald Tribune*, Feb. 1, 1959.

p. 34. Yetnikoff and Levy:

Yetnikoff's investment in Malinowski: Confirmed by Yetnikoff in "King of the Schmooze"; and by Yetnikoff's attorney, Stanley Schlesinger, AI, Sept. 2, 1987.

Investment in Levy horses by Joel, Hall, Frank Weber (Joel's manager), and Tommy Mottola (Hall's manager): AIs with Levy, May 27, 1987; and Adam Levy, Apr. 8, 1988.

"Psychiatric consultation" check: Shown to author by Adam Levy on above date.

pp. 37–40. Levy and the mob:

New York police information: Confidential source.

Description of Carbo: Virgil W. Peterson, *The Mob: 200 Years of Organized Crime in New York* (Illinois: Green Hill Publishers, 1983), pp. 328–29.

Greenwich Village Inn: AI with Levy, July 30, 1988.

"This kid could tear": Quoted in " 'Corky' Vastola: Music and the Mob," *The (Bergen) Record*, Sept. 30, 1986.

Genovese history: Peterson, op. cit., pp. 316–18, 395; and Peter Maas, *The Valachi Papers* (New York: G.P. Putnam's Sons, 1968), pp. 242–45.

Eboli's Promo deal: Confidential source.

FBI warning about Gigante: Levy on NBC's *Today*, Sept. 24, 1986 (Levy did not name Gigante, but the inference was obvious).

Gigante's insanity gambit: "Strange Old Man on Sullivan Street: A New Mob Power," *The New York Times*, Feb. 3, 1988.

The brownstone: "Runnin' Scared," *The Village Voice*, Dec. 8, 1987. The *Voice* reporter, William Bastone, calculated the $16,000 sale price from the transfer tax on the property deed. Levy insisted to the author that he had sold the brownstone to Esposito for exactly what he had paid for it. But the author examined the same deed transfer documents—for 67 East Seventy-seventh Street, Block 01392, Lot 0129, New York County—and reached the same conclusion as Bastone. The clear implication is that Levy paid tribute to Gigante, or laundered money for him, via Esposito. For more evidence of this, see the Ferreira affidavit and "The Godfather of Rock & Roll," *Rolling Stone*, Nov. 17, 1988.

pp. 40–41. Goldner information: "Frankie Lymon, the Teenagers: A Recording History," booklet published by Murray Hill Records & Tapes for five-record Lymon reissue, 1986. For an amusing account of how Goldner formed Red

Bird with Leiber and Stoller, see: Ted Fox, *In the Groove: The People Behind the Music* (New York: St. Martin's Press, 1986), pp. 182–83.

pp. 41–43. Alan Freed history: Ed Ward, Geoffrey Stokes, and Ken Tucker, *Rock of Ages: The Rolling Stone History of Rock and Roll* (New York: Rolling Stone Press/Summit Books, 1986), pp. 69–70, 96; and Steve Chapple and Reebee Garofalo, *Rock 'n' Roll Is Here to Pay: The History and Politics of the Music Industry* (Chicago: Nelson Hall, 1977), pp. 56–57.

"Anybody who says": Ibid., p. 56.

P. J. Moriarty story: Confirmed in AIs with Gayles, June 1, 1987; and Hooke, Mar. 24, 1988. Both these men told the story a bit differently than Levy, in each case making himself the principal foil.

Lew Platt information: Confirmed by Freed authority Jeff Rutledge in July 20, 1989, letter to author.

Earl Wilson interview: "Alan Freed Telling All: Meets Payola Probers," *New York Post*, Nov. 25, 1959. The type size is indeed enormous.

p. 45. Weakness of payola statute: See also: "$1 Million in Suspected 'New Payola' is Probed," *Los Angeles Times*, Dec. 22, 1987.

pp. 45–47. Congressional hearings: *Payola and Other Deceptive Practices in the Broadcasting Field.* Hearings before a Subcommittee of the Committee on Interstate and Foreign Commerce, House of Representatives, Eighty-sixth Congress, second session. See also: "The Entertainer: After Three Decades on TV, Dick Clark Is Busier than Ever," *The Wall Street Journal*, Mar. 25, 1985.

p. 46. Elektra's $27 million loss: "A Wildcatter in the Record Biz," *Manhattan, inc.*, May 1989.

p. 46. "the man who is to the record industry": AI with Smith, July 21, 1987.

p. 48. "Morris gave me back the demo": AI with Cordell, Mar. 21, 1988.

p. 49. "He's entitled": AI with Weiss, Mar. 23, 1988.

p. 49. Lennon case: *Big Seven Music Corp.* v. *John Lennon*, Case No. 2924 (1975), Supreme Court of the State of New York, County of New York. Appellate court opinion: 409 F. Supp. 122 (1976).

p. 49. "You get together": Deposition of Morris Levy, Apr. 18, 1985; *Emira Lymon* v. *Morris Levy*, U.S. District Court, Southern District of New York.

p. 49. "If you screw him": AI with Art Kass, Jan. 14, 1988.

p. 49. "Given where we came from": AI with Weiss, Mar. 23, 1988.

p. 50. Jimmy Weston's incident: "Gigante Asks Probe of D.A. Office in Assault on Cop," (New York) *Daily News*, July 2, 1975.

"Morris told me, Louie": AI with Gigante, Apr. 6, 1988.

pp. 50–51. McCalla information:

Date and details of murder; height and weight: Fort Lauderdale, Florida, Police Department offense report, Case No. 15317 (1980); and Certificate of Death for Nathan Calvin McCalla, State of Florida, File No. 204, Feb. 20, 1980.

Military background; JAMF name; "If I was going to describe": AI with Barry Fredericks, Nov. 12, 1987.

"Nate had a medieval mace": AI with David Nives, Nov. 17, 1987.

Washington police information: AIs with D.C. policemen Carl Shoffler, Feb. 29, 1988, and Joe Quantrille, Mar. 16, 1988. Also: Washington, D.C., police report, June 8, 1983.

pp. 51–53. UJA dinner: All details and dialogue from *Sliced Steak*, a 1973 movie documentary of the dinner, by Richard Perry.

p. 51. Levy requested Smith as emcee: AI with Smith, July 21, 1987.

p. 52. "I was the payola king": AI with Weiss, Mar. 23, 1988.

pp. 53–56. Extortion case:

    Heroin allegations: Oct. 28, 1988, sentencing of Levy in *U.S. v. Levy*.

    Testimonial letters: AI with Levy, July 30, 1988.

    Details of cutout deal: Testimony in *U.S. v. Levy*.

    LaMonte's criminal record: Criminal docket of John Donald LaMonte, Docket No. 438 (1977), United States District Court, Philadelphia.

    FBI wiretaps: Government's exhibits 104, 107, 116, and 138 in *U.S. v. Levy*.

p. 54. Vastola and music:

    Vastola and Freed: AI with Freed acquaintance Bob Rolontz, Mar. 20, 1988; confirmed to author by Gayles, June 9, 1987.

    Vastola and Lymon: Deposition of Morris Levy, Apr. 18, 1985, *Lymon v. Levy*.

    Vastola and Cleftones: AI with Levy, July 30, 1988.

    Vastola and Queens Booking: AI with then–U.S. Attorney for Newark, Thomas Greelish, Jan. 26, 1987; confirmed by Levy in Lymon deposition.

    Vastola and Davis horse farm: Davis's testimony in *Organized Crime in Sports (Racing)*. Hearings before the Select Committee on Crime, House of Representatives, Ninety-second Congress, second session.

4 Goddard and Clive

pp. 58–59. Lieberson information:

    Personal history; Cronkite quote; bons mots (unless otherwise noted): Goddard Lieberson commemorative album, private issue, Columbia Records, 1977; and "Goddard Lieberson, Who Fostered LPs at Columbia Records, Dies," *The New York Times*, May 30, 1977.

    Stool sample: AI with Bruce Lundvall, May 18, 1987.

    Signed his letters "God": AI with Arthur Taylor, Apr. 28, 1987.

    "He spent the whole meeting": AI with John Eastman, Dec. 17, 1987.

pp. 59–60. Paley and Stanton: Metz, op. cit., pp. 243–244; and Halberstam, op. cit., pp. 153–154.

p. 60. Shepard and Lieberson: "Capturing Broadway on Record," *The New York Times Magazine*, July 15, 1984.

p. 61. *My Fair Lady* investment: Metz, op. cit., p. 400.

p. 61. "Big Red" and "Mediocre Orange": AI with Ron Alexenburg, Feb. 10, 1987.

p. 61. Columbia history: Roland Gelatt, *The Fabulous Phonograph: Eighteen Seventy-Seven to Nineteen Seventy-Seven* (New York: Macmillan, 1977).

p. 61. Lieberson and the LP: "Goddard Lieberson, Who Fostered LPs at Columbia Records, Dies." For an amusing account of RCA's discomfiture over Goldmark's invention of the LP, see: Peter C. Goldmark and Lee Edson, *Maverick*

Inventor: My Turbulent Years at CBS (New York: Saturday Review Press/E. P. Dutton, 1973), pp. 141–44.

p. 62. Mitch Miller information: Fox, op. cit., pp. 25–71. Miller denies in his interview with Fox that he loathed rock, but this is flatly contradicted by his own words, quoted by Representative Derounian at the 1960 Congressional hearings on payola: "You would not invite these unwashed kids [rock and roll musicians] into your living room to meet your family. Why thrust them into the living rooms of your audience?"

pp. 62–63. John Hammond information: John Hammond and Irving Townsend, *John Hammond on Record* (New York: Summit Books, 1977), pp. 9–11, 59–60, 95–104, 351–53.

p. 63. "I would go to A&R": AI with Lundvall, Jan. 26, 1987.

pp. 63–64. Distribution system history: AI with Jack Craigo, Oct. 23, 1987, and Bill Gallagher, Mar. 28, 1990.

p. 64. "the Pope"; "confessions": AI with Gallagher protégé Tom Noonan, July 27, 1987.

p. 65. Ertegun and Wexler: "Eclectic, Reminiscent, Amused, Fickle, Perverse," (Profile of Ahmet Ertegun), *The New Yorker*, May 29, 1978 (Part I), and June 5, 1978 (Part II).

Ertegun as "character": Ertegun has consistently got adoring press, the *New Yorker* profile being one prime example. Another is Dorothy Wade and Justine Picardie's *Music Man: Ahmet Ertegun, Atlantic Records, and the Triumph of Rock 'n' Roll* (New York: W. W. Norton, 1990). According to legend, Ertegun's Atlantic paid royalties to black performers when other labels did not. In the otherwise cynical *Rock 'n' Roll Is Here to Pay*, Ertegun tells a story of how another record executive in the fifties admonished him: " 'You're paying those people royalties? You must be out of your mind!' Of course, he didn't call them 'people.' He called them something else."

The fact is, Atlantic's royalty record may have been better than most, but it was hardly impeccable. The reader is advised to take a look at "Atlantic Records Refigures Royalty Status for 35 of Its Vet R&B Artists," *Variety*, May 18, 1988. In it, Sam Moore of Sam & Dave and Ruth Brown both complain of not having received a royalty check in over two decades, despite numerous reissue albums—and they are not isolated examples.

Even Lee Magid, the former A&R man for the notorious Herman Lubinsky, complained about Ertegun. He told the author on Mar. 29, 1990, that the Clovers' version of a song he wrote, "I Played the Fool," was recently reissued on Atlantic—with Ahmet Ertegun listed as the author. Magid said he pointed this out to Ertegun, who apologized for the "mistake."

"he went *legit*": AI with Levy, July 30, 1988.

pp. 65–70. Clive's early history and rise to Columbia president: Clive Davis and James Willwerth, *Clive: Inside the Record Business* (New York: William Morrow, 1975), pp. 7–29. In an AI on Mar. 28, 1990, Bill Gallagher declined to discuss the details of his power struggle with Clive. He said only, "My departure just had to be. It was either him or me."

"I had no A&R training": This and all subsequent Davis quotes in this chapter, unless otherwise noted, are from his autobiography.

p. 66. **Clive and Teller:** AI with Teller, Apr. 13, 1987.

p. 66. **"That ego":** AI with Craigo, Oct. 23, 1987.

p. 66. **"Let me read":** AI with Smith, July 21, 1987.

p. 67. **Clive and the CD:** AI with Rose Gross-Marino, Clive's administrative assistant in the eighties, Feb. 25, 1987.

pp. 67–68. **Clive, Hammond, and Dylan:** Hammond and Townsend, op. cit., p. 355–56; and Davis and Willwerth, op. cit., pp. 49–50. It's interesting to note that the two accounts differ somewhat. Clive wrote that he persuaded Hammond to appeal to Dylan as a friend, and that the singer voluntarily rescinded his letter. I've gone with Hammond's account, in which Clive more or less forced Dylan to remain on Columbia.

p. 68. **Clive and Goddard's wardrobe:** AI with Davis, Apr. 30, 1987. Clive waxed rhapsodic about how Goddard's handkerchiefs matched his shirts.

pp. 69–70. **"needed a buffer"; "the original job"; "Goddard would *never*":** Ibid.

pp. 70–71. **Clive hires Yetnikoff:**

"rough around the edges"; "I wouldn't say Lieberson": Ibid.

Yetnikoff quotes: Joe Smith and Mitchell Fink, *Off the Record: An Oral History of Popular Music* (New York: Warner Books, 1988), p. 334; and Goodman's interview with Yetnikoff, May 26, 1988.

pp. 71–73. **Clive hires Asher:** AI with Asher, Jan. 9, 1987.

p. 74. **"It's hard to overestimate":** AI with Asher, Apr. 21, 1987.

pp. 74–76. **Clive, Monterey, Joplin:** Davis and Willwerth, op. cit., pp. 74–90; Smith and Fink, op. cit., pp. 257–58 ("the creative turning point"; "it was clear"); Ward, Stokes, and Tucker, op. cit., pp. 373–76.

"Clive came back to New York": AI with Asher, Jan. 9, 1987.

"I hope you didn't fuck us": Quoted in "From Ashes to Asher: PolyGram Prexy Leads Way to the Top," *Hits*, June 29, 1987.

p. 77. **"everybody ran to the index":** AI with Yetnikoff, Mar. 30, 1987.

p. 77. **"If there's fallout":** AI with Davis, Apr. 30, 1987.

p. 78. **Clive on Schein's parsimony:** Davis and Willwerth, op. cit., p. 57.

p. 78. **"I bought some suede boots":** Lombardi notes.

p. 78. **"He was tongue-tied":** AI with Lundvall, Jan. 26, 1987.

pp. 78–79. **Clive's ambitions to replace Stanton:** AI with Eric Kronfeld, Clive's personal attorney at the time, Nov. 20, 1987.

pp. 79–80. **Signing of Neil Diamond:** AI with Goldman, Jan. 9, 1987.

p. 80. **The singles meeting:**

Basic description: Davis and Willwerth, op. cit., pp. 203–6; "Talk of the Town," *The New Yorker*, Nov. 27, 1971.

"It was like being back in school": Confidential source.

"There's a story": AI with Yetnikoff, Mar. 30, 1987.

p. 80. **"I thought Clive was terrific":** AI with Asher, Apr. 21, 1987.

p. 81. **Altshuler's sycophancy:** Confirmed to author by a number of journalists who covered Clive's CBS, including Lombardi.

p. 81. **Theobalds Road story:** AI with Asher, Apr. 21, 1987.

pp. 81–82. **Clive's thoughts about his compensation:** Davis and Willwerth, op. cit. pp. 120–30.

p. 82. **Goddard's resentment of Clive:** "Clive Davis Ousted: Payola Coverup Charged," *Rolling Stone,* July 5, 1973.

  "Goddard was so much fun": AI with Yetnikoff, Mar. 30, 1987.

  London snub: Ibid.; and AI with attorney Eric Kronfeld, Dec. 1, 1987.

p. 82n. **"I think Jagger":** Quoted in *The New Yorker* profile of Ertegun.

p. 83. *Corporate Financing* **rumor:** Metz, op. cit., p. 405.

p. 83. **Taylor and Schlesinger:** AI with Schlesinger, Mar. 17, 1988.

p. 83. **Clive's resentment of Taylor:** AIs with Asher, July 1, 1986; and Yetnikoff, Mar. 30, 1987.

p. 84. **"Initially, Clive and I":** AI with Craigo, Oct. 23, 1987.

5 Newark

p. 85. **Announcement of Clive's firing:**

  Alexenburg's recollections: AIs with Alexenburg, July 7, 1986, and Feb. 10, 1987.

  "A funny thing happened": AIs with Asher, Apr. 21, 1987; and Craigo, Oct. 23, 1987. Both men remembered the line exactly the same way.

p. 86. **Clive feels unappreciated:** Davis and Willwerth, op. cit., p. 280. This book is the source of all Davis quotes in this chapter, unless otherwise noted.

  An interesting fact published here for the first time is that over the Memorial Day weekend, just before Clive was fired, his attorney, Eric Kronfeld, was in London, wrapping up a secret deal with L. G. Wood, the chairman of EMI London. EMI was going to hire Clive from CBS and give him his own new label. Then Clive was fired, and a short time later, Wood wrote Kronfeld a letter terminating the deal. In it, Wood refused even to mention Clive Davis by name, saying only that any meeting of "the parties" would be "inappropriate."

p. 86. **Expense-account charges:**

  CBS allegations: *Columbia Broadcasting System* v. *Clive Davis,* Case No. 9634 (1973), Supreme Court of New York.

  "CBS is idiotic": Quoted in "Clive Davis Ousted; Payola Coverup Charged," *Rolling Stone,* July 5, 1973.

pp. 87–88. **Clive and Gamble and Huff:**

  Gamble and Huff history: Ward, Stokes, and Tucker, op. cit., pp. 501–2; "The Day the Soul Train Crashed," *Philadelphia,* June 1983.

  Clive's observations about R&B; details of Philadelphia International deal: Davis and Willwerth, op. cit., pp. 144–47.

  Stax Records deal; "I said, Jesus": AI with Craigo, Oct. 23, 1987.

  Sitdown with Kronfeld: AI with Kronfeld, Dec. 8, 1987.

  Coombs and Gamble dealt in payola: Both men pleaded guilty to violating the payola statute on Apr. 8, 1976, in: *United States* v. *Kenneth Gamble et al.,* Case No. 373 (1975), U.S. District Court, Eastern District of Pennsylvania.

pp. 89–91. **Rudman information:**

  Rudman quotes and history: "Clive Davis Ousted; Payola Coverup

Charged"; "A Pile of Guile Guides the Wheels in Record Style," *Philadelphia Inquirer*, Nov. 18, 1978; "When Kal Rudman Hollers 'Hit,' Every DJ Tries to Swing," *Philadelphia Inquirer*, May 8, 1983; "Kal Rudman: A Rock Paradox," *(Philadelphia) Inquirer Magazine*, Oct. 21, 1984; "Talk of the Town," *The New Yorker*, Nov. 27, 1971; "Pop-Music Scandal Laid to Pursuit of Fast Money," *The New York Times*, June 11, 1973.

"Cowboys to Girls" information: Rick Sklar, *Rocking America* (New York: St. Martin's Press, 1984), p. 94.

Rudman's indie promo clients; $44,000 fee: "The Trouble with Rock," *CBS News*, Aug. 11, 1974.

Wagner on Rudman: AI with Wagner, May 26, 1987.

pp. 91–92. Wynshaw information:

Physical description and early career history; "I loved it": "Witness Details Workings of the Recording Industry," *The New York Times*, June 8, 1973.

"Wynshaw wasn't a very good branch manager"; carried a gun: AI with Craigo, Oct. 23, 1987. Gun also mentioned in Metz, op. cit., p. 380.

"Clive's pimp" and other titles: "Clive Davis Ousted; Payola Coverup Charged." Arthur Taylor also told me on Aug. 27, 1989, that shortly after joining CBS, he encountered Paul Simon at a B'nai B'rith dinner and casually asked the singer if he knew what Wynshaw did. "He's Clive's procurer," Simon replied.

p. 92. Wynshaw, Falcone, Campana, clients:

Falcone and Campana; list of clients: "Investigations, Rumors Mount in Columbia 'Drugola' Scandal," *Rolling Stone*, July 19, 1973.

Smith and Beck death threats: "The Trouble with Rock."

p. 92. Wynshaw, Falcone, and sham companies: Count 1 of indictment in *United States* v. *David Wynshaw and Pasquale Falconio*, Case No. 623 (1975), U.S. District Court, Southern District of New York. Wynshaw pleaded guilty to Count 1 on Jan. 12, 1976, before Judge Greisa. See also: Memorandum Opinion of Judge Lacey in *United States* v. *Frankie Crocker*, Case No. 256 (1976), U.S. District Court, District of New Jersey; and *Columbia Broadcasting System* v. *David Wynshaw and Anthony Rubino*, Case No. 13399 (1973), Supreme Court of New York.

pp. 92–93. Wynshaw, Clive, and false invoices: Letter dated July 29, 1976, from Assisant U.S. Attorney Frank Wohl to U.S. Probation Officer Ronald Rogart in *United States* v. *Clive Davis*, Case No. 625 (1975), U.S. District Court, Southern District of New York; and AI with Taylor, Apr. 28, 1987.

pp. 93–95. Newark moves in on CBS:

Falcone's heroin operation: "Drug Charges Shake the Record Industry," *The New York Times*, June 5, 1973.

Strike force warns CBS: AI with Taylor, Apr. 28, 1987.

Events of Apr. 9; Wynshaw quotes: "Witness Details Workings of the Recording Industry."

Clive at Ahmanson Theater; Paul Simon incident: "Clive Davis Ousted; Payola Coverup Charged."

Clive and Billy Joel: Davis and Willwerth, op. cit., p. 281; Joel interview in Smith and Fink, op. cit., pp. 414–15.

pp. 95–96. Taylor deals with crisis: AI with Taylor, Apr. 28, 1987.

pp. 96–97. Clive's final day:

    Morning routine; firing: Clive's and Willwerth, op. cit., pp. 281–83.

    "He doesn't remember": AI with Yetnikoff, Mar. 30, 1987.

pp. 97–98. Irwin gets Clive's job: AIs with Segelstein, Feb. 18, 1987; and Taylor, Apr. 28, 1987.

pp. 98–99. Asher in London: AI with Asher, Apr. 21, 1987.

p. 99. Wynshaw as government witness:

    Wynshaw's accusations: "Columbia Payola Put at $250,000; Sum Reported Given Yearly to Black Radio Stations for Playing Records," *The New York Times*, June 6, 1973.

    "I'm clean as the Board of Health!": "Pop-Music Scandal Laid to Pursuit of Fast Money."

    Ferretti article: *The New York Times*, June 8, 1973.

pp. 99–100. CBS paranoia:

    Counsel provided for all employees; "There was a tremendous amount of backbiting": AI with Taylor, Apr. 28, 1987.

    Employees believed phones bugged: AI with Alexenburg, July 7, 1986.

    Craigo's thoughts and quotes: AI with Craigo, Oct. 23, 1987.

    Cow Palace convention: AIs with Alexenburg, Feb. 10, 1987, and Bruce Lundvall, Feb. 15, 1987; confirmed by Scully, AI, Mar. 26, 1990.

    Taylor death threat: AI with Taylor, Apr. 28, 1987.

pp. 100–101. CBS News and payola story:

    "irrefutable proof": AI with Asher, Feb. 15, 1987.

    "That piece of *shit*!": AI with Yetnikoff, Mar. 30, 1987.

pp. 101–2. Segelstein as defender of CBS Records:

    Contempt for news coverage: AI with Segelstein, Feb. 18, 1987.

    "Everyone thought": AI with Lundvall, Feb. 15, 1987.

pp. 102–3. Clive sees reputation dismantled:

    Altshuler betrayal: Davis and Willwerth, op. cit., p. 288.

    "Are you kidding?": Quoted in Metz, op. cit., p. 379.

    "After Clive got fired": AI with Goldman, Mar. 19, 1987.

pp. 103–4. Project Sound gathers momentum:

    Goldstein's agenda: AI with Romano, Sept. 23, 1987.

    Targets of probe; names of those indicted: "U.S. Indicts 19 in Record Firms Probe," *Washington Post*, June 25, 1975; and "Payola Indictments Name 19, Including 3 Company Heads," *The New York Times*, June 25, 1975.

    Gamble and Huff financial records; "every time they got a check": Confidential source.

pp. 104–6. Frankie Crocker case:

    Crocker's grand jury testimony: Disclosed in indictment in *U.S.* v. *Crocker*.

    Romano's thoughts and quotes; depiction of trial: AI with Romano, Sept. 23, 1987.

p. 106. Outcome of Project Sound:

    Crocker appeal: *United States* v. *Frankie Crocker*, Case No. 1358 (1977), U.S. Court of Appeals, Third Circuit; and AIs with assistant U.S. Attorney Mel Kracov, Oct. 23, 1989, and Crocker's lawyer, Michael Pollack, Jan. 3, 1990.

Tarnopol case: *United States* v. *Nat Tarnopol et al.*, Case No. 312 (1975), U.S. District Court, District of New Jersey; and AI with Pollack, who also represented Tarnopol, Jan. 3, 1990.

Ruthlessness toward Jackie Wilson: AI with artist manager Joyce McRae, Dec. 15, 1988.

Gamble's plea bargain: "Trial Waived by Philly Intl. Men: 4 Fined $45,000," *Billboard*, Apr. 17, 1976.

pp. 107–8. Clive's recovery from scandal:

Clive's sentencing: *U.S.* vs. *Davis*, Sept. 23, 1976.

Civil case settled: "CBS Lawsuit vs. Clive Davis Settled," *Billboard*, Feb. 11, 1978.

Mail-order rights and Martell award taken as exoneration by Clive: AI with Davis, Jan. 20, 1987.

"Clive was permanently damaged": AI with Goldman, Feb. 16, 1987.

Asher on Clive: AI with Asher, Apr. 21, 1987.

p. 108. "Someone who worked": AI with Davis, Jan. 20, 1987.

p. 109. "Everyone was so scared": Confidential source, a prominent figure in radio.

6 Walter's War

p. 110. "creative wars": Davis and Willwerth, op. cit., p. 279.

p. 110. "One thing I did know": AI with Segelstein, Feb. 5, 1987.

pp. 110–11. CBS in poor shape for successor: Ibid.

p. 111. "wheeling and dealing": AI with Segelstein, Dec. 27, 1989.

p. 111. CBS distribution vs. WEA: AI with Craigo, Oct. 23, 1987.

p. 112. "When I shopped": Irving Azoff, in his keynote address at the NARM convention, Mar. 8, 1986.

p. 113. "After I left CBS": AI with Craigo, Oct. 23, 1987.

p. 113. Goddard and Irwin:

"There was a little too much": Quoted in Metz, op. cit., p. 386.

"I could walk into his office": AI with Segelstein, Feb. 5, 1987.

p. 114. "I would rant": Ibid.

p. 114. "Jewish the way I am": Quoted in "The 101 Years of CBS Records" (advertorial), *Billboard*, Nov. 19, 1988.

p. 114. "I guess I wanted it": AI with Yetnikoff, Mar. 30, 1987.

p. 114. Yetnikoff and Taylor: AI with Taylor, Apr. 28, 1987.

pp. 114–15. "Goddard didn't like the corporate thing . . . I was really pissed": AI with Yetnikoff, Mar. 30, 1987.

pp. 115–16. Taylor, Schlesinger, Yetnikoff:

Sailing story: AI with Schlesinger, Sept. 2, 1987.

"Fuhrer's job" . . . "I got it because": Quoted in Smith and Fink, op. cit., p. 334.

p. 116. Irwin's departure: AI with Segelstein, Feb. 5, 1987.

p. 116. "a brilliant choice": AI with Taylor, Apr. 28, 1987.

p. 117. "I think when Paley began to hear" . . . "I'm just a bad picker": Quoted in "An Intimate Talk with William Paley," *The New York Times Magazine*, Dec. 28, 1980.

p. 117. "Walter was beloved": AI with Kronfeld, Nov. 20, 1987.

p. 118. "How do you feel about Jews?": Quoted in "King of the Schmooze," *Esquire*, Nov. 1986.

p. 118. bar mitzvahs; Fillmore East: AI with Asher, July 1, 1986.

pp. 118–19. Dick vs. Walter on Clive: AI with Asher, Apr. 21, 1987.

p. 119. Walter's ill will toward Clive:

Walter's imitations of Clive: Related by Nat Weiss, AI, Mar. 5, 1987; and David Braun, AI, July 14, 1987.

"I turned to Clive for advice": Quoted in Smith and Fink, op. cit., p. 335.

"Walter went fucking crazy": AI with Record Bar president Barrie Bergman, Sept. 3, 1987.

p. 120. "So I have to follow": Quoted in Smith and Fink, op. cit., p. 335.

pp. 120–21. Beginnings of Walter's War:

GI boots; FUCK WARNER signs: AI with Elliot Goldman, Feb. 16, 1987.

Wickey Bird story; "It became quite vicious": AI with Craigo, Oct. 23, 1987.

"When Walter took that job": AI with Goldman, Feb. 16, 1987.

Walter called statue Mo: AI with Federoff, Apr. 9, 1987.

pp. 121–22. Ostin background and Warner history: Chapple and Garofalo, op. cit., pp. 201–206; and "Steve Ross on the Spot," *New York*, Jan. 24, 1983.

pp. 122–23. James Taylor debacle: AI with Weiss, Mar. 5, 1987.

pp. 123–26. Paul Simon debacle:

"Walter hated his guts": AI with Federoff, Apr. 9, 1987. Federoff added that one year on the first night of Passover, she broke up an argument between Walter and Paul Simon, ordering them both to go home.

Taylor plays along with Walter's threat to Simon: AI with Taylor, Apr. 28, 1987.

Ostin told Tannen he wanted Simon; "Walter thought we reneged": AI with Tannen, Apr. 6, 1987.

"anger and retaliation"; other allegations; CBS denial: *Paul Simon v. CBS Records*, Case No. 20687 (1978), New York State Supreme Court, County of New York.

Walter admits he forbade artists to record with Simon: "Walter Yetnikoff: The Most Powerful Man in the Record Business," *Rolling Stone*, Dec. 15–29, 1988.

Schlesinger's boast: AI with Schlesinger, Sept. 9, 1987.

Playboy interview: Feb. 1984.

Tannen/Orenstein story and quote: AI with Orenstein, Nov. 24, 1987.

"It's outrageous": AI with Tannen, Mar. 15, 1990.

Tannen's client list: AI with Tannen, Apr. 6, 1987.

"Walter turned orange and purple": AI with Wagner, Sept. 14, 1987.

pp. 126–28. The war continues:

"I've never seen a deal made so quickly": AI with Gaff, Oct. 12, 1987.

Off Broadway story: AI with Craigo, Oct. 23, 1987.

"When the Frank Loesser catalog was sold": AI with Orenstein, Nov. 24, 1987.

CBS lost $9 million on McCartney: Confidential source.
"just by sitting on its fanny": Quoted in Fox, op. cit., p. 60.
"banking deals": Ibid., p. 225.
"Warner is probably the best record company": Confidential source.
p. 128. "sort of stupid": Quoted in Smith and Fink, op. cit., p. 335.

Another example of how the war continued well into the eighties was the MTV affair of 1986–87, as described to the author by a confidential MTV insider. MTV had made deals with all the big record companies to get exclusive use of certain videos in exchange for payment. In 1986 CBS Records was the first record company up for renewal. But CBS was bashing MTV in the press over its programming choices and threatening not to renew. Mo Ostin phoned MTV president Bob Pittman with an idea. Suppose the Warner labels renewed their contracts a year early? Would that give MTV leverage in its struggle with CBS? Pittman was gleeful. Once Warner renewed, all the other majors followed—all but CBS. Now the odd man out, CBS found itself in a corner, still fighting MTV in the press but anxious for a way to renew without losing face. In 1987 CBS quietly signed a new contract with MTV.

7 The Troika

pp. 129–33. Geffen information:
Investments: AI with Geffen, July 27, 1987. During the interview, Geffen bragged that he had sold a building he had bought for $800,000 to late Broadway producer Michael Bennett for $3.2 million.
Forbes **estimate:** "The Forbes Four Hundred," Oct. 23, 1989.
Rohan story: "Breaking In, Busting Out: Contract Negotiation and Re-negotiation in the 80s," *Musician*, Nov. 1983.
Geffen's upbringing and career through Laura Nyro: AI with Geffen, July 27, 1987; Geffen interview in Smith and Fink, op. cit., pp. 303–4; Clive and Willwerth, op. cit., pp. 100–102.
Geffen and Crosby, Stills: Wexler ejected him; "He was the most charming person," from Smith and Fink, op. cit., p. 304; "Their last tour was a joke" . . . "don't squeeze the juice": "Eclectic, Reminiscent, Amused, Fickle, Perverse," *The New Yorker*, May 29, 1978.
"I didn't like being called" . . . **"we can *all* have millions"; Roberts deal:** Smith and Fink, op. cit., pp. 304–5.
Asylum to Warner Bros. Pictures; "It was a nightmare"; $1.2 million for Tiffany lamps: "On the Go with David Geffen," *The New York Times Magazine*, July 21, 1985.
Cancer scare; "I didn't know what to do": AI with Geffen, July 27, 1987.
$175 million in revenues: "Geffen's Coming of Age," *Rolling Stone*, July 13–July 27, 1989.
pp. 133–34. Scene in Geffen's office: AI with Geffen, July 27, 1987; Young curses Geffen: Interview in *Rolling Stone*, June 2, 1988.
pp. 134–36. Azoff information:
Background details; Front Line's client list: "MCA Records Chief Softens

Tune," *Los Angeles Times*, Jan. 29, 1985; "MCA Records' Chief Turns the Firm Around by Being Aggressive," *The Wall Street Journal*, Mar. 31, 1986; Ward, Stokes, and Tucker, op. cit., p. 591.

"Poison Dwarf": AI on Oct. 21, 1987, with rock publicist Howard Bloom, who worked with Azoff on the Victory tour. On May 11, 1987, attorney Paul Marshall, who described himself as a friend of Azoff's, said he called him "the *malignant* dwarf."

Hotel story; "Irving's got a fast burn": AI with Fine, Nov. 6, 1987. Azoff confirmed having trashed hotel rooms in an interview in *Hits*, Dec. 18, 1989. He claimed he once had a room next to Joe Walsh of the Eagles at a Holiday Inn in New Haven. "There was no adjoining door," Azoff said, "so I made one."

Burning menu story; "Irving is as fast mentally": AIs with Buziak, Apr. 1, 1987, and Jan. 30, 1989.

Snake story: "Take One," *People*, Nov. 17, 1986.

"He was a master": Confidential source.

pp. 136–37. Azoff and MCA:
  Yetnikoff offered MCA job: See Chapter Thirteen: The Firing.
  "I alleged they were so inept"; parts for Frey and Jennings; "Yetnikoff, Geffen, and Irving are the only three": Quoted in "MCA Records' Chief Turns the Firm Around by Being Aggressive."
  Press accounts of Azoff's turnaround of MCA: See notes to pp. 134–36; and "The Hit Man of the Record Biz," *Newsweek*, Feb. 8, 1988.
  More income from Full Moon than MCA salary; "For MCA to be in the management business" . . . **"crybabies":** "MCA Buys Azoff Firms," *Rolling Stone*, July 3, 1986.

pp. 137–38. Yetnikoff, Azoff, and Geffen on one another:
  Recognized themselves as troika: This is my own analysis, based on conversations with many industry people, among them artist manager Kenny Laguna, who concurred in AI on Sept. 8, 1989.
  "I don't wish to have him in my life": AI with Geffen, July 27, 1987.
  "Once we screamed for two hours"; "Dennis the Menace": Quoted in "King of the Schmooze," *Esquire*, Nov. 1986.
  "I'm waiting to get Irving on the stand": Quoted in "Walter Yetnikoff: The Most Powerful Man in the Record Business," *Rolling Stone*, Dec. 15–29, 1988.

pp. 138–41. The Boston saga: All information except where noted, and deposition quotes, from Jock Baird's excellent article, "Tom Scholz's Battle for Boston," *Musician*, Jan. 1987. Numerous details from article are corroborated in the legal documents cited below.
  One drum track done seven hundred times: Defendant Scholz' Memorandum of Law in Opposition to Motion for Preliminary Injunction, *CBS Inc. v. Donald Thomas Scholz et al.*, Case No. 5995 (1984), U.S. District Court, Southern District of New York.
  "I was Walter's fair-haired boy" and other Engel quotes: AIs with Engel, July 2 and 3, 1987.
  Azoff's "personal understanding"; how CBS would have retaliated against Geffen; "This means war"; CBS withdrew master from MCA: Defendant

Scholz' Memorandum in Opposition to Plaintiff CBS's Motion for Partial Summary Judgment, *CBS Inc.* v. *Paul Ahern et al.*, Case No. 7918 (1983), U.S. District Court, Southern District of California.

"I'm not in the business of incurring lawsuits": AI with Geffen, July 27, 1987.

"absolutely outrageous": Quoted in "Judge Dismisses CBS Move vs. Rock Group's Attorney," *Daily Variety*, Feb. 14, 1985.

Engel's countersuit: *Donald S. Engel* v. *CBS Inc.*, Case No. 7198 (1985), U.S. District Court, Central District of California.

p. 142. "Do you think": AI with Paul Walker, Nov. 30, 1987.

pp. 142–43. Teena Marie case: *Motown Record Corp.* v. *Tina Marie Brockert*, Case No. 420-886 (1982), California Superior Court, County of Los Angeles. "Slave" labor is not hyperbole. The judge in the case ruled that Motown had given her a "contract of adhesion," which is merely a polite way of saying the same thing.

p. 143. "All of a sudden": AI with Engel, July 3, 1987.

pp. 143–44. Today's contracts: See: "Breaking In, Busting Out: Contract Negotiation and Re-negotiation in the 80s," *Musician*, Nov. 1983; "Of Human Bondage," *Musician*, Nov. 1986; and "Music and Money: New Rock Economics Make it Harder to Sing Your Way to Wealth," *The Wall Street Journal*, May 21, 1985. The Patty Smyth story and quote are from the *Journal*.

p. 144. "I would venture to say": AI with Engel, July 2, 1987.

p. 144. "increasingly difficult": AI with Tannen, Mar. 15, 1990.

p. 144. "I know": Notes of interviews conducted between Dec. 1987 and Feb. 1988 by Susan Adams, for her profile of Allen Grubman, "Hitting the High Notes," *The American Lawyer*, Mar. 1988. Hereafter: Adams notes.

8 Grubman

p. 145. Walter meets Grubman: AI with Mottola, Aug. 24, 1987.

p. 145. Grubman's early client list: AI with Grubman, May 12, 1987; article on Grubman in B'nai B'rith gazette, late seventies (date unknown).

pp. 145–46. Grubman history:

Childhood; joining Hofer: AI with Grubman, May 12, 1987; "Hitting the High Notes," *The American Lawyer*, Mar. 1988.

"Everyone in entertainment": Grubman's remarks at New York Public Library forum, Feb. 1988.

Hofer embezzlement information: Deposition of Danny D. Sims, Feb. 20, 1985, in: *Cayman Music, Inc.* v. *Rita Marley et al.*, Case No. 24020 (1984), New York State Supreme Court, County of New York.

"I started with some clients": AI with Grubman, May 12, 1987.

Grubman's longing for Rolls Corniche: AI with Henry Stone, Feb. 17, 1987.

pp. 146–47. Grubman as poor jurist and rock hater:

Finished near bottom of class: "Hitting the High Notes."

"The only piece of paper" ... "The Blarney Stone": Adams notes.

Grubman's hatred of rock: AI with Linda Stein, former manager of the

Ramones and close friend of Grubman's, Nov. 11, 1987. Irving Azoff says in Adams notes, "The three things Allen doesn't do are listen to rock and roll, read, and write."

pp. 147–48. Mottola history: AI with Mottola, Aug. 24, 1987; T. D. Valentine profile, *Blues & Soul*, date unknown; *Sandy Linzer* v. *Allen Grubman et al.*, Case No. 4949 (1984), U.S. District Court, Southern District of New York.

p. 148. "Tommy's a kick-ass little guy:" AI with Jerald Wagner, Sept. 14, 1987.

p. 148. "natural rapport" . . . **"traditional Jewish upbringing":** AI with Grubman, May 12, 1987.

p. 148. "We sat down" . . . **"really and truly your friend":** AI with Mottola, Aug. 24, 1987.

p. 149. Scene in Grubman's office: AI with Grubman, May 12, 1987.

p. 149. Welch story: "Hitting the High Notes."

p. 149. "Allen has taken his shoes and socks off": Ibid.

p. 150. "John would murder his mother": AI with Gaff, Oct. 12, 1987.

p. 150. Grubman's clients: Adams notes; AIs with Grubman, May 12, 1987; and Arthur Indursky, same day.

p. 150. "He is my partner": Quoted in "A Sampler of the Leading Lawyers for the Stars," *The National Law Journal*, Oct. 27, 1986.

p. 150. "Each lawyer": AI with Marshall, May 15, 1987.

p. 151. Grubman's fees: "Hitting the High Notes."

p. 151. "He brags". . . **Mottola's clients:** AI with Mottola, Aug. 24, 1987.

p. 151. Linzer case: All details from *Linzer* v. *Grubman*.

p. 151n. Mottola, Levy, Gigante: Levy described Mottola as a friend and racehorse investor in AI, May 27, 1987. In a subsequent AI, on July 30, 1987, Levy no longer considered Mottola a friend; ever since Morris's criminal conviction, he said, Mottola had been slow to take his calls. The author was interviewing Gigante in his East Bronx office on Apr. 6, 1988, when the priest took a long, cordial call from Mottola. Gigante went on to explain about the movie project, and mentioned that Mottola had met his alleged mobster brother.

pp. 152–53. Grubman and Walter:

"great affection"; "I see this plate fly past my head": AI with Grubman, May 12, 1987.

"Walter asked him to get on his knees": AI with Mottola, Aug. 24, 1987.

"The next thing I know I'm talking to him": Adams notes.

Grubman lends Yetnikoff his apartment: confirmed in Dec. 7, 1989, AI with Grubman.

Represented 30 percent of CBS pop roster; Joel and Springsteen deals: "Hitting the High Notes."

"Walter knows that he is only giving up": Confidential source.

"give me an endorsement": AI with Grubman, Dec. 7, 1989.

Grubman's anxieties: Corroborated by numerous sources close to Grubman, and plainly evident in AI with Grubman, May 12, 1987. When I inadvertently asked Grubman how he accounted for his "hot streak," he winced and said, "Don't tell me 'hot streak.' That gets me crazy!"

"Once I yelled at Allen": Adams notes.

Further corroboration of Walter's role in helping Grubman build his practice: In a Sept. 22, 1987, AI, with industry veteran Elliot Goldman, who described himself as a close friend of both Grubman and Mike Tannen, he said the following: "Walter would have no hesitation [throwing clients to Grubman]. You want to renegotiate your deal? Fine. I don't talk to Mike Tannen. Go hire Allen Grubman and do a new deal. The end result is, [Grubman] does go in and get them good deals. If Walter doesn't like somebody, he's not only going to take a business position, he's going to take a personal position. That's what it's all about. And I would find it very hard to do that. But I think Walter's attitude is, Look, this is a business of people and relationships, and I'm easier to deal with when I deal with somebody I like."

pp. 153–54. T.K. Records and Stone:
  Stone and T.K. history: AI with Stone, Feb. 17, 1987.
  "He's one of the great old-time record men": AI with Grubman, May 12, 1987.
  "Henry Stone ran his record company": Confidential source.
  "very, very possible": AI with Stone, Oct. 12, 1989.
pp. 155–56. Grubman and Joel: Adams notes and confidential source.
p. 156. "legitimate": In an AI on Sept. 21, 1987, Yetnikoff's ex-mistress Lynda Emon commented, "I remember when Grubman said one day, You know, I'm really happy that finally I have a legitimate law firm." As opposed to what? "A schlock law firm. Here he was, representing big clients, making big deals. He was respected by the presidents of record companies. When you have access to record company presidents, you're powerful. Whoever has the most access the quickest, wins."
p. 156. Grubman and Geffen: AI with Elliot Goldman, Sept. 22, 1987. Goldman was senior vice-president of Warner at a time when the company was hoping to win back the foreign rights to Geffen Records.
p. 156. Landau, Grubman, and Springsteen: Confidential source.
pp. 156–57. Winterland deal:
  "the *schmatte* business"; "Irving understands that business" . . . **"Allen needed the fee!":** Fred Goodman's interview with Yetnikoff, June 1, 1988.
  Details of deal: "Bar Talk," *The American Lawyer*, Sept. 1988. Some additional details were provided to me by Susan Adams, who wrote the item, by a confidential source, and by Grubman and Indursky, AI, Dec. 7, 1989.

9 Casablanca

p. 161. Bogart's drug abuse: Denied by Joyce Bogart in AI, July 22, 1987. Confirmed by Danny Davis in AI, July 21, 1987. In an interview with Russ Regan on July 23, 1987, I asked whether he believed drugs hastened Bogart's death. He said, "I can't speculate on that. The man was charismatic, truly a genius. But all I know is, if you put enough chemicals in your body, it's gonna kill you. I don't care who you are." In an AI on Mar. 26, 1990, David Shein, who worked with Bogart at Casablanca and Boardwalk, noted, "I don't think there's anybody in this industry who didn't do drugs at some time. Let's not bullshit each other. Neil was no different. Who the hell didn't in those days?"
p. 161. "If it cost him three dollars": AI with Kass, Jan. 14, 1988.

p. 161. "No question about it": AI with Regan, July 23, 1987.

p. 162. "I always referred to Neil": AI with Grubman, May 12, 1987.

p. 162. "Neil was probably": AI with Levy, Feb. 24, 1987.

pp. 162–63. Bogart's excesses:

$45,000 party: "Play it Again, Neil," *New West*, Oct. 10, 1977.

"In the Navy"; Hansen's cake: AI with Joyce Bogart, July 22, 1987.

"Take Me Home" story and quote: AI with Bleiweiss, Sept. 5, 1985. See also: "A New Act Takes Over at PolyGram," *The New York Times*, Nov. 3, 1985.

pp. 163–66. Bogart's childhood and early career history:

Through 1967: AIs with Joyce Bogart, July 22, 1987, and Jeff Franklin (one of Bogart's closest friends and a business partner), Apr. 14, 1987; and "Play it Again, Neil."

"And over that weekend": AI with Levy, Feb. 24, 1987.

Bogart vs. Klein: "Visions of Sugar Plums," *Forbes*, Apr. 15, 1968.

Kama Sutra and Buddah: AIs with Kass, Dec. 10, 1987, and Jan. 14, 1988; and "The History of Buddah," *Fusion*, Aug. 1972. Information about Sonny Franzese's role reported in: "Tour Shakedowns Alleged," *Rolling Stone*, May 4, 1989.

king of bubblegum; "We are giving kids": "Tunes for Teeny-Weenies," *Time*, July 19, 1968.

Kasenetz and Katz: Ward, Stokes, and Tucker, op. cit., p. 408.

"He was such a terrific salesman": AI with Joyce Bogart, July 22, 1987.

Curtis Mayfield signed by Kass: AI with Kass, Jan. 14, 1987.

Sklar's honesty: In a Jan. 5, 1988, AI, self-styled payola bagman Johnny Bond groused, "We couldn't do nothing with Rick; he was a bastard." Confirmed by veteran song-plugger Juggy Gayles in AI, June 9, 1987.

Reingold anecdotes: Sklar, op. cit., pp. 149–50.

"He always wanted to live that fast life" . . . "I called Morris": AI with Kass, Jan. 14, 1988.

pp. 166–68. Casablanca's early days:

Emerald City: AI with Larry Harris, July 28, 1987.

Kiss information: AIs with Joyce Bogart, July 22, 1987; and Harris, July 28, 1987.

"He went crazy": Confidential source.

Robert Klein's quip: AI with Joyce Bogart, July 22, 1987.

"Not really": AI with Bird, July 28, 1987.

Donna Summer information: AIs with Joyce Bogart, Harris, Bird (same dates as previous refs.). Ward, Stokes, and Tucker, op. cit., pp. 527–29.

$55 million revenues in 1977: "Casablanca Bursting at the Seams After 38 Months," *Billboard*, Mar. 18, 1978.

pp. 168–71. Casablanca under PolyGram:

Increase in head count; purchase of adjoining real estate on Sunset: Ibid.

"Loud. Real loud": AI with Harris, July 28, 1987.

DiNoble's gong; "Everything was at such a fevered fucking pitch": AI with Bleiweiss, Feb. 19, 1987. Gong confirmed by DiNoble in AI, Oct. 16, 1989.

Description of interior: AI with Joyce Bogart, July 22, 1987. Fully stocked bar in Neil's office plainly visible in photo in *New West* article.

"**People were happy**": AI with Bird, July 28, 1987.

Davis background and quotes: AI with Davis, July 21, 1987. The story about the young woman taking drug orders was confirmed in AI two days later with Russ Regan.

pp. 171–72. PolyGram history and management:

History of formation: AI with attorney Eric Kronfeld, Dec. 1, 1987.

"**I always wanted to get out of Holland**": Quoted in "PolyGram: That's Entertainment—Conglomeratized," *Los Angeles Times*, Sept. 30, 1979.

Descriptions of Hix and Kinkele; Kinkele's ice-breaker: AIs with Braun, July 7, 1987, Kronfeld, Dec. 1, 1987, and Harris, July 28, 1987.

pp. 172–74. RSO and Coury:

RSO made a net profit: AI with Guenter Hensler, Oct. 30, 1985.

Stigwood information: AI with Coury, July 23, 1987.

Coury urinated in plant: AI with eyewitness Bob Buziak, Apr. 29, 1987.

"**Al Coury must have broken more hits**": AI with Bleiweiss, Feb. 19, 1987.

"**There was a *Billboard* conference**": AI with Hutson, June 11, 1987. Essentials of Hutson's story confirmed by Coury in AI, Oct. 19, 1989.

Wardlow fired; *Billboard* unhappy with his charts: Confirmed by Wardlow's replacement, Tom Noonan, in AI, July 27, 1987. Noonan added that "we didn't accuse him of anything."

pp. 174–76. PolyGram in fool's paradise:

SNF and *Grease* grosses; $1.2 billion; Solleveld to New York; other details: "Polygram: That's Entertainment—Conglomeratized"; "A New Act Takes over at PolyGram"; "Slipped Discs: PolyGram Had Some Big Pop-Music Hits, but Its Main Goal Now Is to End Red Ink," *The Wall Street Journal*, July 28, 1981; "Transatlantic Surgery for a Slipped Disc," *Financial Times*, Nov. 9, 1980; "Harvey Schein of PolyGram Records: He Sells Sizzle," *The New York Times*, May 4, 1980; "PolyGram Shuns the Limelight," *The New York Times*, Apr. 8, 1980.

One other article bears special mention: "The General Motors of the Record Business," *Washington Post*, May 4, 1980. It is essentially an interview with Solleveld that ends with this ludicrous assertion by the writer, Joseph McLellan: "Where Solleveld and his company will go from here is still uncertain, but the future looks a lot more secure for them than it does for some other companies that have tried to get rich quick by following passing trends." By this time, PolyGram was hemorrhaging money. Either Solleveld was putting one over on McLellan—who did not do his homework in any case—or else the executive was blithely unaware of what was happening to his company. I suspect the latter.

"**All of a sudden**": AI with Hensler, Sept. 17, 1985.

Profit margin slim: AI with PolyGram executive Mel Ilberman, Sept. 23, 1985.

"**Neil ended up selling**": AI with David Braun, July 7, 1987.

"**It sold maybe 3 million**": AI with Harvey Schein, Jan. 8, 1987.

Depots losing $7 million a month: AI with Bleiweiss, Sept. 5, 1985.

"**We built a six-inch pipeline**": AI with PolyGram executive Art Dalhuisen, Sept. 23, 1985.

pp. 176–78. The crash:

"**If I were a wholesaler or retailer**": Quoted in "PolyGram: That's Entertainment—Conglomeratized."

Examples from Casablanca's roster: Culled from Dave Marsh and John Swenson, *The New Rolling Stone Record Guide* (New York: Rolling Stone Press/Random House, 1983).

Casablanca had over a hundred acts; costs of $100,000 per signing before promotion: AI with Hensler, Sept. 17, 1985.

"**Those things hurt**": AI with Harris, July 28, 1987.

"**Neil always spent everybody's money**": Confidential source.

"**Neil had a unique way**": AI with Shein, Mar. 26, 1990.

"**I asked to see the guy**": AI with David Braun, July 7, 1987.

Details of Summer lawsuit: "Summer Sues Casablanca, Asks Contract Terminated," *Billboard*, Feb. 4, 1980.

"**We developed evidence**": AI with Engel, July 2, 1987.

$15 million buyout price: "Bogart Bows His BogArts," *Billboard*, Feb. 23, 1980.

Bird termination: "Regan Named PolyGram West GM in First Stage of Reorganization," *Variety*, Dec. 3, 1980.

pp. 179–80. Schein and Braun:

Schein inadvertently spurred PolyGram's U.S. buildup: AI with Schein, Jan. 8, 1987.

Schein's résumé: "Slipped Discs" *(Wall Street Journal).*

Schein's violent temper: AIs with Braun, July 7, 1987; and Hensler, Mar. 19, 1987.

"**Harvey was a very intelligent man**": AI with Braun, July 7, 1987.

"**Record people are hardly literate**" . . . "**turn out the lights!**": AI with Schein, Jan. 8, 1987.

How Braun got the job; "There were things I did not know" . . . "**see their senior executives fight**": AI with Braun, July 7, 1987.

"**He didn't realize**": AI with Schein, Jan. 8, 1987.

p. 181. $220 million loss: Briefs filed by defendants in: *Federal Trade Commission* v. *Warner Communications et al.*, Case No. 5809 (1984), U.S. Court of Appeals, Ninth Circuit.

10 Joey and Freddy

pp. 182–85. Davis and Isgro:

Davis's suicide attempt; early acquaintance with Isgro; "I was fucking depressed" . . . "**fucking flabbergasted**": AIs with Davis, July 21 and 28, 1987; Nov. 23, 1987; Jan. 7, 1988; Feb. 29, 1988.

Rook owned Good Luck Broadcasting with Isgro: AI with Rook, Oct. 17, 1989.

Sir Lancelot story: AI with Davis, Jan. 7, 1988; he claims he so testified in *Isgro* v. *RIAA*, but his deposition is sealed.

Isgro's military records: National Personnel Records Center, St. Louis. Isgro's service number is M-2195669. Further details about Isgro's military history, along with a precis of his career, can be found in: "Application for Order to Amend Travel Restrictions," *United States* v. *Joseph Isgro*, Case No. 951 (1989), U.S. District Court, Central District of California. A copy of a photo of Isgro and Westmoreland is attached to this document. It shows the general fingering the Purple Heart on Isgro's chest as Isgro salutes. Both men are in civilian dress.

"Un-fucking-believable": Confidential source.

pp. 185–86. Isgro's lifestyle and history through Motown:

$1.4 million marble-floored mansion: Price disclosed in: *Joseph Isgro* v. *Rich Gold*, Case No. 517094 (1984), U.S. District Court, Central District of California. (Gold was the real estate broker who sold Isgro his Encino home. Isgro alleged Gold ran an aerial photo of the home in an advertising circular without permission.) Marble floors mentioned in: Los Angeles Police Department burglary report, Case No. 100625 (1986) (Isgro's July 12, 1986, burglary).

$10 million a year: AI with Isgro, July 29, 1987.

Motown's gross in late seventies: Confidential source at Motown.

Isgro bragged he made more from Motown as indie: AI with Al Coury, July 23, 1987.

Isgro pleased by Burt Reynolds comparison: AI with Davis, July 28, 1987.

"Joey comes out of the limo": AI with Fred Haayen, June 20, 1986.

Date of birth: Made public in LAPD burglary report.

Early career history; "I was dating a girl": AI with Isgro, July 29, 1987. All subsequent Isgro quotes in this chapter, unless noted, are from this interview.

"He was a good kid": AI with Levy, July 30, 1988.

Ales's explanation of how Isgro got Motown job: AI with Ales, July 23, 1987.

pp. 186–87. Isgro as indie promoter:

Scotti Brothers and Streisand: AI with Dick Asher, June 29, 1987.

DiSipio claimed L.A. stations: "A Few Promoters Dominate Record Business," *The Wall Street Journal*, Apr. 18, 1986.

ICE Management: "Joe Isgro Forms ICE Management, *Billboard*, Oct. 3, 1981.

p. 187. Larc and Private I:

Larc's initial good showing: "Larc Off to Flying Start," *Billboard*, Jan. 15, 1983.

"We had a great measure"; Azoff preferred Gary Bird to Isgro: AI with Davis, July 28, 1987.

Grubman represented Private I: Confirmed by Grubman in AI, Dec. 7, 1989.

"Because we were schmucks": Quoted in "The Fault Is Not in Our Stars," *Forbes*, Sept. 21, 1987.

p. 188. Isgro's outside interests:

Hawaii condos: Confidential source.

Isgro's quip about Sinatra: On July 16, 1987, I had an informal chat with Isgro at Stefanino's, during which he made the remark.

pp. 188–89. Tashjian and Craig:

Tashjian and Craig hired in 1981 and 1983, respectively, and nature of

their roles: Isgro deposition of Apr. 23, 1987, in *Isgro* v. *RIAA*.

"Tash the Flash": AI with Juggy Gayles, July 13, 1987.

Craig's encyclopedic knowledge of radio: AI on Sept. 1, 1987, with Ray Fersko, defense lawyer in *Isgro* v. *RIAA* who deposed Craig.

Number of Isgro employees: "Application for Order to Amend Travel Restrictions," *U.S.* v. *Isgro*.

Isgro's description of his job: Isgro's deposition of Apr. 23, 1987, in *Isgro* v. *RIAA*.

Las Vegas sorties: "Payola: The Record-Label Connection," *Rolling Stone*, Apr. 21, 1988.

Tashjian and Craig dealt in payola: Both men pleaded guilty. See p. 324.

"If anybody in this business knows me": Mar. 1986 interview with Isgro by anonymous reporter.

pp. 189–91. Isgro's bodyguards:

Smith and Pond bios: "Briton Involved in Mafia Pop Promotion Scandal," *The Times* (of London), Aug. 21, 1988.

Isgro assault: Los Angeles Police Department assault with a deadly weapon report, Case No. 1016464 (1984).

"Dave is the kind of guy": AI with Davis, Feb. 29, 1988.

Alleged assault of Gordon: *Renee Michelle Gordon* v. *David Michael Smith*, Petition for Injunction Prohibiting Harassment, Case No. 583807 (1986), Superior Court of California, County Los Angeles.

pp. 191–94. Isgro and Armone:

Vesuvio's information: AI with Remo Franceschini of Queens D.A.'s Office, Oct. 19, 1989.

Armone's conviction as member of crime family: Dec. 22, 1987, jury verdict in: *United States* v. *Joseph N. Gallo et al.*, Case No. 452(s)(4) (1986), U.S. District Court, Eastern District of New York.

Armone history; rise of Gotti; "We ain't gonna get nothing"; Armone as underboss and acting boss: Gene Mustain and Jerry Capeci, *Mob Star: The Story of John Gotti*, (New York: Franklin Watts, 1988), pp. 52–53; "The New Godfather" (four-part series), *NBC Nightly News*, Nov. 1987; " 'Twas Silent Night; And He Was Under Wraps for Christmas," (Jimmy Breslin's column), (New York) *Daily News*, Dec. 27, 1987.

Murder of Yudzevich: "Gambino Informer Slain in California," *The New York Times*, Mar. 16, 1988.

Armone/Castellano conversation: Government exhibit 30 (A) in *U.S.* v. *Gallo*.

pp. 194–96. Scotti-Bird incident:

"In the business of independent promotion": AI with Davis, July 28, 1987.

Bird's indictment, plea, and sentencing: *The State of Ohio* v. *Gary F. Bird*, Case No. 180085 (1983), Court of Common Pleas (Criminal Division), County of Cuyahoga.

Y-100 and Scottis: See also: *In Re Metroplex Communication*, Case No. 50 (1987), Application before the Federal Communications Commission.

"secretary of defense": Confidential source.

Police report: Santa Monica Police Department Crime Report, Case No. 4642 (1985), Assault with a Deadly Weapon [i.e., Rick Caseras's hands].

pp. 196–97. McDaniel story: AIs with McDaniel, Aug. 28, 1987, Sept. 18, 1987, Nov. 24, 1987, and Sept. 7, 1989; and Barrie Bergman, Sept. 3, 1987. Also: "Indie Promo Men Trying to Kill Musicstream Firm, Its G.M. Sez," *Variety*, July 24, 1985.

pp. 197–98. DiSipio information:

"It takes him a while": AI with Fred Haayen, June 18, 1987.

"One time, I was in Patsy's": Confidential source.

Year of birth; school history; Gambier Bay: "33 Years: From Nightmare to Dream World" (Larry McMullen's column), *Philadelphia Daily News*, Oct. 6, 1977; Edwin P. Hoyt, *The Men of the Gambier Bay*, (New York: Avon Books, 1979), p. 205.

"He was taking care of things": AI with Eddie Deane, Oct. 26, 1987.

Claimed ninety stations: "The New Payola," NBC *Nightly News*, Mar. 31, 1986.

Racehorses: DiSipio's bangtail, Lucky Larry, won the Garden State in Cherry Hill on Mar. 15, 1986. See: "Inside Track," *Billboard*, Mar. 29, 1986.

Road manager for Martino; "I said, What do you figure he's got, Al?": AI with Danny Davis, Jan. 7, 1988.

pp. 198–99. Isgro and DiSipio:

"When I was vice-president of promotion": AI with Davis, Nov. 11, 1988.

Isgro used Big Mike to guard La Toya Jackson: AI with Isgro, July 29, 1987.

"Big Mike walked into my office": AI with Davis, Feb. 29, 1988.

"One time, Freddy was in my kitchen": AI with Davis, Jan. 7, 1988.

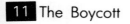 The Boycott

pp. 203–4. Paley and Backe:

"We should have known": Quoted in "CBS Chief's Abrupt Ouster Came Amid Network's Rising Fortunes," *The New York Times*, May 10, 1980.

"I think Backe wasn't secure enough": "An Intimate Talk with William Paley," *The New York Times Magazine*, Dec. 28, 1980.

p. 204. Yetnikoff's pet names for Wyman: AI with Irwin Segelstein, Feb. 5, 1987; and "King of the Schmooze," *Esquire*, Nov. 1986.

pp. 204–7. Asher, Epic, Dileo:

DEPUTY DICK MUST GO!: AI with Epic alum Steve Dessau, Nov. 11, 1987.

"Walter had never even talked to me": AI with Asher, Sept. 29, 1987.

"Frank had that sense": AI with Blond, Oct. 2, 1987.

"I appeared in the door"; "I had so many crazy conversations with Dick": AI with Dileo, July 16, 1987.

"Artists and managers were constantly trying to change": AI with Asher, June 29, 1987.

Asher on Dileo's Rolex; "It wouldn't have bothered me so much": AI with Asher, Sept. 29, 1987. That Dileo received the Rolex from REO was confirmed by two other sources. Neither of those sources wanted to be named; both are ex-CBS employees. One of them is also the source of the quote, "Once I told him he couldn't wear his gold Rolex with his pinkie ring." Dileo declined to comment.

"One day, I took Dileo to Walter": AI with Weiss, Mar. 5, 1987.

pp. 207–9. Warner boycott:

Asher's paranoia about indies: On Sept. 29, 1987, Dick told me, "It became apparent to me that virtually everything I said immediately got to the independents. I don't remember exactly how I found out. I guess various people in the company reported to me that they had heard the independents were upset at me, and this or that guy's out for me. Something like that."

Horowitz information and quotes: AI with Horowitz, Mar. 31, 1987. That Horowitz was the instigator of the Warner boycott was confirmed in AI with Fred Haayen, Jan. 15, 1987.

"Mo hates it": AI with Marshall, May 15, 1987.

Billboard **articles on boycott:** See notes to p. 11. Also: "WCI Is Alone; Other Labels Deny They'll Kill Indie Promotion," *Billboard*, November 15, 1980; and "Indie Promo Reps Blame the Labels," *Billboard*, November 29, 1980.

pp. 209–10. CBS joins boycott: AIs with Asher, May 23, 1986; July 1, 1986; June 3, 1987; June 29, 1987; and Sept. 29, 1987.

pp. 210–13. Network retaliation:

"The indie promoters chose to wipe our noses in it": AI with Asher, June 29, 1987.

"It was *at least* a top five record": AI with Haayen, Jan. 15, 1987.

"Bob Geldof is a lovely guy": AI with Asher, Sept. 29, 1987.

"Dick did not believe" . . . **"Dick shot it down"**: AI with Marshall, May 15, 1987.

"It wasn't a moral judgment": AI with Asher, June 3, 1987.

pp. 213–15. Collapse of boycott:

"I don't think Epic": AI with Asher, Sept. 29, 1987.

"Columbia initially followed us": AI with Horowitz, Mar. 31, 1987.

Maurice White story: AIs with Asher, May 23, 1986, and June 3, 1987.

12 Thriller

p. 216. Asher and Wyman: AI with Asher, July 1, 1986.

pp. 216–18. Yetnikoff and Wyman:

"He always had to be the big *starker*" and subsequent Federoff quotes: AI, Apr. 9, 1987.

"Clive can't take artists" . . . **"voodoo that no one can understand"**: AI with Yetnikoff, Mar. 30, 1987.

Motor scooter story: "CBS Records: Dominant, Lucrative and Troubled," *Los Angeles Times*, Feb. 15, 1987. Confirmed by Stanley Schlesinger, AI, Sept. 9, 1987.

p. 218. Yetnikoff and Wenner:

"I never liked Jann Wenner": Lombardi notes.

"I ran into him": Fred Goodman's interview with Yetnikoff, Oct. 1988.

pp. 218–19. Yetnikoff as womanizer:

"Those women represent": Confidential source.

"Puppy one, puppy two, puppy three": AI with Weiss, June 24, 1987.

"It's hard to hang out with these guys": "King of the Schmooze," *Esquire*, Nov. 1986.

"Playboy of the Western World": AI with Asher, July 1, 1986.

pp. 220–22. Yetnikoff and Emon:

Winter introduced Walter and Lynda: AI with Winter, July 30, 1987.

"It was the biggest wedding of the year" and subsequent Emon quotes: AIs, Aug. 17, 1987, and Sept. 21, 1987.

Lived with Kronfeld: AI with Kronfeld, Nov. 20, 1987.

Riverside Drive address: Cited in *Walter Yetnikoff and Lynda Emon* v. *Lonnie Katz Interior Design*, Case No. 7643 (1984), Supreme Court, New York County. (Walter sued an interior decorator for failing to deliver some dining room chairs.)

"almost a caricature"; Ohga story: AI with Asher, July 1, 1986.

Billboard ad listing Emon as Winter associate: Jan. 21, 1984 (part of Scotti Brothers advertorial).

Husney/Soskin/Emon deal: AIs with Emon, Sept. 21, 1987; and Husney, Oct. 19, 1989.

p. 222. Lundvall quits: AI with Lundvall, Jan. 26, 1987.

pp. 222–23. Teller information: AIs with Teller, Apr. 13, 1987; Jamieson, Sept. 3, 1987; and Asher, Apr. 21, 1987.

p. 224. "Of course Dick was set up": AI with Kronfeld, Nov. 20, 1987.

p. 224. "Asher came in": Confidential source.

p. 224. "hold his blood pressure down": "Inside Track," *Billboard*, Aug. 21, 1982.

pp. 224–26. *60 Minutes* affair:

"We're looking into the role": "*60 Minutes* to Spotlight Record Promotion," *Billboard*, Feb. 13, 1982.

Yetnikoff quotes: Fred Goodman's interview with Yetnikoff, June 1, 1988.

Incident at Waldorf; "He says, Listen": AIs with Wallace and Hewitt, Oct. 24, 1989.

p. 226. Men at Work story:

Basic details: AI with Bob Jamieson, Sept. 3, 1987.

"We put it out": Confidential source.

pp. 226–28. Thriller information and Jackson quotes: Michael Jackson, *Moonwalk* (New York: Doubleday, 1988), pp. 189, 198–200, 205–7.

pp. 228–31. Dileo information:

Dileo a friend of Isgro's: Confirmed by Isgro in AI, July 29, 1987.

"That campaign cost about $100,000": Confidential source.

"Uncle Tookie": "Is Michael Jackson For Real?," *Rolling Stone*, Sept. 24, 1987.

"He has made observations": Quoted in special advertising section to salute Victory tour in *Billboard*, July 21, 1984.

"Everyone turned fucking green": AI with Jerald Wagner, Feb. 9, 1987.

Dileo's house: Grant Deed for Lot 7 of Tract 13022, City of Los Angeles, July 11, 1984.

License plate; cabana description; Dileo quotes: From author's visit to Dileo's home and interview on July 16, 1987.

Dileo's arrest records: *Commonwealth of Pennsylvania* v. *Frank M. Dileo*, Case No. 7702351A, May 5, 1977; and *Commonwealth of Pennsylvania* v. *Frank M. Dileo*, Case No. 7803525A, July 20, 1978. Both times Dileo pleaded guilty to two counts: 1) poolselling and bookmaking; and 2) possession of an instrument of crime (the rice paper). The first time, his punishment was a $1,000 fine; the second time, a $300 fine. Go figure.

The first arrest form carried this descriptive paragraph: "On Mar. 28, 1977, pursuant to a search warrant for the actor and his premises, 163 North South Drive, Ross Township, Pa., the police found the actor had possession of a sheet of rice paper on which was recorded $2,305 in sports bets on the result of the college basketball game between Marquette and North Carolina colleges. Both phones on the premises rang intermittently, answered by the police officers, and the callers placed sports bets on the aforesaid game, totaling $670. Also found on the premises were three sheets of paper indicating apparent owes and 25 sheets of rice paper."

Dileo failed to collect on insurance: He complained about this vociferously to my source, who did not want to be named.

pp. 232–33. Branca information:

Braun's enmity with Walter over UA lawsuit: AI with Braun, July 14, 1987. See also pp. 152–53.

Walter helped Branca hold on to Jackson: AI with Asher, Sept. 29, 1987.

"Controversy is bad": "Michael's Main Man," *The American Lawyer*, Dec. 1985.

"John is a power broker": AI with Kronfeld, Nov. 20, 1987.

"Michael Jackson is the biggest star": Confidential source, active participant in the Victory tour. The source confirmed that Azoff did little actual work on the tour.

"I have been accused": Quoted in "Michael's Main Man."

"The only attorneys": AI with Branca, July 21, 1987.

13 The Firing

p. 234. Yetnikoff before the analysts: The meeting, on Mar. 15, 1983, was depicted in: "CBS Sees Strong First Quarter," *Billboard*, Mar. 26, 1983.

pp. 234–35. Yetnikoff and MCA offer: "Yetnikoff to Stay at CBS," *Billboard*, Apr. 9, 1983.

pp. 235–36. Asher's thoughts prior to firing, and quotes: AI with Asher, Sept. 29, 1987.

p. 236. "Just before Dick arrived": AI with Jamieson, Sept. 3, 1987.

pp. 236–39. Account of Asher's firing: AI with Asher, Sept. 29, 1987.

p. 239. "Dick would only consider it": AI with Schein, Jan. 8, 1987.

p. 239. "Dick had a very naive attitude": AI with Braun, July 14, 1987.

p. 239. "When he was fired": AI with Dileo, July 16, 1987.

pp. 239–40. Yetnikoff and the Rolling Stones:
Steven Wright quip: *I Have a Pony*, Warner Bros. Records, 4-25335.

$28 million: Widely accepted as the correct figure, though never confirmed by CBS. Reported, probably not for the first time, in: "Pop Records Go Boom," *New York*, October 31, 1983. Confirmed in Nov. 20, 1984, AI with lawyer Eric Kronfeld. Kronfeld said he was set to become Jagger's attorney until Walter prevented it—if true, another example of Yetnikoff's ability to influence who represented his company's artists. Kronfeld also confirmed that Ertegun's bid was half that of Walter's.

"So we're in the Ritz": "King of the Schmooze," *Esquire*, Nov. 1986.

pp. 240–41. Yetnikoff and Emon birthday parties: AIs with Emon, Sept. 21, 1987, and Oct. 20, 1989; Winter, July 30, 1987; and confidential guest at Emon party (on cocaine use).

pp. 241–42. Yetnikoff before the analysts—again: CBS Records transcript of security analysts meeting, Nov. 8, 1983.

p. 242. "That's unheard of": Quoted in "Walter Yetnikoff: The Most Powerful Man in the Record Business," *Rolling Stone*, Dec. 15–29, 1988.

p. 242. "Michael Jackson would ask Walter": AI with Schlesinger, Sept. 2, 1987.

pp. 242–43. Yetnikoff and Warner negotiations: AIs with Elliot Goldman, May 13, 1987, and Schlesinger, Sept. 9, 1987. Goldman, who handled the negotiations for Warner as senior vice-president, allowed me to see some internal memos he had written on the subject. In early 1984 Steve Ross asked Goldman to study the possibility of having Walter Yetnikoff replace Ahmet Ertegun as head of Atlantic. The study had a code name—the "YGP" project—to prevent leaks. YGP stood for Yetnikoff, Guber, and Peters. Apparently, Walter was offering himself to Warner as part of a package that would include Peter Guber and Jon Peters (see pp. 318–19). Goldman suggested that Walter be given a five-year contract with an annual salary of $500,000, plus a $1 million signing bonus. He was less enthused about Guber and Peters. "GP's talents in the record industry are virtually nil in my judgment," he wrote in a March 1984 memo to Ross. By October, Goldman informed Ross that he was more and more convinced that the YGP deal would not close, and that Walter was "simply using the process to get CBS as high as he can." He was right.

pp. 243–45. Asher after the firing: AI with Asher, Sept. 29, 1987.

Fox, Reed, and Loshak were forced out: confirmed in AIs with Reed and Loshak, Mar. 23, 1990.

"Dick walked over to Dempsey": AI with music publicist Richard Gersh, Sept. 29, 1987.

14 Clive Redux

p. 246. Whitney's effect on Arista's bottom line: Disclosed at a Bertelsmann Music Group press conference, Jan. 30, 1989, Plaza Hotel, New York. Houston's first two albums, it was revealed, grossed more than $200 million in the United States alone.

pp. 246–47. Arista history:
Clive's job offers; "I felt that if I was going to be signing": AI with Davis, Jan. 20, 1987.

For more on Davis and Hirschfield, see: David McClintick, *Indecent Exposure: A True Story of Hollywood and Wall Street* (New York: William Morrow, 1982), pp. 70–71, 109.

Naming of Arista; "His ambition"; AIs with Elliot Goldman, May 13, 1987, and Sept. 22, 1987.

pp. 247–49. Dobbis and Clive: *Richard Dobbis* v. *Paul Marshall and Clive Davis,* Case No. 23455 (1984), Supreme Court, New York County; and AIs with Dobbis, Mar. 11 and Apr. 30, 1987; Goldman, May 13, 1987; Davis, Oct. 12, 1989; and Marshall, Oct. 19, 1989.

pp. 249–51. Clive and Whitney:
Details of discovery, signing, and breaking of Houston: "Duet Again," *Manhattan, inc.,* Jan. 1987.

Marshall quotes: AI with Marshall, May 15, 1987.

CBS was the third bidder; "I couldn't believe it": AI with Davis, Apr. 30, 1987.

"It came higher"; "totally contrived artist": "Duet Again."

"When the record came in": AI with Fine, Nov. 6, 1987.

Griffith's reason for leaving Arista, as stated in *Manhattan, inc.:* Confirmed by Griffith in AI, Oct. 16, 1989.

15 Dick Redux

pp. 252–53. Goldman at Warner: AI with Goldman, Sept. 22, 1987. Ertegun story provided on good authority by Eric Kronfeld, AI, Dec. 1, 1987.

pp. 253–54. Timmer information: AI with Timmer, Dec. 15, 1986.

pp. 254–56. The merger proceeds:
Horowitz's thoughts: AI with Horowitz, Mar. 31, 1987.

Goldman memo to Ross: From Goldman's private "chrono" file, made available to author.

"He became furious": AI with Goldman, Sept. 22, 1987.

Nature of Asher's job at Warner: AIs with Goldman, Sept. 22, 1987, and with Asher's then-secretary, Cynthia Lane, Feb. 24, 1987.

"I saw a lot of things": Quoted in "From Ashes to Asher: PolyGram Prexy Leads Way to the Top," *Hits,* June 29, 1987.

Goldman came up with ingenious solutions: AI with Kronfeld, Dec. 1, 1987.

pp. 256–57. Yetnikoff's attack; collapse of merger:
"PolyGram, Polydor": Lombardi notes. Yetnikoff made the remark on Apr. 4, 1986.

"patently illegal," etc.: "WCI-PolyGram Ties Blasted by Yetnikoff," *Billboard,* July 9, 1983.

"we were more concerned": AI with Horowitz, Mar. 31, 1987.

Walter asked to testify in Yiddish: The story is somewhat apocryphal, but not out of character for Walter. Told to author on Mar. 5, 1987, by Nat Weiss.

FTC suit: See notes to p. 181.

"My guess": AI with Kronfeld, Dec. 1, 1987.

"That was the kiss of death": AI with Willis, Aug. 21, 1985.

"sliced up": AI with Goldman, Feb. 16, 1987.

pp. 257–59. Hensler and his removal: Quotes and details accumulated by author between Aug. and Oct. 1985, in preparation for: "A New Act Takes Over at PolyGram," *The New York Times*, Nov. 3, 1985.

p. 259. Timmer's change of heart on Asher: AI with Alain Levy, Dec. 18, 1986. Levy said, "I was one of the people who Timmer was listening to, but he was listening to a lot of people. I regarded Asher very highly. I frankly didn't like the way CBS treated him. I recommended him, but a number of other people had a voice in that decision." Oberstein declined an interview. Billy Gaff, artist manager and founder of PolyGram's Riva Records unit, told me on Oct. 12, 1987, that Oberstein definitely insisted on Asher over Hensler.

pp. 259–61. Goldman at RCA:

"I was never offered PolyGram": AI with Goldman, July 21, 1986.

Diana Ross and Kenny Rogers deals overly generous; $25 million in unsold albums: AIs with Buziak, Apr. 1, 1987, and Jan. 30, 1989.

$35 million loss: Disclosed by Bertelsmann at Jan. 30, 1989, press conference.

Buziak's accomplishments: "The Rap on RCA Records," *Los Angeles Times*, Sept. 18, 1988.

At least $1 million in severance for Goldman: Reported by gossip columnist Liz Smith in the New York *Daily News*, Sept. 29, 1987. Goldman told author the amount was a "safe assumption" on Sept. 15, 1987.

"Clive, God bless him": AI with Goldman, Sept. 15, 1987.

p. 261. Teller's promotion and reputation:

Walter disliked Teller: AIs with Debra Federoff, Apr. 9, 1987; and Nat Weiss, June 24, 1987.

"If you are a fierce competitor": AI with Teller, Apr. 13, 1987.

Teller and H-bomb: Confidential source at Epic.

pp. 261–63. Asher at PolyGram:

Dick's claim about spotting Bon Jovi early: *Hits*, June 29, 1987.

"Truth be known": Smith delivered this wisecrack at the T. J. Martell dinner honoring Irv Azoff on Apr. 11, 1987.

"After you've finished": "A New Act Takes Over at PolyGram," *The New York Times*, Nov. 3, 1985.

"I was amazed"; "three in three": Quoted in "Asher Beats His PolyGram 'Secret' Goal by a Year," *Radio & Records*, October 23, 1987.

"Columbia West": AI with former PolyGram executive Rick Bleiweiss, Dec. 2, 1986.

Asher delighted in hiring Bill Fox: AI with Asher, Apr. 21, 1987.

"You know what I did the other day?": Fred Goodman's interview with Yetnikoff, Oct. 1988.

16 The Board Meeting

p. 264. "The record industry has created": AI with then–Bee Gees manager Dick Ashby, Sept. 25, 1985.

pp. 264–65. Indie promotion in 1985:

Ostin and Thyret opposed to indies: On Nov. 23, 1987, Danny Davis told me, "Joe [Isgro] carried on about Mo Ostin—I didn't know he was so dead set against [indie promotion]. Although Russ Thyret loves the fact that he paid less for indies than anybody else. He was delighted when he didn't have to use them."

What Warner and CBS spent: Made public in *Isgro* v. *RIAA*. It was further disclosed that MCA spent $9 million (as stated on p. 265), and that A&M spent more than $2 million.

***Rolling Stone* estimate**: "Payola: The Record-Label Connection," *Rolling Stone*, Apr. 21, 1988.

Walter's relationship with Fred DiSipio: "King of the Schmooze," *Esquire*, Nov. 1986, quotes Yetnikoff: "I am—I've said it before and I'll say it again—a *friend* of Freddie DiSipio's. Fred is good at what he does; Joe Isgro is good at what *he* does, on the West Coast."

p. 265. Azoff, Geffen, and indie promotion:

Isgro's boast about Quarterflash: Mar. 1986 interview with Isgro by anonymous reporter.

Azoff's attack on R&R: "MCA Pulls Trade-Paper Ads in Feud," *Los Angeles Times*, July 7, 1985.

Azoff accuses Walter: *Esquire* quote from "King of the Schmooze"; deposition quote made public in a pretrial brief in *Isgro* v. *RIAA*.

Circumstantial evidence that Azoff was trying to rein in Walter's use of indies can be found in the text of a letter disclosed in a brief in *Isgro* v. *RIAA*. In the fall of 1985, Sid Sheinberg, Azoff's boss, wrote to Tom Wyman, Walter's then-boss: "In our judgment, the questions raised by rumors concerning the practices of independent promoters in the record industry require the attention of corporate management."

p. 266. "conspiracy of silence": Quoted in "Payola Investigation Launched," *Washington Post*, Apr. 3, 1986.

pp. 266–68. Oct. 1, 1985, RIAA meeting:

MCA, Motown, and Arista; text of resolution: Disclosed in various briefs in *Isgro* v. *RIAA*.

Tally of vote; Gartenberg's objections: "A Few Promoters Dominate Record Business," *The Wall Street Journal*, Apr. 18, 1986.

"You know I have a temper" . . . **"Watergate break-ins"**: Lombardi notes.

p. 268. Nov. 7, 1985, legal committee meeting:

"They were going to use": Ibid.

Schoenfeld's memo: Attached to brief in *Isgro* v. *RIAA*.

pp. 268–69. Asher and RIAA investigation: AI with Asher, June 29, 1987.

pp. 269–70. Jan. 23, 1985, RIAA meeting:

Moss and Craigo voted no: AI with Craigo, Feb. 10, 1988. Craigo denied CBS pressure, same interview.

"And since three companies": Lombardi notes.

pp. 270–71. Yetnikoff, DiSipio, Empire Records:

Empire deal: To my knowledge, first publicly disclosed in "Payola Charges Rock Record Biz," *Rolling Stone*, Apr. 10, 1986. Four excellent sources told me about Empire, including Nat Weiss, in June 24, 1987, AI.

"the hand inside the glove": AI with Davis, Apr. 4, 1988.

Landau article: "The Thin Line Between Payola and Promotion," *Rolling Stone*, Aug. 2, 1973.

"First of all": AI with Landau, Oct. 13, 1989.

17 The Evening News

p. 272. Ross and Silverman information:

Background details: "NBC's Intrepid Investigators," *Washington Journalism Review*, June 1986; "TV's Toughest Reporters," *Us*, June 1, 1987; "The Big Story Is Apt to Be Theirs," *The Philadelphia Inquirer*, Mar. 30, 1986; " 'Danke Schoen,' Las Vegas," *The American Lawyer*, Mar. 1987.

pp. 272–78. How NBC got the story: AIs with Ross, Apr. 8, 1987, May 29, 1987, June 16, 1987, June 29, 1987, Sept. 30, 1987; and Silverman, Apr. 4, 1988.

"the reports of my demise": "Cox Airs from Hospital," *Billboard*, Mar. 15, 1986.

"shouldn't have such a big mouth": "Truth and Consequences?," *Rolling Stone*, Apr. 24, 1986.

Walter Lee and the cattle prod: *William Bartlett* v. *Capitol Records et al.*, Case No. 633615 (1987), Superior Court, Los Angeles County.

Federal agents encountered one another: "Promoters Key Issue in Record Industry Fracas," *Los Angeles Times*, Apr. 24, 1988.

Gotti discussed record business: Mustain and Capeci, op. cit., p. 24.

p. 278. *Godfather* theme music anecdote: Brian Ross told me on May 29, 1987, "After the Grammys, the night after our first piece, there was a big CBS Records party at a fancy restaurant in Los Angeles. Isgro enters—and I got this from four different people who were there—on Yetnikoff's specific instructions, they played the theme from *The Godfather*."

pp. 278–79. Feb. 26, 1986, RIAA meeting: AI with Asher, June 29, 1987.

p. 279. "$50 million or $60 million": Goldman's keynote speech at NARM convention, Feb. 14, 1987.

pp. 279–80. The labels drop the indies: Corporate press releases.

pp. 280–81. Isgro's reaction to story and suspension:

"Cocksuckers," etc.: Mar. 1986 interview with Isgro by anonymous reporter.

"I'm destroyed . . . insidious innuendo": Quoted in "Joe Isgro: Promoter Under Fire," *Rolling Stone*, Apr. 24, 1986.

pp. 281–83. Pisello/MCA scandal: The best primary sources are: Government's Sentencing Memorandum Pursuant to 18-USC-3577, *United States* v. *Salvatore James Pisello*, Case No. 818 (1984), District Court, Central District of California; and trial transcript in: *United States* v. *Salvatore James Pisello* (1987), District Court, Central District of California.

The "organized crime concept" remark made by Newark prosecutor Bruce Repetto at Oct. 28, 1988, sentencing of Morris Levy in *U.S. v. Levy*.

There has been an enormous body of press coverage on this subject as well, ever since William Knoedelseder of the *Los Angeles Times* broke the story on May 10, 1985. For further reading, I recommend:

From the *Los Angeles Times:* "MCA Audit Details Ties to Pisello," May 10, 1985; "Probe Points to Mob Role in Record Deal," Mar. 3, 1986; "Salvatore Pisello: A Shadowy Figure in Records Deals," May 4, 1986; "Prosecutor Benched After Getting His Man," Jan. 22, 1989.

And: "Death of a Mob Probe," *The American Lawyer*, July/Aug. 1988; "MCA and the Mob," *Regardies*, June 1988; "Risky Business," *Rolling Stone*, June 2, 1988; "Spinning Web of Intrigue Around MCA," *Los Angeles Herald-Examiner*, Mar. 12, 1989.

pp. 283–84. Isgro and Ross:

"Freddy, hey!": "TV's Toughest Reporters."

"Cameras, boom mikes": Mar. 1986 interview with Isgro by anonymous reporter.

Parker-Meridien story: AIs with Isgro, July 29, 1987; and Ross, June 16, 1987.

p. 286. Disbandment of Empire and Private I: "CBS Ended Private I Deal Before Scandal Re: Indie Promoters," *Variety*, Apr. 9, 1986; and "Payola Charges Rock Record Biz," *Rolling Stone*, Apr. 10, 1986. Altshuler quoted in *RS*.

Mottola's denial and quote: AI with Mottola, Aug. 24, 1987.

pp. 287–88. Yetnikoff's reaction to Mar. 31, 1985, story:

Walter demanded that Wyman react: Confidential source.

"What did they prove? . . . Never use the stuff": Quoted in "King of the Schmooze," *Esquire*, Nov. 1986. According to article, Yetnikoff said this on Apr. 2, 1986.

"If I took," etc.: Lombardi notes. This section from Apr. 4, 1986.

pp. 288–89. Asher quotes and Isgro/Grubman story: AI with Asher, June 29, 1987.

pp. 289–90. Gore's press conference: "Payola Investigation Launched," *The Washington Post*, Apr. 3, 1986.

p. 290. Manager complaints in Billboard: "Managers Irate over Indies," *Billboard*, Mar. 29, 1986. Dileo quoted in sidebar to story: "Dileo on Indies: 'It's a Shame What the Labels Did.' "

pp. 290–92. Indies after suspension:

Lawyers unable to serve DiSipio: AI with defense lawyer Peter Gelblum (Chrysalis, A&M, RIAA), Jan. 25, 1988.

Leyte Gulf christening: "Street Talk," *Radio & Records*, Oct. 2, 1987.

Intercontinental and MidAtlantic: I attended the 1987 Bobby Poe convention—the biggest Top 40 gathering—on June 26-27 of that year. During the convention, I met Ron Kyle, Matty Singer, and Helene Masiko, employees of Intercontinental and MidAtlantic. I got the company names from them. Curiously, neither company was listed in the phone book.

Profile story and Robbins quotes: "Indies' Clout Still Strong," *Rolling Stone*, June 5, 1986.

"reliable sources": "PDs on Indies: Phones Have Gone Quiet," *Billboard*, Mar. 22, 1986.

Isgro tabs; "Am I doing anything different?" . . . "information through them"; names of managers and acts: Isgro's Apr. 22–23, 1987, deposition in *Isgro v. RIAA*.

"Very often, I'm asked directly": AI with Asher, Sept. 29, 1987.

Island and Virgin: "Virgin Named in Mafia Payola Case," *(London) Observer*, July 24, 1988.

pp. 292–93. Deane and Betancourt fracas: AIs with Asher, Apr. 17, 1986, and June 29, 1987 (quotes); "Exec Sues PolyGram for Slander," *The Hollywood Reporter*, Mar. 3, 1988.

p. 294. Rudnick on payola case: AI with Rudnick, May 18, 1988.

pp. 294–95. Ross and Dantzer: I was with Ross in Los Angeles later that day (July 9, 1987), and he told me the story. If you watch Dantzer's lips in the broadcast, you can make out the words.

p. 295. Davis leaves Isgro: AI with Davis, Apr. 4, 1988.

p. 295. Martell dinner: That Azoff stiffed the Martell Foundation became inadvertently known to me during a July 31, 1987, interview with publicist Norman Winter, when Winter took a phone call from chairman Tony Martell to discuss the problem.

There is a further irony in the industry's so honoring Azoff while excommunicating Isgro. Up until the first NBC story broke, both Isgro and DiSipio were on the Martell Foundation's advisory board, according to pre-1986 dinner program booklets.

pp. 295–97. "I applaud them . . . I'm a gangster and every other fucking name. . . .": AI with Isgro, July 29, 1987.

p. 296. "He thought he was doing us a favor": Quoted in "King of the Schmooze," *Esquire*, Nov. 1986.

pp. 492–94. Collapse of MCA probe: See articles cited in notes to pp. 281–83.

Transfer of case; Rudnick handling FOIA requests; Rudnick's termination: AI with Rudnick, Dec. 12, 1989.

pp. 298–99. Denouement of Isgro lawsuit:

"Isgro thought he was thumbing his nose": AI with PolyGram defense lawyer Ray Fersko, Sept. 1, 1987.

"They said to me, Do you know John Gotti?": AI with Davis, Jan. 7, 1988.

Countersuits: *MCA Records* v. *Joseph Isgro*, Case No. 2110 (1988), Central District of California; *Warner Bros.* v. *Joseph Isgro*, Case No. 547 (1988), Central District of California.

"charming little house": AI with Danny Davis, Jan. 7, 1988.

18 The Big Score

pp. 300–302. Yetnikoff's dreams of the Big Score:

"I am probably the most the most powerful": Lombardi notes.

$4 million net worth prior to Sony deal: AI with Schlesinger, Sept. 16, 1987.

"I hope he does make his big score": AI with Weiss, Mar 5. 1987.
"Every time I talk to Walter": AI with Federoff, Apr. 9, 1987.
"It's the immigrant fear": Adams notes.
Ruthless People soundtrack to have been on Empire: AI with Nat Weiss, June 24, 1987.
$2 million from Disney: AI with Schlesinger, Sept. 2, 1987.
"The goy upstairs": Quoted in "King of the Schmooze," *Esquire*, Nov. 1986.
pp. 302–5. Wyman, Turner, and Tisch: "Gambling on CBS," *The Business World (The New York Times Magazine, Part 2)*, June 8, 1986; "A Tisch Is Still a Tisch," *Channels*, Feb. 1987; "Changing Picture: How the CBS Board Decided Chief Wyman Should Leave His Job," *The Wall Street Journal*, Sept. 12, 1986.

Dayan story: AI with Joe Rosenberg, manager of Loews' investment portfolio, Oct. 1986.
pp. 305–6. Yetnikoff and Tisch:
"Velvo": "King of the Schmooze."
"pisch" and "Tischburg": AI with Schlesinger, Mar. 17, 1988.
"the evil dwarf": Fred Goodman's interview with Yetnikoff, Oct. 1988.
"the kike upstairs": AI with Lynda Emon, Sept. 21, 1987.
"Ha! A major cost saving": Quoted in "Sony and CBS Records: What a Romance!," *The New York Times Magazine*, Sept. 18, 1988.
Tisch's ideas on decorum of Jewish executives: AI with Joe Rosenberg, Oct. 1986.
Walter's threats to Tisch; drug charges against CBS News: Unpublished interview with Tisch by Neil Koch of *Channels*, June 13, 1988.
"There's no big scandal . . . we'd all be in trouble": AI with Tisch, Oct. 29, 1986, for article in *Channels*, Feb. 1987.
pp. 306–7. Walter's wedding:
DiSipio and Levy at wedding: Confirmed by confidential source.
Other guests: Liz Smith's gossip column, (New York) *Daily News*, Mar. 24, 1987.
"divorce settlement": At a private dinner party on Sept. 17, 1987, Lynda Emon introduced me to her friend and attorney Sandy Katz as the person who had negotiated her "divorce" from Yetnikoff. I do not think she was being facetious.
"I feel like the beheaded queen": AI with Emon, Aug. 17, 1987.
pp. 307–8. Tisch puts records on the block:
Memo expressing "complete confidence" in Derow: "Tisch Acts Fast to Exert Control at CBS, Backing Top Executives; Sauter Resigns," *The Wall Street Journal*, Sept. 12, 1986.
Americana Hotel: "Gambling on CBS."
"Our licenses": Quoted in "Sony and CBS Records: What a Romance!"
"I screamed and yelled": AI with Yetnikoff, Mar. 30, 1987.
pp. 308–10. Sony's interest in CBS Records: "Sony and CBS Records: What a Romance!"
"The sign-on bonus . . . all my *business* dreams": AI with Yetnikoff, Mar. 30, 1987.
Wall Street Journal article: "CBS Records Head, Yetnikoff, Is Restive Under Tisch, Company Sources Say," Jan. 5, 1987.

Sony, the Betamax, DAT: This is my own analysis. I note that author Peter Boyer reached a similar conclusion in "Sony and CBS Records: What a Romance!"

"stealing": Lombardi notes.

pp. 310–11. Walter, Tisch, renewed Sony interest:

Numerous details: "Sony and CBS Records: What a Romance!"

Walter screaming in Tisch's office: Confidential source.

"Larry, bless his soul": "Tisch Does What CBS Feared in Turner," *The Wall Street Journal,* Nov. 20, 1987.

Walter did not play the market: Interview with Schlesinger, Sept. 2, 1987. He said Yetnikoff liked safer investments, such as Treasury bonds.

pp. 312–13. Mottola at CBS:

"I think one of the more interesting facts": Quoted in "The 101 Years of CBS Records," (advertorial), *Billboard,* Nov. 19, 1988.

Champion managed John Eddie on Columbia: AI with Mottola, Aug. 24, 1987. Mottola further acknowledged on that date that he had a production deal with CBS Records, but declined to give details.

$3 million bonus: Confidential source.

pp. 313–14. Walter continues to attack Tisch:

Tisch tried to pin the cutback on Stringer: Peter J. Boyer, *Who Killed CBS?: The Undoing of America's Number One News Network* (New York: Random House, 1988), pp. 329–30.

UJA, cognac, Dileo: "Sony and CBS Records: What a Romance!" The Dileo story was confirmed to me by a confidential source.

Gun story: Related to author by the *Rolling Stone* reporter, Fred Goodman.

p. 314. Employee lawsuit and counterclaim: *Ralph F. Colin Jr. and Robert T. Kennedy v. CBS Inc. and Laurence A. Tisch; Walter R. Yetnikoff, Seymour Gartenberg, and Does 1-10, Additional Counterclaim Defendants,* Case No. 4447 (1988), Supreme Court, New York County. All details of CBS allegations are from interrogatories filed by CBS. See also: "CBS Says Disc Boss Cooked the Books," *New York Post,* Sept. 20, 1988.

pp. 314–17. Shareholders' meeting: Gartenberg made his disparaging remarks to me in the museum lobby. I took down all the other details and remarks in a notebook. Freelance reporter Stu Stogel provided me with a tape of Walter's press conference, which I attended.

p. 317. "Disgraceful"; "Walter is an animal": Neal Koch interview with Tisch, June 13, 1988.

p. 318. CBS vs. Warner on pop albums: " '89 Chart Share: It's WEA by a Mile," *Billboard,* Mar. 3, 1990; "Music to Warner's Ears," *Los Angeles Times,* Mar. 20, 1989; and "A Cold Spell for CBS Records," *The New York Times,* May 17, 1989. Quotes are from *NYT* article.

p. 318. Walter's marital troubles; sojourn at Hazelden; "superb fighting condition": "Sony Boom," *Los Angeles Herald-Examiner,* Sept. 29, 1989 (Mitchell Fink's gossip column). See also: "A Well-Timed Rehab for Walter Yetnikoff," *New York Newsday,* Oct. 25, 1989.

pp. 318–19. Details of Guber-Peters deal: "Walter Yetnikoff's $300 Million Mistake," *Forbes,* Dec. 11, 1989 (Gubernick quote); "Sony Taking On an Even

More American Look," *Los Angeles Times*, Oct. 16, 1989 ("Why 8.08 percent?"); "Behind the Scenes of the Big Deal," *(Los Angeles Times Sunday) Calendar*, Dec. 31, 1989; "Sony Bid to Enter U.S. Film Market Faces Setback as Battle with Warner Heats Up," *The Wall Street Journal*, Oct. 16, 1989; "Yetnikoff to Head Record and Movie Committee at Sony," *The Wall Street Journal*, Oct. 13, 1989.

pp. 319–21. Asher leaves PolyGram; purchase of Island and A&M: AI with Asher, Dec. 6, 1989; prospectus dated Nov. 7, 1989, for initial public offering of thirty-two million shares of PolyGram. Fine quotes from "P'Gram Defends Exec Exits," *Billboard*, Mar. 31, 1990.

19 The Reckoning

p. 322. "The evidence I've got": Quoted in "Payola: The Record-Label Connection," *Rolling Stone*, Apr. 21, 1988.

pp. 322–23. Indictments: See notes to p. 12.

p. 323. Walker co-chaired a "Just Say No" program; "ridiculous":"The New Payola," *NBC Nightly News*, Feb. 26, 1988.

p. 323. "heavy-handed," etc.: "Tashjians, Craig, Wilson Indicted," *Radio & Records*, Mar. 4, 1988.

pp. 323–24. Judgments in Tashjian and Craig cases:
   Charges against Valerie thrown out: "Valerie Tashjian Tax Charges Dismissed," *Radio & Records*, May 19, 1989.
   Ralph's guilty plea: "Tashjian Pleads Guilty to One Payola Count," *Radio & Records*, May 26, 1989.
   Craig's guilty plea: "Craig Pleads Guilty to Payola Charge," *Radio & Records*, Oct. 20, 1989.

p. 324. Isgro, Moore, and 20th Century–Fox: AI with Isgro, Aug. 3, 1989; and "Isgro, Fox Plan Film on Hoffa," *Daily Variety*, Dec. 29, 1989.

pp. 324–25. Indictments of Isgro, Anderson, and Monka: *United States* v. *Joseph Isgro et al.*, Case No. 951 (1989), U.S. District Court, Central District of California.

p. 324. Monka a drug offender: "Payola Probe's 'Mystery Man' Had State Political Entree," *Daily Variety*, Dec. 7, 1989.

p. 325. Arrest of Monka and Isgro; Isgro's confrontation with Silverman: AIs with Silverman, Dec. 13 and 15, 1989.

pp. 325–26. Isgro's bail hearing: "Record Promoter Accused of Ties to Mob," *The (Santa Monica) Outlook*, Dec. 6, 1989.

p. 326n. Smith's incarceration: "King of Spin, or Just a Kingpin?" (Jerry Capeci's "Gang Land" column), (New York) *Daily News*, Dec. 19, 1989.

p. 326. Tashjian's sentencing: "Tashjian 'Turnaround' Spurs Light Sentence," *Radio & Records*, Dec. 15, 1989.

p. 326. Craig's sentencing: "Craig Gets Probation, 60G Fine," *Daily Variety*, Dec. 19, 1989.

p. 326. Indictment of Goodman: *United States* v. *Howard Goodman*, Case No. 20305-H (1989), U.S. District Court, Western District of Tennessee.

p. 327. "I will defend my innocence": AI with Isgro, Dec. 14, 1989.
p. 327. "I can't wait": AI with Rudnick, Dec. 12, 1989.

The following people not cited in the above notes generously made themselves available for interviews: Fred Ansis, Frank Barsalona, Bob Brundige, Bill Cataldo, Max Collins, Syd Connor, Betty Cordes, Herb Corsack, Al DeMarino, Joel Denver, Bob Feiden, Dizzy Gillespie, Michael Klenfner, Cal Mann, Leonard Marks, Tony Martell, Bhaskar Menon, Bob Pittman, Ed Rosenblatt, Peter Sarasohn, Paul Schindler, Ekke Schnabel, Bruce Schoen, Tom Silverman, Barbara Skydel, Jim Sotet, Mike Stewart, Frank Wohl.

A few people whose actions are depicted in this book declined to be interviewed: Joseph Armone, Irving Azoff, Allen Davis, Don Dempsey, Fred DiSipio, Ahmet Ertegun, Bob Krasnow, Ron Kyle, Dennis Lavinthal, Maurice Oberstein, Mo Ostin, Paul Simon, Ralph Tashjian, Frank Weber, David Wynshaw.

INDEX

About the Author

■

REDRIC Dannen, a contributing editor at *Vanity Fair,* was a co-recipient of the Overseas Press Club's 1986 Morton Frank Award for business reporting from abroad. His articles have appeared in *The New York Times, Institutional Investor, Rolling Stone,* and *Barron's.* He lives in New Jersey.